D0895303

Lotte Lehmann

ALAN JEFFERSON

LOTTE LEHMANN

1888–1976

Julia MacRae Books

A DIVISION OF WALKER BOOKS

First published in Great Britain 1988 by
Julia MacRae Books, a division of Walker Books
87 Vauxhall Walk, London SE11 5HJ

Jefferson, Alan
Lotte Lehmann: a singer's life.
1. Lehmann, Lotte 2. Singers —— Biography
I. Title
782.1'092'4 ML420.L33

ISBN 0-86203-311-X

Designed by Douglas Martin

Typeset by
J&L Composition Ltd, Filey, N Yorkshire
Printed in Great Britain by
Adlard & Son Ltd

For Fernando Córdova

and to the first Young Composer in Ariadne

Musik ist eine heilige Kunst,
zu versammeln alle Arten von Mut
wie Cherubin um einen strahlenden Thron . . .

Music is a holy art,
which brings together all the Powers
like Cherubim round a shining throne . . .

Hugo von Hofmannsthal

Contents

Illustrations

Introduction

Lotte Lehmann first entered my conscious thoughts when I heard her as the Marschallin over the 'wireless' on 4 May 1938 in that performance of Act I of *Der Rosenkavalier* from Covent Garden when she broke down.

Thereafter it was those twenty-one large, red-labelled 78s of *Die Walküre* Act I and *Der Rosenkavalier* excerpts, as well as numerous others of songs and arias, which kept her in mind during and after the War.

In 1957 and 1959 I sat in the audience for some of her Master Classes in London and then, at last in 1971, I met her at a private party and had the opportunity to talk to her for a few moments apart. She kindly replied from Santa Barbara to two letters I had written to her, and then in 1976 she died.

Somehow she remained a potent force in my life, so when I suggested a biography to the London publisher, Julia MacRae, it was partly because of my (long-distance) love-affair with Lotte Lehmann, partly because no 'independent' biography existed, and also because the centenary of her birth in 1988 needed to be celebrated. Her own accounts of her life leave huge gaps that need to be filled, and I have been sufficiently attracted to her to want to do this.

It seemed reasonable to approach Lotte Lehmann's companion of thirty-eight years, who was still alive, still living in Santa Barbara, to ask for her advice and assistance. This was not forthcoming in any shape or form. She also denied me entrance to the Lotte Lehmann Archive in Santa Barbara, housed in the University Library there and intended by Lotte herself as a source of information for students and writers. So much for that.

Most of my letters to Lotte's friends and colleagues in the USA received no answer, or else excuses, and it seemed as though the 'sole executrix' was firmly exercising her powers all round. To those who did reply positively I am doubly grateful.

I occupied my time, until I found a mode of expression, in compiling a discography of all Lotte's gramophone records. It kept me close to her, it taught me a lot. Eventually this work was completely overtaken by a Dutch discographer of standing, who published his own compilation in a German specialist publication. It was far ahead of my own efforts, but seemed to offer, in its excellence, the right sort of approach. If I was to be kept away from details of Lotte's personal life and denied access to the collected source material, the best factual approach was going to be through published data, not only the records, but the printed ephemera.

These details were available in Hamburg, Vienna, Munich and Salzburg. I already had the information needed for Lotte's performances in London between 1914–1938 (and the master-classes which were performances too); the Met, Chicago and San Francisco Operas sent me theirs, and there were several people who were delighted to talk to me about Lotte.

Desmond Shawe-Taylor, the distinguished critic and a lifelong admirer and personal friend of Lotte's, gave me considerable encouragement and allowed me to read his sheaf of her letters. So did Archie Drake, one of her pupils from Santa Barbara, who had more letters and plenty of anecdotes. He introduced me to Ron Holgate, a fellow-student with Lotte, who was appearing in London in 'Lend me a Tenor'. Alfred Levy, who had known Lotte in the 1930s, provided me with pictures and stories and was the only person to answer my appeal for correspondents which I had placed in *The Times*. Isidore Lichtman from Chicago, who had not only heard Lotte while being an usher in the Opera House, but had carried a spear in *Lohengrin*, gave me programmes and details about the early 1930s. Jürgen Borchert, who lives not far from Perleberg in the DDR, provided information about the place of Lotte's birth, also photographs and other valuable information. K. A. Pollak, son of the conductor Eugen Pollak, became an excellent source of reference for details about the conditions pertaining in Austria and Germany up to 1934, and sent programmes, gave advice and generally became a means of obtaining quick answers.

In 1985 I went to Hamburg where I was very kindly received at the Music Library of the University and given the files of actual playbills from 1910. In Vienna, thanks to Herr Hofrat Dr Brosche, Director of the Music Collection in the Austrian National Library, the same applied, and I was also free to peruse many books there which are not easily available in England. Munich offered information about the very few performances Lotte had sung there – it was not one of her places – but the open shelves in the three libraries I visited yielded a marvellous collection of reference books and historic magazines. Salzburg was equally hospitable in the person of Herr Jaklitsch, the archivist at the Festspielhaus, who gave me his guard books and photograph albums to inspect and then arranged for me to have copies of what I wanted.

When I reached home again, I had enough material to begin to write, in addition to which, Robert Tuggle of the Metropolitan Opera New York had sent me a great bundle of photocopies of all kinds of important pictures and cuttings. There was another pile from the Santa Barbara Public Library, and from friendly people in Australia and New Zealand.

Floris Juynboll, the Dutch discographer, has kept in close touch and eventually asked to read the typescript before it was finished. His comments, corrections and suggestions have continued to be of enormous help, and he has been a kind of pre-editor as the book progressed. His agreement to allow inclusion of his considerably amended and expanded discography as well as his appraisal of Lotte the Recording Artist is very greatly appreciated, as is the part played by Jim Seddon.

In Vienna I was housed and fed by Christopher Norton-Welsh, a significant person in the gramophone world, and together we visited a number of singers who remembered Lotte.

The following people and, in a few cases the institutions they represent, all receive my grateful thanks and acknowledgement for their help and encouragement: Peter Andry, EMI; John Ardoin, Dallas; Professor Dr B. Barcowioch, Munich; Fru Kron Bucht, Operan, Stockholm; Grace Bumbry, Switzerland; Claudia Cassidy, Chicago; Sarah Boslaugh, Boston, Mass.; Thaddeus Crenshaw, Paris; Joan Cross, Great Glenham; Elizabeth Duschnitz, New York; Francesca Franchi, London; Dr R. O. Martin Elste, West Berlin; Jeremy Geidt, Cambridge, Mass.; David Hamilton, New York; Peter Heyworth, London; John Higgins, London; Dr Robert Jones, London; Alfred Kaine, DGG Hamburg; Dr Götz Klaus Kende, Vienna; Lotte Klemperer, Switzerland; J. C. Lamb, Montevideo; William Mann, Coleford; Peter Morse, Honolulu; Frau I. Pahlitzsch, Dresden; Jim Pearse, London; Charles Strafford; Sonia Sharnova, Chicago; Frau Doktor Martha Schneider, Vienna; Stroma Sutherland, London; Paul Wilson, Aldeburgh; Dr. Dagmar Wünsche, West Berlin; Also to the late Gustl Breuer, Paul Hirschman, Aenne Michalsky and Gerald Moore.

Public Libraries and other sources of information: Public Library Auckland, New Zealand; Forschungsinstitut für Musiktheater, University of Bayreuth; Akademie der Künste, West Berlin; Landesarchiv, West Berlin; Public Library, Boston, Mass.; Hungarian National Opera Archive, Budapest; State Opera Archive, Dresden; Public Library,

Dunedin, New Zealand; University Theatre Collection, Hamburg; British Library, Bloomsbury and Colindale, London; Royal Opera House Covent Garden Archive, London; Polish Cultural Institute, London; Westminster Music Library, London; Wiener Library, London; Bavarian State Library, Munich; German Theatre Museum and Library, Munich; Bavarian State Opera Archive, Munich; Metropolitan Opera Archive, New York; Church of Latterday Saints, Plymouth; Public Library, City of Plymouth; Czech National Theatre Archive, Prague; Public Library Santa Barbara, Calif.; Allgemeinbibliothek, Schwerin, D.D.R.; Australian Broadcasting Commission Archive, Sydney NSW; Austrian National Library Music Collection, Vienna; Public Library Wellington, New Zealand.

I am grateful to the following publishers and organisations for permission to quote extracts from material which is their copyright, or to authors whose copyrights have reverted to themselves: Jonathan Cape – *My Many Years* by Arthur Rubinstein; William Collins – *Too Strong for Fantasy* by Marcia Davenport; *More than Music* by Alec Robertson; *The Correspondence between Richard Strauss and Hugo von Hofmannsthal* translated by Hanns Hammelmann and Edward Osers; Duckworth & Co. – *Puccini: A Critical Biography* by Mosco Carner; Faber & Faber – *On and Off the Record* by Elisabeth Schwarzkopf; Victor Gollancz – *The Last Prima Donnas* by Lanfranco Rasponi; Hamish Hamilton – *The Baton and the Jackboot* by Berta Geissmar; *At the Piano – Ivor Newton* by Ivor Newton; Secker & Warburg – *Ring Resounding* by John Culshaw; Internationale Richard Strauss Gesellschaft, Vienna, Correspondence between Richard Strauss and Ludwig Karpath. Every effort has been made to trace holders of copyright material. If, however, any query should arise, it should be addressed to the Publisher.

Deviock, Cornwall 1987 Alan Jefferson

Chapter One

Family and Teachers

1888–1910

From Hamburg you drive east to Lauenburg and over the River Elbe to the frontier-crossing into the Deutsche Demokratische Republik (East Germany). The road becomes Route 5 to Berlin. The countryside is sandy, with scrub and pine trees as far as Ludwigslust. Here the road leads north to handsome Stettin, and thence to Wismar on the Baltic, only 67Km away. But south, which is the way we are going, it leads to Perleberg, at a cross roads that does not mean much nowadays, and the way ahead leads to Berlin: 140Km.

Perleberg is just inside the DDR. A bulge in the frontier between East and West falls short by only 16Km, barred by the River Elbe. This is the state of affairs today, but there have been civilisations in Perleberg for the last 10,000 years, they say.[1] In the middle ages, the Slavs who lived there gave way to German races who made it a prosperous town in the fourteenth century. Within the district of Prignitz, it had its 'Perleberger accent' spoken for some way round, and then, in 1701, it came under absolute control of Brandenburg and the Prussians.

Perleberg has some interesting buildings, some of Dutch architecture, while the large, sandstone figure of the medieval Roland,[2] Perleberg's symbol of 'special freedom, jurisdiction, municipality and trade' still stands on guard in his medieval, knightly armour in the market place.

Roland and Lotte Lehmann are the two individuals who represent Perleberg, and, for most people, Lotte Lehmann is the better known of the two.

She was born in Perleberg on 27 February 1888,[3] at 11 Pritzwalker Strasse, during a heavy fall of snow. Her mother, Frau Marie (née Schuster) already had a four-year-old son called Fritz, who carefully protected and championed his little sister throughout their lives.

Both the Lehmann parents had come to Perleberg from Prenzlau, then in Pomerania, now at the eastern end of the DDR, close to the Polish border. They probably moved westwards from Mecklenburg into

Brandenburg round about 1880. Fräulein Schuster had been engaged to a young man whom she had known for most of her life. He was killed at the beginning of the Franco-Prussian War in 1871 'fighting heroically for the Fatherland'. The Schuster family were prosperous millers in Prenzlau, living comfortably without the need to economise; but suddenly Marie's father died, and the large family was left without means when the business collapsed. As the eldest daughter, Marie bore much of the responsibility for trying to rehabilitate her ailing mother as well as her brothers and sisters, developing the start of a nervous gastric complaint that was never to leave her.

Although it was considered proper to allow a long period of mourning before a girl looked for another suitable husband, Marie was obliged, by the circumstances, to look in the direction of a young man called Carl Lehmann, who was at the outset of a safe and respectable career as a junior official in the *Ritterschaft*, a national benevolent society. They were married in 1873.

Shortly after Lotte's birth her father was promoted to be local secretary in the Perleberg district of the *Ritterschaft* and the family moved to a larger house provided at 51 Berliner Strasse. It had a large garden, which was Carl Lehmann's pride and joy.

Lotte describes her grandparents as 'simple old people' and her grandfather was simple in another way. Owing to an accident he was weak in the head and always thought he was at home in Frankfort-on-the-Oder, no matter where he really was. He never comprehended any change of scenery and shook his head in disbelief. His wife was skinny and bad-tempered. She did not get on at all with her daughter-in-law when she came to stay, and it greatly upset Lotte to see her mother in tears after the many rows which used to go on between the two women. It seemed that Carl Lehmann was his mother's pet. His sister, Lotte's aunt Lenchen, was 'deformed, sickly and embittered' although she could sing like an angel.

Singing seemed to run in the family. Carl Lehmann belonged to the Perleberg Choral Union (unkindly called 'The Half-Lung' by Fritz) and sang tenor with great enjoyment and vigour. Lotte's mother possessed a far better voice, a rich and smooth mezzo which should probably have been trained. Her father had been completely against any such nonsense, even though a professor of music who had heard Marie sing in Prenzlau, offered to give her free tuition.

Marie Lehmann did not like Perleberg. Her family had now all moved to Berlin, and she wanted to be near them. So she urged Carl to apply for a transfer, but it was unsuccessful and they were obliged to stay put.

In 1894, Lotte went to the primary school, where she loved to sing. At an early age she was given a solo part in the end of term entertainment, impressing people with the quality of her voice and the expressiveness of her little performance. Father Lehmann shut his ears to the polite comments of other parents – 'the makings of a voice, she should have training' – because he had a good, safe job in mind for Lotte, either she would be a secretary or some such, with a pension of course. Lotte's mother, perhaps regretting her own lost vocal opportunity, was in favour of at least giving Lotte a chance in this direction.

Whenever Carl Lehmann got a bonus payment from the *Ritterschaft* they went by third class train to Warnemünde by Rostock on the Baltic. There they were all at their best: mother forgot her stomach cramps, father's eyes wrinkled with laughter and he gave out modest sums of pocket-money. Baltic breezes are particularly effective in producing a tan on the face and whatever other parts of the body are exposed. Warnemünde was a fashionable resort with its large hotels, casino and Kurhaus on the front. Lotte used to press her nose to the windows of the Kurhaus restaurant, watching the rich people eating the luxurious foods, always to be far beyond her means, she thought. By contrast, the Lehmanns stayed at a small pension some hundred metres or more behind the fashionable houses and buildings.

At the age of fourteen, in 1902, Lotte was confirmed in the Lutheran Church, and very soon after that, Carl Lehmann obtained his long-sought transfer to the headquarters of the *Ritterschaft* in Berlin. At last, and after many domestic squabbles, Frau Marie was reasonably satisfied at the prospect of being near her relatives again.

Brother Fritz had been forced to abandon his ambition of going to sea; the parents had not been able to afford the funds to send him to a marine college, so he found a job as a clerk in Berlin, and went on ahead of the others. They moved to Hochmeister Strasse in a lower-middle-class district of North Berlin, and Lotte was sent to the *Ulrichsche Höhere Mädchenschule* (Ulrich's High School for Girls) named after the principal. Most of the girls were in love with 'Ulli', as they affectionately called him, and he seemed to be a thoroughly sensible and intelligent man. 'Go your own way,' he told the girls, 'don't follow the herd. Be individuals, but each of you be true to yourself. This is the best thing in life. It lies before you: so live it!'

Lotte left Ulrich's school in tears in the summer of 1904, and the family moved again, to a rented flat (with garden) in Gross-Lichterfelde, right across Berlin to the South. There Lotte helped her mother with the housework and sang as she dusted and brushed and washed up.

Sometimes she went to the piano and accompanied her own ballads and folk-songs. As yet she knew very little serious music.

One day their neighbour from upstairs, a Frau Kühnen, came in to their apartment and congratulated Lotte on her singing, which she had been listening to with pleasure. Had she not thought of having her voice trained? Lotte and her mother replied that they could not possibly afford it, though it was what they both desired. Frau Kühnen offered to help. Her uncle was connected with running the canteen at the *Königliche Hochschule für Musik*. This august institution was founded in 1869 under the direction of Joachim as part of the *Akademie der Künste* (Academy of Art).[4] It was one of the finest in Germany with outstanding musicians on the staff who, after 1872, used to give public concerts with the advanced students. It is not far from the Tiergarten.

On the day after Frau Kühnen's first visit, she returned with news that the entrance examination for new students was in a week's time, and an advanced student (who was already taking pupils) would listen to Lotte that very afternoon. Lotte had heard only two performances of opera: *Lohengrin*, and *Mignon* with Emmy Destinn, and full of apprehension (for her father had not been told) Lotte and Frau Kühnen arrived together at the School of Music. The advanced student's name was Erna Tiedke, 'a very superior-looking girl' who had gone out of her way to impress, with imitation jewellery, a shawl trimmed with ostrich feathers and a grand attempt at sophistication and worldly knowledge. Lotte followed her as she sang, and went up to top C. This pleased Tiedke who thereupon said she would prepare her for the examination.

'You have a very pretty voice,' she said, 'and my lessons cost two marks each. But in your case this audition is free. Bring Siebel's aria from *Faust* and the aria 'Jerusalem' from *St. Paul*. I shall see you again tomorrow.'

As they had only a week to prepare, they concentrated upon the aria from Mendelssohn's oratorio, and Lotte immediately discovered two things about herself: her sense of rhythm was weak, and she had to alter her natural way of singing to conform with the instruction she was receiving.

Then she had to confess to her father what had been going on. A mild man, he took it calmly – almost as if he was expecting it – and promised to go with her to the audition. Then he would enquire whether it was felt that Lotte had it in her to become a capable singing-teacher. If not, she must go to the commercial school.

They arrived at the *Hochschule* with Lotte feeling not unduly nervous. The Mendelssohn aria had been thoroughly rehearsed but the *Faust* item was hardly touched because Fräulein Tiedke felt certain that it would not be needed. Thirty-two applicants were applying for eight places and were auditioned in alphabetical order of surnames. Thus L came about half way, and it seemed that most of the aspirants had already sung 'Jerusalem'.

Lotte was called in eventually, and found herself in front of a long table at which Professor Adolf Schulze, head of the singing department, presided. Then Fräulein Tiedke was called in and Lotte noted, with interest, how all her fine airs had disappeared, and she had shrunk to student status, though she seemed elated at being invited to sit with the panel of adjudicators.

When asked what she was going to sing, Lotte's reply was greeted with groans. They had already heard 'Jerusalem' far too often that day – had she nothing else? Fräulein Tiedke went pale and did her best to persuade Professor Schulze to allow Lotte to sing her chosen piece, but in vain. It had to be Siebel's aria! So she began, receiving no encouragement from Tiedke, but as she progressed, she noticed approval in the faces of those listening to her. At the end, they turned to Fräulein Tiedke and congratulated her, thanking Lotte, and asking her to come back on the following day.

Erna Tiedke rushed out of the room after Lotte and embraced her. 'You've passed, you idiot!' she cried in her youthful excitement, and to Lotte's father: 'She must go on the stage!'

'Not a singing teacher?' he asked, hesitantly.

'I shall become a concert singer,' said Lotte proudly.

On the way home in the tram, Carl Lehmann told Lotte that he was going to enquire whether she was eligible to receive a grant. 150 marks for the course was out of the question.

When Professor Schulze received Lotte and her father in his office, he confirmed that she had been awarded a place for the coming term, and her professor would be Fräulein Helene Jordan. A scholarship? No, not for the first term, but thereafter it might be possible. Schulze considered Lotte's voice to be ideal for oratorio: she should be thinking in that direction.

'Don't let your child go on the stage, though,' he advised Carl Lehmann, 'she is entirely unsuited to the opera. But when her voice has been trained, she will certainly be able to earn her living.'

Carl Lehmann applied to the *Ritterschaft* for a loan of one hundred and fifty marks, but was given a dusty answer. In his position it was considered unethical to ask for an advance or a loan for this purpose. He was most distressed and more or less gave up the whole idea of trying to find the money. Lotte's mother and Fritz were spurred on to help her, and somehow the money was found: goodness knows where it came from, but 150 marks were scraped up and paid over. Lotte began.

Fräulein Helene Jordan was a patient and pleasant woman who had to start absolutely from scratch. At the age of sixteen, most girls in Germany had already received some musical education, but not Lotte. She had to go through breathing, placing the voice, scales, sol-fa and all the rest of it. But whenever she was able, Lotte ran off to listen outside the door of the opera class where Erna Tiedke and others, nearly ready to be launched in their careers, made Lotte extremely envious.

Fräulein Elise Bartels was in charge of the elocution class. Lotte afterwards believed that it was due to her that she was able to enunciate so clearly. Lotte enjoyed this, and the Italian classes, and piano – her second subject. But she did not like any of the theory classes. They were as incomprehensible as arithmetic had always been at school, and she was the despair of the theory professor.

This did not seem to have counted too much against her, for when it came to the end of term and she sang Schumann's 'Was will die einsame Träne' as a test-piece, she afterwards heard that she had won a scholarship for free training during the rest of the course.

Everything seemed set for her, but then Lotte's mother became very ill, and there was nobody else to look after her and the house. Lotte took leave, became a housewife, did the cooking – an art at which she was at first spectacularly unsuccessful, though later she improved. In the course of time she was able to return to the *Hochschule*, but found that she had missed a great deal, and was obliged to work harder than ever in an effort to catch up. Carl Lehmann's job was changed, and he became a superintendent with a rent-free flat in Augusta Strasse only a little way north of Lichterfelde, but in a pleasanter district.

Now it was Lotte's turn to be ill. A fellow-student, with whom she had become friendly, needed nursing desperately, but died. Lotte was so upset that her nerves suffered and she had to take a cure – with her mother – at the expense of the *Hochschule*, thanks to kind Professor Schulze.

In the summer of 1907 the Lehmanns discovered an island in the Baltic where it was possible to live very cheaply. It was a resort for artists, known as the 'Hiddensee Riviera'. They went by steamer from Stralsund, some 85Km east of their old haunt, Warnemünde, to the long thin island off the west coast of the far bigger island called Rügen.

During Lotte's second year at the *Hochschule*, Fräulein Jordan was taken ill, and Professor Schulze, who was still advocating oratorio to

Lotte, passed her on to another teacher whose name we do not even know. She was the wrong person, and Lotte had no confidence in her, nor was she progressing at all. Since she was determined to become an opera singer, Lotte wrote to Frau Etelka Gerster, whose private singing school in Berlin was a famous institution, saying that she was determined to reach the opera stage, but had no money.

Some days later a reply came, inviting Lotte to sing for Fräulein Eva Reinhold. She went along, and sang, and the 'friendly, dark-haired' woman told Lotte that she had a beautiful voice. She would recommend that Frau Gerster heard her, but there were no scholarships available at the school. Nevertheless, she might be prepared to take on Lotte as a non-paying student.

Lotte could not believe her good fortune and presented herself to the *Maestra*, Frau Etelka Gerster-Gardini,[5] to give her full name. She was fifty-two when Lotte first met her, a Marchesi pupil and possessed of a remarkable coloratura soprano voice. Verdi had recommended her to the Fenice Theatre in Venice where she made her début as Gilda in *Rigoletto* in 1877. She then travelled all over Europe, and in the USA between 1879–87 there was bitter rivalry between her and Adelina Patti. Gerster then returned to Berlin and opened her singing school in 1896.

After hearing Lotte's voice, Gerster promised her free tuition – as a very great exception – for she acknowledged her beautiful voice. Fräulein Reinhold would be Lotte's first teacher, and then she would take care of her, and shape the voice herself.

Frau Gerster's Singing Academy was a very different kind of place from the *Hochschule für Musik*. Many rich, foreign students attended, gratefully paying the high fees and treating it as a kind of finishing school. Among them Lotte noticed an elegant girl called Betty Kalisch, who was one of Gerster's favourite pupils. By comparison, Lotte felt extremely dowdy and even a nonentity, and this mood seemed to hang over her during the time she was at the Gerster Academy. Fräulein Reinhold's methods did not suit her, and although she worked very hard, she appeared to be making little progress.

One afternoon, Frau Gerster's own teacher, the famous Mathilde Marchesi, visited the school and was fêted. The most celebrated Gerster pupil, Julia Culp,[6] gave a recital for Marchesi, and the students of the school were present, including Lotte. She was full of admiration at Culp's skill and beauty of tone, feeling herself a long way from such finish and assurance. It left her feeling quite miserable.

During a visit to Perleberg in the holidays, Lotte was invited by the wife of her father's old director there, Herr von Saldern, to give a concert. This led to an audition with Baron Joachim zu Putlitz, Intendant of the Stuttgart Ducal Theatre. To prepare for it, Lotte asked Fräulein Reinhold for help and she (not at all pleased at her pupil's presumption) arranged for Professor Bake to coach her. He then accompanied Lotte when she sang Agathe's aria from *Der Freischütz* and Elsa's Act II aria from *Lohengrin*, both vital in her subsequent career.

Professor Bake did not approve of Lotte, especially when she took her own tempi and often sang wrong note-values (known as 'swimming'). He and Reinhold discussed her deficiencies in front of her, and they both came to the conclusion that Lotte wasn't trying. Even so the audition went very well and the Baron, enchanted by Lotte's voice, expressed the wish that she apply for another audition and 'a definite agreement' when she was ready to accept her first engagement.

So back to school, the flush of success from the audition dampened by Fräulein Reinhold and her method. Towards the end of 1908, Lotte was given 'Dove sono' to study (the Countess's aria from Act III of *Figaro*). It went from bad to worse, and instead of laying it aside for a week or so, Reinhold kept Lotte hard at it until, of course, there came a psychological block. Reinhold's impatience and Prussian stubbornness made matters worse, and Lotte remembers that even at the first notes of the aria's introduction, she began to tremble.

At the end of the year she was summoned to Frau Gerster. She showed no friendliness, no sympathy, and when Lotte left the academy that afternoon she knew in her bones that she would never enter that building again. She wrote to Fräulein Reinhold. It was an unfortunate letter, long and recriminatory, suggesting different singing methods and calculated to offend an even less haughty Prussian singing teacher. It was the kind of over-confident letter she was to write throughout her life.

On New Year's Eve, Lotte received a command to see Reinhold in her house. There she was harsh and severe in manner and in speech. Lotte had sung badly of late; she and Frau Gerster were completely disenchanted with her; and she must consider her studies at the academy to be at an end. And she had *no suggestions to make*: they had written off Lotte entirely.

If this was unkind and unhelpful, the last sting from Fräulein Reinhold came with the post for poor Lotte sitting at home as though paralysed. It was a sofa cushion that she had made as a Christmas present for Reinhold – returned with a letter, written on behalf of the Principal, who apparently would not condescend either to dismiss Lotte herself, nor to correspond with any of the Lehmanns. The letter contained such expressions as: 'take up a practical career', 'none of my pupils has ever been such a disappointment', 'Frau Gerster requests me to tell you that your progress is not even that of a mediocre pupil, and that even as a paying pupil you would have been expelled'.

Lotte's mother helped her to bed, her father kept back his comments in the silence, and Fritz stayed beside her until, near dawn, she was able to sleep.

An advertisement to be a companion to some aristocratic old lady got no reply, and there seemed nothing else but to agree to beginning a secretarial course that was due to start on 15 January 1908. Unless . . .

Now the real Lotte showed herself, the Lotte who would not be put down, who knew herself and her capabilities, as 'Ulli' had known them – how long ago? The Gerster experience seemed to have lasted a lifetime. She kept the letter for evermore.

Lotte wrote to Frau Mathilde Mallinger[7] in Berlin.

Born in Zagreb in 1847, Mallinger made her début as Norma in Munich in 1866 and then became principal soprano at the Berlin Court Opera between 1869–82. After teaching singing in Prague, she opened her Berlin school in 1895. Mallinger is best remembered, though, as the creator of Eva in *Die Meistersinger* in Munich. During a long and tiring rehearsal under Wagner in June 1868 in the Hoftheater, everybody was thoroughly exhausted and out of sorts. When it came to Mallinger singing her last line for the umpteenth time: 'Keiner wie du, so hold, zu werben weiss!', while placing the Master Singer's wreath on Walter's brow, she introduced a trill on the word 'werben'. It immediately released the tension and there was general laughter. Wagner looked at her and said: 'Well, have your fun. You may keep your trill if you like it so much.' And it has stayed in the score.

She seems to have been a sensitive, attractive and good-natured woman. She carefully read Lotte's enormously long letter that set out all her hopes, her fears, her dreadful experiences at the Gerster Academy, and her treatment there. All she asked for was an audition, to set her mind at rest again, to be reassured about her voice. Might she even take some lessons from a pupil whom Frau Mallinger recommended?

'The Mallinger' replied in a few days, inviting Lotte to come and sing to her. This helped efface all Lotte's misery and filled her with the self-confidence which had been drained away by Gerster and Reinhold.

She duly arrived at 'a real artist's house' full of mementos. Among them Lotte was amazed to read a card attached to a faded wreath and bearing the words: 'To the immortal Elsa – Ludwig II'. The stately old lady (she was sixty-one) greeted Lotte, told her to forget her misfortunes and to *sing*! There were pupils sitting round and listening, and after Lotte had finished, Mallinger sent them away while she spoke privately to Lotte. But first of all, she didn't speak: she sang. She sang personally to Lotte, Mallinger the idol of a King! The effect was devastating: this was the way, with open throat and with joy in the voice and Lotte could not help singing with her.

'The Mallinger', with her big, beautiful, laughing eyes, was entranced. 'No talent indeed,' she scoffed, 'I'll show you!' Then she looked serious for a moment, for she could not give free tuition. All the same, she invited Lotte to come often and listen at the classes where there was much to be learned, while she considered a way to manage the fees.

'Come when you like,' she told Lotte, 'I teach all day – but in any case come and see me again tomorrow.'

Lotte kissed her hand and left, dancing on air and with her heart full of love for the old lady who had, in such a short time, reversed all the events of her previous school. It was a different, laughing, bubbling Lotte who reached home to tell them what had happened. Even her father seemed pleased and encouraging, and said he heartily wished that she would be able to become one of Frau Mallinger's pupils. This was a surprise. The good old man had been working away behind the scenes after witnessing and sharing his daughter's unhappiness at the Gerster débâcle. He had written to the Baron Konrad Gans Edler Herr zu Putlitz, who lived in the stately home of Gross-Pankow, some twenty-five kilometres distant from Perleberg, on the road to Pritzwalk. Carl Lehmann had worked under the Baron whom he had met officially, but was not on social terms with him. The Baron's brother was Stuttgart's Intendant who had already heard and liked Lotte's voice.

Carl Lehmann knew that Baron Konrad zu Putlitz was a patron of the arts, and had been to meet him in Berlin to ask whether he was able to consider supporting his daughter in her singing lessons. After confirmation from his brother, the Baron promised to pay for the tuition himself. This whole episode shows great credit so far as Carl Lehmann was concerned, for going outside his social *Kreis* in a begging manner, yet with evident stature and confidence.

Lotte wrote to the Baron, attempting to express her gratitude, whereupon the Baroness invited her to have tea with them all in their Berlin house in Tauentzienstrasse, where they always spent the winter. Erika zu Putlitz[8] recalled Lotte's appearance at that first meeting. She wore a simple white blouse and dark skirt. Her blonde hair was fastened back with a small black slide, but it was her eyes, her large blue eyes which looked at them shyly, almost uneasily, while her movements were unsure and restrained.

Lotte thought that the Baroness was a lovable woman whose Prussian severity was a thin mask for her big heart. The Baron,[9] an idealist, had a very artistic nature, for as a young man he had lived among theatre people when his father, Gustav zu Putlitz, had been the Intendant of the Royal Theatre in Karlsruhe. The Baron was tall, slim and fair, with penetrating blue eyes, a neatly-trimmed beard and an aristocratic bearing. There were three sons and two daughters, Erika and Elisabeth. Elisabeth, the younger girl, played the piano well, and accompanied Lotte when she sang the *Freischütz* aria and some folk-songs. They took to her as readily and as affectionately as she to them.

Lotte made tremendous progress under Frau Mallinger's guidance and encouragement, and her voice developed gloriously. Although the old lady sometimes lost her temper – or seemed to – Lotte knew perfectly well that she didn't mean what she said, and was only exhorting her to greater effort or closer comprehension. Mallinger was, without doubt, the right teacher for Lotte, and kept her for a year. She studied her first role of Agathe in *Der Freischütz* with Arthur Arndt, the coach at Mallinger's school before he opened his own successful academy of singing in Berlin. Knowing the notes of the arias and concerted pieces in an opera is not at all the same as learning the whole role, as Lotte soon discovered. But Herr Arndt not only prepared her for the part, but carefully prevented her from making ordinary singing mistakes at the same time, so that it was, in effect, a singing lesson as well.

At Eastertide 1909, Frau Mallinger said to Lotte: 'Off you go now and get yourself an engagement. I'll make the appointments for you to sing to some agents.'[10] But even Mallinger's name was of no avail in the usual chicken-and-egg situation which bedevils all beginners in the theatre: 'What was your last job? You haven't had one yet? Well, go and get one first. Don't call us . . .'

Mallinger exhorted Lotte to present herself better, to put on grander airs and to stop behaving like a country cousin. This Lotte could never do, and all the auditions ended in the same way; so she wrote to Baroness zu Putlitz, whose husband seems to have set wheels in motion with one of the largest agencies in Berlin. They paid more attention, were kinder and more helpful, but still they failed to get her an appointment.

Probably at Arthur Arndt's suggestion, Lotte had lessons in deportment and movement with Herr Dahn, the stage manager of the Royal

Berlin Court Opera, who took her through Agathe, trying to help overcome her native clumsiness. She said she felt as thought she had too many arms and legs which got in the way all the time.

Part of Lotte's holidays were now spent with the Putlitzes at Gross-Pankow. There the Baroness organised a strict daily plan for everyone, family, guests and servants, that began with morning prayers at 7 o'clock sharp, and was kept punctually until last thing at night. Lotte became especially friendly with Erika, who was slightly younger than herself, but they both treated Elisabeth like a child. Erika possessed her mother's efficiency, combined with her father's clear mind, though without his dreamy nature.

Sometimes the Baron took them out in a horse-drawn chaise which he drove himself, and often Lotte sat beside him. He teased her by asking what the crops were as they passed his fields, knowing that she had no idea of the difference between corn and barley, wheat or rye. They all teased her, in turn, about eventually becoming a *grande dame*, beautifully dressed and perfumed and unlikely to know them any more. Lotte loved it all, they were so kind and easy to be among that it was like a second home.

She sang again for the Baron Joachim when he came to his country house from Stuttgart, and a few days afterwards, at a tennis party, Baron Konrad told Lotte a great secret: she was about to be offered a contract for one year at 150M a month to go to Stuttgart. The Baroness told her not to worry about having no clothes: she would supply them, and would also arrange for her accommodation.

Although this sounded too good to be true to Lotte, Baron Konrad was less satisfied. He warned her that there would very likely be jealousy and intrigues against her when it became known that she had a personal link with the Intendant; she might do better elsewhere, at an opera house which had no such connection between her and the management. He said he would continue to look round on her behalf. Lotte trusted him completely and felt certain that whatever he said was right for her.

Then Herr Dahn told Lotte that a certain Herr Halpern was looking for singers to take on a tour to Bucarest, and had put her name forward. Lotte's mother was aghast and Fritz thought his sister was already in great danger. Carl Lehmann, now fully behind Lotte, could not do enough in her interests and went from Dahn to Mallinger to Halpern and eventually to the chief Court Conductor, von Strauss (who was not, of course, Richard Strauss). He had no enthusiasm for the tour and strongly recommended against it. Carl Lehmann was much relieved at such good advice from one in authority, but Lotte was furious. Because she had to have the contract countersigned by her father, and he refused to do so, she was forbidden to go. And they were offering her 160M a month, with (impressively) *second*-class travel.

Strauss was right, and so was Carl Lehmann, for only a short time afterwards Lotte read in the newspaper that Director Halpern's enterprise had folded in Sofia – they had not got as far as Bucarest.

In the holidays which followed, Lotte again spent several glorious weeks at Gross-Pankow and, while there, learned that Harder, her agent, had secured a contract for her at the Hamburg Operntheater for three years, starting at 200M a month, rising by 100M a year. Riches! And so far as Carl Lehmann was concerned, it offered considerable security, which was always important to him.

As she was leaving Gross-Pankow on her way home, the Baron held her hand and said affectionately, with a tear in his eye: 'Bleiben Sie, wie Sie sind.' ('Stay just as you are.') And back to the family, to the red plush and heavy furniture, to the prospect of her dream coming true at last. Her mother was overcome by the Baroness's present to Lotte: her first evening gown of white chiffon.

The parents could not bear the thought of leaving her alone in Hamburg, and had already decided, at the time of the Stuttgart offer, that they would go with her to her first place of work.

It was August 1910.

Chapter Two

The Apprentice

1910–1912

In mid-August 1910, Lotte and her parents packed up and went through the upset of their move from Berlin to Hamburg. Fritz had to remain behind because of his job but the parents, determined not to let their daughter face the wicked world of the opera alone, willingly gave up their lives to her protections. She was twenty-two.

Hamburg was then an independent city within its own small state inside the boundaries of Prussia, always important as the largest port on the North Sea, even from 1241 when it joined Lübeck to form the Hanseatic League. Hamburg's independence extended to its opera, founded in 1678 and altogether different in character from the Royal and Ducal Court Theatres to be found in every principal city. Their tradition was Italian-based: Hamburg's was German.[1]

The city's riches, though, did not extend to the Opera Company. The Hamburg Stadttheater[2] was under the control of Councillor Max Bachur and embraced both the Opera in Dammtorstrasse and the theatrical company with altogether nearly four hundred people on the payroll. They included sufficient personnel to withstand sudden changes of plan and to carry them out, for performances were given every night of the year, including Christmas Day and matinées every Sunday, for ten months out of the twelve. Sometimes there were mixed performances: a play followed by an opera, but usually the two companies performed quite separately. Normally the Opera Company played Hamburg, and the Theatrical company in Altona, at the Schiller Theatre.

Altona[3] was a suburb of Hamburg at the other end of the Reeperbahn, and still is, though in former times it had been part of Denmark. This may have accounted for the different temperament of its audiences: far more tolerant and easy-going than those at the Stadttheater. Consequently, opera performances at Altona were often fair game for ad-libbing and an opportunity to play broadly, even fooling about. The singers followed the actors' example after performances and adjourned to their *Lokal*, the Schiller Café.

Councillor Max Bachur[4] had been more of an accountant than an impresario when he was first appointed to Hamburg, but he had managed to keep the enterprise going in a determined but not exactly exciting or inspiring manner for he lacked an imaginative artistic policy. Hamburg's status as the second important Opera after Berlin depended largely on the voices, but by 1910 Bachur's Company had become so financially run down that he was forced to appeal to the Senate for a subsidy. The Stadttheater was a private concern, out of which the Director was entitled to take the profits. But there had not been any profits for several years and so Bachur was obliged to resort to short-term means by which he hoped to encourage full houses. These included the engagement of famous personalities in guest appearances, such as Enrico Caruso, Artur Nikisch and others; and he also gave his audiences liberal doses of the trivia that they enjoyed, laced with solid German fare. There were always three cycles of Wagner's *Ring* every season.

Perhaps the most notable deficiency at the Hamburg Opera was a musical director. The post had been vacant since Gustav Mahler left Hamburg in 1897 to go to Vienna; from 1903 Gustav Brecher had been principal conductor though without the status of his predecessor and mentor. For the 1910–11 season, Brecher had engaged a young conductor to assist him, one who had already made a name for himself at the German Opera House in Prague: Otto Klemperer.

Hamburg was an instant delight to Lotte from the moment she arrived there. It is a city of trees and water; and, in spite of its massive shipping and industrial core, remains clean and fresh. The Alster lake in the middle of the city is bordered by walks along the water's edge, and these were very appealing to the girl. Her parents had found an apartment close to the Alster at No.94 Isestrasse in the residential part of the city, and Lotte was easily able to walk across to the jetty which stretches out into the lake, from which she watched the pleasure boats crossing and re-crossing the Alster. It was all so much more welcoming than Berlin. Hamburg is neither grand nor imposing and Lotte felt at home there at once. She was overjoyed at her good fortune in coming to work and to sing in such a lovely place.

It was another short distance from 'home' to the Opera House, the Stadttheater, where she went to report her arrival and prove her identity with the contract.[5] She had frequently been warned that officials in the theatre are, without exception, immoral creatures, given to preying on young girls; so it was with protracted parental preaching, considerable misgivings and fast-beating heart that Lotte entered the stage door and asked to be directed to Councillor Bachur.

Perhaps naïvely, she had written to him in advance, expressing her thanks for the engagement and promising to work hard and to be a good girl. Bachur received her in his office with great civility and instead of a monster she saw a short, grey-haired man who seemed impressed that both Mathilde Mallinger and Baron Putlitz were her sponsors. He promised that he would watch her progress with great interest and then, with a slightly absent-minded glance of fatherly benevolence through his spectacles, he went back to what he had been doing before her arrival.

The opera season[6] began on 2 September with *Die Zauberflöte* in which Lotte had been cast as the Second Boy. Four days later she was to become the Second Page in *Tannhäuser*, a Bridesmaid in *Der Freischütz* and then an Apprentice in *Die Meistersinger*. The thought of having to encompass all these roles within four weeks, together with a real one – Freia in *Das Rheingold* – made her head spin.

Lotte was sent to the coach, Felix Landau, a stout little man with a perpetual bad temper, who assumed her to be ignorant, stupid and unmusical. Opera house coaches are an interesting breed and, like stage doormen in their sphere, are much the same the world over. They have spent their lives in assisting, moulding, building the same roles over and over again, always finding that the singers who come and go are exhibiting the same faults and foibles. The coach either becomes an efficient conductor, or else he is satisfied with his lot and remains at the rehearsal piano for ever, growing more frustrated as the seasons roll by. There is then only his celesta for *Zauberflöte*, recitatives to accompany, or the off-stage band to control. His world stretches no further.

Herr Landau was one who tried to impress the singers by announcing all kinds of recommendations – if he liked their voices. It was not long before he told Lotte that he would put her name forward for Bayreuth; but she soon discovered that this meant nothing at all. Landau needed flattering, and she did this so effectively that very soon he was working with her at all hours perfectly willingly.

Although the *Zauberflöte* was a repertory piece and generally went on 'cold' each season, it so happened that a number of principals were new to the production and Brecher called a full dress rehearsal with orchestra. It was the first time that Lotte had set foot on a stage and she was terrified. The First Boy of her trio was a delightful girl from Merseburg near Leipzig, some four months younger than Lotte and had been at

Hamburg for a season already. Her name was Elisabeth Schumann. The Third Boy was Annemarie Birkenström who was no newcomer either. The two of them did their best to help and cheer poor Lotte who looked as miserable as she felt.

The producer was Siegfried Jelenko[7] (known as 'Yelle'). He was a large, aggressive-looking man with a red face, but who was in reality gentle and kind. His position forced him to put on a blustering act for much of the time. Lotte's woeful countenance made him shout at her to look more cheerful, and not to present the appearance of a mourner. She reminded him that this was the first time she had sung with an orchestra, but that made no difference. She felt a complete failure at being reprimanded in front of the whole company.

Nor had she been taught how to use make-up. Annemarie helped her at first, but the result was not very sensitively applied. She followed her two companions down the stone steps on to the stage for the performance, absolutely convinced that every member of the cast, the chorus, the ballet and all the stage hands were staring at her. Then *on*, pushed by Annemarie, into the light. At first Lotte saw only the gleam of Brecher's white cuffs, then the orchestra, and beyond them her *enemy*, the audience!

Suddenly something unusual happened. In her numbed condition Lotte became aware of Brecher's spectacles flashing as though to attract her attention, and having done so, his hands seemed to be magically drawing out the melody for her until her voice, like a fluttering bird, settled on his hands, and then hovered, to wing its way out into the huge, wide partial-darkness of the auditorium.

It is a wonderful experience to be accompanied by an orchestra and Lotte's description is a good one. Whether one allows the voice to settle upon the conductor's hands or on the orchestral sound doesn't matter. It must be given over for the conductor to manipulate in exactly the same manner as he is already doing with the orchestral instruments. Nobody can have taught Lotte exactly how to let her voice go like this: it was probably her natural instincts, coupled with Brecher's skill, which allowed that audience to hear the voice of Lotte Lehmann in a performance for the first time. She found the result elating.

Her second role was by no means as successful. The three other *Tannhäuser* Pages were Grete Schlegel, Magda Lohse, and Annemarie Birkenström again; but Lotte's line in the quartet went awry at an exposed moment, and Brecher's look of fury at the resulting discord lost her the little role.

Lotte was terribly upset, not that she particularly wanted this part, but the shame and indignity hurt her. Annemarie cheered her up with the thought that such a miserable part can stick for years, and she could remain identified with it. She was sure that Brecher had already forgotten about it. Lotte waited outside the conductor's room after the performance until he returned from taking his calls, burst into tears and begged him to let her keep the horrid Second Page. He was tired, irritated by the howling girl, and remained adamant. She never sang it again.

In spite of what she considered, at the time, to be a major disaster, she was still allowed to tackle Freia in the *Rheingold* which was being conducted by the great Arthur Nikisch. Freia is the goddess of youth who tends the apples which keep all the gods young; she is taken away as a hostage by two giants against payment for the building of Valhalla which Wotan, father of the gods, cannot afford to give them. At the orchestral rehearsal, Lotte let out such an agonised 'Wehe! Wehe! Wehe!' at being seized that Nikisch stopped the orchestra. He called Lotte to come down to the footlights where he could speak to her. In complete silence and with everyone's eyes on her, Lotte made her slow way down the 'rocks' in her long dress, trying not to trip over it and feeling quite terrible.

Nikisch was very gentle with her. He knew she was a novice and urged her not to be so frightened of him. He smiled and said 'Let's try again.' So back she went, comforted by the kind words of the great Hungarian conductor, then at the peak of his fame and who, if he wished, could be an absolute terror.

Lotte's performance as Freia, nursed by Nikisch, seemed to go well, and she received so many congratulations from her colleagues and from the conductor too, that she sent a telegram to Fritz in Berlin, telling him of her success. Next morning, though, they all read that the Hamburg critics had thought otherwise. Some of their comments were scathing: 'Touching ungainliness . . . throat constricted with extreme nervousness . . . she looked more like a dear little kitten than an imposing goddess . . .' The 'dear little kitten' infuriated Lotte, and she wrote to the critic concerned and to the editor of the newspaper – a silly thing to do. Newspapers always have the last word. Lotte expected that Councillor Bachur would support her campaign, but of course he knew better. Her complaints to him continued long after the event had been forgotten by the rest of the Company.

The musical press in Hamburg at that time had two distinguished critics, Ferdinand Pfohl[8] of the *Hamburger Nachrichten* and Heinrich Chevalley of the *Hamburger Fremdenblatt*. Chevalley was a composer in his own right and also contributed to the influential German magazine, *Die Musik*. He and Pfohl had both been critics on the staff of these papers throughout Mahler's régime in Hamburg and Pfohl had been a student with Mahler in Leipzig. They were men of substance and their opinions can be accepted as informed and reasonable.

Lotte was still complaining about her harsh treatment when she was launched into her fourth role as the First Bridesmaid in *Der Freischütz*, again with Schlegel and Lohse as companions. Eight days after that she was one of the Apprentices in *Meistersinger*, girls trying to be boys (and usually failing to succeed, visually). This was in a production that as very popular with Hamburg audiences, Hans Sachs was sung by the bass-baritone Max Dawison,[9] a celebrated Bayreuth Alberich, whose career in Hamburg lasted until 1926; and the Eva was Bella Alten whose career, to a certain extent, paralleled Lotte's own, though in a less distinguished manner.[10]

Lotte's next new role – for some of the earlier ones had already been repeated – was a Choirboy in Meyerbeer's *The Prophet*, a long-winded, semi-religious work. In mid-October Caruso came to Hamburg for three performances. He sang the Duke in *Rigoletto* (with Dawison as the Hunchback); in *Martha* and in *Carmen*. Ottilie Metzger, one of the greatest German contraltos, was Hamburg's Carmen, and Katharina Fleischer-Edel, a delightful woman and a firm favourite in Hamburg, sang Micaela. Her range was similar to Lotte's and consequently her roles were those on which Lotte already had her eye. Oh to be singing Micaela opposite Caruso and under Klemperer's baton! For he was given the task of conducting all the three Caruso performances while Lotte only saw and heard the great tenor from a distance.

Otto Klemperer,[11] a giant of a man, had occasioned great mirth – and severe criticism – when he sat down to conduct a concert in Hamburg, for conductors were meant always to stand. But his height, accentuated by his gauntness, was immense. He had come to Hamburg at Mahler's emphatic recommendation: 'Grab Klemperer!' had been his laconic telegram. His arrival there had coincided with Lotte's.

She now exhibited the first example of a trait which was to repeat itself throughout her career in the opera house: to aim at and to court affection and protection from the musical director. Later this was extended towards composers, publishers and anyone in a position of authority who was able to support her and advance her, especially when there was competition. She thought she had fallen in love with Klemperer and wrote him poems, anonymous but self-confessing in their authorship. She even persuaded a young composer she knew to set some of them, but Klemperer tartly remarked that he found the music preferable to the words.

Lotte soon discovered something else about Klemperer which may have caused her to ease up. He was a manic depressive of a particularly tempestuous kind, near to hysterical joy when 'up', black and nearly suicidal when 'down'. But he was an influential person in Lotte's life and received as much pestering from her as she bestowed on Brecher, Jelenko and Bachur; but in Klemperer's case it was an altogether different approach. Her imagined love for him, his appearance and his aloof attitude never made her feel comfortable in his presence.

In 1910, Klemperer was usually in a 'down' mood and when in this state he had no time for women, least of all a dumpy, clumsy, unprepossessing young person like Lehmann who did not interest him in the least. Even so, he had noticed one of the prettiest young sopranos and asked her name. 'Elisabeth Schumann', he was told.

Lotte's attention to the Hamburg management and her nuisance value – as well as her undoubted hard work – seem to have paid off, for only three months after the season had begun she was singing the rewarding little role of Anna Reich (Annette Page) in Nicolai's opera *The Merry Wives of Windsor*.[12] Anna's scenes included a love duet and a recitative and aria, perhaps not one of the most memorable in the work, but a challenge and a real opportunity for a young singer. Lotte appears to have come through it favourably, the only criticism being about her nerves and her inexperience that would surely be overcome with the passing of time. Her voice was admired.

In the next four days, Lotte had two more new operas. The first was a new work that somewhat unjustifiably failed because its companion-piece was so poor. *Fortunios Lied* by Offenbach contained two breeches roles for Lotte and Elisabeth and was conducted in exemplary style by Klemperer. The second new part, on 12 December, was the First Esquire in *Lohengrin*, her first direct introduction to this opera which was to become so important to her future career.

With the approach of Christmas, *Hänsel und Gretel* made their seasonal appearance in a cluster of performances with Elisabeth as Gretel and Lotte as the Sandman. This completed her assumption of ten new roles in fourteen weeks.

From the end of 1910, everybody in Hamburg was talking about Richard Strauss's new opera, *Der Rosenkavalier*, which was in rehearsal for its world première at Dresden towards the end of January. Hamburg had secured the rights to produce the opera less than a month afterwards, and of course the usual canvassing was being brazenly carried on by the principal – and the not-so-principal – singers. Bachur intended that the Hamburg production would be a superlative one and had invited Caruso to sing the small role of the Tenor Singer at the Marschallin's levée. But he asked as much for this tiny cameo as for a complete performance and Bachur's purse was unable to stretch that far. The world was deprived of what would probably have been an extraordinary experience, perhaps even followed by a recording.

Lotte had hoped that she would be given the important and delectable part of Sophie von Faninal, and had so persuaded herself of the fact that she came to believe that she had been promised it, and learned Sophie's part assiduously. But due to the request of the Octavian, Edyth Walker (Gustav Brecher's mistress), Elisabeth Schumann was cast as Sophie on the first night.

Lotte got herself into such a state over this 'treachery' that Jelenko was practically besieged in his own office. To extricate himself, and to soften the blow – as Lotte saw it – Jelenko told her that she would sing the highly gratifying role of Lola[13] in *Cavalleria Rusticana* on the night before the first Hamburg *Rosenkavalier*. Actually it was entirely unsuited to Lotte's personality and she sang it only twice, and with the second cast. She continued to nurse a grudge against Elisabeth Schumann whom she regarded as her worst enemy, though nothing can have been further from the truth. At the time, Lotte couldn't see any reason for the loss of Sophie, other than through perfidy and the undermining of her career by jealous rivals.

Suddenly the clouds cleared, and Lotte was allowed to sing her cherished Sophie, on 10 and 17 April, which was fortunate, for Bachur suddenly received a call for help from Leipzig. Dr Hans Loewenfeld, the opera director there, needed a Sophie for their *Rosenkavalier* on 20 April. He had no understudy available. Elisabeth Schumann was committed to Hamburg on that day, but . . . their second Sophie was note-perfect, the young Lehmann. Loewenfeld accepted her gratefully, she went, and was well received. It made her feel very important. Thereafter she alternated in Hamburg with Elisabeth, and it was Lotte's dropped handkerchief which closed the 1910–11 season there.

Lotte's parents had, of course, been kept well up to date with most of what had gone on during the season and had attended many of the performances. How soon Carl Lehmann came to the conclusion that he had been right in allowing his daughter to become an opera singer, is hard to guess, but it is certain that nothing he now said would divert her. The three of them went off to Sylt for a few weeks where they were joined by Fritz in an atmosphere of relaxed family affection. Lotte was full of her successes, equally full of criticism of her rivals, but glad and happy at the way in which her first season had turned out. She did not forget her exercises or her diet, for she was inclined to dumpiness – not suitable for a *Meistersinger* apprentice – though her thoughts were always on real roles.

The first part of the 1911–12 season in Hamburg was probably the most vexatious for Lotte in all the time she spent there. She was singing a few Sophies and not as many as Elisabeth, but this was not enough. The wretched small parts continued and so did her pleas, her letters, her protestations to the management. She was always able to squeeze out some tears when they might help: she must have been a real trial to those in authority.

Her growing friendship with Elisabeth Schumann – at last – and the understanding of her colleagues may have helped to give Lotte another step up. She was given her first principal role of Agathe in *Der Freischütz*. Weber's super-romantic opera of 1821, so very German, is as much a cornerstone of their operatic tradition as *Die Zauberflöte* and *Fidelio*, extending the tradition which was to become formalised in the late nineteenth century by Richard Wagner. It might be thought that taking Agathe in *Der Freischütz* was an honour for any soprano, and it is surprising that Lotte remarks on it without any emphasis in her first autobiography: 'I often sang Agathe in Altona'.[14] She may not have liked the effects and emphasis on the Wolf's Glen taking precedence over the domestic scenes in which she was involved (Max does risk his salvation for love of Agathe!) but Agathe has some wonderful arias, scenes, and a moving finale.

Lotte's first Agathe at the Stadttheater was for a matinée on 8 October.[15] Elisabeth Schumann was the Ännchen; the steady and reliable tenor Hochheim was Max; and Fritz Windgassen (father of Wolfgang, the post World War II Heldentenor) was Kilian. Neither a performance in Altona, nor a Hamburg matinée was as prestigious as an evening in Hamburg, and Lotte seems to have resented this second-rate début. Her ingratitude was visited upon her when she was reduced to First Page in *Tannhäuser* that very evening.

Lotte was delighted six days later when she appeared in Goldmark's setting of an adaptation of Charles Dickens's short story 'The Cricket on the Hearth' (*Das Heimchen am Herd*). Lotte sang May, the 'heroine' and Elisabeth Schumann was the Cricket who first appears from 'a brightly lit rosebush' and is the moving spirit of a simple plot. It is a charming work and has a delightful love duet for May and her lover, Edward.

On the very next night, Lotte was cast as Eurydice in Gluck's opera, with Ottilie Metzger as Orpheus and Elisabeth Schumann as Amor. The advertising and programmes all stated that this opera would be performed after *Pagliacci*, in which Caruso was making the first of his three annual performances. But the star always comes at the top of the bill, that is to say he goes on last, and *Orpheus und Eurydike* began the evening.

Lotte tells how Caruso, always more than punctual, and very nervous, stood in the wings wearing his *Pagliacci* costume and makeup, listening to the Gluck opera. When Lotte came off, he grasped her hand and smilingly declared: 'Ah, brava, brava! Che bella voce! Che magnifica voce! Una voce italiana!'[16]

Lotte was in her seventh heaven, and while she was in her dressing-room, changing from her costume, Jelenko came in and told her that Caruso had taken such a liking to her that she was invited to 'a small dinner party' at Bachur's on the following day. Jelenko made it clear that he did not agree with such a junior member of the company being favoured in this way, but 'what Caruso says, goes.' She hurried down to the stage in order to listen and watch.

She was completely entranced by Caruso's performance and, for the first time, she understood what acting means: the complete transformation of one's own personality into that of the character one is playing. Lotte refers to this as a miracle, and of being reborn. Caruso's art made a lasting impact on her.

On the following evening, after Caruso in *Carmen*, only the top principals – and Lotte – were present at the party, all in what she calls *grande toilette de soirée* while she, in a cheap dress covered as far as possible by a shawl, sat next to the great man. They were unable to communicate properly, though, because Caruso knew no German and Lotte could speak neither Italian nor French. An interpreter told her that because Caruso liked her voice so much, he had just told Bachur that he wanted her to sing Micaëla to his Don José. Jelenko, who was listening, said this was quite impossible, because Lotte had never sung Micaëla – it was far too risky even to contemplate it. Poor Lotte was totally deflated and sat with a red face. Caruso, full of sympathy, tugged at one end of her shawl under the table.

On the following morning she received a telegram from him, inviting her to supper at his hotel after the performance. All the warnings about men that Lotte had received in the past, seemed to be clanging in her ears, and with the aid of a French dictionary she wrote a polite refusal. She was on the point of delivering it when she overheard two members of the company discussing 'the party'. When she asked them 'What party?' she was told that everybody had been invited by Caruso. She felt very foolish, but relieved at having avoided making an absurd *gaffe*.

Caruso seemed exhausted at the dinner and didn't, at first, react to Lotte in the way she expected, but he later brightened a little and gave her a caricature of himself on the back of a menu. This was in exchange for her address. On the following morning she received a large photograph dedicated: *Mademoiselle Lotte Lehmann, la charmante et jolie Eurydike, très sincèrement – Enrico Caruso*.

After this flash of glory, Lotte returned to her small roles and was annoyed when, on the 125th anniversary of Weber's birth, there was a special performance of *Der Freischütz* – without her. The senior soprano, Luise Petzl, sang Agathe. But on Christmas Eve, Lotte sang her usual Sandman in *Hänsel und Gretel*, on this unique occasion doubling the Dew-Fairy.

She need not have felt in the least dissatisfied so far. Lotte had achieved far more and in a shorter time than her young companions among the Pages and Esquires, with the exception of Elisbeth Schumann, but she had been there a year longer. Lotte had the impatience of youth and a burning faith in her own capabilities which, she knew very well, were far more than 'they' (the management) realised. If Jelenko had noted Caruso's talent-spotting for Micaëla, or if the great man had mentioned it to Bachur, it came to the same thing. On 10 January, Lotte was cast as Micaëla opposite Paul Hochheim, and with Ottilie Metzger as Carmen – at Altona. Recommendations such as this had, it seemed, to come from outside.

Micaëla became one of Lotte's best and favourite roles in her early career, one that she continued to sing for over a decade; she did not get the chance to sing Micaëla in Hamburg until the following May, though. These try-outs took time to register.

There were two clear months ahead of her at the end of the season, so Lotte and her parents went to Sylt. For all her later assumption of the successful role of a Viennese, Lotte belonged to North Germany, with sand from the dunes under her feet, and the Baltic breeze shining her face and cleansing her lungs. Then back to Hamburg, refreshed, excited and determined.

When she greeted old Haake, the stage doorman, Lotte was at once aware of changes inside the theatre. A year earlier, Max Bachur had failed to attract any financial support from the Hamburg Senate and had consequently resigned. The previous season had been his year's notice. An impressive-looking man had been coming and going throughout the

1911–12 season, though nobody has said much about him. This was the new director, Dr Hans Loewenfeld from Leipzig, whom Lotte knew.

Loewenfeld[17] was a Berliner who had gained his doctorate in music at Berlin University. He was a minor composer and some of his operas, mainly of a humourous or satirical nature (such as *The Merry Niebelungen*) had been staged. At Leipzig, during the past three and a half years, he had successfully shown his ability as a reformer, especially in his production of *Die Zauberflöte* with its then unusual expression of a gentle, poetical and lofty work, instead of being interpreted at the 'Papageno-level'. Loewenfeld's musical training and dramatic ability seemed likely to make him the ideal director of both elements in the Hamburg Stadttheater.

Loewenfeld looked a Prussian, with his hair *en brosse*, a thick, though not curled or waxed, moustache clearly divided in the middle, a full mouth and a cleft under the lower lip. Direct, dark eyes completed a picture of the man who is accustomed to giving orders and having then carried out immediately. On the other hand, there was a softer, more indulgent side to him. Already, at thirty-seven, he had a double chin and more than a little of the *Genussmensch* lay behind the stern stare.

The musical staff had lost Gustav Brecher (and Edyth Walker had also left), and his replacement, with the title of Artistic Director, was Felix von Weingartner from Vienna. Unfortunately he was not, by nature, a man of the theatre[18] and was far more effective as an orchestral conductor, though he composed eight operas which held the stage temporarily. He always managed to inspire either love or hate in people, was extremely intelligent, self-important, and never ceased to exaggerate a concealment of his humble background and upbringing. Weingartner was to weave his way in and out of Lotte's life for many years to come.

Loewenfeld and Weingartner were together seen as a vital means of saving the Hamburg Opera and bringing to it a 'new look', as well as a new, clear music policy. Jelenko continued to deal with the day-to-day running of the two companies, the planning, casting and handling of the artists and staff.

Otto Klemperer remained on the conducting staff and was joined by a new man, Arnold Winternitz, married to a dramatic soprano, Martha Dorda, who had been at Hamburg since 1910. There were other more junior conductors on the music staff, but Bachur's and Brecher's going had involved the company in a major shake-up.

Lotte was more confident now, at the start of her third season, and after performances, rehearsals, coaching and singing lessons she was beginning to find more time than hitherto in relaxing with her four contemporaries, and especially with the three small-part singers, Annemarie Birkenström, Magda Lohse and Grete Schlegel. They were not jealous of Lotte nor unfriendly, but they quietly envied her 'push and shove' methods that seemed to have achieved wondrous results. They shared a dressing-room and became close, taking part in outings and getting up to the most ridiculous antics, not only outside the Theatre. But there they were in awe of the wardrobe-mistress, Hulda Wulf, who inspired terror in them and in the tailors.

The fifth member of this band, Elisabeth Schumann, was married and consequently lived rather a different private life.

Lotte had become friendly with two girls outside the opera house, Cilly and Liesel Loewengard. Their father was music critic of the *Hamburger Korrespondent*, and consequently of some importance to all singers. Klemperer knew Loewengard quite well, and suggested that he ask Lotte to sing for him at home and invite Dr Loewenfeld to be present. Klemperer had noticed Lotte's voice, rather than her personality, and was enthusiastic about encouraging her progress. Loewengard agreed to Klemperer's proposal and Director Loewenfeld was made aware of an important young singer in his company, one who probably deserved promotion. Evidently he and Klemperer had decided to stretch Lotte's capabilities and gave her three new roles to sing within five days: Ortlinde in *Die Walküre*, Wellgunde (instead of Freia) in *Das Rheingold*, and the cameo of Pepa in Eugen d'Albert's *Tiefland*.

This last role was in preparation for Martha in *Evangelimann* a month later, and was the one which fell flat. Lotte reports that she was given Martha to sing first but it failed; yet this seems unlikely because the records state clearly that she sang ten performances of Martha that season and six in the next whereas she gave only two Pepas, and never again.

After the disappointing Pepa, Loewenfeld lost interest in Lotte who had seemed to fail him. So Klemperer advised her to hand in her resignation rather than face the prospect of being dismissed – something of which Loewenfeld was capable. So Lotte asked her agent, Harder, for his advice. He made enquiries on her behalf at other opera houses and was soon able to assure her that a number of managements, big and small, were showing interest in her, including the Berlin Court Opera. Sensing that Klemperer's advice was right, Lotte asked to be released from her Hamburg contract to which Loewenfeld agreed without hesitation. He had decided that her voice was not sufficiently 'rich' and condemned her acting entirely.

Stung by this criticism, she asked Loewengard about changing her teacher, and he recommended Alma Schadow, one of the most prominent in Hamburg, to whom Fleischer-Edel and Elisabeth Schumann both went. Lotte's voice immediately blossomed under the right tuition, and so quickly that Loewenfeld was sensible enough to change his tune and to realise that he had been wrong about Lotte's voice. He asked her to forget about what he had said and to remain in Hamburg for at least another year because he felt sure it was the best thing for her to do. With this encouragement, Lotte agreed, and in any case she was in no particular hurry to move. It was now only November, a bad time to change horses, and she stayed put, under the watchful eyes of Klemperer and Loewenfeld.

Round about 20 November Klemperer sent for Lotte. She imagined she was still in love with him and his close proximity still made her feel confused and ill-at-ease. He told her that the two sopranos who normally sang Elsa in *Lohengrin* were unavailable for the next performance of the opera on 29th and he had persuaded Dr Loewenfeld to let her risk it. Would she?[19]

Lotte needed no second asking. It was her habit to notice and to study principal soprano roles when she was singing the smaller ones, and she had already 'marked' Elsa which suited her own voice perfectly. But this was entirely insufficient for Klemperer: from his point of view she did not know it at all. Lotte never forgot those terrible *Lohengrin* rehearsals with Klemperer whose presence and performance at the piano she likened to an evil spirit, a demon, with hands like tiger's claws. She was hypnotised by him and, in spite of the dreadful experience, she did all he asked, with clenched teeth.

It was probably the first time in her short stage career that Lotte had taken heed to the lesson Caruso had taught her in his total dedication to the character being played. She, too, subjected herself, subordinated herself entirely to Elsa. Hamburg's leading tenor Pennarini sang opposite her as Lohengrin (and was not at all keen about it either); the visiting Ortrud, Theo Drill-Orridge, was horrified at the antagonism which Lotte's assumption of a major role was causing. Dr Loewenfeld was peeping out from his box at her and Klemperer was furious at each tiny mistake she made. The stage director had trained Lotte 'like a poodle'.[20] What she had been forced to do in rehearsal did not stick, and in the performance she let herself go, moving and expressing exactly what came most naturally to her. She may, she said, have done 'things that were silly', but she was certain that it was better that way, coming out of her 'own being'.

'I was just Elsa', Lotte recollects and, when one reflects on the pure and simple character of Elsa, it is easy to understand how Lotte triumphed by forgetting the director, the conductor, the tenor and everybody else who interfered with her sole task of *being Elsa*.

The critics praised her in a qualified manner, acknowledging her 'lovely bright soprano' but admitted that it was a trial performance. Chevalley's hope that 'the bud will develop into a lovely blossom'[21] was sufficient for Dr Loewenfeld. He forgot everything about a further year on trial and extended her contract with a higher salary. Lotte was fully aware that this first Elsa was immature in many ways, but she regarded it as 'one of the sacred high-points' in her life, and believed that it had really made life worth living! It was the start to her success as an opera singer.

Chapter Three

Fulfilment in Hamburg

1912–1916

Lotte felt happy, grateful and full of hope for the future after her first Elsa, and her parents were inordinately proud of her. But other excitements caused far more general interest in Hamburg and even outside it.

During rehearsals for *Lohengrin*, Klemperer[1] had changed from a 'black' mood to an euphoric state. On 21 November he conducted a performance of *Figaro* with Elisabeth Schumann as Cherubino, and became extremely attracted to her. On the night before Lotte's Elsa, there was a performance of *Rosenkavalier* which Klemperer was rehearsing jointly with *Lohengrin* and in which Lotte was the Sophie and Elisabeth Schumann the Octavian. Her voice was too light for this role, and because it was unfamiliar to her she needed careful, individual rehearsal. Klemperer was more than delighted to give this to her at his apartment in Gross Flottbek, a residential suburb beyond Altona, where the romance swiftly took wing. At a late stage-rehearsal, Klemperer (as the Marschallin) demonstrated how he wanted the love scene to take place. In speaking the words of love to Elisabeth he knew for certain that there was now no going back.

He made no secret of his attraction for Frau Puritz-Schumann and they dined publicly together, so people did not take them seriously nor suspect that there was very much in it. And while Walther Puritz resented the amount of time his wife was spending with the conductor, he allowed that it was probably going to be beneficial to her career.

On 28 November Elisabeth Schumann sang her one and only Octavian in Klemperer's one and only *Rosenkavalier* performance in Hamburg. The reviews were not flattering but Lotte was commended for her Sophie. On the following evening she sang her first Elsa, and Elisabeth was among the audience to listen. Afterwards, Klemperer and Elisabeth Schumann vanished. Puritz was told by his wife's maid that her mistress had eloped with Herr Klemperer. He informed the police.

There is a good deal of confusion as to what happened next. The conductor, Egon Pollak received the runaways who sheltered with him in Frankfort.[2] They had both broken their contracts by leaving the Opera as they did, and had consequently put themselves outside the possibility of engagement by any other opera management in Germany, once the fact was published. For whatever reasons, and perhaps in the chill light of several dawns, they had both returned to Hamburg by 5 December, for on that evening Elisabeth Schumann was singing in Humperdinck's opera *Königskinder* (about some silly geese!).

Elisabeth Schumann did not return to her husband, and according to the social behaviour of the time he was in honour bound to challenge Klemperer to a duel. Klemperer made several excuses and then declined the challenge, though he was apparently in some fear of assault, travelling in cabs with the blinds drawn and eventually absenting himself from the Opera for nearly a fortnight. It says much for Loewenfeld and Weingartner that they were tolerant enough to put up with this behaviour, though it may have brought more interest and support to their organisation than ill-will.

The crisis occurred on Boxing Day 1912. It was Lotte's second performance as Elsa, and Klemperer was conducting again. During the first two acts of the opera some seats immediately behind the conductor in the front row of the stalls had remained empty, but during the second interval, Puritz and some male friends occupied them. Elisabeth Schumann saw this from her box and tried, unsuccessfully, to warn Klemperer when he appeared to begin the third act.

At the very end of *Lohengrin* there are twelve bars of orchestral coda to bring down the curtain, and when the singing had stopped Puritz jumped to his feet, called out '*Klemperer, umdrehen!*' ('Turn round!'), at the same time taking a riding whip from his sleeve, and slashing the conductor twice on his face. Klemperer was knocked over by the suddeness of this attack, but began to climb back from the bottom of the orchestra pit where he had fallen 'like a huge, black spider' as Lotte described him.[3]

Puritz was surrounded protectively by his companions and by other members of the public, and while he was being escorted out of the auditorium, a pastor stood between Klemperer and the exit. 'As a friend of the family' he tried to explain the reason for Puritz's action, but Klemperer, to the huge amusement of everybody, shouted out: 'Herr Puritz has attacked me because I love his wife. Goodnight!' And he disappeared.

The disappearance was real, and for the second time in a month,

Klemperer and Elisabeth Schumann absented themselves from Hamburg. He and Puritz both issued statements about what had happened and the press regarded the whole business with delight during the usual post-Christmas period of flatness for news. But this kind of publicity was too much for Loewenfeld, and Klemperer was dismissed *in absentio*.

The sad thing about the whole business was rooted in Klemperer's character. By the summer of 1913 he was no longer infatuated with Schumann. She returned to her husband in August and stayed with him for another four years. For her, though, it had been the real thing, 'the red thread in my life' she said, many years later.[4] She dwelt on her love for Klemperer as long as she lived, but he refused to mention it or to associate himself with her, even indirectly. He and Lotte did not meet again until very much later, while she and Elisabeth remained the closest of friends wherever they happened to be, together or apart.

Weingartner had brought his latest wife, Lucille Marcel, with him to Hamburg.[5] She was an American soprano and had been a pupil of Jean de Reszke. Early on in the season Weingartner and Marcel were crossing the back of the stage during a matinée performance while Lotte was singing. 'What a voice!' exclaimed Marcel in admiration, believing that Lotte had a great career in front of her. For her part, Lotte also admired Marcel, who had sung Aida at the opening performance of this season, and considered her voice to be deep and velvety and her character exotic and seductive. So, apparently, did Weingartner, to the exclusion of real interest in other sopranos. Lotte found him far too remote to expect any special interest or advancement from him. In his autobiography, Weingartner does not hesitate to place Marcel and himself on the same level as Caruso (in 'a triple constellation') when the tenor came back to Hamburg and sang a *Carmen*, an *Aida* with Marcel and a *Traviata*. But Lotte did not have a place in any of these casts.

At about this time, the Baron Konrad zu Putlitz was attending the funeral of one of his wife's relatives in Bremen, and passed through Hamburg. There he saw Lotte and took her to a coffee-house where he gave her a poem he had written for her, and asked her to read it to him. She was so excited that her hands trembled and she had to lean her arms on the table to conceal her emotion. It was a love poem: 'The Baron and his Protégée'. The word 'protégée' can have several meanings, and she read into it the implication that something was due to be returned to the one who 'protects'. It was this aspect which upset her because the Baron, a person greatly respected by her father and regarded almost as a supernatural being by herself, had shown himself to have feet of clay. It was a great shock, for the Baron, who had already given her the means to complete her training, as well as his hospitality and affection, seemed to have transferred his fondness to the human plane, to the masculine-feminine.

It remains a secret to them both how far the relationship went and the Baron probably visited her in Hamburg more than once. She afterwards tried to redress his approaches by telling him that he had fallen in love with Elsa, not with Lotte. Some ten years later, the Baron fell in love with one of his nieces who was helping him to translate Dante's 'Divine Comedy' into German. His children, who had rather resented his attachment to Lotte, now regarded the old man's soft spot for young girls with more understanding.[6]

The other Baron zu Putlitz in Stuttgart had managed to pull off something of a theatrical *coup* by attracting Hofmannsthal and Strauss to the smaller of his Court Theatres which seated only 800 people. That is how it seemed to zu Putlitz at the time, thought it seems more likely that, with his enormous musical power in Germany at the time, Richard Strauss insisted upon his opera receiving its première there in preference to any other house in the land – for what they were about to do was rather different from *Der Rosenkavalier*. As it turned out, zu Putlitz lived to regret his accommodation of the 'foreigners' who behaved in a high-handed manner.

On 25 October 1912, *Ariadne auf Naxos*, preceded by a new translation of 'Le Bourgeois Gentilhomme' was given with a Moravian soprano, lent by Vienna at Strauss's demand. She possessed a wonderful voice, a stunning appearance and great acting ability. Her name was Maria Jeritza and she had taken Vienna by storm now that she had joined the company of the Imperial and Royal Court Opera there. Everybody in the operatic world had heard about her including Lotte, but Vienna was far away from Hamburg, further and more remote even than Berlin.

Hamburg seemed ideal for the new and optimistic undertaking since Loewenfeld's theatrical and operatic companies were there to be welded together if necessary, and with the least amount of difficulty, unlike the resources of other cities. Indeed, Berlin's production was to come after Hamburg's (thanks to the prudish nature of the Kaiserin, who had been affronted by certain aspects of all Strauss's operas so far, including the last one, *Der Rosenkavalier*, for which a specially 'cleaned up' text had been made for Berlin audiences before it was allowed to be staged there).[7] There were to be many important musical visitors to Hamburg where the production created quite a stir on 17 January 1913, when *Ariadne* was first heard there.

Lotte sang the role of Echo, the middle-voiced of three nymphs attendant on Ariadne (sung by Theo Drill-Orridge), with Hedwig Francillo-Kaufmann as Zerbinetta and Otto Mařak a superb Bacchus. There were some very great voices and operatic personalities in Hamburg during these years, many of whom are known only to collectors of acoustic gramophone records. Some were heard in London during Thomas Beecham's early seasons at Covent Garden and His Majesty's Theatre,[8] partly because it was more convenient for them to come from Hamburg than from Berlin and the voices were not only as good, but less expensive.

Among the preliminary performances of the new Strauss opera Lotte had her first Irene to sing in *Rienzi*. The idea of an opera house mounting such complicated operas simultaneously gives some idea of the administrative ability of Loewenfeld and Jelenko. A week later, on 28 January, Lotte sang Antonia in *Tales of Hoffmann* for the first time, a role which suited her in every way, and in which she grew in intensity and pathos during her stay in Hamburg.

She carried on singing unimportant, as well as the few principal, roles she had been given, treating them with equal care and respect as a good trouper should. Her three friends were glad that she still wished to share her spare time with them offstage, and sometimes to be light-hearted with them on stage too.

On 12 March Lotte sang the exacting role of Dorabella in *Così fan Tutte*. Though not as demanding as Fiordiligi, taken by Winternitz-Dorda, it nevertheless called upon every ounce of her skill. Mozart was still not coming easily, but under Loewenfeld's hand in production and Pohlig's baton, she got through seven performances that season but has nothing to say in her books about any of them. One wonders how she sounded in '*Smanie implacabili*'.

Five days later, there was a revival of Leo Blech's short opera, *Versiegelt*, which had been given its début at Hamburg in 1908. Now it disappeared after only three performances, so Lotte's effort to learn the role of Else seemed to have been to regrettably little purpose. Likewise the small role of Stella in Wolf-Ferrari's *Jewels of the Madonna* gave Lotte only two performances before she dropped it.

Richard Wagner intended that his last 'sacred stage festival work' *Parsifal*, should be performed only at Bayreuth. After his death in 1883, the Wagner family exercised the right to maintain its copyright until the last day of December 1913 for staged performances. Although this dictat was broken wholesale in the USA and South America, it was respected in Holland, Switzerland and Germany where not even concert performances nor selections from the score were given. Weingartner had been attracted to *Parsifal* for many years, having heard it at Bayreuth.[9] He possessed a full score, and realised the importance of mounting a full production of it as soon as conditions allowed. Meanwhile, he gave a concert performance of selections at Easter 1912. All the Kundry scenes were omitted. Parsifal was taken by the celebrated Bayreuth tenor, Heinrich Hensel who was now principal Heldentenor at Hamburg. Lotte sang in the choir.

On 6 April, Lotte was 'off' for the first time in her career. No reason is given, but Winternitz-Dorda sang Antonia in *Hoffmann* for her. It was unusual for Lotte to succumb, for even when she was not feeling at her best, whether or not it was a major role, it was of the utmost importance to her that she fulfilled her obligations to the public and appeared when billed.

Singers have colds, the usual complaints and indispositions just like ordinary people, but they learn to sing over a cold and to put up with the rest of it, generally by becoming the character, as Caruso taught Lotte to do. In April she sang Antonia with the tenor Paul Schwarz. A Viennese, he had come to Hamburg that season to stay there and to remain a firm friend of Lotte's. The next performance of *Hoffman* was exceptional, for Winternitz-Dorda sang all three soprano roles, a most unusual thing to do at the time.

After a top-price *Carmen* with Ottilie Metzger and Otto Mařak, and Lotte singing Micaela, she took her last new role of the season on 30 May as Gutrune in *Götterdämmerung*, with guest Siegfried and guest Brünnhilde who were clearly being tried out for Hamburg, but who both afterwards vanished without trace.

The 1913–14 season opened for Lotte with more Wagner: as Ortlinde in *Die Walküre*. This was a new production by Loewenfeld who was succeeding in brushing some of the dust off Hamburg's more ancient sets, and either restoring them in brighter productions or else commissioning entirely new scenery.[10]

True to form, Weingartner had left Hamburg after the end of the last season, taking Marcel with him, and Selmar Meyrowitz had become the new musical director. He had prepared and carefully rehearsed Gluck's *Iphigenie in Aulis*, which Dr. Loewenfeld produced with Lotte as Iphigenie. The Director now regarded her as one his 'most highly-esteemed associates' and during rehearsals for this opera they had reached complete artistic sympathy and understanding.

Elisabeth Schumann had rejoined the company and was calling herself Elisabeth Puritz-Schumann, though to make her reappearance as

Cherubino, as she did on 4 September, seemed to be conjuring up reminiscences of the last time she had sung that ardent boy.

Lotte felt that if she had not completely 'made the grade' in Hamburg, she was on the way to doing so; and consequently it did not call forth the usual recriminations when Fleischer-Edel and not she was cast as Elsa in Hamburg's five hundredth *Lohengrin* on 6 October.

Caruso came for only two performances this year, and again there was no part for Lotte in either *La Bohème*, where his Mimi was sung by the American soprano Mary Cavan; nor in *Girl of the Golden West*, when the extraordinarily demanding and exhausting part of Minnie was taken by the talented English soprano, Florence Easton. Caruso had been the first Dick Johnson in Puccini's American opera at the Met with Emmy Destinn, in 1910. In 1912, Jeritza had created even more of a sensation as Minnie in Vienna. But Vienna was far away.

Lotte was very happy, had given her heart to Hamburg, and went on learning new roles, practising assiduously and taking regular lessons. On 28 December, after a good deal of thought and no little anxiety, she decided to accept the offer to sing the Countess in *Figaro*, remembering that second aria which had almost finished her in Berlin. It was courageous, to say the least.

This was, in itself, an interesting piece of casting for a girl of only twenty-five, with a newcomer to Hamburg as the Count, the thirty-five year old baritone, Wilhelm Buers.[11] He had arrived with solid experience from Berlin, Vienna, Leipzig and the Met, but was now to remain in Hamburg for the rest of his life. The other principals in this *Figaro* were Elisabeth, of course, as Cherubino; Hedwig Francillo-Kaufmann as Susanna; and the jovial Max Lohfing as Figaro. The others helped Lotte to enjoy herself in this wonderful opera.

On 9 January she first sang a role which was soon to qualify her to sing in three out of the four *Ring* operas (there never could be anything in *Siegfried*) and to lay the foundations for one of her best-loved and internationally acclaimed assumptions in the future: Sieglinde in *Die Walküre*. Meyrowitz put on a single performance before his projected *Ring* cycle five weeks later, but there is no indication of how far Dr Loewenfeld had taken Lotte through the varying shades of emotion in this marvellous role – which she had already heard others singing many times – nor how much of what she was later to crystallise into *her* interpretation was carefully built up over the years. But here it was, for a start, with the splendid American tenor, Francis Maclennan, as Siegmund, and his wife Florence Easton, as Brünnhilde.

A week later, on 23 January, Hamburg Stadttheater presented its first performance of *Parsifal*, a great event and one in which nothing had been spared in the production by Dr Lowenfeld. Taking advantage of Weingartner's preparatory work nearly a year before, he and Meyrowitz used some of their best singers in relatively small but important roles. Hensel sang Parsifal and the first four beguiling Flower Maidens were Elisabeth Schumann, Mary Cavan, Martha Winternitz-Dorda and Lotte. Ottilie Metzger's husband, Theodor Latterman, made a profound impression as Gurnemanz.[12]

Among the other Flower Maidens were, of course, Lotte's young friends with whom she still dressed. They used to fool about, inventing new methods for ensnaring Parsifal in the next performance, vying with one another on stage, later, for the hero's favours. When Hensel was not singing Parsifal, it was Otto Mařak (shortly to marry Mary Cavan); but when the girls went too far and got out of control so that their intonation suffered, it was always Winternitz-Dorda who brought them back with her infallible musicianship.[13] There were twelve performances of *Parsifal* in this first season's introduction of the work, and it always played to full houses.

In Meyrowitz's first cycle of *Der Ring*, Lotte sang Freia, Sieglinde in *Die Walküre*, and she sang Third Norn and Wellgunde in *Götterdämmerung* instead of Gutrune. But in the second cycle in April she returned to Gutrune.

April also saw Lotte's first Pamina in *Zauberflöte*: pure Mozart to which, as she admitted, she was not altogether suited. She made a very sympathetic character in the excellent company of Francillo-Kaufmann as Queen of Night, Ziegler as Tamino and Lattermann as Sarastro.

Lotte's next role was probably the lightest she had yet taken: the sparkling Eurydice in Offenbach's *Orpheus in the Underworld*. Humour had been apparent in several of Lotte's past performances, but of a different kind: that in the *Merry Wives* is heavy and anticipatory; in *Rosenkavalier* it is sophisticated; in *Così* it is high comedy allied to farce; and in *Figaro* it is again high comedy. Now, in the Offenbach work, the whole atmosphere is frivolous, and Lotte revelled in it. She had sung two of her scheduled performances that season (there were altogether thirteen – rivalling *Parsifal* in popularity) when an event of enormous importance occurred.

She was preparing to go on as Micaëla in *Carmen* on 7 May when somebody remarked jokingly to her: 'Sing up tonight! Director Hans Gregor from Vienna is in front to hear Ziegler. If he likes you, he may engage you too!'[14]

Ziegler, who had been Lotte's Tamino in the *Zauberflöte*, was undertaking a series of guest performances in Hamburg. It was usual for talent-spotting directors to hear prospective voices on home ground first before inviting them to audition in a full-scale performance at the new opera house. Hans Gregor had succeeded Weingartner as Director of the Royal Court Opera in 1911. He was from Dresden, had been an actor, a theatre manager, had founded and run the Komische Oper in Berlin most economically, and, exceptionally (for a Royal and Imperial concern), he had come to Vienna through a musical agency. Gregor was forty-five years old when he arrived there, with an unprecedented seven-year contract, and typifying what has been called the 'modern manager', for first and foremost, Hans Gregor was a businessman. He was a tall, bald and fat bespectacled Prussian with a bull-neck and an aggressive voice, not calculated to appeal to the Viennese. But he made it quite clear to the two musical directors, Bruno Walter and Franz Schalk, that he was in charge, and that he did not necessarily believe slavishly in the 'composer's view first' principle. Indeed, it seems that Gregor had little music in him. His purpose in travelling round to hear voices was to 'buy cheap'.[15]

Lotte went on and sang a good Micaëla (her eighteenth) and thought no more about it. Vienna was too far away to ponder on, and Hamburg was so beautiful, her colleagues and friends so dear and familiar to her, the fans so loyal. Hamburg was not to be exchanged for anywhere else.

The agent, Norbert Salter, had accompanied Gregor to Hamburg. He was one of the best in the business. Much to her surprise, Lotte was summoned to Salter's hotel on the following morning.[16] She had met him before, thanks to an introduction from Theo Drill-Orridge, who had taken an interest in Lotte and was convinced that she had the ability and inspiration to go a long way further, if placed in the right hands. Up until now, though, Salter does not seem to have given Lotte much thought. But he was now very friendly, bade her sit down and wait while he finished making some telephone calls. She could not help hearing the astonishing amounts being bandied about as he fixed contracts between managements and artists – thousands of marks!

He then gave Lotte his full attention. Director Gregor, he said, had come to Hamburg especially to hear the tenor, Ziegler. Gregor had listened carefully to Ziegler, but afterwards, when Salter had presented him with a contract to sign, Gregor had pushed it away and said: 'I want the Micaëla for Vienna – Lehmann, isn't it. Please arrange.'

There was a dramatic pause and then Salter gently pushed a piece of paper in Lotte's direction. 'Here's your contract.'

She was speechless.

Seizing a pen, she was about to sign. She did not see much except the huge salary figure, a long term of engagement. . . . But what about Loewenfeld, who had been so kind to her? What about her parents? What would they think, what would they wish for her? How would her Prussian father take to Vienna, in any case? She put down the pen, and said she wanted to take the contract away and think about it all. Of course the offer was marvellous, it was a heaven-sent opportunity, but for it to come at this very moment when she was so blissfully happy in Hamburg was as totally unexpected as it was confusing.

When Jelenko heard what had happened, he went straight to Dr Loewenfeld in a state of great anxiety and pother. If he was prepared to raise Lotte's salary to 12,000 Marks a year, she would remain in Hamburg, Jelenko suggested; but Loewenfeld considered that his puffing, red-faced administrator had gone mad. Lotte and Vienna were merely 'trying it on'.

The Lehmann parents came to the conclusion that it was in their daughter's best interests to sign the contract and go to Vienna, and they were prepared to go with her. Jelenko was enraged. He never believed that Lotte would leave them. But he always preferred the status quo to upsets of any kind – he had to face too many of them daily. Eventually, and without any persuasion on her part, she recognised that Loewenfeld was not going to be held to ransom, and so she signed.

'Please wait, little Lehmann,' Jelenko besought her. 'The *Herr Direktor* is bound to give in and then you can stay here with us.' He collapsed into his chair, wiping the sweat from his large, red face with an enormous coloured handkerchief. But once she had signed, Lotte had committed herself. The only defence which Loewenfeld still had was to withhold Lotte's release from Hamburg and keep her there until the end of her present contract-term: until the end of the 1915–16 season.

With the contract signed, Lotte was now a desirable property for her agent, who immediately arranged some engagements for her outside Hamburg. Since the one Sophie in Leipzig she had not been invited elsewhere. There was London, the Cologne Festival in June, and the Zoppot Festival in July.

Sir Joseph Beecham's lavish season of opera and ballet at Drury Lane Theatre included *Zauberflöte* and *Rosenkavalier* with Claire Dux as both Pamina and Sophie. She was unable to sing the two last Sophies and so Lotte travelled to London to appear instead. A director of the Hamburg-America Steamship Line and his wife, who Lotte had met socially, chaperoned her from Hamburg to London, where she had never been before.

Neither of the evenings when Lotte sang her Sophie[17] was a press night and there were no reviews; furthermore the programme wrongly showed her as singing Octavian, and the true Octavian (Joanna Lippe) as Sophie. Lotte sang with the Dresden creator of the Marschallin, Margarethe Siems, on the first night of her appearance in London, and with Frieda Hempel, the first Berlin Marschallin, after that. But Lotte was too shy to speak to either of these two great ladies offstage.

After looking at Covent Garden Theatre from the outside, among the squashed fruit and vegetables, Lotte's Hamburg friend, John Naht, remarked: 'You'll sing there next time!' (He was right).[18] Naht and his wife accompanied Lotte to Cologne where she was met by her mother. Frau Lehmann was suffering from stomach trouble, and Lotte paid for her to go to a spa at Bad Neuenahr, not far from Cologne.

Lotte sang Agathe there, and was glad to see Gustav Brecher again. He was delighted at her news, though he did not conduct the performance. The producer and director was the German composer, Hans Pfitzner who afterwards wrote to Lotte, predicting that she would become 'one of the greatest hopes of German opera'. He begged her to go on working as hard as she was then doing, and never to believe that she had reached perfection – *dass man niemals am Ziele sei'* (you never get there).

After the pleasant engagement in Cologne, Lotte went to collect her mother, who was feeling better, and they walked together along the Ahr river valley near Remagen. Lotte's increased salary had lifted many of the family's former financial worries, and they were already discussing the move to Vienna. Carl Lehmann, however, was not to be tempted away from his usual summer holiday at Sylt.

Lotte's next 'date' was also in that direction: at Zoppot, a prosperous seaside resort on the Baltic near Danzig, known as 'the Monte Carlo of the North'. In 1909 the first operatic entertainment had been promoted there for holiday visitors in a natural theatre among the woods, the *Zoppot Waldoper*, with singers drawn from provincial German houses and musicians from the Danzig State Orchestra. *Tannhäuser, The Bartered Bride* and other, lesser-known works had been performed there, one a year, until 1914 when *Der Freischütz* was billed for these ideal surroundings.[19]

If the weather was fine, swarms of gnats, attracted by the greasepaint, settled on the singers' faces. If it rained, which was not often, the audience did not become unsettled and performances were seldom interrupted, but the string players were often unable to continue for fear of damage to their instruments.[20]

In 1914, Zoppot was in East Prussia, a long railway journey from Hamburg, via Berlin. Lotte enjoyed herself there. The Baltic air suited her in any case and it became a kind of working holiday. Richard Tauber sang Max, Otto Goritz was Kaspar and Georg Zottmayr the Hermit. It all took on a 'festival' air and any singer who appeared at Zoppot has told how easy it was to sing in the open air, despite initial fears for vocal projection being difficult. Likewise, conductors found that they were able to support the voices easily without any fear of ever swamping them, so it was an immense pleasure for all concerned.

Richard Tauber was a wonderful partner under circumstances which encouraged lightheartedness. Lotte recalls how she had won a bet from him, and he had agreed to give her a bar of chocolate though when she least expected it. During a duet in *Freischütz* one evening, in a fully-lit scene, he pressed something into her hand. Not realising what it was, Lotte put it down on a bench where the silver paper glittered magically under the overhead lighting battens. Then the Ännchen, Paula, Ulm, sat down and broke it with a loud crack. Lotte and Tauber did not dare to look at one another; but afterwards some friends from the audience came round and congratulated Lotte upon the moving duet she had sung with Tauber. They were so committed to the emotion of the moment, it appeared.[21] In an irregular sort of way, this is a good test of a performer's control over his feelings and it happens everywhere, from time to time, in operas and plays, especially if there is a joker about. Lotte had already experienced this kind of horse-play in Altona.

On 1 August, Prussia declared war on Russia and within the next few days the Zoppot Festival came to an end. Rail traffic back to Hamburg was delayed because of troop trains taking proud, cheerful and optimistic young men eastwards to the front, believing, as both sides seemed to do, that it would all be over by Christmas. Lotte wondered whether the Stadttheater would stay open. She had never experienced war and the conditions it imposed were still unknown to her and to her contemporaries. The Stadttheater remained open, and more. Realising the importance of spiritual comfort through music in times of stress, Hamburg's singers gave their services generously to the wounded in hospitals and at 'military matinées' once a week.

Lotte had been asked to sing Eva in *Die Meistersinger* at her 'proving performance' in Vienna and Loewenfeld was helping her to the extent of letting her sing some Evas in Hamburg. She was also invited by Pathé to make a few records. Only two of them have survived and are extremely rare (See Discography Nos 1 & 2). Although it is possible that she recorded as many as six sides, no more were issued.

Arthur Nikisch arrived in Hamburg at the beginning of the 1914–15 season to conduct his *Ring* cycle. Lotte sang Sieglinde in the *Walküre*, but did not appear in any of the remainder, perhaps because she was getting up another new role for its première on 1 October. This was Christine Hofer in Alfred Kaiser's patriotic opera *Theodor Körner*. Körner was a philosopher and poet during the war against Napoleon in 1813, and became a national hero after he died, aged only twenty-two, fighting the French. His poems were gathered together by his father afterwards, and their passionate battle-cries were exceedingly popular. More popular, it seemed, than Kaiser's opera about him which, in spite of its suitability in the present war, vanished after only five performances.

On 11 October there was a 'Fatherland Concert' at which Lotte sang Lieder by Hugo Wolf, Brahms and van Eyken. It was repeated with an identical programme a week later. Then on 20th, Lotte appeared for the first time as Octavian in *Der Rosenkavalier*. At her present age of nearly twenty-seven, he was more appropriate to Lotte than Sophie, but she had to learn to walk like a man and as far as possible to try to think like one in this opera, with its overtones and passions that need to be so different from a woman's. Winternitz-Dorda was the Marschallin and Max Lohfing the thoroughly experienced Ochs, while Frl. Jansen was the Sophie.

On 27 or 28 October, Lotte left Hamburg for Vienna and describes how she drove through the 'City of Dreams' with a beating heart.[22] It was so to many people, and certainly to opera singers, for Vienna was still the old Imperial city, full of charm and gaiety, and so far away in spirit from the war that many elsewhere believed the Emperor Franz Josef had begun.

Lotte was enormously impressed by the Royal Court Opera House on the Ring, and entered it as though in a dream. She was over-awed by the manner of Franz Schalk, the first conductor, a Viennese through and through, to whom everybody who lived outside his city was a mere provincial, and deserved to be treated as such until he or she had fully absorbed and adopted the ways and customs and habits of incomparable *Wien*. She detected a hint of mockery in his otherwise impeccable approach and greeting.

Wilhelm von Wymetal, the Vienna Court Opera's producer since 1908, was courteous and considerate towards Lotte. He escorted her personally to the wardrobe where he showed her the Eva costumes which Alfred Roller had designed for the current *Meistersinger* production. 'Of course if you don't like them,' he told her, 'there are many others, and you can choose which you prefer to wear.' Lotte was overwhelmed.[23]

By comparison with this elegant behaviour and lavishness Hamburg dwindled into a thoroughly provincial background, as though Schalk's opinions were already taking root in her mind. Everybody was courteous, friendly and helpful, and at the rehearsal she found herself among artists whose names were uttered with reverence in the singing world outside: Friedrich Weidemann, the Sachs; Richard Mayr, Pogner; Viktor Madin, Nachtigall; Georg Maikl, David. Singing opposite Lotte as Walther von Stolzing was the American tenor, William Miller. Schalk conducted.

Before the performance, Lotte was in her hotel when a mysterious stranger, to whom she refused to open her door, said he had come about the claque. Lotte would have nothing to do with him and he went away. Shortly afterwards, when she had gone downstairs, another man with a foxy face who introduced himself as Herr Freudenberger, appeared before her in a strange, bemedalled coat, bowed ceremoniously and also said he had come about the claque. He was enraged to hear that his rival, Wessely, had already been, and after displaying postcards, letters and old newspapers to Lotte, he finally convinced her that it would be to her benefit to employ him for the night. He promised to ensure that he and his minions would applaud her frantically.[24] 'Standing on the stage behind the closed curtain I wanted to listen to the Prelude. But when the first bars sounded, in all their splendour, I had the sensational feeling that I had never heard it before. On the wings of this orchestra [the Vienna Philharmonic] the music sounded almost unearthly beautiful to me.'[25]

Lotte remembers that she was dazed by the performance, during which she listened a lot to the marvellous voices singing round her. The 'finest opera orchestra in the world' allowed her voice to rest upon it and be carried to the furthermost corners of that great house. She was grateful for a very friendly reception and at the end of the third act she heard a few vociferous cries of 'Lehmann!' among those for Mayr, Miller and the rest, at which she felt terribly ashamed. The critics were also friendly on the following day. Ludwig Karpath, one of the most influential (and viperish) declared that Lotte might easily become a favourite singer in Vienna.

She returned home knowing that her contract had been confirmed by the *Meistersinger* performance, and that she had nineteen months more in Hamburg before she would be leaving there to become a Viennese. In some ways she felt a traitor to Hamburg where she – a true German and no Austrian – had now lived and worked for four years. Until Gregor's arrival on that fateful *Carmen* night, she had expected to stay, but she had to recognise this future as her destiny, as Carmen had recognised her own.

The dear old Stadttheater, when Lotte saw it again, was no longer quite as welcoming as she had known it to be – in fact it looked exceedingly dingy – and in some ways she wanted to leave it now, and for ever, and get on with her new life. Her public and her fans were overjoyed at her success and her fan-club increased in size until it became rather unmanageable. She never wanted for flowers, for applause (and without claque-payment) or for real love from those who had watched and encouraged her progress from the terrified Second Boy in *Zauberflöte* to today's assured principal soprano – perhaps to be a world star.

Lotte moved to An der Alster 18,[26] the Holzdamm right on the Alster itself, and was now determined to make this last period of her time in Hamburg the happiest. She had only half a dozen performances in November, and all important ones now (Octavian, Elsa, Eva, *Figaro* Countess, Antonia and Pamina) because she was studying and rehearsing two new roles for December. The first was Margiana in Peter Cornelius's attractive and humorous 'eastern' opera, *The Barber of Bagdad*. The simple story is about a young man's (Nureddin's) efforts to marry the Caliph's daughter Margiana, with the connivance of that ever-resourceful operatic character, the Barber (Abu Hassan). And on Christmas Day Lotte assumed for the first time the 5th Flower Maiden in *Parsifal*, rather than the 4th whom she had been singing since March 1913. This was not at all an easy transfer, because she had first to unlearn and shut her ears to her former cues for the 4th Maiden in this close writing for six solo voices above a chorus.

On Sunday 10 January there was a special concert in the Stadttheater called 'German House-Music in Song', a popular concert of favourite songs among which Lotte sang two groups perhaps for the first time in public, in Hamburg. The songs were by Mendelssohn, Mahler and Richard Strauss, which spoke highly of the audience's musical taste.

On 23 January a scheduled performance of *William Tell* was suddenly cancelled owing to the illness of the irreplaceable tenor. *Der Freischütz* was substituted and Lotte was hastily summoned to sing Agathe again.[27] She had done so in Altona on the previous evening. In early March she appeared in the new, fairly light role of Angèle in Richard Heuberger's operetta, *Der Opernball*. An Austrian, Heuberger was a critic on the *Neue Freie Presse* (where he had followed Hanslick), and also reviewed for a Munich paper. *The Opera Ball*, first produced in 1898, contains the well-known aria (for Lotte) 'Im chambre séparée'.

By far the most important and taxing role was the new one of Elisabeth in Wagner's *Tannhäuser*, which she first sang on 29 March, with the American tenor, Francis Maclennan, as Tannhäuser; Theodor Lattermann as Wolfram. Arnold Winternitz conducted. The character of Elisabeth does not appear in the first act, but opens the second with the celebrated *Hallenarie*, or greeting aria *'Dich, teure Halle'*. This was such a sensation that Lotte had conquered the audience within the first few minutes. Two nights later she took part in a 'Bismarck Festival', an all-Wagner programme of excerpts. She sang Elsa in the finale to *Lohengrin*. It was the centenary of Otto von Bismarck's birth on the following day, 1 April.

2 April was Good Friday, with a suitably religious and devout programme for the concert in which Lotte sang two solos. She was the principal soprano in Bruckner's *Te Deum*, and then gave Mahler's *'Um Mitternacht'*, the last of the five Rückert Lieder which has the oft-repeated words of the title ('at midnight'). These require a different inflexion each time. Mahler's Lieder are invariably set for low voice, and although Lotte was singing more roles which took the second line, she by no means could be considered a mezzo-soprano.

The phase through which her singing was going was certainly emphasised by Lotte's next new role: Prince Orlovsky in *Die Fledermaus* on 14 April. This is a mezzo (if not mezzo-contralto) breeches part and she sang it eight times altogether, always in Hamburg. It seems that she may have been in the position to demand roles that she wished to sing, and her singing teacher may have recommended that she take several to deepen and to strengthen the voice. The penultimate Hamburg season closed for Lotte at the end of May with the 5th Flower Maiden in *Parsifal*. She had three months uninterrupted holiday, most of which she spent in Sylt.

There was no festival at Zoppot between 1915–19 on account of the war whose privations were beginning to bite, although there was little evidence in Hamburg when Lotte returned there to sing Elsa in *Lohengrin*, her twentieth performance in Hamburg of the role in which she had first triumphed. This character thus had a special significance for her and for her audiences.

In the 1914–15 season, Lotte had sung twenty-four different roles, but she had scaled them down slightly to twenty-one, including three new ones. These changes were not necessarily at Lotte's request, for she had left a few treasured characters behind; the opera house had to vary its repertory, and apart from those works which were bad box-office and had consequently been dropped, there were others that were being rested, or were not ideal for the present company of soloists. Fashion and the war had also to be considered.

The salary scale, prepared by Loewenfeld for the 1915/16 season, was this:[28]

Heinrich Hensel (Heldentenor)	5 x 6,400	32,000M
Maclennan	(9 weeks)	28,000M
Paul Schwarz (Buffo-tenor)		6,000M
Lohfing (bs)		19,000M
Fr. Drill-Orridge (dramatic soprano)		25,000M
Fr. Winternitz (coloratura soprano)		18,000M
Easton/Lehmann (1st sopranos)	each	15,000M
Sabine Kalter (1st contralto)		15,000M
E. Schumann (soubrette)		9,000M
Rose Ader (coloratura soprano and very young)		4,500M

Lotte surprised her fans by returning for two performances of Eurydice in the Gluck opera. Not since that unique occasion almost four years before, when Caruso had congratulated her on her 'bella voce Italiana', had she been heard in this classical role. Again Elisabeth Schumann (still Puritz–) was the Amor.

Lotte was 'off' as Elisabeth in *Tannhäuser* – a rare occurrence as we know – and Florence Easton stepped in to give a much tougher performance of the gentle Landgrave's niece. Easton was born in Middlesbrough, England and gained a reputation for being a quick learner and for being able to take over from an indisposed soprano, of almost any range, at short notice.

On 13 November, Lotte wrote from her parents' address, Dammtorstrasse 11, to Pathé Frères:

> I shall be pleased for an extension to my contract until 31. March 1916. I shall be grateful if you will send 400 Marks to my account.[29]

But no more interest in her seems to have been evinced by Pathé, even though she gave her address as the Vienna Court Opera from 1916.

Lotte was again 'off' as the Countess in *Figaro* in November, and Winternitz-Dorda took her place. Just over a fortnight later, Lotte returned to sing the Countess, as billed, but Winternitz-Dorda was the Susanna!

The shadow of Felix Weingartner was temporarily over Lotte on 20 January 1916 when she was cast as Ada in his 2-acter *Kain und Abel* for which he had written the libretto as well as the score. In Weingartner's own words his opera concerns:[30]

> . . . the dispute between the first two human brothers about a sister whom I called 'Ada'. I took the name from Byron, who in turn had taken it from the Bible. Though deviating from Byron's conception where the motive of erotic jealousy was lacking, I allowed myself to be so far influenced by the poet as to transfer his Lucifer into a demon, who in true opera style took on the form of a beautiful woman, drawing Cain into her toils while secretly feeding his love for Ada, in order thus to prepare the way for the innocent Abel's death.

At the third of the four performances of this curious work, Lucille Marcel returned to Hamburg to sing Ada. A short musical comedy by Eugen d'Albert, called *Solo Flute*, followed the Weingartner opera, and is notable only for the fact that it was produced by the young Otto Erhardt at the outset of his career as an international opera-producer.

On 6 February there was a performance of *Carmen* with Elisabeth Schumann due to sing Micaëla because Lotte had the first night of a new opera for her on the 7th. In the event, Elisabeth was 'off' and Lotte went on for her – a remarkable thing to have done, considering that the next day she had to sing Rachel in Halévy's *La Juive* (which, in German-language houses is Recha in *Die Jüdin*). It is a long and complicated work with a slightly uneven score lifted, at moments, to musical greatness. It was to be in Lotte's repertoire when she reached Vienna, so probably her grateful Hamburg management were allowing her to cut her teeth on it now.

The two most interesting roles in *La Juive* are those of the old Jewish goldsmith, Eléazar and his supposed daughter, Rachel. Caruso used to sing the rather troublesome, ranting old fellow who was ill at ease in a Christian community. At the end of the five acts, both Eléazar and his daughter are burnt as heretics. Lotte found massive scope for vocal and dramatic achievement and her 'father' was none other than the tenor, Ziegler, who had failed to be taken up by Gregor for Vienna in 1914.

A large turnout of soloists and principal singers from the opera participated in a matinée on 20 February which had the full title of 'Patriotic Concert for the Benefit of Dependants of those from the Reserve Infantry Regiments 76 & 216 who have lost their Lives'. Lotte sang Mařenka's aria from Act III of *The Bartered Bride*. She never recorded it nor sang it in the opera, nor again so far as can be determined. It seems to have been given here out of any context unless she was studying the part and subsequently decided not to continue with it.

On 1 March, Gustav Brecher resumed friendly relations with Hamburg by returning as a guest conductor for *Götterdämmerung* in which Lotte sang Gutrune. Walker was the Brünnhilde. At the Good Friday Concert, Lotte sang three of Wagner's Wesendonck Lieder (omitting the 2nd & 3rd) with orchestra, and just before the end of the season she put the clock back by singing Freia in *Rheingold* under Nikisch. This was of less importance than the first Hamburg production of Eugen d'Albert's *Toten Augen (Dead Eyes)* on 18 March. Lotte's success in it was enormous and enduring, for she not only repeated performances on her return there in subsequent years as a guest, but recorded an aria, and demonstrated it much later in her master classes. In Lotte's words, *Toten Augen* 'set the seal' on her operatic career in Hamburg. She remembers that Loewenfeld, who was producing, 'really let himself go' with the colours, and spent many hours choosing exactly the right shades and materials for the garments and furnishings.

The story concerns a Greek girl called Myrtocle who is blind. She is married to a hideously ugly Roman proconsul called Arcesius (sung by Wilhelm Buers) whom she loves, unaware of, and therefore totally unaffected by, his appearance. Mary Magdalene restores Myrtocle's sight by a miracle, and the first man whom she sees is the handsome Captain Galba. She worships the sight of him, taking him to be her husband, for such was her mental impression of the man to whom she is married. When she discovers that she is in love with a man who is not her husband, the delusions and sins that sight can afford make her decide to go blind again. She achieves this by staring into the sun until it burns away her eyes.

It was d'Albert's wish that, after receiving her sight for the first time, Myrtocle should ask for a looking-glass:[31] this would be surely be every woman's first desire, to see herself. Lotte disagreed and refused to obey the text and the score at this point. In spite of d'Albert's protests, she persisted and declared that she would rather give up the part of Myrtocle altogether.

d'Albert was nonplussed, but Loewenfeld assured him that Lotte was certain to make the scene work if she was allowed to play it her own way. And so it was. Meyrowitz, who was conducting, expressed great satisfaction at the dress rehearsal, and d'Albert was also pleased with the way it went. This particular scene worked perfectly well but the finale was a triumph for Lotte.

Loewenfeld tried in every possible way to persuade Vienna to release Lotte from their contract. He offered Lotte any fee she asked, so long as she stayed in Hamburg, but everybody knew she was legally bound to leave them. She wanted to stay now! In the hour of her greatest success it all seemed so wrong to think of going. But in retrospect, what better time?

Her eleventh performance of Myrtocle was her farewell performance (*Abschiedsvorstellung für Frl Lehmann* it said on the bills). She remembers dragging herself miserably up the oh-so-familiar stone steps to her dressing room for the last time, and weeping at the sight of banks of flowers there. The once so-feared wardrobe-mistress, Hulda Wolf was standing beside Lotte's dresser, Else, both of them in tears and Lotte in tears too.

After the specially emotional performance, the audience simply would not let her go. Nor would her fans, later on, who followed her home and stood beside the Alster opposite her house until Lotte came out on her balcony and begged them to let her sleep in peace. '"Hurrah for Lehmann" is too noisy for a lullaby', she told them.[32]

In the *Hamburgische Fremdenblatt* in the morning, Heinrich Chevalley said that they were all so proud of her in Hamburg and loved her so much that to see her leave them was like losing a favourite child from the family.

Chapter Four

Vienna

1916–1918

Before going to Vienna, Lotte had eventually prevailed upon her parents to stay behind in Hamburg and let her – at least – begin her new career and find her feet alone in Vienna. For, after all, a person of twenty-eight is no longer a child. With much good advice from the old Lehmanns, and promises from her to bring them to her when the time was right, Lotte took the train on its long journey through Berlin, Dresden, Prague and eventually to Vienna.

She took lodgings at Keilgasse 13,[1] in the Third District near the Botanical Gardens and the Südbahnhof, in preparation for her first appearance on 18 August.

This was to be in the familiar role of Agathe in *Der Freischütz*. A whole year and ten months had passed since her proving performance in Vienna, and the effects of the war were now plain to see there. Vienna looked dirty and unkempt, the streets had not been swept for ages. Lotte found this distasteful and slovenly. Vienna was no longer the gay and charming city it had been in 1914 on her short visit: the former *Kaiserstadt* of story and legend, which she had been fortunate to glimpse, had gone.

Apart from the dirt and the dereliction, there was strict food-rationing. A singer has to eat properly in order to provide the physical strength which the voice demands. Great meals were a thing of the past in Hamburg, admittedly, but Lotte had found enough there to sustain her, including the warmth from family, friends and fans. These were now lacking. To be a stranger in Vienna, and hungry as well, made poor Lotte feel very miserable.

She presented herself at the Court Opera and met Hans Gregor. 'So I've really caught you!'[2] he chuckled, rubbing his hands. He evidently took a shine to her, and was from the start giving her more than expected support, as will soon be seen.

Hans Gregor[3] was born in Dresden in 1866. He began as an engineer in Berlin, but following a strong inclination towards the theatre, he was trained by the actor, Heinrich Oberländer. Gregor was not only an actor but a manager, and after appointments in Breslau, Königsberg and Berlin, he became director of the Stadttheater in Görlitz on the Polish border, East of Dresden. A more prestigious appointment followed in 1898 in Barmen-Elberfeld. There Gregor and the conductor Fritz Cassirer were responsible for helping to promote the music of Frederick Delius, as well as that of Richard Strauss, but in 1905 Gregor moved on to found the Komische Oper in Berlin. He profited by a comfortable niche for the kind of works scorned at the Court Opera: *Carmen, Tosca, Die Fledermaus* as well as new and out-of-the-way modern operas. In 1911 the enterprise collapsed for lack of funds, but fortunately for Gregor this coincided with the demise of Felix Weingartner as Director of the Vienna Court Opera. It was decided to employ a man of the theatre, for the first time, instead of a practising musician. Gregor was appointed.

His North German accent caused Lotte to warm to him at once: it was almost like being at home again. But Gregor considered himself Viennese and promised Lotte that she, too, would fall in love with the city. He likened the experience to taking a hot bath: unpleasant, even impossible at the outset; then gradually more comfortable until, when you fully enjoy it – hey presto! you have become Viennese yourself!

Gregor was being slightly cynical for, as he well knew, there is far more to Vienna than 'the heat of the bath-water'; and the curious nature of this city and its folk has been well described by John Culshaw, an Englishman who lived there, on and off, as a record producer in the middle of the present century. Vienna has not changed that much since Lotte's time:[4]

> Vienna is a village in more senses than one. Its people do not behave like the inhabitants of a great capital city, and there is generally a remarkable unawareness of the rest of the world . . . Vienna still lives in its past, with what I suspect to be highly coloured memories of the days of the Habsburg Empire and dear old Franz Josef . . . The famous coffee-house tradition of gossip and scandal – another village trait – has shown no sign of waning . . . and has no parallel that I know of elsewhere, largely because in other big cities most people are too busy or too taciturn or too ambitious to indulge in sustained malice with such abandon. Minding one's own business is strictly unknown to the Viennese. It takes a while to become accustomed to this, and to learn not to take offence: to accept, in fact, that the English [or German] approach to life is as far removed from the Viennese as can be imagined . . .

In consequence, Lotte's arrival at the Opera was regarded with intense interest by everybody, who attempted to pry into her personal life and background. They all took a great interest in their clothes, their appearance, their manners and in the conventional courtesies of the Opera and of Vienna itself, whether they were 'real' Viennese or otherwise.

Lotte was amazed to see, once again, the expensive costumes laid out for her to wear as Agathe,[5] and indeed in the whole range of luxurious clothing and costume properties in the wardrobe. If she didn't like anything there, not only might she choose elsewhere, but this time, because she was one of them now, they would make her a new costume according to her demands. Her surprise and embarrassment was taken by the wardrobe staff as an indication of Lotte's indifference to her appearance and to finer points of her dress both on- and off-stage. This did not go down at all well.

Wilhelm von Wymetal, the producer, was amused at her unsophisticated ways and assured her, as Gregor had done, that she would soon be a changed person, taking far more care over her dress. Wymetal was a good influence on her. He did not, at first, know what to make of her attitude, mistaking it for a kind of prima-donna-ish approach put on to seek attention. Lotte's impulsiveness and – to most of her colleagues – sheer rudeness were far removed from the courtly manners that were *de rigeur*. If they considered her crude in her ways, then she thought they were a lot of hypocrites, especially when she heard that complains about her had already landed on Director Schalk's desk.

Gregor brought up the question of Lotte with Schalk.

'Well, what do you think of our new acquisition?' he asked.

'Oh, she's just another of them,' Schalk replied, 'she'll be away at the end of the year.'

'Not her, Herr Kappellmaeister, you can forget that,' Gregor answered, 'not her.'

Schalk was certain that Gregor was 'backing' Lotte's progress, but, in his usual way, said nothing more.

Schalk thoroughly disapproved of Lotte's Prussian coldness and stiffness, and told Wymetal to do something about it. So he took her aside one day and gently suggest that she might perhaps, well for a start, consider conforming to the accepted practice of extending her 'Good morning!' when meeting or passing a senior member of the Opera, to 'Good morning, Frau Kammersängerin!' (a title of Royal patronage, approaching our Dame of the British Empire) or even to ask after her health. Lotte replied curtly that she was not in the least bit interested in anybody's health. It took a little time, but eventually the 'temperature of the bath-water' became a good deal more comfortable.

The principle singers in Vienna at that time were very great personalities as well as being wonderful artists, all stars in their own right. Perhaps the most unusual of them all was Jeritza.[6] Born Marie Jedlitzka in Bohemia, she was possessed of a radiant beauty, a marvellous voice of strength, range and brilliance, great acting ability and with it a streak of crazy comedy. She was trained and first sang in Brünn before going to the Operetta in Munich, thence to the Vienna Volksoper. This organisation duplicated some operas given at the Court House, but also staged far lighter ones which appealed to a different public.

Mimi Jeritza, as she then called herself, appeared in the Volksoper's world première of the contemporary Austrian composer Wilhelm Kienzl's *Der Kuhreigen* as Blanchefleur. A year later, in 1912, by special order of the Emperor Franz Josef, who had been entranced by her at a private soirée where she sang, Jeritza was transferred to the Imperial Court Opera. In that year she was lent to the Ducal Opera in Stuttgart to sing Ariadne in the Strauss-Hofmannsthal work at its world première, by special request of composer and librettist.

She was a breath-taking Salome in Vienna, and achieved a tour de force with her Minnie in Puccini's *Girl of the Golden West*, as has already been mentioned. Jeritza soon commanded a far higher salary, influence and presence than any other singer in Vienna. She was in most ways an exceptional person, and a formidable one. In her unsatisfactory autobiography (unsatisfactory in that it ends in 1924 and she lived for another sixty years) she claims[7] to sacrifice everything to her art. There were no late nights, no parties, a special diet with its emphasis upon pineapple juice, all of which make her sound a somewhat dull person. She cannot have been that. Yet she was so different from homely, friendly Lottchen that on the occasions when (later on) they both sang in the same opera, their two sets of fans had to be separated to avoid riots, and consequently the two sopranos were directed to different and widely separated exit doors after the performance.

Jeritza's stamina and vocal powers were amazing. She had been well trained, she had experienced the rough and tumble of both the Munich Operetta and the Vienna Volksoper, and she was a professional in every respect. If there was any adverse criticism that could be levelled against Jeritza's characterisations, it was a very full-blooded, sometimes very slightly inelegant way in which she put them over, and a lack of subtlety, resulting from a humble upbringing. But she was able to turn this to advantage with breath-catching visual tricks and *coups-de-théâtre*, out-daring all other singers. Combined with her ravishing appearance and her astonishing voice, Maria Jeritza always captivated her audiences and was paid very handsomely for doing so. This mattered a great deal to her.

Among the roles which Lotte brought with her to Vienna were an uncomfortable number already being sung by Jeritza: Elsa, Elisabeth, Sieglinde, Agathe, Antonia, and later others. These roles were not exactly Jeritza's exclusive property, but were much in demand from her. Jeritza was very curious about Lotte, having made certain that she had found out all about this new addition to the Vienna sopranos. For a short time, Jeritza believed that she had nothing to fear from this dowdy young thing from – where was it? Hamburg? – who was so abrupt, so badly dressed, so plain. ('Young!' Jeritza made out that she was only four months older than Lotte, but it has at last been revealed that Jeritza was born in November 1882 and was therefore five years older than she admitted).[8]

For her part, Lotte was in awe of Jeritza, to whom she took an instant dislike on account of her superciliousness, her superiority and her intolerance of a calculating kind. Jeritza was definitely somebody to be reckoned with, somebody who was cunning and accustomed always to getting her own way. This was clear to Lotte from the start and she was angry with herself that Jeritza always made her feel small, inferior and uncomfortable.

Among the other sopranos, Marie Gutheil-Schoder was entirely different. Lotte greatly admired her and referred to her as her 'model'. Much later she admitted that she had had 'a great crush' on Schoder, who had been the first Elektra and Octavian in Vienna and was already part of the tradition. In 1916 she was over forty, and was still singing wonderfully, even though, when Mahler had first engaged her in 1900 she was maliciously called 'the singer without a voice'.[9]

Lucy Weidt, another great Viennese soprano and the first Marschallin there, was still singing that role nobly. She was also an Elisabeth and Sieglinde, and Lotte greatly admired her. Weidt was twelve years Lotte's senior and beautiful in a stately way. Berta Kiurina had been at the Vienna Opera since 1905 and was now thirty-four. A true coloratura, she sang Eva among her many roles.

Selma Kurz has become famous for her endless trill, and is consequently thought to be only a coloratura, but in fact she began as a lyric soprano. She and Jeritza were regarded as the two prima donnas of the Vienna Court Opera, and at forty-one, Kurz was still in prime of voice.

Naturally none of these singers expected to sing every role in their repertoires without sometimes sharing them. But Lotte had been the reigning queen of song in Hamburg and was not at all keen on competition. Furthermore, she swore that she was never going to allow herself to be considered as a second cast principal. If there were to be two casts for any opera, she was going to lead the first one. It was to be *prima inter pares*.

The singer who was kindest to Lotte in the early days, really kind and not merely Viennese-courteous, was Bella Paalen, the principal contralto. There could be no vocal competition between her and Lotte – which helped. She was Hungarian, had been at the Court Opera since 1906 and was seven years older than Lotte.

There was also a wondrous collection of male singers: Leo Slezak, Erik Schmedes and Alfred Piccaver among the tenors; Emil Schipper, Hans Duhan and Friedrich Weidemann as famed baritones; and the incomparable Richard Mayr leading the basses.

Lotte made her début as a member of the Imperial and Royal Court Opera of Vienna as Agathe in *Der Freischütz* on 18 August 1916, which was the opening night of the new season.[10] William Miller was her Max (he had also sung Walther opposite her in 1914) and the performance was conducted by the routinier, Hugo Reichenberger, one of Franz Schalk's assistants. Lotte's performance was later described in the *Allgemeine Musik-Zeitung* of Berlin as 'graceful and technically accomplished'.

Jeritza sang Elsa in *Lohengrin* two evenings later, and then, on 25 August, Lotte repeated her Eva with William Miller, and with Schalk as the conductor. Again she found it an exciting as well as a musically ennobling experience. Two days later she sang Martha in Kienzl's *Evangelimann* which she had given ten times in the 1912–13 Hamburg season but very seldom since. She was amazed to find herself singing opposite the great Erik Schmedes as Mathias, and he was again her tenor partner in *Tannhäuser* two days later, when Hans Duhan sang Wolfram.

On 11 September Lotte may well have overparted herself. She had been singing Antonia in *Hoffmann* fairly regularly since 1913. It suited her well and she was able to extract the maximum of pity from it. But on this one and only occasion she sang Giulietta in the Venetian scene as well as Antonia! It is unlikely that she stood in for an indisposed mezzo because the part was strange to her, so for some inexplicable reason she took it on, and it lies far lower than Antonia.

Lotte returned to more familiar territory on 16 September when she gave her first Viennese audience the chance to hear her as Micaëla. She found it very stimulating to be appearing with Gutheil-Schoder, in one of her celebrated roles as Carmen, and with Miller again, as Don José. A week later she sang Recha in *Die Jüdin*, again with Miller (who was being worked hard) as Eleazar. There was a repetition of *Carmen* on 26th, but not with Gutheil-Schoder, and Lotte was thrilled to find herself singing with Alfred Piccaver as Don José.

Piccaver[11] had been born in Lincolnshire, was of Spanish forebears, brought up in New York and became an electrical engineer at Edisons. Finding he had a voice, he was trained by Angelo Neumann in Austria, and was engaged by the German Opera in Prague. In 1910 he visited the Vienna Opera with an Italian Company led by Bonci and Battistini, but it was not until Gregor took over that Piccaver was snapped up and made his début there opposite Jeritza in *The Girl of the Golden West*.

'Pikky' to his fans, and to most Viennese but 'Teddy' to his friends[12] – 'The Albany Boy' to Gregor[13] – Piccaver became part of their city and was there throughout Lotte's association with the Opera. 'Pikky' was often found either watching or playing football on Saturday afternoons; and while of a genial nature, he tended to consider his health (and that meant his voice) very seriously. 'I will sing', or else 'I will not sing tonight' came over the telephone to the management of the Opera on each morning when he was billed to appear.

Piccaver's voice was considered to be the most beautiful of any in his generation of tenors. When asked many years later about her favourite tenor, Lotte unhesitatingly replied, 'Oh Piccaver! It was like being surrounded with velvet.'[14] The ardent quality of his voice matched hers extremely well; but it was his *pianissimi* and the perfectly placed top notes, combined with the marvellous lyricism that he expressed which made him the darling of Vienna in spite of the fact that he never learned to act at all.[15]

The Strauss-Hofmannsthal *Ariadne auf Naxos* had been proving too unwieldy and too expensive for many opera house managements since its first production in Stuttgart in 1912. Soon afterwards, its two creators seriously considered doing away altogether with the play and its actors, and making an introductory *Vorspiel*, or Prelude, to explain the circumstances under which this opera was being sung.[16] The revised version of *Ariadne auf Naxos* was scheduled for its first appearance at the Vienna Court Opera in October 1916. Jeritza was again singing Ariadne, but more interest had begun to centre upon a new and endearing character, that of a Young Composer, whose opera *Ariadne* was supposed to be. He was to become the central figure of the Prologue and Marie Gutheil-Schoder was cast in the role.

Gregor had reservations and, preferring to have two strings to his bow, he told one of the musical assistants at the Opera to take Lotte aside and coach her in this grateful part so that she became, in effect, an unofficial understudy. Schalk knew nothing about it. At the preliminary rehearsals, Gutheil-Schoder failed to stir anybody's emotions with her characterisation and seemed awkward.[17] Perhaps, at the age of forty-two, it was difficult for her to carry off the youth and ardour of this 'Young' Composer.

Before the first orchestral rehearsal of the Prologue with the singers, Gutheil-Schoder failed to turn up. According to Gregor's *Memoirs* the conversation, first in Strauss's office and then in the auditorium, went like this:

STRAUSS: How kind of her! So the whole of today's rehearsal has gone to the dogs.

SCHALK: There's nothing to be done. [*Exit*]

GREGOR [*in conspiratorial fashion*] I have an understudy, musically prepared. Dr Schalk doesn't know anything about her, so far as I'm aware. While the scenery is being got ready, might I suggest you hear her? She is very intelligent and you will find her satisfactory. May I send for her?

STRAUSS: All right, all right.
[*Exeunt to Auditorium where Schalk is at the conductor's desk. Strauss storms up to him.*]

STRAUSS: Listen, Schalk, the Director has made it known to me . . .

SCHALK: Ach! Ah! I know, I know, that Lehmann has been rehearsing. Not with me though. Anyway, it's useless.

STRAUSS: But we haven't got much time . . .
[*Schalk shrugs his shoulders indifferently, and a moment later 'Gregor's understudy' is there. Gregor steps back into the darkness of the auditorium to observe the outcome with expectation.*]
[*At Lotte's first phrase, Strauss is completely taken by surprise and turns his head to see where Gregor has gone. Then, at the first 'break' he is at Gregor's side.*]

STRAUSS: Hey! That girl, she's . . . who is she then? What's her name? – Lehmann? Lehmann? Any relation to Lilli?

GREGOR: No idea.

STRAUSS: Tell me, can that talented young thing over there have an hour with me alone this afternoon? (*With an ironic laugh*) So far as Gutheil is concerned tomorrow morning . . .

GREGOR: Certainly she can.
[*On the following morning, Gutheil fails to turn up again. Strauss seeks out Gregor in his office alone and*:]

STRAUSS: Listen to me, Director, your Hamburg girl is a hundred times better than the first-cast Composer will ever be. In spite of all the circumstances, you must let her sing the première.

GREGOR: Doctor!

STRAUSS: If you're scared of telling Gutheil, I'll do it.

GREGOR: Oh no! That would only make it worse. Confound it! What excuse can I make? Frau Gutheil will be mortally offended.

STRAUSS: My sincere apologies; but the creator's word carries more weight than the irritability of an artist when the question of the right characterisation is concerned.

GREGOR: Very well then.

Lotte stood before Gregor, pleading and tearful, when she received the news that the first night bills were going to carry her name. 'Oh for God's sake, don't do this to me,' she urged him, 'the great Frau Gutheil will be my enemy for ever more!'

'*Your* enemy?' replied Gregor, laughing, because never before had he known a soprano offer to give up an important role for the sake of a colleague. '*Your* enemy? In that case I'll go and find her and suggest that she helps you bear your burden!'

Lotte's version of the event is rather different. She records that, with some surprise, she went to the piano rehearsal as requested, and Strauss played, taking her through the role. She observed Hofmannsthal and Gregor listening. (Gregor never once mentions Hofmannsthal in his *Memoirs*.) Eventually Strauss turned to Lotte and said, quite simply and with a smile, 'You will sing at the première!'

She pleaded with him because she admired Gutheil-Schoder so much, but Strauss, amused at her ingenuous behaviour, told her that she had to accept. He wanted her to sing the Young Composer and so did Director Gregor, so she had to accept.

On the evening of 4 October 1916, half an hour after the first performance of the revised *Ariadne auf Naxos*, everybody in Vienna knew the name *Lotte Lehmann*. Or in Gregor's words: 'Yesterday she was Miss Nobody: today – Lotte Lehmann.'

But Gutheil-Schoder blamed Gregor entirely and never spoke to him again – not even giving him a 'Good morning!'

The influential critic, Richard Specht, in the magazine *Der Merkur* gave credit to Jeritza as the 'pompous and slovenly prima donna of the Prologue' who, in the opera, is changed into a towering goddess 'with such nobility of expression that one is amazed at her security and abundance of her talents'. And then he remarked on the extraordinary good fortune of the young Lotte Lehmann who sang the youthful Composer in the Prologue 'with so fresh, sweet and full-voiced a manner and with such animation that had not been heard in Vienna since the days of the great Marie Renard. The storm of applause and tumult after the Prologue was greater than for any other Strauss première in Vienna.'

Strauss was present, though Schalk conducted. The Zerbinetta was Selma Kurz, who delivered the big aria perfectly and fearlessly, and so that night Lotte was between the two prima donnas and getting more applause than either of them. Her impassioned aria at the end of the Prologue, a dramatic-musical coup if ever there was one, with its urgency, fury and youthful charm, is always certain of the biggest ovation of the evening.

Lotte refers to this evening as the one when she was 'pushed to the front' and soon became aware that she had put Jeritza's nose out of joint. Such a grand success after a mere handful of performances since her arrival (there had been only eight) did not please this Queen of Vienna. Lotte was made aware for the first time of real professional hostility and realised that once an artist is set on the upward path, she may expect competition and behaviour of the most unpleasant kind.

Lotte was unequal to this kind of opposition so early in her career, yet she continued to move upwards in spite of it. Her own lack of animosity – a kind of purity in itself – was her protection. She did not try the same kind of behaviour on her new enemy, because that was not her manner. However, this was Vienna, and she had to learn to live with their ways.

Lotte sang the Young Composer twenty times in her first season, more than in all the later seasons put together, and it established her as a valuable asset to the Vienna Court Opera, perfect in the youthful, ardent – and the sympathetic – roles. She possessed star quality. Nobody could compare her with Frau So-and-So's performance as the Young Composer because nobody else had sung it, until 13 November, when Gutheil-Schoder sang it at last. But there is a silence surrounding that occasion.

Ariadne and the Young Composer never come face to face in the Prologue, so Lotte was spared a duet with Jeritza; but she had the love scene with Zerbinetta, about which she had no complaints. Selma Kurz was a professional of the old school, secure in the knowledge that nobody had a trill like her own, so consequently she bore no grudges, no ill-will, tried no tricks and was a good colleague. She was especially helpful to Lotte because in the past, and before turning coloratura, she had sung the more lyrical roles, especially Sieglinde and Eva under Mahler's baton.

It may well have been at Strauss's suggestion that Lotte was given Octavian to sing in the following January. She knew the role well after more than a dozen performances in Hamburg. She again appeared in breeches, with sword this time, in a noble cast that included Lucy Weidt as the Marschallin and the incomparable Richard Mayr as Ochs.

Then there was *Manon*. Massenet's opera was a firm favourite in Vienna where, in contradistinction to Prussian preference in Hamburg, a French flavour was popular. Such works as *Faust* (always known as *Margarethe* in German-speaking countries so as to differentiate Goethe's revered classic), *Mignon*, *Carmen* – and *Manon* – all had roles for Lotte.

She sang eight Manons in her first season, establishing herself in the guise of the sweetest, most fickle and enchanting young miss to have been seduced by a handsome nobleman so as to avoid taking the veil. But with what results. Her agonising death scene was a complete foil to the earlier acts, and in spite of others' achievements here, Lotte's assumption was unrivalled.

Lotte's first Des Grieux was the ugly but beautifully voiced Hungarian heroic tenor Béla von Környey. He had sung Bacchus in the new *Ariadne*, and had been in Vienna for only a year before Lotte's arrival. Perhaps because of Környey's sudden death in full voice, a decade later after he had left Vienna, the *afficionados* of the Opera remember only the other tenor who frequently (but not exclusively) sang Des Grieux with Lotte, Alfred Piccaver.

In Lotte's first season she sang seventy-three performances in forty-three weeks; and while she had sung more often than this in Hamburg, she had now adopted more taxing roles, the house was larger, so was the orchestra (meaning that there was a greater distance over a heavier weight of sound to surmount). Also the standard in Vienna was considerably higher, and there could be little playing about in the Imperial and Royal Opera.

Naturally, Lotte was extremely happy about her success, but Jeritza's shadow seemed to be over her wherever she went, an unfriendly, dominating shadow. Jeritza was adept at manipulation and was determined that the little upstart from Hamburg was not going to outshine her. Had Jeritza not feared Lotte's ability, to some extent, she would not have continually behaved so badly towards her. Lotte was unable to dazzle with sheer beauty of features: she had not got them. Lotte's voice had always to be carefully nurtured: she had not Jeritza's iron lungs and throat. Lotte had humour all right, but not of the crazy, almost circus kind which Jeritza used to extraordinary effect at unexpected moments. Yet Lotte had an incandescent spirit that shone through her characters and gripped the audience by its quality of *goodness*, for none of the girls and women (and boys) she played was really bad, and one could always identify easily with them.

Lotte had to put up with this competition and make the best of it; although Jeritza denied that it existed. She was too grand, and *never* took an insignificant role – as she persuaded herself Lotte did. Second Rhine-Maiden, Fifth Flower-Maiden, are not exactly star roles: Micaëla and Gutrune do not exercise control over the action in *Carmen* or *Götterdämmerung*. Nevertheless Lotte sang them all full-out as individuals, irrespective of their relative importance. And this is being professional.

Lotte had another première, in February 1917. The Austrian-Dutch composer, Jan Brandts-Buys's *Die Schneider von Schönau* had one soprano role: Lotte as a rich widow called Veronika Schwäble among a cast of men including Richard Mayr, Hermann Gallos and the wonderful bass, Nickolaus Zec as three tailors, all in love with her. It vanished after only five performances.

Towards the end of the season, in May 1917, a dazzlingly handsome Norwegian tenor came to sing guest performances. His name was Karl Aagard Oestvig. Not only had he the appearance of a Nordic hero, but he possessed a voice to match. Lotte found him too beautiful for words when he sang Don José opposite her Micaëla, and then gazed at his Bacchus in *Ariadne*, making love to Jeritza, of course.

On 6 June, and a week before the season ended, there was a concert in aid of widows and orphans of Austrian soldiers killed in the war. Stars of the Opera gave their services in a rather mixed bag of works conducted by Franz Schalk. They included Jeritza, Kurz, Piccaver, Slezak, Mayr, Weidt and Lotte. She sang two orchestrated Strauss songs, *Wiegenlied* and *Cäcilie*.

From time to time, after her *Ariadne* success, Lotte had been invited to appear as a guest outside Vienna, but her requests to do so had all been turned down by Gregor. She should have realised that her numerous appearances in her first season were more than enough, for the managerial argument ran: we dare not let you work you voice outside in case, when you return, it has suffered. Your first duty is to the Emperor's Opera. Lotte pleaded, cajoled, burst into tears, lost her temper – quite in the old manner against Jelenko. She also wrote letters to Schalk with all manner of unfounded accusations.

However, in May, and since it was not far from the end of the season, she was allowed to go to Hamburg for two events: a special concert and a performance in *Lohengrin*. At the first, Lotte sang a 'Liebeslied' from Klemperer's unfinished opera *Eros* in a concert of his compositions on his thirty-second birthday.[18] Two evenings later on May 16 she repeated her much loved Elsa at the Stadttheater to a fond, appreciative audience, delighted to hear 'our Lotte' back home again.

The famous singer, as she now was, spent a well-earned rest with her parents on the Baltic, but did not neglect her practice. The parents were overjoyed at her success, and although Papa did not fully understand her need to go on singing to the birds and the waves, he was immensely proud of his daughter.

She returned refreshed to Vienna for her first appearance in the new season as Frau Fluth in *The Merry Wives*, a role she had been singing towards the end of the previous season. There were also two *Manons* (one with Piccaver, the other with Környey), Antonia, and the Young Composer with the original cast, all in October, and Lotte was looking forward to her next Octavian.

However, Jeritza had been talking to the Management. She would sing all the Piccaver *Manons*, and Octavian as well. The Composer was not within her scope, and Ariadne suited her far better, but she insisted on the two other pieces of casting and almost got them. When Lotte examined the cast lists on the stage door notice-board she discovered that after her first *Manon* with Piccaver, she had no more with him, and no Octavians. He was shared between Jeritza and Gutheil-Schoder.[19]

Lotte was allowed back to Hamburg for four peformances in October. They included one Myrtocle, which she had not sung since her farewell performance in the previous May; a Margarethe, Mignon and Elsa. *Mignon* was certainly a novelty in Hamburg.

In December 1916 and early 1917, Lotte made a substantial number of acoustic recordings for Grammophon-Polydor in Berlin (see Discography Nos 3–23) with two very surprising items: from *La Bohème* and *Eugen Onegin*, neither of which was even remotely in Lotte's repertoire.

There were concentrated rehearsals in December for the forthcoming cycles of *Der Ring*. In the January 1918 cycle Lotte sang Freia in *Das Rheingold*, Sieglinde in *Die Walküre* and Gutrune in *Götterdämmerung*. Her Sieglinde on 8 January was another of those occasions when the whole of Vienna was saying her name. With Schmieter as Siegmund and Zeč as Hunding, Lotte showed what she could do with a passionate and frustrated Sieglinde, bursting into intoxicated passion with her brother-lover. In the second act Lucy Weidt was the statuesque Brünnhilde. Another *Walküre* was promised at the end of the season so that the public might have another opportunity of hearing Lotte's Sieglinde.

It is somewhat tragic to have to record that at this moment there were strikes and mutinies in Vienna as a result of the way the war was going for the Austrians.[20] The Communists were agitating at a time of indecision and disgust at the lack of adequate leadership in the Austrian army, letting it become no more than a subordinate force for the Prussians to thrust into battle. However this seemed to matter not at all to the enthusiastic audiences at the Vienna Court Opera.

We know that Lotte had never considered herself a Mozart singer. Remembering her terrible experience as a student in Berlin with the *Figaro* Countess's second aria, she had conquered that horror with sixteen performances over her last three seasons in Hamburg. Now she found herself singing it again in Vienna with a superb cast: Richard Mayr as Figaro, Hans Duhan as the Count, Lotte Schöne as Cherubino and Bella Alten (a very experienced newcomer) as Susanna. Richard Mayr was very friendly to Lotte, had been almost from the start. It was partly thanks to him that she was able to get enough to eat in the early days, for he had his farm at Salzburg and did not want for dairy and vegetable produce. This he shared with those singers who had no other sources.

It should have been a performance of *Ariadne* on Sunday 7 April 1918, and the theatre bills had already been printed when, at the Emperor's Royal Command, there was a charity performance instead, with an exact repeat four days later. The programme consisted of the spectacular Mahler VIII ('Symphony of a Thousand') and Schumann's *Scenes from Faust* in which Lotte sang the Penitent.

The delayed *Ariadne* was the first that Strauss conducted in Vienna and also the first time that Lotte had sung under his baton. It formed part of a Strauss Week, although Lotte did not sing in any other opera. It was a delight, and a wonderful experience to be singing the Composer for, if not *to*, the man who had made it possible for her to rise so spectacularly. She loved him for it and poured out her heart *à l'outrance*.

But Lotte discovered that Strauss the man and Strauss the conductor were two very different beings.[21] With an immobile expression on his face, and very small gestures from his desk he seemed to register nothing and to put up an impenetrable barrier between himself and the stage; yet everything was so completely under control that nobody had cause to worry that he was at all remote from them – though it looked like it.

Julius Korngold, the music critic of the *Neue Freie Presse* and no friend of Richard Strauss's, was very complimentary about Lotte's Young Composer on this occasion, congratulating her on the 'complete abandon' with which she sang the role. He also referred to her in his review of the concert at the end of the Strauss Week when Lotte sang three of Strauss's songs with orchestra: 'Das Rosenband', 'Wiegenlied' and 'Cäcilie' which Strauss conducted. They were the only vocal items in an otherwise orchestral concert of three tone poems. Korngold admired Lotte's ample voice, produced at the dictates of both head and heart, and whose reception afterwards was 'stormy'. But he offered the suggestion that in the 'higher middle range a tremolo creeps in'.

In May Lotte had two very enjoyable performances with Aargard Oestvig: a *Lohengrin* at close quarters (Elsa), which was delightful, and an *Ariadne* at long range (the Composer). How she longed to sing the Greek heroine opposite his Bacchus. Another charity performance followed, for Crown Prince Otto's Orphans' Home, and this was a *Meistersinger*. Leo Slezak was singing Walther von Stolzing, and at a Slezak performance anything was likely to happen. He had practically no respect for the Royal stuff and nonsense.

Slezak[22] was formerly a gardener and keeper from Bohemia, and he had been another of Mahler's 'finds' at the Court Opera in 1901. Later he studied with Jean de Reszke to great advantage, and his strong, ringing tenor voice, which also possessed sublime tenderness, made him an ideal Wagnerian and Verdian. And he was a practical joker. Nothing seemed serious to him, least of all the most tragic opera. *Meistersinger* and *Aida* afforded him opportunities to 'express himself' to the cast, for in both operas there is a stage full of singers round him at a time when he has very little to do except stand and look important. With his back to the audience, Slezak used to make the most excruciating faces in the direction of the chorus, and on at least one occasion (in New York) the complete chorus was fined by an irate stage manager for behaving in an unseemly manner when it was all Slezak's fault. Slezak would not have that, and paid all the fines himself. He enjoyed life to the full and wrote a number of highly amusing anecdotal autobiographies. His son, Walter Slezak, collected a further volume with his father's 1896 Brünn début in mind as Lohengrin, and called it 'When Does the Next Swan Leave?'[23]

Lotte was not alone in adoring Slezak for his huge teddy-bear appearance, the wrinkled eyes about to launch one of his enormous, infectious bellows of laughter, and his wonderful voice. He was in Vienna for many years – until 1934 – with Lotte.

The 1917–18 Viennese opera season ended early on account of the war that was reaching its climax in the bloody trenches of Flanders. It seems incongruous, if not downright callous, that the Royal Court Opera should be carrying on with its lavish productions as though nothing else mattered and as if nothing important was happening in the rest of Europe. Even so, leaders of Austria's musical life were already looking forward to the possibilities of a radical change in their Opera, a change that was closer than anyone could realise.

Chapter Five

The Strauss Régime

1918–1924

Between 1908 and 1919, Richard Strauss was under contract to conduct about ten concerts of the Philharmonic in Berlin every year.[1] After he had relinquished his permanent conducting post at the Royal Court Opera in 1910, he still kept a foot in the capital with the Philharmonic, where his concerts were a feature of every season.

Before Hans Gregor left the Vienna Court Opera at the end of 1918, a certain Baron Andrian was made manager for a short time, to keep the organisation on an even keel in very troubled times. Andrian was a lifelong friend of Hugo von Hofmannsthal, who proved to be the link between Strauss and Andrian when it came to appointing a new Director. Naturally, with Gregor still there, these negotiations were carried out in great Viennese secrecy.

In this complicated business, made more so by Andrian's own exit after only four and a half months, Strauss was invited to share the directorial duties with Franz Schalk, in spite of the fact that Hofmannsthal foresaw that it would never work.

Strauss and Schalk seemed complementary in effect: the one was composer and conductor and possessed enormous prestige; the other was conductor and administrator and already had a great deal of experience in both aspects of the Vienna Court Opera since the beginning of the century, where he applied his talents with more than ordinary zeal.

It was not thought advisable for Schalk to continue with the task of running the Opera unaided, for he lacked the ability to make quick decisions and implement them; and when other contenders, and a 'dreadful muddle'[2] organised by Ludwig Karpath (in the Ministry of Education that bureaucratically controlled the Opera) had been cleared away, Hofmannsthal came round to backing Strauss. His appointment was then ratified, and he became due to take over his directorship in the following December. It was unfortunate that, in the course of another muddle, no proper terms of reference between Strauss and Schalk had been drawn up or defined; nor were there terms between them and the Ministry. The lack of any firm guide-lines was to have disastrous results later.

Strauss seemed to make his own views quite plain in a letter to Hofmannsthal in August 1918:[3]

> 'Since I compose only in the summer, I have resolved to devote five winter months for the next ten years or so to my work as a conductor – and since Berlin claims a little more than two months, I could well imagine myself spending the other, longer, half – and if necessary part of the spring – in Vienna in a kind of advisory capacity (*along with* a full-time Director) in the building up of a truly artistic repertoire, with a say as to the manner of its execution. . . . Let me tell you that it has been my devoutest wish for the past thirty years to assume the *de facto* supreme direction of a big Court Opera House on the artistic side. . . . If therefore a *modus* were to be found for such an "Indian Summer" enabling me to pursue in Vienna the kind of directing activity . . .' etc., etc.

Strauss was fifty-four years of age, and had now completely reconciled himself to having lost a fortune during the war (it had been deposited in London at a high interest rate), and to the fact that he must continue conducting to earn the required income which composing alone could not yield. The prospect of Vienna was ideal.

Before the season had begun, Lotte was playing fast and loose with first Gregor and then Schalk, demanding more money and stating that the 28,000Kr salary she had been offered was not nearly enough. Hamburg, she told them, was offering her the equivalent of 50,000Kr to return there. Schalk approached Strauss, clearly enraged about Lotte's behaviour, but Strauss replied:[4]

> 'Don't be too angry with Lehmann. She will remain with us if you bide your time! Loewenfeld has indeed offered her 50,000 but where is that coming from? Has everybody got to put money first these days? Haven't we still got a Vienna Court Opera? Shall I not be a boss there myself in the autumn? Haven't we still got an Austria?'

And remain with them she did.

The 1918–19 Vienna season opened for Lotte with rumours about all this directorial news circulating freely in the streets of the city and in the corridors of the Opera House. Her first performance was as Sieglinde, and the third as Martha in *Evangelimann*, a role she had sung twice in her first Vienna season, but not since. Both September and October were fairly light months, with only five performances in each; then, after an *Ariadne* under Schalk on 1 November, Lotte went to Hamburg for four guest appearances that included two Myrtocles. It was on the way home to Vienna, after the last of these, that Lotte heard about the collapse of the Austro-Hungarian Monarchy, the end of the war, and defeat. This was on 11 November.

As always happens there, the sands of popularity were running out for the Director of the Vienna Opera. Hofmannsthal refers to him at this time as 'that accursed man Gregor'[5] (and only because Selma Kurz had sung Zerbinetta too infrequently); and the board of the Opera were looking for a reason to oust Gregor and make Schalk the sole Director, *pro tem*. This turned out, conveniently but curiously, to be pinned on Gregor's decision and stubborness to mount Strauss's *Salome* – with Jeritza – in 1918.[6] This was its Viennese première, for the Church had previously been successful in keeping it off the stage.

There were clearly going to be great changes in Vienna – so Gregor imagined – and while the Emperor Charles I renounced all participation in affairs of state but did not abdicate, Gregor (whose pernicious activities[7] Strauss now referred to) kicked the dust of Vienna off his boots at the end of 1918, departing gratefully to become Regisseur in Hamburg. One cannot help but wonder whether Gregor wanted Lotte to involve herself with his move.

But Vienna never changes much. Down came the Imperial Crown and Eagles from the building and the programmes, and overnight it became the Vienna Operntheater, still in business, and with Franz Schalk as sole Director until Strauss joined him.

They both discussed the singers and the everlasting salaries. 'Jeritza pulls them in most of all,' wrote Strauss to Schalk.[8] 'After her 70 evenings and 100,000+ to the Box Office, it is Piccaver, Weidt, Mayr, Oestvig and Lehmann that are each worth their 1000/1200Kr a performance.'

In December, Lotte was rehearsing for a new role which should have suited her to perfection: Lisa in Tchaikovsky's *Queen of Spades* with Slezak as Hermann. He had sung this role of an introspective Russian officer at the Met opposite Destinn in 1910. It was greatly to Lotte's advantage that he should be repeating his portrait in Vienna. Something went wrong for Lotte, because she abandoned Lisa after only four performances, and gave no clue as to the reason. It seems to have been rather a doubtful investment.

She had a habit, which infuriated Schalk, of playing the *grande dame* when she was offered a new role.[9] He sent her the score with a letter, encouraging her in honeyed words to read it and then – surely – to agree with him that it was absolutely ideal for her: vocally well-suited, dramatically powerful (or sympathetic, or attractive in a new way, or in vogue, or seemingly created just for her, or as the case might be). Whatever it was, Lotte instantly returned the score to Schalk with a brisk note, informing him that it was out of the question for her to undertake it – for a number of reasons that she seemed to pull out of a hat.

Schalk then resumed the attack, reinforcing his previous arguments, swearing that Lotte was the only singer in Vienna who could do justice to the role, and imploring her to look at it again and to let him know quickly, because he was faced with the need to cast the opera and wanted, above all, for her to shine in it.

Again Lotte returned the score, sometimes regretting, sometimes reiterating her previous reasons. And so the charade went on, with Lotte playing less hard to get until at about the third, or even fourth, attempt on Schalk's part, she held on to the score, graciously but reluctantly, and then got to work. Once she had agreed to settle for the part, the to-ing and fro-ing was not at an end. She didn't bother Schalk any more, but her coach now suffered from her sudden decline in self-confidence when, on bad days, she slammed the score shut and declared that to be an end to it. Then it was the coach who had to convince her that all was really well, and that she was already making a marvellous characterisation after such a short time spent on it. Getting Lotte into a role thus appeared to be a battle of wits and of patience every time.

But once she had mastered it, Lotte put every ounce of herself behind the role and always revealed a new and complete interpretation. Her acting was improving all the time.

So it was rather a pity that after Lisa, Lotte went on with another doubtful adventure: the role of Frederike in Bittner's *Der Musikant*. This was a revival of the original, 1910 production during Weingartner's first engagement in Vienna, and Richard Mayr repeated his creator's performance of Oberstierberger, a bassoon player who becomes involved with two women, one of whom is Friederike, a female violinist. Lotte took over Gutheil-Schoder's old role.

Julius Bittner's opera did not hold the stage beyond one season, when Lotte sang the six performances, but by then she was thinking about her next new role – in breeches. This was the 17-year old Silla, pupil of Palestrina, in Hans Pfitzner's opera of that name, which was receiving its first Vienna production. The work has no significant female roles, the two principal ones are *en travesti*, Silla and Palestrina's 15-year old son Ighino, sung on this occasion by the contralto Hermine Kittel.

The mounting of this production was Hans Gregor's last piece of organisation before he left Vienna, and might not have happened if Strauss had already arrived as co-director. He and Pfitzner did not get on at all well, which raised the subject of whether a composer of operas should be the director of an opera house at all. Mahler had been mainly a symphonist, but Strauss was always very concerned that as many of his operas as possible remained on the maximum number of stages. After the bad notices *Der Rosenkavalier* had received in Vienna after its first night there, it looked like being dropped altogether by Gregor; and it was only thanks to Alfred Roller's persuasion and abiding faith in the work – for after all he had played a large part in its realisation – that it held its place long enough for the public to appreciate its worth and vitality and demand its constant repetition.

Strauss was already planning for the world première of his next opera to be given in Vienna in October 1919. Lotte enjoyed working with him, and in advance of his arrival as director she had written to him in endearing, though respectful, terms, calculated to keep her in his mind – or so she hoped.

There were two cycles of *Der Ring* in March and April as usual, but Lotte had no Sieglinde (forfeit, as it were, to Jeritza), though she sang the Freia and Gutrune in both cycles. Strauss came as a guest to conduct *Ariadne*, with Lotte in her beloved role, and two nights later she appeared in yet another guise that, in the event, did not please her at all.

Apart from the Viennese composer, Julius Bittner, there was another who, from time to time, was honoured by having his genius-son's operas performed. Julius Korngold's son Erich had his two one-act operas *The Ring of Polykrates* and *Violanta* performed in Munich in 1916, and now they were scheduled for Vienna, especially as father Julius exercised an ambivalent attitude towards Strauss in his newspaper. To him, Strauss the composer and director in Vienna was chastised for allowing Strauss the conductor in Berlin to interfere with his more important work.

Gregor had prevented the two operas from reaching the stage of the Court Opera, believing them to be more suitable for the Volksoper. Now Lotte was cast as Laura in the story about a legendary Greek tyrant who is lured to the mainland from his well-defended island stronghold, and crucified. Piccaver was also taking part and the first opera went well, but only as a curtain-raiser for *Violanta*, starring Jeritza as a tigress of an Italian Renaissance lady who, in attempting to murder the seducer of her sister, falls under his spell instead. As usual, Jeritza stole the show and at the end of the evening, which had been conducted by the twenty-two-year-old composer as a guest, *Polykrates* had been erased from the memory of the audience by her majestic – and highly-coloured Renaissance – performance.

Lotte was furious at being so successfully upstaged by her rival, and sang only one further performance of Laura, but not until nine months later. Her fury was altogether assuaged on the next night, when Strauss conducted a perfect *Zauberflöte* in which Lotte sang Pamina. With Piccaver as Tamino, Mayr as Sarastro and Berta Kiurina as Queen of Night, the performance which Strauss nursed along so that it breathed love and tenderness, proved exhilirating and beautiful to cast and to audience alike. For Strauss the agnostic, Mozart was god; and for Lotte singing Pamina, even that hurdle 'Ah, ich fühl's' came much more easily.

Lotte's two last performances of the season were as the Fifth Flower Maiden in *Parsifal*, and that of 1 June was in celebration of fifty years since the Opera House on the Ring was opened. The date was adrift by a week, but it was a splendid event.

Many severe restrictions, shortages and a valueless currency all followed in the wake of the war's end. Electricity was also rationed and so was transport. But the Opera still went on, and planning for the coming season was in full swing before the season closed in June, promising Lotte less holiday than usual before September.

Since the beginning of the war in 1914, Hofmannsthal had been working with Strauss – on and off – at 'their *Zauberflöte*',[10] a fairy-tale opera in the form of a parable that extols procreation with all the joys it brings to a married couple. There had been many delays in meetings and in correspondence during the war between the two creators through illness, family worries and Hofmannsthal's unavailability while an intelligence officer in the Austrian army. As a result, the opera, already somewhat cumbersome and obscure, had lost a little of its shape along the way. Strauss's initial spark had become dimmed with the long passage of time until he was able to complete *Die Frau ohne Schatten* (*The Woman without a Shadow*) so that it emerges as a flawed work, yet one of great beauty and feeling with some really inspired moments in both story and score. It was to be the first important première in Vienna after the war, due at the beginning of October, and requiring the first month of the season for stage rehearsals. The magical plot needs many scenic tricks and illusions which had to be perfected, among which was the essential absence of visible shadow from one of the principal sopranos, as the title suggests.

Casting had been in the minds of both Hofmannsthal and Strauss for some time, and had lain in Strauss's mind while he was composing. There are three principal female characters: an Empress who is half human, half fairy, and whose vocal line lies very high, sounding pure and bell-like. The second is a poor Dyer's Wife whose tessitura is lower, but she is given to intemperate – and strenuous – ranting between lyrical and romantic passages. The third is a mezzo-contralto, the malevolent Nurse to the Empress, who hates and despises mankind for she is from Elsewhere. Her role is so very difficult and tiring to perform as Strauss wrote it that nowadays it is extensively cut.

Strauss was originally considering Jeritza for the Dyer's Wife, Lotte as the Empress and Lucy Weidt as the Nurse. It will be noticed that the characters' names are stylised: there is only one who has a name and that is Barak the Dyer, the principal baritone. There is also a Heldentenor, the Emperor, whose vocal powers are pushed a long way.

Strauss had told Jeritza that he was giving her the Dyer's Wife, the most important character, composed with her in mind; and that she, and only she was going to be able to do it justice. At any rate this is what Jeritza said to the press during the summer of 1919. When Strauss, who certainly did have Jeritza in mind for most of the first act, was composing the second act, he began to realise that she had all the authority, and presence and *beauty* for the Empress, who is light as air and casts no shadow. Strauss was fully aware of the animosity which existed between Jeritza and Lotte, and found himself in an awkward situation when Jeritza gratefully accepted the Empress, leaving Lotte to believe that she was being landed with her opponent's cast-off role.

When, in early July 1919, Franz Schalk sent Lotte the score[11] of the opera and it was clear to her that her role had been switched 'after Strauss had composed it specially for her' she flew into a rage. Together with the score was a letter from Schalk saying that he must have her agreement to singing the Dyer's Wife as there was no time left for the usual convention which they had adopted between themselves over new scores, and to pretend that she had already received it and had returned it.

Lotte was amused by Schalk's approach, but was not initially won over. It needed Strauss's added weight and personal charm to convince her, and this came in his letter of 22 July. As Lotte had already written to him personally to complain at the state of affairs, his reply was not only natural, but skilful:[12]

> . . . What Ochs or, let us say, what opera-composing colleague has talked you into believing that this role is too strenuous for you?

Practise at the piano, when a couple of important points must be gone over will result in what seemed difficult being conquered by you that evening. Think, for God's sake, what a fuss there would be if you, the first youthful-dramatic singer, do not sing this most lovely youthful-dramatic role. If Frl. Jeritza has to take over your role because Frl. Lehmann herself cannot master it – you couldn't allow that! That would be suicide! . . .

You have only to come here as soon as possible and I promise you that in 3 days you'll be cured after you've been twice through the lovely role (it really is lovely – and marvellously grateful) with me. Eventually we'll alter things a little bit, cut little bits until the dress fits perfectly . . . Thus: we expect you here as soon as possible, my wife invites you to stay with us (have you not received my last letter?) and so [here Strauss notated Zerlina's words from *Don Giovanni*] 'You'll see, my dear, if you're good, how I'll cure you!'

and he concludes, even more comically, with

Your ready and most provoking
Dr Richard Strauss

Lotte was at Gmunden, halfway between Salzburg and Linz on the Trauensee with the score of *Die Frau*. Fortunately she encountered two musicians there, Jascha Horenstein, at that time 'a rather wild-and-woolly-looking bohemian' and the pianist, Leo Sirota, who agreed to help her through the Dyer's Wife. Consequently when she arrived at Strauss's estate in Garmisch she had a fairly good idea of the role.[13]

Lotte records how amazed Strauss was at her artistic and technical understanding when he gasped 'I did not imagine that anybody could learn this!'[14] He used to work all morning and it was during the hours with him that Lotte got to know the Strauss behind his mask which was always in place when he was in public. The warm, sensitive artist, sometimes near to tears revealed himself to her.

Otherwise Lotte was astonished at the relationship which existed between Strauss and his wife, Frau Pauline,[15] who derided, scolded, upbraided him and treated him as though he were a stupid yokel. She never missed the opportunity to compare her own background and parentage with his – to his disadvantage, and should anything in the house, or the garden, happen to go wrong, she blamed Strauss with a fierce torrent of invective no matter who was there. At first, Lotte tried to intervene, but Strauss asked her never to do so for it would make it far worse if she tried to defend him against his wife.[16] His 'angelic patience and adaptability'[17] were what appealed to Lotte under these circumstances; but when he played his Lieder, as he sometimes did after the intensive rehearsals of Lotte's Dyer's Wife, everything was different. Then the couple showed how much they loved one another and 'Frau Pauline would embrace him sobbing in one of her violent outbursts of tenderness.' [18] Old memories would be awakened and they carried on like an engaged couple of youngsters. Yet when this was over, Frau Pauline would, like as not, resume her role of the tyrant. She found an actual delight in arguing with him for argument's sake, and often left the rudest letters about the house, addressed to him.

On 28 August the setting rehearsal for *Die Frau ohne Schatten* was held at the Opera House, but (unusually) without Hofmannsthal being there. He had absolute faith in Alfred Roller, who had made the prompt book for *Der Rosenkavalier* at Dresden in 1911 and was in every way a man of the theatre. Lotte had only an Octavian to sing on 4 October, and Elsa on the 8th, otherwise the rest of the month was purposely free for her to rehearse.

Neither Lotte nor Jeritza has anything to relate about the rehearsals, and there is another regret. No recordings were made of the creators' performances in these dazzling roles. Richard Mayr sang the patient Dyer, Barak (who has to suffer under his Wife's tongue and behaviour the same kind of insults as Lotte witnessed in Garmisch); and Karl Aargard Oestvig was the Emperor.

Puccini had an opportunity to look at the score in Schalk's office one day and, after perusing only a few pages, closed it and put it down with the remark: 'It's all logarithms!'[19] For many musicians, the score of *Die Frau* seemed unnecessarily difficult and complicated, and while rehearsing for the Dresden production shortly afterwards, one of the violinists remarked: 'It seems more suited to the gynaecological ward than the opera house.'[20]

The opulent *Frau ohne Schatten* was first heard in Vienna on 10 October 1919 at inflated prices twice over: once because of the debased Austrian currency (when a gallery seat cost the same as a pre-war season ticket in the stalls), and also because this first performance was in aid of the Opera's Pension Fund. It was hardly appropriate in a defeated and starving Vienna, except that even under these depressing circumstances, the Opera was still the most important feature of Viennese life.

For Lotte it was a trial and a triumph. In interpretation of the ambivalent character of the Dyer's Wife, she revealed a lovable woman beneath all the shrewishness, which is exactly what so many of her successors have failed to do. Jeritza was also praised for displaying such strength in the Empress, combined with a calmness in her voice and person. (The Empress has to undergo several fearsome ordeals.) Schalk always conducted the opera and it was a great sensation during the whole of October, when eight performances were given to full houses, four with each of the two casts. Lotte had no other roles to sing that month, but in every performance of *Die Frau ohne Schatten* there were several intimate scenes with Jeritza who had always to appear subordinate.

On 31 October, Lotte made her début in Prague as Elsa, receiving a long and flattering review in the German language newspaper, *Bohemia*. They most admired her warm and poetic reading, devoid of all theatricality, though intense and emphasising a personal beauty. She next appeared as Margarethe in Gounod's *Faust*, with Nikolaus Zeč from Vienna as Mefistopheles, and was equally well received. They liked her 'brilliant' Jewel Song, and were delighted that she had left all traces of Gounodisms behind by presenting the character as a plain, middle-class German *Mädchen*. Her last performance was as Myrtocle in *Toten Augen*, apparently a work that was entirely new to the German Opera House in Prague. The critic looked forward to hearing Lotte again, in projected performances of *Meistersinger* and *Rosenkavalier*, in the coming May.

Lotte's last Octavian had been in Vienna at the beginning of October and before the *Frau ohne Schatten* stage rehearsals, *Generalprobe* and performances. There had been a placing rehearsal for the *Rosenkavalier* on stage on 4 October morning which had been specially called by Strauss for Acts II & III on account of a new soprano in the company who was singing Sophie. She had joined with her husband, who was a very good pianist and coach and a thoroughly reliable conductor. He was Karl Alwin and she was Elisabeth Schumann.

When Elisabeth and Lotte greeted one another warmly in front of the company ready to begin Act II, Lotte clasped her and whispered urgently into her ear: 'For God's sake don't tell anyone what we got up to in Hamburg. They all think that I'm pure and virtuous in Vienna!'[21]

Elisabeth Schumann was then almost unknown in Vienna, as seems evident from the playbill of this performance when her name was spelt 'Schürmann'. In her first month there she sang Micaela, Antonia, Eva, Sophia and Pamina, all which – except for Sophie – can be thought of as 'Lotte roles'. But such was their friendship that Lotte was delighted. Nor did Elisabeth sing any Wagnerian role heavier than Eva, while in *Freischütz* it was always Aennchen, never Agathe.

12 November was the anniversary of the Republic of Austria when Lotte sang Pamina in a subdued gala performance. She had a new role to sing in December, and apart from one Dyer's Wife she had a reasonably

gentle time before 16 December. This was the date of her first Mimi in *La Bohème* (with Piccaver as Rodolfo) her first Puccini heroine. The heavy, untubercular figure of Lotte would not seem to represent an ideal Mimi, but she perfectly convinced her audience of that frailty which is the essence of the pathetic little seamstress. Her interpretation, which deepened and was enhanced with further subtleties as time went on, always fascinated her, and continued for three or four performances a season until the late twenties. It became an important operatic event in the calendar, and the house was always sold out.

Lotte strikes at the root of Mimi in her observation about the death scene.[22] This is the culmination of the story, for Mimi is dying from the moment she first appears to Rodolfo in the garret; thus Lotte emphasised the death itself, with her body stiffening and the muff falling to the floor with her last breath. Lotte also observes, à propos Italian opera in general though with special reference to *La Bohème,* that the aria is not only a wonderful chance for the singer to show off, but it must be seen and heard as an integral element of the whole work.

Now that Strauss was a fully-fledged co-Director of the Vienna Operntheater he appeared more often on the rostrum, but never for the *Frau ohne Schatten* which he left entirely to Schalk. Lotte was very happy singing under his direction in *Lohengrin, Ariadne* (twice), *Walküre, Götterdämmerung, Rosenkavalier* and *Freischütz* (twice) during the first quarter of 1920. *Freischütz* was a particularly favourite opera of Strauss's, not only because of its importance in the German operatic tradition, but because it was the first opera he had heard as a boy of not quite eight years of age. So far as Lotte was concerned, it also remained a constant enjoyment with the vocal opportunities that Agathe offered her.

The *Rosenkavalier* with Strauss was the first time that she had sung Octavian for him. Lucy Weidt was the Marschallin, and still Strauss's avowed favourite singer for this part, but instead of Richard Mayr as Ochs, it was Michael Bohnen from Berlin, a sturdy bass-baritone who was cast by Hofmannsthal in the silent film *Der Rosenkavalier* a few years later,[23] not the opera. It is a story which uses the same characters (and the Feldmarschall) and situations, but is complimentary to the plot as we know it.

Lotte fulfilled her Prague engagement in April, but instead of the expected *Meistersinger* and *Rosenkavalier* it turned out to be two Mimis and a Sieglinde, which attracted ecstatic reviews in *Bohemia.* After that she went to Hamburg for almost a month. It was like a holiday! She had seven performances, and they especially asked her to sing her new creation of Mimi as well as Elsa, Elisabeth, Octavian, Eva, Myrtocle and

Sieglinde. She was fussed and fêted and the weather was kind during this April and May.

During her absence, there were two performances of the *Frau ohne Schatten* and an *Ariadne* in which Elisabeth Schumann sang the Young Composer for the first time. It was a piquant performance, lighter and less dramatically risky: anybody else who attempted to reproduce Lotte's anguished boy was in danger of overdoing it and appearing ridiculous. Lotte had it so nicely balanced that one was caught up in the situation when the Young Composer finds he has to cut his cherished classical opera to make way for the harlequinade, and Lotte always had the audience supporting her. Looking at the end of the prologue coolly, it is a ridiculous situation – a piece of purposeful Hofmannsthal-irony.

On her return to Vienna, Lotte had a few rehearsals for a most unusual production of *Carmen* – the part (of Carmen herself) that every soprano *except herself* wants to sing, according to Lotte. The fated Gypsy in this case was, surprisingly, Jeritza in a blonde wig, leaping on and off tables, smoking cigarettes as she sang, dancing, playing the castanets and rushing about in varying moods of elation, depression and anger. She certainly presented the character in a manner never before seen in Vienna – or anywhere else. Lotte, being as usual at the edge of the drama as Micaela, gave her normal, touching performance which was seen, from Don José's aspect, as more of a passive foil to Carmen than usual.

Strauss conducted with zest, gave Jeritza full rein, and appeared to be enjoying it all thoroughly. There were four performances at which Ziegler – the tenor whom Gregor did not accept for Vienna in 1914 – sang three Don Josés and Aargard Oestvig the fourth.

Lotte's varied season ended happily when the Rodolfo in *La Bohème* on 16 June was Richard Tauber, her old friend from Hamburg, Altona and Zoppot, deputising for Piccaver. He was making several guest performances during Vienna's quest for new tenors, having recently joined the Berlin State Opera from Dresden. Before this *Bohème*, the leader of the Vienna claque came round to ask for Tauber's subscription, which he refused to give, so the man darkly said he would be round again afterwards. However, Tauber sang so beautifully and earned his own applause that the fee was not demanded.[24]

July and most of August were free for Lotte without a large Strauss score to learn, but there was an important assignment waiting for her in October, the month of Vienna's next new production. Lotte thought it wise, in any case, to capitalise on the popularity of the composer concerned: Giacomo Puccini. She was to sing two roles in his *Trittico*; and she had asked to sing *Madam Butterfly* in addition.

She appeared for the first time as Cio-Cio-San on 10 September 1920 opposite Piccaver as Lieutenant Linkerton ('Pinkerton' is impolite in German). Although she had not the figure for a Japanese girl, any more than she looked like the consumptive Mimi, until she began to sing, Lotte was again able to win all hearts with her pathetic oriental, persuading her audience that she *was* petite, fragile and totally lost among westerners and their ways.

Then came the rehearsals for Puccini's 'Triptych' of three one-acters. The first is a *verismo* work called *Il Tabarro* (*The Cloak*), almost a three-hander about a Parisian bargee and his wife, Georgetta. Her attempts to leave her brutish husband for a handsome stevedore causes the young man's death by strangulation at the hands of the jealous husband. What happens to Georgetta after the curtain has fallen has to be left to the imagination.

The second opera, *Suor Angelica,* has an all-female cast and takes place in a convent. Sister Angelica, daughter of a noble Italian family, has taken the veil because of the scandal caused by the birth of her illegitimate baby boy. When her Aunt, the Princess, comes to the convent to obtain Angelica's signature on a legal document, she casually tells the girl that her son has died. Angelica takes poison, but in the moment of death she prays to the Blessed Virgin for forgiveness, and sees her leading the boy towards her.[25]

The third opera, *Gianni Schicchi,* is a rousing comedy about a family round the death-bed of a rich old rogue who is only pretending to have passed on so as to assess which of his dependants truly loves him. It depends to a large extent upon the buffo baritone of Schicchi, and the one soprano aria does not demand a prima donna.

The two heavily contrasted roles of Georgetta and Angelica presented Lotte with a challenge which, from the composer's point of view, she was unable to meet. Puccini seems to have decided, rather late in the day, that there was need for an altogether different personality as Georgetta, especially as Lotte's Angelica was a thing of great beauty and sensitivity. Consequently it might have lost part of its purity and artistic value by being associated with the same singer's Grand Guignol Georgetta.

Maria Jeritza recalls[26] that she was in London in the middle of October when a telegram from Puccini in Vienna implored her to take over Georgetta with, in Jeritza's words, 'Only two days in which to learn the role. I actually lived with the score from the moment I had wired him my acceptance . . . and I do not believe I ever worked harder in my life.'

This probably turned out for the best. Lotte put everything she had into Angelica and Puccini was so fascinated and moved by the dress rehearsal that he openly wept. Lotte was satisfied so far as this went – it is not often that a composer can be so moved by his own work – but she was piqued that Jeritza had once again succeeded in stealing a role from her. Yet in this instance, bearing in mind the *Polykrates* and *Violanta* incident of a short while before, Lotte saw Jeritza's curtain raiser of *Il Tabarro* as preparation for the centrepiece of the evening's entertainment; and after *Suor Angelica,* the comedy was merely to send the audience away in a cheerful frame of mind. Without doubt, *Angelica* is the most touching and far-reaching of the three.[27]

When Puccini returned to Italy, he wrote to his friend Sybil Seligmann in the following January about the *Angelica*:

> In Vienna it was the most effective of the three, with the good Lehmann (she's German, it's true) but a fine, delicate artist – simple and without any of the airs of a prima donna, with a voice as sweet as honey![28]

Mosco Carner, who was at the première, added that the part might have been written specially for Lotte, who lent the opera a poignancy not experienced since.

Lotte was somewhat puzzled and disappointed when Puccini did not come round to congratulate her afterwards. But he sent word almost immediately: he was weeping, and ashamed to show himself, so Lotte would have to wait to see him when he had calmed down.

There were five performances of the *Trittico* and a Mimi in the Puccini line, before Lotte returned to Hamburg for four different operas during the first half of December. They included one *Tiefland,* which had by now become a Lehmann rarity, and, of course, a Myrtocle. Try as she might, Lotte was unable to persuade Strauss and Schalk to mount *Toten Augen* in Vienna. It is unlikely that either of them had been present at one of Lotte's performances in Hamburg or Prague (she gave it nowhere else) to see that its potential rested upon the singing-actress at the climax of the opera, rather than its score.

In February 1921, Lotte appeared for the first time in Vienna as Marta in Eugen d'Albert's *Tiefland,* the most successful of the twenty operas that he composed.[29] It is a *verismo* work based on a Catalan play. A shepherd called Pedro is given Marta by the rich landowner, Sebastiano, provided he takes her away to the Lowlands (the opera's title). When Marta confesses to Pedro, whom she loves, that Sebastiano had seduced and tired of her, Pedro forgives Marta and then strangles Sebastiano when he tries to take her back. Her two appearances as Marta were the only ones she ever gave in Vienna and she was glad to surrender her to Claire Born, a newcomer to the opera, although she was Viennese and shared many of Lotte's roles.

Another new character, specially studied, and which profited her little, was the Widow Helene in Bittner's *Die Kohlhammerin* with only two out of four performances and never again.

In May, Lotte went to Hamburg and gave them her 'three E's' Elsa, Elisabeth and Eva; then to Prague for two nights as Elisabeth and Butterfly. Her Elisabeth was very successful because of its varying qualities of tone and for the intensity in portrayal. And while other singers had been known to 'refine' their technique when singing Butterfly, Lotte gave her full heart to the role, singing out and projecting the character's sadness in Act II instead of attempting to *imply* it. (After all, *Madam Butterfly* is no more Japanese than *Carmen* is Spanish!) It was also noticed in Prague how effectively Lotte's complicated arrangements for her death scene had been devised. 'The sold-out house overwhelmed their beloved singer with applause'. These turned out to be Lotte's last guest performances in Prague.

At the end of April, Richard Strauss conducted his *Frau ohne Schatten* for the first time, though not with Lotte in the cast. The number of singers now trained to sing in this large and complicated opera was growing, which Strauss hoped would make performances more likely elsewhere with guest singers supplied by Vienna. Although there were sufficient tenors able to sustain the heroic role of the Emperor, that of the Nurse was proving to be exceedingly difficult for nearly every contralto except Lucy Weidt and Bella Paalen to sing as it stood in the score; several others who had tried to learn it had found themselves overparted.

The new season of 1921–22 (Lotte's sixth already) opened for her in gentle fashion with Eva, Elisabeth and Octavian. She was preparing for her new role of the season, Blanchefleur in Kienzl's *Der Kuhreigen* (*Cowbells*). Jeritza was not in Vienna so Lotte picked up the role with which Maria had established herself at the Vienna Volksoper in 1911. But three performances in quick succession were all that Lotte sang at the Opera, Maria Rajdl succeeding her. Another doubtful enterprise on Lotte's part.

After four performances in Hamburg (but no Myrtocle for a change) Lotte resumed her famous partnership in *Manon* with Piccaver – twice; and on Christmas Eve she sang an Eva under Schalk's baton in which the three singers, Lotte, Aargard Oestivig and Alfred Jerger were so young that their combined ages did not reach one hundred.

There was now an event of great significance in Lotte's personal life, which was to extend over it for the next seventeen years.[30] At the end of the war, the Baronin Gutmann of Vienna, a widow and member of the very rich Jewish banking family, realised that her four children were much in need of a step-father, especially as three of them were boys. She met and married a tall and strikingly handsome Hungarian ex-cavalry officer called Otto Krause. He had been born in Budapest in 1883 and was also Jewish. He was an excellent horseman and very musical, being particularly fond of opera. He had a permanent stall at the Operntheater and had become a fan of Lotte's, but from a distance. He used to tell his wife about her, for the Baronin was not at all interested in opera and did not accompany him to performances.

On 29 January, which was Otto Krause's birthday, the Baronin gave a dinner party for him, and mischievously told him that he would not get his present from her until the dinner was in progress. He asked the meaning of an empty chair next to his at table, but his wife laughed and said he must wait. Krause was very perplexed.

During the meal a guest was ushered into the room and expressed her apolgies for lateness, though the Baronin knew that she was otherwise engaged. She was led to the empty chair beside Krause and sat down. 'Here is your birthday present, Otto!' said his wife. Fatal words: it was Lotte Lehmann. The unfortunate Baronin did not know that it was the worst kind of present – from her own point of view – that she could have given her husband, for it was love at first sight between him and Lotte.

They began seeing one another clandestinely until Lotte had to tell her lover: 'I am going to Buenos Aires and Montevideo with an opera company for three months. I do not want to hear from you during the time I am away; but if, after those long three months, we still feel the same about each other as we do today – well, then we must decide what is to be done about it.'

Lotte's performances in Vienna this season were limited because she had leave of absence, together with several other principals from Vienna and Berlin, and the Vienna Philharmonic Orchestra under Felix Weingartner, to visit South America.[31] The company was a two-part affair, led by the Italian impresario, Walter Mocchi, who strutted about like a little Latin Diaghilev and who had collected an excellent set of principals including Gilda Dalla Rizza and Mariano Stabile, with the conductor Vincenzo Bellezza and the composer-conductor Pietro Mascagni. Weingartner, for his part, had taken temporary leave of the Vienna Volksoper, where he was now chief conductor, and had collected a strong cast of Wagnerian singers for the first *Ring* cycle ever to be performed in Buenos Aires. They were Helene Wildbrunn as Brünnhilde; Walter Kirchhoff as Siegmund and Siegfried; Emil Schipper as Wotan-Wanderer; Carl Braun as Fafner, Hunding and Hagen; and Lotte as Freia, Sieglinde and Gutrune.

While Lotte was preparing to leave Vienna, rumours about her and Otto Krause were rife, since there can be no such thing as a secret there. Stories soon reached the Baronin's ears, but her husband professed complete ignorance of such calumnies. On marrying into the Gutmann family he had been given a sinecure job and was financially very well cushioned.

The ship sailed from Genoa and on the voyage the Italian and German singers got on well together (except for Mascagni) in spite of the fact that they had been on opposite sides in the war.

It took three weeks before they reached South America where Lotte was enchanted by the sights, especially the people whom she found fascinating, though she admitted to feeling desperately homesick. No doubt she longed for Otto and for her parents, who were staying with Fritz and his wife in Sylt, while she was away.

Not only were the Argentinians unfamiliar with the *Ring*, but so, it seemed, was Mocchi, and there was considerable difficulty on Weingartner's part in persuading him to allow *Das Rheingold* to be played without an interval. In his autobiography, Weingartner recalls that he and the Germans had always to be fighting for 'their rights', whether it be a proper presentation or adequate rehearsal time. At one time it seemed that the *Ring* might not be extended beyond *Siegfried* to its conclusion,[32] but eventually Mocchi was bound to admit that the Wagnerian performances had saved his tour from financial disaster; and this was partly due to an influential Wagner Association in Buenos Aires. For them the mounting of the *Ring* Cycle amounted almost to spiritual salvation.

Weingartner thought that Lotte was so beautiful and so feminine as Freia in *Das Rheingold* that for once it made sense that the two giants were struggling against the gods with her between them. The company went on to Montevideo in Uruguay for one performance of *Die Walküre* on 21 August when Lotte and Helene Wildbrunn were the stars of the occasion. Fortunately these two sopranos were on the best of terms and spared any jealous feelings. The newspaper *La Mañana* recorded 'The end of the first act was outstanding, giving this scene an extraordinary brilliance.' This was at the Urquiza Theatre (now no longer standing).

Suddenly Otto Krause arrived. He could no longer bear to be without Lotte so they came to the decision that they were destined to stay together. She went on to Bahia Blanca in Argentina where she gave two Lieder recitals and Otto Krause had to begin to learn his duties as 'husband' of a prima donna. Lotte admits that she had hardly embarked upon Lieder singing ('that holy of holies') and in any case her audience had no previous experience of it at all.[33] They expected her to flounce about, snapping castanets as if it were a Cante Flamenco. At first they were uncomprehending, if not disappointed, that she merely stood there in an evening dress without moving; but gradually they were drawn in to the beauty of Song and accepted what was, to them, an entirely new convention. It was such a success that she gave a repeat concert shortly afterwards.

The company returned home on a German ship to Hamburg, calling at Tenerife en route, and passing through storms which extended their voyage to four weeks. But with Otto beside her, Lotte found peace and calm: everything was suddenly new and exciting, and so different.

In 1920, Lotte had moved her belongings to Schönbrunnerstrasse with her parents. Because of the new life before her, she decided to buy the old people a house of their own in Hinterbrühl, some fifteen miles to the south-east of Vienna, near Mödling. From pictures, it was a charming little place, and one that suited them admirably. It suited her too, that they were at some distance – much as she loved them – but it took a little time for the house to be made ready. She knew that her father would object to her illicit relationship, more especially as Otto was married and was Jewish: so she did all she could to prevent him from finding out about the *affaire*.

The Baronin had heard more than rumours before Otto left her to go to South America, telling her that it was a business visit. Then everything she hoped could not be true became a realisation. She suffered a stroke or else a palsy and from then on she was confined to a wheel-chair.

When Lotte returned to the Opera, and met members of the Company, they expressed to her their intense sorrow and shame at 'what she had done' to the Baronin Gutmann. Marie Gutheil-Schoder and Selma Kurz, the acknowledged senior members, rebuked Lotte severely, reminding her that this would bring discredit on the Opera and everyone in it. For some time she refused all invitations, believing herself to have been placed outside Society. Her father soon heard all about it and was extremely upset, refusing her his blessing if she was intending to urge Otto to seek a divorce in order to marry her. Consequently they remained unmarried but lived together at Schwindgasse 10 in the Fourth District.

Lotte was relieved to have a contract with the Berlin State Opera in

October, placing her at some distance from her own Company at the beginning of the season. She sang Eva, Elsa, Mimi and Butterfly at 5,000 marks a performance and an extra 2,000 marks for travel.[34] (The exchange rate at the end of 1922 of 1,750 marks to the £1 sterling made the German currency of the Weimar Republic most unenviable and the contract worth very little in real terms). Nor was the visit especially pleasing, for Lotte found herself to be no longer attuned to Berlin and its inhabitants: they seemed lacking altogether in the warmth which was all part of life in Vienna.

So it was with mixed feelings that she returned to the stage of the Vienna Operntheater for her Butterfly on 7 November, the first of fifteen performances before the end of the year, and her first since the previous February. The applause and the friendship which greeted her on both sides of the curtain made up for the pangs of conscience and months of professional unhappiness that she had been suffering. She had evidently weathered the storm.

Butterfly with Oestvig; *Jüdin* with Slezak; *Werther* with Piccaver; and a *Rosenkavalier* with Lucy Weidt, Elisabeth Schumann and Josef von Manowarda as Ochs was all like coming home again after a long time among strangers, and Lotte sang to Vienna with her whole heart.

On 2 December, Lotte's second *Butterfly* was conducted by a new assistant to Schalk called Clemens Krauss, another of the Schalk-Strauss management's 'new men' and one who was there very much at Strauss's instigation.

He had been born to Clementine Krauss, a dancer at the Imperial Opera in 1893 and his father – so it eventually came to be known – was Count Baltazzi, a courtier, and uncle to the Baroness Maria Vetsera.[35] It was she who had died with the Archduke Rudolf, heir to the Austro-Hungarian throne, at Mayerling in 1889, changing the whole future of the Austrian monarchy, even perhaps of Europe's history. Count Baltazzi, a keen horseman and show-jumper, bequeathed this passion to his natural son Clemens.

Clementine Krauss had been obliged to leave the Imperial Ballet on account of her peccadillo, but began a new career as 'Clemy' Krauss, singer at the Volksoper, where she took important roles; later she was the first woman to produce opera there. Her son, Clemens, was born in Vienna, took her surname, and when he was of the right age he joined the Vienna Boys' Choir. As he grew up he took on the appearance and manners of his noble ancestry and stood out in a crowd. He was exceedingly musical and quickly proved himself a willing and apt pupil to the composer-teacher Heuberger and others. From an early age he had been a keen disciple of Richard Strauss, who arranged for his transfer from the Frankfort Opera to Vienna where, after all, he belonged.

Lotte admired Krauss tremendously and found him physically attractive from her first sight of him. She was to sing a great deal under his baton, with diminishing enthusiasm, and to share his fondness for riding in the Prater, which was one of her own great enjoyments. But now she experienced his careful and helpful style on the rostrum.

On 14 December, Lotte sang her first Desdemona in *Otello*, conducted by a junior Kappellmeister and with Slezak as the Moor. Desdemona is a woman of tenderness and compassion, and a Venetian senator's daughter who can be assertive when roused in defence of her honour. This suited Lotte perfectly, and although she did not sing Desdemona very often in Vienna, it was thought to be unmatched in its subtle shades of characterisation. Slezak was like a savage bear in Otello's wrath: soft and gentle in the love duet, and always singing that searchingly high *tessitura* with effortless ease and great beauty.

After this role, Lotte was preparing herself for two more in this season, one entirely new but in line with her personal policy; the other very familiar and greatly coveted.

Proceeding with her leading characters in Puccini's operas, ('a series of generically identical works' as described by Hofmannsthal who did not much care for them),[36] Lotte was now about to tackle *Tosca*. It was clear to everyone that she could not – dare not – attempt to outface Jeritza in one of her most famous roles, so Lotte must sing and act it in an inimitable manner and give her character her own authoritative stamp. Jeritza was at the Met and the Viennese coast was clear.

Four out of her five performances were opposite Piccaver, which was a great help (the penultimate was with Laurenz Hofer), but Lotte's characterisation was never one that altogether pleased her, though she went on trying to improve it for the next twelve years. She writes little about it, merely remarking that she knew she lacked the 'flashing temperament'[37] which the passionate Roman prima donna exhibits so forcibly. Yet Lotte always hated to be thought of as a *prima donna* and rejected the title. She was of the people and tried never to inflate herself – except to opera managements. Perhaps this is what was missing in her Tosca: the *prima donna assoluta* attitude on which Jeritza thrived (and, much later, Maria Callas too). A report that Puccini 'seemed quite satisfied' with Lotte's Tosca is no criterion. Every composer is satisfied when his operas are performed regularly, and after all, Puccini had much to be grateful for in Lotte's other assumptions of Sister Angelica and Mimi.

A month after this, Lotte changed Italian dress for Grecian and sang Strauss's Ariadne for the first time on 23 February. It was a special event with top prices and Strauss conducting. Aargard Oestvig sang Bacchus – Lotte's ambition achieved – and Selma Kurz was the Zerbinetta. This was, at the same time, not without a pang of regret, for her attachment to the Young Composer was now of six-and-a-half years' standing. She often used to stand in the wings and listen to others singing 'her' paean to Music at the end of the Prologue and regretted having lost it. But now she had moved into Ariadne's sphere, a more gentle and tragic place which she was able to occupy with great distinction. It was another sensational evening for her and she was often to sing this role in Vienna.

Massenet's *Manon* had been firmly entrenched in the repertoire of the Vienna Opera since November 1890, when it was first heard there sung by Marie Renard and Ernst van Dyck. Three years later, in Turin, Puccini's opera on the same subject received its world première, and to avoid confusion (which he did not altogether manage) he called it *Manon Lescaut*. In both cases the plot follows the Abbé Prévost's novel of 1731 fairly closely, though neither has time to illustrate fully enough all Manon's infidelities. Massenet's five-act work 'of discreet and semi-religious eroticism' (to quote Vincent d'Indy) called upon two librettists: Puccini had five for his four acts, one of them being Giulio Ricordi, his music publisher.

It was not surprising that with the current demand for Puccini in Vienna, it was decided to mount *Manon Lescaut* and with the two principals who had become so identified with the characters of the Chevalier Des Grieux and Manon: Piccaver and Lotte.

But *Manon Lescaut* was not a success, probably because the Viennese preferred Massenet's more subtle handling of what is, *au fond*, a highly-coloured and slightly sordid plot. After the eighth performance of *Manon Lescaut* had clearly failed to win any further acclaim (Lotte sang six and Claire Born the other two), Massenet's version returned on 30 November to instantaneous and unbridled delight. This was the score they liked and the only one they wanted.

Lotte had a *Bohème* with Tauber; a *Walküre* and two *Ariadnes* with the beautiful Aargard Oestvig. One of these was conducted by Strauss, and the other, for the first time in Lotte's experience, by Clemens Krauss who was fast becoming a 'Straussian' and a close friend to the composer. At the time Lotte did not see any reason why this should affect her one way or the other.

She took time off to visit Budapest, with Otto acting as her guide and interpreter, for one Elsa, one Desdemona and one Margarethe. Her

Lohengrin was Herbert Leuer from Vienna, the rest of the cast for all performances were Hungarians, but Lotte sang in German, to universal applause. The critic of the *Pester Lloyd* likened her characterisation of Desdemona to a combination of Gounod's Juliet and Thomas's Mignon.

Lotte had, for some time, been dissatisfied with Grammophon, the independent German branch of HMV, for not having given her an opportunity to make any records since 1921. The company had been in difficulties, mainly over copyright, since the war and, as nothing was forthcoming, she transferred her allegiance to Odeon in Berlin.[38] In February, March and April 1924, in three sessions, she recorded twelve arias and the famous duet from Korngold's *Tote Stadt* with Richard Tauber. She sang this role of Mariette-Marie at the Berlin State Opera in March, conducted by a brilliant young Hungarian called George Szell. She also sang Elsa, and Mimi with Tauber, both under the batôn of Êrich Kleiber.

Lotte returned to Vienna for two performances in between her recordings. The first was a *Bohème* with the Rumanian tenor Trajan Grosavescu as a guest. He had recently joined the Volksoper but was now on his way to the Operntheater. He had a specially good voice for the Italian repertory, though it had what has been described as 'a metallic edge'. His most famous role in Vienna was the Duke of Mantua in *Rigoletto*. Three nights later Lotte and Piccaver sang their last *Manon Lescaut*, a performance that seemed to have been popped in to try to catch the audience off their guard. But it was the last. In early May Lotte reappeared with Piccaver in the *real* Manon, as if to cleanse the ears of Puccini's work. The applause was rapturous.

Jeritza was back in Vienna, singing Octavian and Sieglinde, two roles that Lotte had very much in mind at the time, one in a negative, the other in a positive fashion.

As she had given up the Young Composer in favour of Ariadne, she now thought it was time to move from Octavian to the Marschallin. She had trailed her coat to this effect in Vienna but without any response. Strauss was very satisfied with Lucy Weidt's performance, and she did not wish to move or to be moved.

In the spring of 1924 a British Empire Exhibition was held at Wembley in North London. In connection with an expected influx of thousands of foreign guests, the Grand Opera Syndicate of Covent Garden had formally invited the Vienna State Opera to present a season there in May and June. For the past three years a native company called the British National Opera (BNOC) had occupied Covent Garden giving performances in English with British singers. The Syndicate's decision to close its doors to the BNOC in 1924 because they paid an uneconomical rent was only one of several reasons why they were excluded. The main intent of the Syndicate and its Society supporters was to encourage a return to the glorious days of the International Opera Season which had not happened since July 1920.

Owing to 'bad feelings' about this in England (generally expressed the loudest by those with the least interest) the invitation to Vienna was cancelled. Not to be outdone, though, the Syndicate decided to ask some of the Vienna Opera's singers to participate in an *ad hoc* season, and the same was arranged for the Italian and French works.

One of the principals who had been approached personally in Vienna was Lotte. The official in London who had been informed about – or who had remembered – her appearance in *Der Rosenkavalier* in 1914 was under the impression that she sang the Marschallin,[39] and offered her four performances of the role, together with two Sieglindes and two Ariadnes. Hearing that Bruno Walter was to conduct the *Rosenkavalier* and that Elisabeth Schumann, Richard Mayr, and Delia Reinhardt (from Berlin) were to be in the cast, she signed for fear of losing the engagement.

After all the time-wasting that had gone on in London before the final arrangements were made, the first prospectus did not appear until 7 April for a first night on 5 May. Yet everything settled down and was put in order for the opening opera, *Das Rheingold*, introducing the first *Ring* cycle, in which Lotte was not singing. Her Covent Garden début was on 21 May as the Marschallin, fulfilling the prophesy made to her by Herr Naht, the Hamburg shipping magnate in 1914.

Lotte recalls[40] that when she reached London and met Bruno Walter, she had to confess to him that she had never sung the Marschallin – although she was not entirely unfamiliar with the opera or the role, having been a Sophie or an Octavian to many different Marschallins during the past thirteen years. This was no excuse for Walter, who was thoroughly shocked; but as one of his many abilities lay in simple but profound explanations from his own extensive knowledge, Lotte profited from his instruction in London to such an extent that her performance was another outstanding success. Critics and public were alike in their enthusiasm for the new Marschallin in an opera that was new, too, for many of them. For the second time Lotte had caused a sensation by appearing in a Strauss opera almost by accident. From now on she was regarded in London as the best Marschallin of her generation of sopranos. Owing to her personal *éclat* as well as to Richard Mayr's endearing Baron Ochs, there were two extra performances of the opera, though Frida Leider sang the Marschallin in one of them.

Lotte's career so far, and her reserve of strength, can be judged by her ability – and willingness – to sing her first London Sieglinde on the night following her first Marschallin. It was a test that today few sopranos would care to risk. In the event she was greatly admired for the human quality she expressed and the variety of fear and horror in the trials of the unfortunate Sieglinde in the second act after her perfect joy and exultation in the first.

The revised *Ariadne* was given for the first time at Covent Garden on 27 May. In spite of Lotte's beautiful and poetic Ariadne, Elisabeth Schumann's Young Composer and Maria Ivogün's marvellously secure Zerbinetta, the public seemed unprepared for it and stayed away. The second performance was even more sparsely attended.

After her success in London, and grateful for the warmth expressed by the Covent Garden audiences, Lotte was disappointed to hear that the Grand Opera Syndicate was not intending to promote another season in 1925. They had made too great a loss – mainly from the rather weak Italian side of their promotion; though it was also unfortunate that the opera-going audience in London was being split three ways by concurrent performances of the BNOC and the Carl Rosa Opera.

Lotte returned to Vienna and finished her scheduled performances on 28 June with Piccaver in *Manon*. Nevertheless, her success as the Marschallin in London had reached the Operntheater, and she had been promised a performance in the coming autumn on home ground.

She was hoping for an untroubled summer holiday, but Richard Strauss was knocking on her door again. After his *Frau ohne Schatten* he had decided to embark upon a very different kind of opera, and to give Hofmannsthal a rest. Strauss approached several writers, notably Hermann Bahr (husband of the great dramatic soprano, Anna Bahr-Mildenburg) and asked for a libretto based upon events in the lives of a composer and his wife, that is to say, Strauss and Frau Pauline. These events, which Strauss related as being based on fact, caused Bahr to shy away from treating Frau Pauline at face value – tantrums and all – when he would be obliged to meet her socially. No other writer seemed at all keen to tackle the libretto, so Strauss wrote it himself.

As well as being lifelike, performed in a contemporary setting and dress, Strauss was contemplating an altogether new (for him) musical expression and architecture. After the huge orchestra in *Frau ohne Schatten*, he was resuming his chamber music idea of the revised *Ariadne* to allow the voices to come through the texture from the pit. Since the singers in the new opera would be speaking as well as singing, it was all the more important that they were completely understood and not drowned. (Strauss wrote an illuminating preface to the score of this work, called *Intermezzo,* dealing authoritatively with the question of audibility in opera.)

Intermezzo was soon to be given its première in Dresden, Strauss's ideal house for introduction. Fritz Busch was the musical director there and responded positively to the suggestion. He did not agree, however, with Strauss's request that Lotte should come as a guest to sing the leading soprano role of the composer's wife, Christine. (The composer's name in the opera is Robert Storch – R.S.) Vocally and temperamentally, Lotte reminded Strauss of his wife, and he insisted.[41] Otherwise, he told Busch, he would present *Intermezzo* elsewhere.

Lotte's contract was eventually drawn up with Dresden, and in order to make it worth her while to rehearse the new work and sing four performances, she was to appear in four other operas.[42] She carefully studied the role during the summer and after six appearances in Vienna up to 21 September, she went to Dresden where rehearsals had already begun.

The atmosphere was not altogether friendly, and in spite of the coaching she had received from Karl Alwin, Lotte was checked for inaccuracies by Fritz Busch. When Strauss arrived for later rehearsals and saw what was happening, he stopped the proceedings and said: 'If you think Mme Lehmann is not singing exactly what I wrote, you are correct. But when Lehmann "swims" it is still far preferable, so far as I am concerned, to others who may sing absolutely correctly.'[43]

Joseph Correck played the composer in a mask that exactly resembled Strauss's features, and the designer, Adolf Mahnke, had reproduced parts of the Strauss villa at Garmisch and its furniture in his stage sets. After Lotte's visit there before *Die Frau ohne Schatten* in 1919, she had become familiar with the house, and was perfectly at home in this reproduction.

The little comedy, in two acts but with 'filmic' scenes, often of short duration and quickly changing, was first heard on 4 November 1924. Frau Pauline was present, and is said to have behaved outrageously during the performance, though afterwards she said how much she had enjoyed it. Lotte not only copied her mannerisms exactly but used her inflexions when raising her voice. (The opera begins with Christine calling for her maid, Anna: the Strauss's maid was called Anna too, and was as stupid as the one portrayed in *Intermezzo*).

It says much for Lotte that she did not flinch from her task, even when she knew she must meet Frau Pauline afterwards. All through her life, Lotte seems to have stood up bravely before people when she was forced to do so on a matter of principle or – as in this instance – professionally. This was one of her great strengths. Her weakness lay in the supposed insecurity which may have stemmed from the ill-advised Frau Tiedke and the Countess's aria in Berlin, a lifelong wound which was never completely healed.

Dresden found Lotte's performance miraculous. Eschewing comment about any similarity with living persons, the *Dresdener Anzeiger*'s critic stressed the apparently soubrettish role performed with distinction and containing far more beneath it than was at first apparent, both in characterisation and vocalisation. The 'speech-sung' role, at first misunderstood, caused another critic to come out with the surprising statement: 'Lotte Lehmann can really sing.'!

The *Intermezzo* première was, from the operatic point of view, a great joy to Strauss, but on that day he received bad news from Vienna, brought to him by his friend, Ludwig Karpath, the Austrian Education Ministry's theatrical adviser.

Strauss's relationship with Schalk had never been an easy one and had been deteriorating almost from the start. Strauss saw it in this light:[44]

> For some time there was no friction between Strauss and Schalk. But then the composer noticed how Schalk was trying to sabotage him. He made arbitrary decisions in Strauss's absence that went beyond his competence and neglected agreed preparations for new productions, etc. When Strauss returned to Vienna and expected that a work had been prepared, he found that not to be the case and that he had to start with the work from the beginning. Schalk was accused of lack of initiative. He was called an eternal no-man who fought against the studying of any new work. Every such suggestion by Strauss was answered with a shrug of his shoulders and Schalk was unable to stir himself to make any suggestions of his own . . . Nevertheless, Strauss called Schalk a competent musician who never did anything that was not artistically in order . . .

Because Strauss was only in Vienna for five months of the year and Schalk was there all the time, the 'resident director' was in a far better position to gain the support of the officials who controlled the Opera from the Ministry. Schalk had quietly negotiated a contract for himself in which there was a new clause, giving him the authority to make all decisions whenever Strauss was absent.

With the clause a *fait accompli* in Schalk's contract, Strauss had no option but to resign when he had read it. All the same, Strauss realised that it was not so much a resignation as a dismissal, and Schalk obtained the new title of 'Director General of the State Opera' which pleased him greatly.

Lotte managed to conduct a warm relationship with both men, and this rift between them did not unduly affect her, though she was unhappy about it. So far as Strauss was concerned, he had found an ideal portrayer of his roles in Lotte, and he promised that he would write his next leading soprano part with her in mind. That was her reward for the success she had made with Christine.

Chapter Six

Singing for Strauss

1924–1930

Lotte returned to Vienna after her triumphant Dresden visit to sing a *Bohème* with Tauber. On 12 December, twelve days later, musical Vienna – which in any case means all Vienna – was plunged into mourning for Puccini's death which had occurred on 29 November. There was a grand memorial concert in the Operntheater: Mozart's Requiem followed by a performance of *Suor Angelica* conducted by Franz Schalk and with Lotte in her original role. This performance affected her deeply and she had to exercise great control over her emotions, remembering Puccini's reaction to her performance.

1925 began with Lotte singing a wide variety of roles from Mariette/ Marie with Tauber in *Tote Stadt*; Elsa with Richard Schubert; Recha with Slezak; Manon with Piccaver; Mimi, Lotte and Tosca with either Oestvig or Piccaver; Sieglinde with Oestvig and Cio-Cio San with Grosavescu. Apart from showing the extent of Lotte's work at the time it also demonstrates the strength and the variety of world-class tenors in Vienna. One wonders if it can ever have been matched since throughout the world, let alone in one house.

Lotte was feeling happy because she had no rivals until Jeritza returned from her usual Met performances in January to sing Elsa, Sieglinde, Mariette and Tosca – all 'Lotte roles' but all handled quite differently by this Moravian prima donna who was now preparing to take Vienna by storm in the revival of one of her most famous pieces.

This was Minnie in Puccini's *Girl of the Golden West*, which she had first given in Vienna in 1912. Again she scored a great triumph, galloping about the stage, with Piccaver as Dick Johnson and Alfred Jerger as the villainous Jack Rance. If anything, Lotte was amused and impressed. This was no part for her and the reason is well summed-up by Lanfranco Rasponi:[1]

> Minnie . . . is considered by some musicians to be the equivalent of a dramatic Wagnerian heroine. The orchestration is in fact

> very heavy; and unlike the Wagnerian dramas, which develop slowly, *Fanciulla* is a crescendo of passions that can easily carry an emotional soprano right off balance. . . . Divas who have appeared in this meaty part have managed, in some cases, to create a believable character, but rarely with sufficient vocal resources.

So far as Lotte was concerned, Jeritza might sing it every night. In one week Jeritza sang Minnie on Monday, Salome on Wednesday and Santuzza on Friday, then disappeared from Vienna for the time being. But not to recuperate. Her iron throat and lungs seemed to need no rest.

There was always something outrageous about a Jeritza performance, something that went just too far, either for credibility (even in opera), or for that dangerous, indefinable element called good taste. In *Tosca* she always sang 'Vissi d'arte' lying flat on her stomach,[2] leaving her Scarpia standing like a lemon against the back wall of the set. As Santuzza, she actually rolled down the church steps. A permanent arrangement with the tenor needed a push from him to initiate her extravagant descent. On one occasion, legend has it, the tenor was Piccaver and he didn't push her. When she furiously upbraided the temperamental fellow afterwards he merely replied that he didn't feel, as Turridu, in such a mood on that particular evening, and desisted.[3]

Lotte had no recording sessions scheduled with Odeon for the spring, which was in many ways a pity. They gave her enough warning to enable her to get leave from Vienna and to secure appearances at the Berlin Opera. When she came to hear that the Berlin Staatsoper were producing *Intermezzo*, it was too late. Vienna claimed her in March and April.

The Berlin *Intermezzo* received its première on 28 March in a production conducted by George Szell. Maria Hussa was cast as Christine and Theodor Scheidl as Storch. Shortly afterwards there were three records made by Polydor: the Skat Scene at the beginning of Act II and the final scene of reconciliation between Christine and Robert. Scheidl and the other Berlin singers in the Skat Scene recorded their roles on three sides, but Grete Merrem-Nikisch sang Christine with Scheidl, on the other three. Thus Odeon missed an opportunity of recording Lotte as the creator of Christine, for record companies were highly jealous of their contract artists and did not allow them to 'cross over' to rivals. Nothing of Lotte from *Intermezzo* exists on record, which is more than a pity, considering how closely she identified with Frau Pauline Strauss. It might have been something of an historic document.

Jeritza was back in New York and so Lotte had no compunction about singing the Mariette/Marie again with Tauber. She had made her Vienna début in this double role on the previous 6 January, repeating the powerful duet they had given in Berlin and had recorded there in the previous year. (Discog. No.64)

A celebrated French soprano called Germaine Lubin was in Vienna, singing Ariadne and Elsa. She was also a famous Isolde, but was not heard in more than the other two roles at present. Madame Lubin was not one to exhibit any modesty about herself:[4]

> Echoes of my terrific notices as Elsa reached Vienna and I was invited to make my début there under Clemens Krauss's direction. I had to relearn the role in German, but the reviews were ecstatic there too. . . . And I was invited to sing *Ariadne auf Naxos* . . . with Strauss conducting. Again another triumph, and the participation of Elisabeth Schumann as one of the nymphs was unforgettable.[5]

Clemens Krauss, idol of many middle-aged (and not so middle-aged) women, was conducting some *Ariadnes*, *Rosenkavaliers* and *Lohengrins*, but none with Lotte. Nevertheless, he was given (or demanded) superb casts including Gerhart, Oestvig and Jeritza – when she returned to Vienna in May.

Lotte had a première in that month in an opera called *Don Gil*, based on the Don Juan legend and in which her character was Donna Juana. But it was not a success. The minor composer Walter Branfels' work had a second performance two days later, a third in the following season, and no more in Vienna. After its second performance, Lotte went to London for three performances of her now famous Marschallin, with the same cast as in the previous year. The house was sold out on all evenings, for *Der Rosenkavalier* had become an immense draw in London. Lotte also sang two performances of Elsa, in which role she had never before been heard at Covent Garden. It was received rapturously, and the second act's *scena*, with Olszewska as Ortrud, was especially successful.

The 1925 Covent Garden season had only materialised when Mrs Samuel Courtauld volunteered to become responsible for its finances after the Grand Opera Syndicate had withdrawn. Mrs Courtauld appointed Lieutenant Colonel Eustace Blois to be her new syndicate's managing director. He was a businessman who nevertheless possessed a first-hand knowledge of singing and of opera stage-management, an altogether unusual combination of expertise.

Blois achieved wonders in organizing and mounting the 1925 Grand Opera Season at Covent Garden within two months. With a little more time to spare some of the casting might have been improved upon, but all in all it was a gigantic achievement and was artistically a success.

Maria Jeritza appeared at Covent Garden for the first time in 1925, as Tosca and as Fedora in Giordano's opera to another libretto by Victorien Sardou. It follows his play very closely – the play with associations of Sarah Bernhardt, Eleanora Duse and Mrs Patrick Campbell. *Fedora* had not been heard in London since its single performance (with Lina Cavalieri) in 1908 – and after Jeritza it has not been given at Covent Garden again. Not that this implies that she was inadequate: on the contrary, she was ideally cast in the lush and passionate role of the Russian princess with a fated lover. Because of Jeritza's advance publicity, all her performances were sold out immediately booking had opened,[6] and a black market in her *Tosca* tickets prevailed. She had a great personal sucess in both works.

Back in Vienna, Lotte sang a *Manon* with Piccaver, and a *Tosca* with him again, with a young baritone of great vocal beauty – and promise – as Scarpia. This was Alfred Jerger, who was now to be an important member of the company.

The new season saw the first of what might be called Lotte's 'established' Marschallins in Vienna, the wonderful character that she was to sing there for more than another forty performances. Coming late to the role, but at the very age that Strauss specified for his Princess of Werdenberg, Lotte's London performances, her tuition from Bruno Walter, and the awareness that she was *becoming* Marie Theresa with every new assumption, caused it to become her favourite of all roles on the opera stage.

In her book, *My Many Lives*, Lotte devotes a long chapter to 'The Marschallin'.[7] She gives only a synopsis of the opera plot, highlit with some observations from the Marschallin's point of view, rather than about her. She includes important points relating to the playing (but not the singing) of Octavian and Sophie from her own experience. Yet there is nothing about how she *sang* the role, which is a pity, and which makes the content of her writing not so different from the chapter called *Der Rosenkavalier* in her book *Singing with Richard Strauss*.[8]

For instruction on Lotte's vocal interpretation, one has to go to the various records, the first of which, the aria 'Die Zeit die ist ein sonderbar Ding' from Act I, was not made until 1928. Perhaps HMV were already envisaging a large selection and stayed their hands. But more of that later.

Lotte had clearly deepened her interpretation since her previous Marschallin in Vienna a year before; and although acceptance there came slowly, for Helene Wildbrunn was still active, Lotte had made her mark.

In October she went to Berlin for some more recordings (Discog. 66–77) which included the early 12″ side of the Marschallin's 'Die Zeit', prefaced by 'O sei Er gut, Quinquin'. She also made second recordings of both Elsa's 'Einsam in trüben Tagen' and Eva's 'O Sachs, mein Freund' on 17 October. Five days later she recorded three more 'repeat' arias (Discog. 72–4) less than a year, as it was to turn out, before the end of the acoustic era.

With only Micaëla, Manon and Mimi among a solidly German list of heroines to sing in Vienna, Lotte nevertheless kept Pamina, and was encouraged with another Marschallin to sing on Christmas Day. Two guest performances in Hamburg made it clear that – for whatever reason – she was giving Myrtocle a rest.

On 28 January 1926, Lotte had another début, as the Countess Madeleine de Coigny in Giordano's French Revolution opera, *Andrea Chénier*. Trajan Grosavescu sang Chénier and Emil Schipper was Gérard, the servant turned revolutionary and still in love with his employer, the Countess Madeleine. It is a stirring, blood-and-thunder piece whose première in Vienna had taken thirty years to arrive from La Scala, Milan where it was first heard in 1896. Franz Schalk now conducted, but later handed over some performances to Robert Heger. Likewise, the tenors became Pattiera or Piccaver. After six performances of Chénier, Lotte sang another Marschallin with Gutheil-Schoder as Octavian, Elisabeth Schumann as Sophie and with Strauss conducting – a great pleasure and a treat for Lotte.

On 8 March, she and Tino Pattiera gave a recital in the Vereinhaus, Dresden. It included two duets from *Andrea Chénier*, the love duet from *Otello*, the Act I duet from *Tosca* and several groups of songs. Pattiera's Neapolitan songs, which he did so well, were very popular, while Lotte sang four by Richard Strauss: 'Zueignung' and 'Wiegenlied'; then 'Ständchen' and 'Cäcilie', presented in exemplary fashion. Rolf Schroeder, from the Dresden Staatsoper, accompanied them throughout on the piano. A Bechstein, it was provided by Herr F Plötner who owned the music shop from which it came, sold the tickets and took the profits from this concert which he had organised as a special event in Dresden's musical life.

Lotte's father had now reconciled himself to accepting Otto Krause as a son-in-law, and as there was no longer an impediment to the marriage, Otto and Lotte were quietly joined in matrimony in Vienna on 28 April. Thereby, Lotte became an Austrian citizen.

Their short honeymoon was followed by the annual visit to London, a season which was overshadowed by the general strike in Britain, lasting from 3–13 May. The main consequence was a dearth of reviews during the first fortnight of the season when no newspapers were printed. Only later, in the periodicals, were there some limited, 'catch-up' notices, but they came too late to be of any support to the box-office.

Bruno Walter opened the season with *Figaro* in German: an unusual opener and an unusual language, but there was no doubt about the 'genuine, pure and unadulterated artistry' of the performance. Beside Lotte as the Countess, Delia Reinhardt (Bruno Walter's lifelong love) sang Cherubino; Elisabeth Schumann was the delightful Susanna; Richard Mayr the Figaro and Josef Degler, Count Almaviva.

Two nights later, Lotte sang Eva in a strongly cast *Meistersinger* conducted by Heger, whom Walter had brought to assist him during this heavy season. There was one complete *Ring* and extra performances of *Die Walküre* and *Götterdämmerung*. Lotte and Lauritz Melchior sang in *Die Walküre*, but this was her only *Ring* appearance. Melchior was found to be more attractive then previously, and of course Lotte's ardent Sieglinde was greatly admired and roundly applauded.

Lotte's first London concert in 1925 had been such a success that she planned another three for 1926. The first of these was at the Royal Albert Hall, and again Bruno Walter was her accompanist. This was on 30 May. The programme consisted of Wagner and Strauss, began with one of her favourite large-scale openers, 'Dich, teure Halle', was followed by three of the Wesendonck Lieder ('Träume' being especially noticed), and then went on to Strauss. The concert ended with the Final Scene from *Salome*, the only known occasion when Lotte sang the taxing *scena*. To attempt it with piano, not orchestra, at least gave her the vocal advantage which her personal resources needed. This according to *The Times* critic, 'was sung, not screamed out and Bruno Walter was a fine accompanist though he inclined to overemphasize the melodic notes in his part'.

At the beginning of June there were four performances of Verdi's *Otello* at Covent Garden with the great, but ageing, Giovanni Zenatello as the Moor; with Mariano Stabile as Iago for three performances, and Lotte as Desdemona throughout. The twenty-year-old Walter Legge, present at the third performance, believed that he would never hear a finer Desdemona, thought Zenatello marvellous, but fifteen years past his prime, and disliked Stabile's wobble intensely.[9]

That particular performance was something of a trial for Lotte. On the previous evening there had been a gala occasion to celebrate Dame Nellie Melba's retirement. Among other items she sang the first scene of

Act IV of *Otello*: the Willow Song and Ave Maria. For Lotte to have to rise above this in her complete performance on the following night was, in the event, possible because their voices and interpretations were so different. Indeed, having just passed her sixty-fifth birthday, Dame Nellie's still sweet voice and awesome presence were more remarkable than her limited dramatic ability. Lotte's fuller, more expressive voice and her powers to encompass each phrase in Desdemona's tragic life gave not an inch to the *prima donna* of the night before, had any fortunate person been at Covent Garden for both events.

Much of Dame Nellie's Farewell Performance of 8 June was recorded and has been reissued since. Some quite sizeable fragments of the Zenatello *Otello* on 17 June were also recorded, all by HMV. Because Lotte was under contract to Odeon, the HMV machines had to be stopped whenever she appeared on the stage and not a note of it was taken.[10] Consequently, her two versions of the Willow Song (Discog. 62 & 193) are all that have come down to us from what seems to have been one of her outstanding roles, and sung in Italian, too.

On the evening before the Melba event, Lotte had sung the first of only three performances of Donna Elvira in *Don Giovanni* that can be traced in her whole career. Bruno Walter's particular affection for the opera had enabled a spectacular cast to be assembled: Frida Leider as Donna Anna, Elisabeth Schumann as Zerlina, and Mariano Stabile as the Don. The final sextet was sung, probably for the first time at Covent Garden, but to those who can still remember it, the production was marred by long waits during inefficient scene-changes, and evidence of inadequate rehearsal time.[11] Nor was the opera a familiar one to the younger members of the audience. The last time it had been given at Covent Garden was in 1914. Jean Aquistapace sang Leporello then, as he did again now, in 1926.

Donna Elvira 'is a treacherous part', said Jarmila Novotná,[12] 'for it is written very much in the middle of the voice, and finding the right interpretation is most problematic. She is a bore, complaining all the time to the sound of lovely melodies, and yet somehow one must make the public feel sorry for her. The way she pursues Don Giovanni is not dignified, and at the same time Da Ponte has written that she is a noblewoman of great breeding.'

Lotte was evidently soon aware that it was not the part for her, but it was Bruno Walter's wish that she should learn it. 'There are very few singers who have the ideal combination of flawless technique and passionate feeling, and I am not one of them', she said.[13] This applied to

Donna Elvira, alas, although there was no lacking the 'passionate feeling'.

Jeritza was in London again, appearing in three operas. *Thaïs* and *Jewels of the Madonna*, mounted especially for her, were rapturously received, but have never been heard at Covent Garden since. This reflects credit on Jeritza as the last of a line of particular *prime donne* who specialised in this kind of highly-charged opera. Her Sieglinde in the second *Walküre*, though, was another matter. Ernest Newman, in his weekly *Sunday Times* article took her severely and mockingly to task in a piece entitled 'Arms and the Diva'. He wrote that he preferred Thaïs when she was accompanied by Massenet's music; for he considered Jeritza to be 'vamping' Melchior/Siegmund like a Thaïs in the first act of *Die Walküre*, waving her arms about and generally behaving 'with emphasis rather than insinuation'. She was never heard at Covent Garden again although it was intended that she should return in the following year.

It was altogether a remarkable season, for apart from the operas and singers in the German part of the programme, there was Chaliapin in *Mefistofele* and as Don Basilio in *Il Barbiere*; Stabile in *Falstaff* with the majority of Toscanini's supporting cast from La Scala, conducted by Bellezza; Fanny Heldy, a famous French Manon in the role with which Lotte had become closely identified in Vienna, but which she never sang in London (perhaps because she would have had to learn it all over again in French).

Towards the end of June, Lotte and her husband were back in Vienna. Her return performance was on 25th as the Marschallin, although this playbill still showed her as 'Frl. Lehmann'. This error – for they must have known of her marriage two months earlier – was corrected for her next appearance in *Tosca* two nights later, when thereafter she was shown as *Fr.* Lehmann. Frau Lehmann ended her contribution to the Vienna season with Piccaver in *Manon* on 29 June.

Most of Lotte's holiday was spent in moving house with Otto from Schwindgasse to Arenbergring 16 in the Third District (now called the Danneberg Platz).[14] They were to remain there for the next twelve years. Quite often, the fans sent Lotte rose bushes instead of bouquets until eventually their garden in the Arenbergring had over 1,000 growing there. In early August she had some lightweight songs to record in Berlin with Dajos Bela and Mischa Spoliansky. (Discog. 85–9). It is a great pity that the Schumann 'Nussbaum', recorded at this time, was never published.

Although there had been festival performances of many kinds in

Salzburg, over the years, most of them connected with Mozart, it was not until after the war that a Festival Society was formed by Max Reinhardt, with Hugo von Hofmannsthal, Richard Strauss and Franz Schalk as its founder-directors.

The Salzburg Festivals began slowly, almost carefully, which was wise, with their opening in 1920. Hofmannsthal's play 'Jedermann' (Everyman) was given four times in the Cathedral Square, and has been given there almost every year since (except between 1938–45, because Hofmannsthal was Jewish). In 1921 there were nine concerts of Mozart's music and three performances of ballet by Karsavina and Novikoff; but in 1922 there were productions of four Mozart operas, beginning with *Don Giovanni,* conducted by Strauss. This was a great step forward, reversed in 1923 with only plays, and in 1924 with no festival at all, because of the Austrian financial crisis.

The Salzburg Festival was firmly established in 1925 when Max Reinhardt's production of 'The Miracle' was first presented. As well as the singers Anna Bahr-Mildenburg and Alfred Jerger in the cast, Hans Thimig, Oskar Homolka and Luis Rainer were among the actors, headed by Lady Diana Manners[15] who astonished everyone by her beauty and her assurance as the Madonna. Besides opera, ballet, orchestral and chamber concerts, there were Lieder recitals by Richard Mayr; Joseph Schwarz; Maria Ivogün and her husband Karl Erb; and Lotte Schöne singing Strauss.

By 1926 there was a formula which, with few variations, was perpetuated with enormous success until 1943. Usually there was a single conductor who bore the brunt of the work, and who was largely responsible for planning the special flavour of each season. In 1926 it was Franz Schalk, with Bruno Walter as a strong second for two operas and one concert.

The musical side of the 1926 Salzburg Festival opened on 9 August with *Die Entführung* conducted by Bruno Walter. It was followed by *Don Giovanni* under Schalk. *Die Fledermaus* under Walter, and *Ariadne auf Naxos* (in the revised version, of course) was conducted twice by Clemens Krauss and once by Strauss himself. Krauss had been released by the Frankfort Opera, where he was the Musical Director, at Strauss's special request. Lotte sang the first Ariadne on 18 August, and Claire Born sang the two others.

Strauss could stay no longer than 21 October because he had to go on to Leipzig for a Strauss week which had been 'exemplarily rehearsed and, in part, magnificently conducted by Brecher'.[16] This was Gustav Brecher from Lotte's Hamburg days.

In advance of the Salzburg Festival, Strauss had complained to Hofmannsthal that this *Ariadne* with a 'hand-picked cast, with a conductor specially invited for the occasion (Krauss) and the best available producer (Wallerstein), is *expensive*, so expensive that even fully booked a deficit for each night of ten to fifteen million Aus.Sch. must be expected.'[17]

A photograph exists of a rehearsal for this year's Salzburg *Ariadne*, with Strauss present,[18] and the principals in the cast grouped round a piano, the women in large hats and long dresses of the period, the men with bow ties and 'co-respondent' shoes.

Krauss had been brought in by Strauss, for the younger man had acquired what might be described as a 'taste' for the composer's music and longed to conduct more of it, preferably at the Master's knee. He was later to play a vigorous part in the Salzburg Festivals, one which was to affect Lotte directly. Krauss had introduced the tenor, John Gläser (a Berliner), to sing Bacchus. He had good reviews but never returned to Salzburg and remained in Frankfort until the end of his singing career. Otherwise the *Ariadne* singers were all from Vienna: Maria Gerhart as Zerbinetta and Maria Rajdal – who was much liked – as the Young Composer. But the most glowing tribute came to Lotte from the Salzburg Chronicle's critic who adored the 'golden colour of her classical singing throughout Ariadne's difficult and demanding moments. The house listened to the magic and shimmer of the Lament, and at the end it was greeted with unbridled joy.' It was a great success for Lotte and her only appearance in Salzburg that year, but it opened the doors to future engagements there.

Lotte went on to Munich, whose annual festival – and that at Bayreuth – are held at about the same time each summer. This Munich engagement, however, was Lotte's first, and had been made before Salzburg over which it had to take precedence although Strauss may have wanted Lotte to sing all three Ariadnes. In the rather stiffer surroundings of the Munich Nationaltheater she sang the *Figaro* Countess on 21 August under Karl Böhm; Eva in *Meistersinger* on 25th under Hans Knappertsbusch; and Sieglinde on 28th under Krauss. This was her first association with 'Kna' whom she liked very much – as nearly every other singer did. Her associates in Munich were interesting as singers as well as musicians, but Lotte was glad to find three friends there: Elisabeth Schumann (the Susanna); Gertrud Kappel (Brünnhilde); and Emil Schipper her Hans Sachs.

Lotte returned to Vienna immediately to sing Elsa at the opening of the season on 1 September. Otto Wolf (who had been her Siegmund in Munich) was opposite her again, as Lohengrin, as a guest tenor, and he was also her partner in the *Meistersinger* on 5th with Schipper as Sachs. Wolf was a very respectable Heldentenor who had made his début as long ago as 1897, and was called to Munich in 1909. He was their first Emperor in *Die Frau ohne Schatten* and now, with only two singing years left before he retired, he went as a guest to Vienna. Such was his training and technique.

At the end of the month Jeritza sang Recha in *Die Jüdin* with Slezak as Eleazar, and squeezed every gram of drama from her role – so differently played from Lotte's manner. Lotte was fulfilling a number of her normal, repertoire roles while preparing and rehearsing for another that one might imagine to be outside her capabilities.

On 14 October and with a rest of eight days since her last stage appearance (as the Marschallin), Lotte gave the Vienna première of Puccini's last opera, *Turandot*. Slezak sang Calaf; Berta Kiurina, Liù; and Franz Schalk conducted. There were two casts, and that which followed the first night had Maria Nemeth, Jan Kiepura (as guest), and Luise Helletsgruber. Afterwards, Lotte used to say: 'Turandot! Oh yes, I enjoy that when Nemeth sings it!'[19]

In Vienna it is Nemeth's impersonation of the cruel Chinese Princess that is remembered, not Lotte's. 'Perhaps I should never have accepted Turandot,' she once confessed, 'for it is a voice wrecker, although musically most fascinating and imaginative . . .'[20]

Turandot *is* 'a voice wrecker', a 'killer' and all the other uncomplimentary epithets often applied to the role. Lotte sang it for several reasons, and not only in Vienna: firstly because it was offered to her to sing; secondly by accepting it she was able to beat Jeritza to the role; thirdly because it was a useful addition to her series of Puccini heroines; fourthly because Lotte had a strong feeling for the composer's memory and wanted to sing Turandot 'for his sake'; and lastly because, like the climber and the mountain, it had to be attempted 'because it is there'.

Lotte was an acknowledged Wagner-Strauss singer (though she did not essay the toughest, dramatic soprano roles of Isolde on the one hand, or Kundry; nor Salome or Elektra). She was not a dramatic soprano and was treading dangerously to have taken on Turandot. Yet it is the very kind of voice that Lotte possessed that is more suitable for Turandot than the Italian-trained voices, very few of which can manage it.[21] Even the strongest have quailed at it. And today several of the most adaptable and indomitable sopranos have made recordings of *Turandot* but have never dared attempt it in performance, where there can be no rest, no repose, no going back.

Nevertheless Lotte got through the role of Turandot nine times in this

1926–7 season, and thrice in the following year. She also sang it three times in Berlin over two seasons, and twice in Hamburg.

For Lotte's third *Turandot* in Vienna on 20 October she had Jan Kiepura as Calaf from the second cast. He was a Pole, and in 1926 was only twenty-four years old, dazzlingly handsome and possessed of a strong, lyric tenor voice. He could pitch a top C, and again, and again to order, which is how (it is said) he was accepted as a guest tenor at the Vienna Opera.[22] Between 1926–38, Kiepura gave performances there, more or less to suit his own inclination and convenience. He was welcome as a guest all over the world, including New York. His fan club was immense, and after he had gone into films (one showed him singing from the top of a taxi) they demanded this 'act' after each performance in Vienna, as soon as he had emerged from the stage door.

Kiepura was a wonder. He acted beautifully and without affectation, he was truly musical, and his value as an operatic tenor was greatly enhanced after his films had been seen. From his début as Cavaradossi opposite Jeritza in Vienna, his desirability was assured.

Turandot had been produced by Lothar Wallerstein as a guest, with splendid sets by Alfred Roller and no expense spared. It was sung in German, however, which (fortunately) limited Lotte's areas of performance. The production was, as a whole, so successful that Wallerstein was taken on immediately as chief producer. Richard Strauss had already estimated his ability.

After the second performance, with Nemeth and Kiepura, one wag of a critic remarked that is was especially hard on Calaf to have to answer Turandot's riddles when her Hungarian-German was as difficult to understand as his Polish mixture.[23]

Lotte's 'Turandot demon' was driving her on, forcing her, for example, to sustain a Marschallin on 3 December, Turandot on 4th and two more Turandots within three days. The demon was also preparing her for another Viennese première.

On 15 January she sang Christine in *Intermezzo*. Strauss had not only insisted that she take the role on home ground, but also that he conduct the first run of six performances in January. Alfred Jerger sang Robert and the production was an even greater success in Vienna than it had been in northern Dresden.

The delay in presenting *Intermezzo* in Vienna had been caused by the resignation of Strauss in 1924. However, since then, the City of Vienna had been making overtures to him and a happy arrangement had been reached whereby he would receive the freehold of his property in the Jacquingasse in exchange for the score of his next opera and one hundred conducting performances at the Opera. Strauss's good nature and business sense prevailed in this 'deal', though his relationship with Schalk had not thawed.

In the middle of February, Lotte went to Berlin to make some strenuous recordings in the new electrical system (but at 80 rpm rather than the subsequently conventional 78 rpm). Strenuous, because they consisted of two arias from *Turandot*, the big 'Ozean' aria from *Oberon*, and 'La mama morta' (in German) from *Andrea Chénier*. (See Discog. 90–94.) These were followed by some far lighter songs (Nos. 95–9). She also appeared in a concert and at the Charlottenburg Opera where Bruno Walter was always anxious for her services.

While she was away from Vienna, a tragedy there made the headline news for over a week. Trajan Grosavescu, the Rumanian tenor, with whom Lotte had often sung, was due to appear in Berlin as a guest. When he returned home to his apartment in the Lerchenfeldstrasse after a performance of *Rigoletto*, his jealous wife, Nelly, accused him of going to Berlin to carry on an *affaire* with somebody else. Nelly Grosavescu had recently suffered a miscarriage and was in a bad nervous condition. After a dreadful argument, she shot him dead. The Viennese newspapers took sides, and the pros and cons went to and fro. Even if Nelly had reason to doubt her husband's fidelity, it was an extreme action, and the opera was robbed of a good voice. Grosavescu was only thirty-three.

Lotte's performances with Bruno Walter in Berlin reflected her recordings of that week. On 20 February her concert items included the *Oberon* aria, and her stage appearances embraced a *Turandot* with Jan Kiepura and Lotte Schöne. She also sang a *Walküre*, with Oestvig as Siegmund, and a *Faust*, with Kiepura and Ludwig Hofmann.

Lotte returned to Vienna immediately for a month of intensive rehearsals and only four stage performances during March (including one *Intermezzo* under Alwin) before her next première. It was to be another milestone in her career.

1927 was the centenary year of Beethoven's death, and Vienna was celebrating the event with – *inter alia* – a new production of *Fidelio*. Lotte was cast as Leonore and Piccaver as Florestan. It was Schalk's idea to cast the two leading singers as lyrics, not dramatics as hitherto: an adventurous if not risky enterprise. But Schalk knew his two singers well enough to have absolute faith in their abilities and experience which, he was certain, would lend the opera an extra touch of humanity and beauty. Alfred Jerger was cast as the villainous Pizarro and Richard Mayr was to be Rocco the jailer.

The characterisation of Leonore was – on the evidence – of no great difficulty to Lotte (Martha Mödl later said 'it is a treacherous part unless you are able to identify completely with this courageous, anguished and clever woman'). It was the demands that Beethoven makes on the soprano, more especially in the great Act I aria 'Abscheulicher!' and its last five bars, which are daunting even to dramatic sopranos. Lotte averred that it was her husband's enormous understanding of her capabilities which persuaded her to sing Tosca, Turandot and Leonore. Perhaps one questions his judgment with regard to the Puccini operas, but in the case of *Fidelio,* Otto was right. And so was Franz Schalk who, after all, proposed it.

The music critics were jubilant after the first *Fidelio* on 31 March, and many were persuaded that they were never going to be convinced by a Leonore and Florestan played and sung in the 'old' manner. Lotte's sheer professionalism had triumphed but she said that it was her trust in Schalk that had taken her through to success.

Schalk counted the performance as the highpoint of his career. He had been deeply affected by Lotte's performance which he called 'the pivot'. It must have been an extremely exciting occasion for them both, for they had become very close artistically speaking, and possibly in Schalk's case it was more than that.

During the month of April, Lotte sang in three more performances of *Fidelio;* a *Manon* with Piccaver (just to keep the legend alive);[24] an *Intermezzo* with Richard Strauss conducting; and a *Meistersinger* with Weingartner unexpectedly back as a guest.

On 21 April, Jeritza returned to present her own, inimitable and stunning interpretation of Turandot, full of the kind of tricks no other soprano would dare attempt. Instead of descending the staircase during the riddle scene so that her face was always visible, 'she came down front all the way up to the Emperor. After the first riddle, she swept down one third of the stage, hovering over Calaf to confuse him with her presence. But she stepped over the train while racing downstage; the train was lined in vibrant red. So when she sang the second riddle, her black and gold costume stood in a puddle of red. Second riddle is: *Blood!*'[25] Lotte watched all this from the artists' box. Is this kind of tricksiness and *Kitsch* a kind of defence? Jeritza's voice was capable of negotiating the fierce *tessitura* of the score without apparent strain.

In early May, Lotte was back at Covent Garden where she opened the season in *Rosenkavalier* and gave four further performances. In addition there was one *Walküre* with Melchior, all occasions conducted by Bruno Walter. She shuttled to and fro between London and Hamburg giving three performances in her old theatre: Elsa and, for the first time there, Leonore and Turandot.

In London there were two performances of *Fidelio*, but not with Lotte. Casting had been done before her success in Vienna and Helene Wildbrunn (vocally fast fading) was partnered by Fritz Kraus.

Jeritza had been expected in London again for three more *Toscas* and for the first London performance of *Turandot*, but she was taken ill in Vienna and did not cross the Channel. Her place was taken by Göta Ljungberg in *Tosca*; and by Bianca Scacciati in the first *Turandot* – subsequently Florence Easton took over at very short notice. Lotte was not invited because she had contract engagements to fulfil in Vienna during June, when the four performances of *Turandot* were given in London.

The Viennese Ludwig Karpath (though originally from Budapest) and a great friend of Strauss's from the time they first met at Bayreuth in 1894, was one of the most influential musical writers and administrators in the city. He gave Strauss a long resumé of the declining Operntheater in the year 1927, partly blaming those in the highest office for the institution's condition. At the end he remarks that Lotte Lehmann, in her industry and ability, is a model to them all.[26]

She travelled to Munich at the beginning of August, for two performances in the Festival: Eva on 4th and Sieglinde on 7th. The *Meistersinger* was conducted by Eugen Pollak, who was highly regarded as a conductor, did some good work in Vienna as a guest, but was never taken on there permanently. This was the last time that Lotte appeared in the Munich Festival. It might have been possible to combine it with Salzburg each year, but her heart was already in that rainy and mountain-locked Austrian Festival town, for which she wanted to keep a fresh voice.

This year's operatic accent in Salzburg was on *Fidelio*. Franz Schalk conducted *Figaro* and *Don Giovanni* twice each, and *Fidelio* four times. It had a memorable cast, almost the same as for the Viennese première in the previous March, though Elisabeth Schumann sang only the first Marzelline. Thereafter it was Adele Kern, an attractive soprano from Frankfort who, from now onwards, was to be associated exclusively with Munich. Schalk's enthusiasm for 'his' *Fidelio* was undimmed, and it remained a yearly event in Salzburg – like 'Jedermann' and the works of Mozart – until 1938, with Lotte singing Leonore in ten out of those twelve Festivals.

The 1927–28 Vienna Opera season's new première at the end of October was to be Korngold's *Wunder der Heliane* ('the Miracle of Heliane'). Schalk had decided – perhaps owing to local pressure – to mount this work and had asked Jeritza to play the lead. She turned it down, and Lotte was invited next. Rather unwisely, as it transpired, Lotte accepted, perhaps because she thought she might make a success of the role of Heliane, and prove Jeritza wrong. Once more, though, Jeritza was proved right for although it seemed to be a success and the press were enthusiastic, *Heliane* lacked staying power.

The *Vienna Zeitung*'s critic declared: 'Lotte Lehmann, now at the peak of her singing and creative development, is one of the greatest – in fact, the greatest of the dramatic singers of our time.' The first cast, with Lotte, Jan Kiepura (whom she detested) and Alfred Jerger gave six performances, another was cancelled, and single performances until the following Easter caused *Heliane* to fade away.

Erich Korngold had previously given his views on Lotte and Jeritza in these terms: 'One half of Vienna is for the fascinating Jeritza, the other for the sweet Lotte Lehmann. Who wins? I am more for heart and head, for the elemental and womanly and therefore: Lehmann is my motto!'

This was the last Korngold première in Vienna, with sopranos like Helene Falk (from Hamburg) and Vera Schwarz eventually taking over the unwelcome, if not despised, Heliane. Lotte, on the other hand, felt some affection for it, and gave one performance in Hamburg during November, also one *Turandot*.

She travelled straight to Berlin after Hamburg to record a clutch of Schubert songs (Discog. 100–109). Odeon took advantage of Jan Kiepura's presence there to record two duets from *Tosca* in Italian (110–111). Lotte also recorded the Marschallin's admonitory address to Octavian towards the end of Act I of *Der Rosenkavalier*, and part of Leonore's taxing aria from *Fidelio*: 'Abscheulicher!' She never recorded the first part of this, but started with 'Komm, Hoffnung' (Discog 112–13), contrary to what it says in the 78 catalogues and on the label. Then finally in this most interesting and beautiful group of records (Discog 114–19), there was 'Porgi Amor' in German, first made ten years earlier.

Bruno Walter had secured Lotte's services again at the Charlottenburg Opera, well in advance, to coincide with her recordings. He conducted all her performances: *Ariadne* (with Ivogün as Zerbinetta); *Fidelio*; two *Turandot*s and a *Lohengrin*. This was Walter's first experience of Lotte as Leonore, and he found it amazingly beautiful and moving. She returned to Vienna for a *Fidelio* on Christmas Day, and the year ended with another performance of *Wunder der Heliane*.

Lotte was very busy for the first two months of 1928, in Vienna, with an Ariadne and two Christines under Strauss's baton. On 2 February she sang a new role in a relatively old opera, Hermann Götz's version of

The Taming of the Shrew, first heard in Vienna in 1875. Lotte was Katharina and Emil Schipper sang Petruchio – a baritone rather than a tenor hero. The opera was not entirely unknown to Lotte for she had recorded the best-known soprano aria from it as early as 1920: 'Es schweige die Klage' (Discog 30) meaning 'Let the complaining stop!'.

At the end of February she had a new Florestan to save. His name was Joseph Kalenberg and his début in Vienna had been as Parsifal. This, and his subsequent Florestan were so well received that – attracted by his enormous repertoire – Schalk engaged him as a leading tenor and he remained with the Opera until 1942.

For the whole of March, Lotte was in Berlin and Hamburg. Her five appearances for Bruno Walter again were in *Die Walküre*, *Faust*, *Turandot*, *Ariadne* and *Fidelio*. The Wagnerian opera had Nanny Larsen-Todsen as Brünnhilde, Alexander Kipnis as a vicious and inky Hunding, and a tenor new to most people called Erik Enderlein whose Florestan was not especially remarkable. (When, later, he arrived at Covent Garden, he was known as 'End O'Line'). This *Fidelio* was produced as well as conducted by Bruno Walter.

Fidelio was, in any case, at the centre of an inter-house rivalry in Berlin. In the previous November, Otto Klemperer, now music director of the experimental Kroll Opera, had mounted his own production of *Fidelio*. He was always facing opposition not only from Walter at the Städtische Opera but also from Erich Kleiber at the Staatsoper unter den Linden, the former Royal Court Opera. Klemperer was encumbered from the start and at a great disadvantage when trying to build an ensemble and repertoire, although he had the advantage of an intelligent and co-operative committee.[27]

An enigmatic character called Heinz Tietjen was at the root of the trouble. He was born in Tangier of a German father and an English mother, was a trained musician and operatic producer who became Intendant at Trier when only twenty-six. Now he was Intendant of both the Städtische and Kroll Operas with an eye to becoming General Intendant in Berlin, an ambition which he soon accomplished. He was a truly German edition of the Vicar of Bray, as will be seen; looked shifty, never met anybody's eyes, was devious, untrustworthy, and utterly ruthless. His notebooks of vital points in conversations gave way to secret recordings of meetings from concealed microphones. 'Did Tietjen ever live?' was the catch-phrase.[28]

Tietjen decided to veto some of Klemperer's operas scheduled for production, and some of the singers he wanted for them. When Klemperer asked for Frida Leider to sing 'Leonore and Donna Anna in his opening productions . . . Singers of that calibre Tietjen made plain, were reserved for the Linden Opera.' So Klemperer had to be content with a small group of singers that he had heard and encouraged over the past year, and since, 'like Mahler, Klemperer was more concerned with intelligence and musicality than with purely vocal attainments . . .' he had a 'closeknit ensemble' of artists like Rose Pauly, Moje Forbach, Jarmila Novotná and Fritz Krenn.

Klemperer was very handicapped by having to share the Kroll with the Linden Opera while their own theatre was undergoing protracted alterations. These should have been finished before his tenure of the Kroll in 1927, but building delays had kept the Lindenoper staff in the offices, and singers on the stage of Klemperer's building. It was altogether most unsatisfactory.

However on 19 November 1927, Klemperer's opera company made its début with *Fidelio*. Rose Pauly sang Leonore in a performance 'marred by a heavy vibrato'. Hans Fidesser's Florestan was regarded as 'lacking in tragic stature'.

So in March 1928, Lotte found herself a heroine in one sense, but from Klemperer's point of view an anti-heroine. She gave a stupendous performance which completely outshone Pauly's interpretation, both vocally and dramatically – though Pauly was no tiro. Lotte Schöne sang Marzelline for Walter, again preferable to Klemperer's casting.

Three months later, Kleiber put on his *Fidelio* at the Linden Opera with Frida Leider as Leonore, Richard Tauber as Florestan and Friedrich Schorr as Don Pizarro. These names look wonderful on paper but that does not mean it all worked out on the stage. Nevertheless, nobody doubted the superiority of Lotte's Leonore over the other two.

In April Richard Strauss was much in evidence on the rostrum then suddenly not so. Lotte sang Ariadne, the Marschallin and Christine all under his baton, and then he set up another *Rosenkavalier*, only to disappear and leave the conducting on 25 March to Reichenberger. Certainly Strauss was needed in Berlin for the reopening of the Linden Opera and a week of operatic festivity. A new production of *Der Rosenkavalier* there with Barbara Kemp as the Marschallin, Delia Reinhardt as Octavian and Marion Claire as Sophie was Strauss's main interest and parts of it were recorded, as were sizeable sections of the *Meistersinger* on 22 May, given on the 150th anniversary of Wagner's birth. The singers included Schorr as Sachs and Robert Hutt as Walther, with Elfriede Marherr-Wagner as Eva.[29]

While all this splendour was an excellent chance for Strauss to excuse himself from Vienna, he did so with tongue in cheek and with a mischievous twinkle in his eye. The *Rosenkavalier* had Lotte as the Marschallin and Jeritza as Octavian! Neither singer has left any reminiscence of the occasion; and while they had appeared together in operas in the past, there had never been anything resembling a love-scene between them. The reason for this provocative casting soon became evident, and it must have been a performance of performances!

Covent Garden had no *Rosenkavalier* to offer in May, but Lotte sang four performances of Wagner. After Sieglinde and before Gutrune in the *Ring* she went to Paris where Schalk had assembled a company of Viennese singers for a special season at the Paris Opéra. It opened with *Fidelio* on 6 May and besides Lotte there was Tauber as Florestan, Elisabeth Schumann, Alfred Jerger and Richard Mayr. It was a gala occasion and the Parisians took instantly and warmly to Lotte who thereafter bore the title bestowed upon her by the *Figaro* critic: 'La Reine de Paris'.

This cannot have been particularly well received by Jeritza who was also in Paris and who, on 15th, repeated her performance as Octavian to Lotte's Marschallin. This was the reason for the trial 'double-act' in Vienna during the previous month, to make certain that it was going to work. Apparently it did, and there were no (reported) scenes of jealousy or temperament.

Jeritza's presence in Paris added to the glittering cast, for she was there principally to sing Tosca. Lotte had come to and fro from London, where she returned for her two last performances after giving Sieglinde at the Opéra on 17th.

Back in Vienna, Lotte had an exceptionally disturbing experience. Much has been made of her association with Richard Strauss, sometimes so far as suggesting that they were lovers. In the context of Strauss's mode of life, of his wife's character and possessiveness towards him, and of his habit of not favouring one artist at the expense of another, such a proposition is unlikely. Pauline Strauss trusted her Richard with the flighty Elisabeth Schumann on a tour of the USA in 1920, with only their son Franz Strauss as chaperon. So she must have been assured of her husband's fidelity – or his lack of interest.

Strauss greatly admired Lotte as an artist and wrote her many gentle and affectionate letters; she was devoted to him, to his Lieder, and to the roles which suited her in his operas. By the middle of the 1920s she had so identified with his musical expression that when she was singing Strauss roles abroad, the time she spent away from Vienna did not count against her leave. Strauss, as co-director, saw to that, for he considered

Lotte one of the most active exponents of his operas, and that meant royalties.

From the moment when she triumphed as the Young Composer in *Ariadne auf Naxos* in 1916; went on to sing the Dyer's Wife in *Frau ohne Schatten* in 1919; had a great and lasting success as the Marschallin in London in 1924; and triumphed as Christine in *Intermezzo* in the same year – the latter, of course, intimately bound up with Strauss's own life – he had it in mind to write another role especially for her. Lotte was absolutely convinced that after *Intermezzo* he said to her: 'I shall write my next opera for you!'

He probably did say that, out of gratitude and because he knew her voice so well and enjoyed her personality with its tantrums. And here lies the difficulty in interpreting what he had intended. Strauss completed the score of *Intermezzo* while in Buenos Aires in 1923 with one of Mocchi's tours – 'a wretched season'. On 14 September 1923, Hofmannsthal wrote to Strauss with a faint sketch for *Die Ägyptische Helena* (*The Egyptian Helen*)[30], proposing Jeritza as the most beautiful woman in the world. Simultaneously, Strauss had suggested to Hofmannsthal 'a second *Rosenkavalier*'. That turned out to be *Arabella* (not staged until 1933). So on the day that Lotte had her success in *Intermezzo, Die Ägyptische Helena* was well on the way and with much of Act I composed.

So can this have been the opera promised to Lotte – a work partly written and already with another soprano in mind for the principal role? Unlikely. If, on the other hand, the 'next opera' was to be that which was little more than a twinkle in the eyes of Strauss, and rather less in the case of Hofmannsthal, it may have been what the composer intended. However, events were to take over and cause a rift between Strauss and Lotte that was never – professionally speaking – completely healed.

Dresden was again to be the place for the *Helena* début, and the Vienna production a few days later. Hofmannsthal was still supporting Jeritza as 'the person born for the part', until she demanded a fee of 6,000M a performance – 5,000M above that authorized by the Theatre Guild of Germany. This put her outside the Dresden première (though not the Viennese) and forced Strauss and Hofmannsthal to look elsewhere for their soprano. As the composer wrote to his librettist on 27 October 1927:[31]

> . . . I fear the Jeritza business is hopeless. . . . Jeritza will not and cannot sing in Dresden and probably not even in Vienna which has meanwhile acceded to the convention of the Bühnenverein. Last

summer in Berlin she demanded 12,000M per night . . . If she were now to sing in Dresden for a *mere* 6,000M (Schneiderhan wrote me that she last demanded $1,500 in Vienna and got approximately that much) Berlin would be up in arms! Now Reucker in accordance with the rules of the Bühnenverein, is offering her 1,000M (a sum with which even people like Bohnen and Lehmann content themselves nowadays) plus 200M per rehearsal: how is that to come to anything like 6,000M? No, it's impossible . . . we shall simply have to do without Jeritza! In which case Mme Rethberg is still the best we've got: superior to Mme Schenker in maturity, beauty of voice and singing technique . . . She enjoys a great international reputation and, lastly, she is a native of Dresden . . .

This letter was in answer to Hofmannsthal's cry of anguish at the thought of Elisabeth Rethberg being cast as Helena. For, he believed:

Mme Rethberg may sing like a nightingale, I understand nothing about that; what I do know is that she is worse than mediocre as an actress and this will ruin Helen, completely ruin her . . . [32]

Strauss was working overtime to try to attract Jeritza after Hofmannsthal's fears that the opera would be ruined by somebody whose face was not exactly capable of launching a dozen barges. 'I shall in the end have to take the line of asking Mme Jeritza outright if she would sing in Dresden *for nothing*. But I doubt whether the publicity will seem to her worth the sacrifice.'

Neither of them suggested Lotte as an alternative, but they were still up against the resistance of Reucker, the Dresden Opera Director, to 'outsiders' singing star parts. In the end Rethberg did sing it, and Jeritza was still allowing herself to hang in the balance over the Viennese première, scheduled for 6 June 1928.

At first Jeritza seemed a certainty, but then she began to behave in a manner that Hofmannsthal described as 'part and parcel of that whole *prima donna* business'.[33] Hofmannsthal had never cared for Lotte personally, on account of her middle-class background which he seemed to see reflected in her work, but he recommended her to Strauss for the Vienna Helena in preference to Margit Schenker-Angerer who was also a contender.

Lotte was incensed that she had not been offered the première first, and refused it outright, also still believing that she had a right to the Dresden première as well. So there began a policy of pacifying Lotte and trying to bring her round to singing Helena in Vienna. In January 1928 Strauss told his librettist:[34] 'Mme Lehmann is already fully pacified, she is . . . only waiting for Jeritza's refusal to take over Helen at once. . . . Lehmann is now right at the top, both in singing and in acting.'

Three days later Strauss continued:[35]

> I asked Mme Lehmann today whether, even if Jeritza still accepts, she wouldn't like to sing the part in turn with her. She didn't say NO, provided matters could be so arranged – perhaps by way of two premières – that she is not regarded as a second cast.

Now they had two prima donnas making up their minds, Hofmannsthal put his ear to the ground in Vienna and, via a friend who knew Lotte's singing teacher, believed he had the reason why she was[36]

> frightened of so beautiful and inviting a part. It relates to certain real or imaginary risks in the vocalisation which make her fear for her voice which is indeed at present perhaps the most beautiful and least strained in Europe. She is said to have in mind a few, not many, passages that could be dealt with by what is called 'rephrasing' . . .

Five days later, Hofmannsthal took this back, having spoken to Karl Alwin who was coaching Lotte in the role of Helena:[37]

> My indiscreet information concerning Mme Lehmann was obviously inaccurate . . . the reason why she does not want to sing the part is resentment over Jeritza. For three weeks Alwin has exerted all his great tenacity (to the point of self-abasement as he himself says) in an all-out effort to win her over. Some personal influence, too, is apparently being brought to bear on her (a very self-willed singing teacher who is just studying Isolde with her); in short there is obviously no hope, I would not say for ever, but in any case for the immediate future . . .

Between them, Jeritza and Lotte had upset and frustrated the whole machinery of the Viennese *Helena* production; and through bitter jealousy and rivalry, Jeritza had all too cunningly made it impossible for Lotte to accept, even in a second première, for Lotte did not consider herself, quite rightly, as *second* material. She had always been in first casts in Vienna, and now was not the time to demote herself.

In the end, when she saw that she had won the battle, and had successfully kept Lotte out, Jeritza sang the Vienna première of *Helena* under Strauss's baton for her stipulated 6,000M paid in dollars, then three more performances over the next ten days.

There seemed to be something connecting Jeritza with staircases, or at any rate stairs and steps. In *Cavalleria Rusticana* she liked to roll down the

Church steps; in *Turandot* she made great play with the stairs and now, in *Die Ägyptische Helena*, one of the memorable moments was when 'at the beginning of the interlude . . . she . . . rose from the great divan on which she had been reclining and slowly made her way down a huge flight of stairs' – according to Marcel Prawy who was there.[38]

It was customary for Jeritza to go to New York in the winter, over the turn of the year, and Strauss had not given up hope of persuading Lotte to sing Helena while her rival was away. In October, Strauss wrote to his friend Ludwig Karpath:[39]

> It is a tragedy that poor Lehmann is so deluded. Shame over such a wonderful talent and rare voice. But nobody will be able to do anything about it . . .

Karpath had warned Strauss in great confidence that Lotte was absolutely refusing to learn the part of Helena and could think of nothing else but Isolde. That role, he was sure, would bring her ruin.[40]

The news that Lotte was studying Isolde will have surprised many people, then and now. It is a role that demands – in a stage performance – the utmost reserves of strength and control, with a truly dramatic-soprano voice able to ride the huge waves of orchestral sound. So far as womanliness and tenderness – and sheer passion – were concerned, Lotte was ideal for Isolde, but the vocal consideration was altogether another matter. She had conquered what had always been considered a 'dramatic' role with Leonore, but Isolde is a long way beyond that. Can one believe that Otto Krause sympathised?

After a short holiday, Lotte went to Berlin for more recordings. One was a charming number, with spoken recitative, from Lehár's *Eva*, the only time Lotte actually speaks on a commercial record and the result is endearing; the other a 'Zauberlied' by Meyer-Helmund: both lightweight, but done with such charm and elegance as to raise them beyond mere trifles. (Discog. Nos xxx–xxx). Then she returned to her beloved Salzburg for three performances of *Fidelio* – that was all. A visiting Russian opera company was the reason.

Lotte was horrified to hear that Franz Schalk had been given notice to quit his conductorship-directorship of the Vienna Opera in one year's time at the end of August 1929. The same system that had upheld him against Richard Strauss in 1924 had turned on Schalk. It was a murky business which was – and still is – commonplace in opera houses. Bruno Walter suffered it with Tietjen in Berlin, and so have many others who believed, as Walter and Schalk did, that they had sweated blood for the masters they served in the cause of art. It is often the case that these 'masters' are inartistic people. . . .

Franz Schalk never got over the wound he suffered from this dismissal. His very life was the Vienna Opera, where he had worked since 1900. It undoubtedly shortened his life. Lotte had come to rely on him and to love him as a father-figure and fount of good advice. He, in turn, had greatly mellowed towards her, valued her art enormously and had exercised a strong, guiding hand over her during the past dozen years. The announcement of his going was a personal blow to Lotte.

The new director was to be Clemens Krauss from Frankfort, and he was going to become music director and administrator of both the Vienna Opera and the Salzburg Festivals, starting in September 1929 (after that year's Festival). Lotte met this news without much concern, for she had got on all right with Krauss so far. But only so far.

Some recordings in Berlin for three days in early September included six folk-songs, some Bach, Schumann and Handel popular Lieder, as well as Ariadne's lament, of which two different versions of the first side were issued (Discog. 120–36).

Lotte sang a rather special Mimi on 2 October. Piccaver shared in the festivities as Rodolfo and after the performance that fairly tingled with excitement and joy, there was a celebration when Lotte was promoted to *Ehrenmitglied* – life member – of the Vienna Opera, deserving an asterisk after her name on every subsequent playbill when she was singing.

Some more performances of *Die Ägyptische Helena* were given during the last three months of the year with either Rose Pauly (whose two main arias were recorded) or Vera Schwarz as Helena; while for two performances at the end of November, a very tall, lanky conductor with a huge head and an insatiable desire for the opposite sex, came to conduct *Figaro* as a guest. His name was Wilhelm Furtwängler.

Lotte gave three performances in Hamburg that included the Marschallin – her first there. How many sopranos have sung all three *Rosenkavalier* roles on the same stage? Then she went back to Berlin and, accompanied by a violin-cello-piano trio, she recorded the whole of the Schumann 'Frauenliebe und-leben' cycle on eight 10″ sides in November (Discog. 137–44). This was a great favourite of hers at recitals and few other singers have been able to match her variety of emotion so excitingly, from first sight of the beloved, through a passionate engagement, to marriage, a happy partnership, motherhood and widowhood.

After several appearances in Vienna in early December – Desdemona and Recha with Slezak; Manon, Elisabeth and Eva – Lotte returned to Berlin for yet more recording. She had become a valuable property to

Odeon and her royalties had now become appreciable. This time they made a famous pair of records that are still regarded as thoroughly representative of operetta singing in the late 1920s. The first was the finale to Act II of *Fledermaus* and the second Act I and II finales to *The Gipsy Baron*, both with Richard Tauber, Grete Merrem-Nikisch and Waldemar Staegemann, all from Dresden. 'This famous record will not be easy to supersede', wrote Desmond Shawe-Taylor in 1951[41] of the *Fledermaus*. (Discog. 149–52).

On 22 February Lotte appeared in Stockholm (once only) during the Vienna State Opera's visit. She sang Leonore and received overwhelming applause. Schalk conducted nobly. Again to Berlin for a new recording of Agathe's aria from *Freischütz* and some traditional and religious 'pot-boilers', some with chorus and organ (Discog. 153–60).

In the Spring, Richard Strauss returned to Vienna to conduct two *Rosenkavaliers* with Lotte and one *Helena* with Jeritza. Hofmannsthal and Strauss had worked hard to secure the success of their opera, so blighted from the start by its casting difficulties. It cannot be said to have approached the kind of acceptance which they had expected, to judge from the world-wide popularity of *Der Rosenkavalier* by direct contrast. From hindsight, one might be led to suppose that Lotte did the right thing in refusing Helena, irrespective of what she thought had been promised, of what happened with Jeritza, and of her friendship with Strauss. Jeritza guaranteed full houses whenever she appeared, and no other singer in Vienna could say the same, not even Rose Pauly and Vera Schwarz when they sang Helena.

History was made at Covent Garden on 22 April when Act I of *Rosenkavalier*, with Lotte, was broadcast live by the BBC – the first such transmission of an opera. There were two different Marschallins this year, Elisabeth Ohms and Frida Leider who gave less warm and human interpretations and did not altogether benefit from Lotte's annual assumption of the role since 1924 – or that is what it had seemed (though actually there were two years in which the opera was not billed).

Between her commitments in London, Lotte dashed over to Paris to sing Elsa at the Opéra opposite the Irish tenor John Sullivan, arriving back in Vienna at the end of May in time for *Manon* with Piccaver. In her absence there had been a visit by the Scala Milan Company, with Stabile in *Falstaff* and Toti Dal Monte in *Lucia* conducted by Toscanini. Had the Italian conductor heard Lotte, instead of Nanny Larsen-Todsen singing Leonore in Vienna, Lotte's career might have taken a different turn.

Her season ended with *Rosenkavalier*, in which Vienna had completely accepted her as the Marschallin, and this performance was conducted by Franz Schalk for the last time as Director of the Vienna Opernttheater.

After recordings in Berlin (Discog. 161–74) Lotte was in Salzburg for three performances of *Fidelio* under Schalk whose contract still held for the festival. She also sang five Marschallins under the new Director's baton. Krauss was already asserting his position in Vienna by using Salzburg as rehearsal for his forthcoming new production of *Der Rosenkavalier*.

The English music critic, Ernest Newman, was covering the Festival at Salzburg this year, and wrote that Lotte 'as the Marschallin and Richard Mayr as Ochs were naturally unequalled and at the top' of their class. In *Fidelio* 'we had the credible and heart-moving Leonore, Lotte Lehmann' as well as 'a really thin tenor (a rarity) who looked as though he might well have been a couple of years in jail.'[42] This was Josef Kalenberg. And Newman considered that *Fidelio* was best of the opera performances, since he questioned the manner in which Krauss directed some aspects of *Rosenkavalier*. Nor did Newman care for Vera Schwarz as Octavian, nor Adele Kern's Sophie.

Lotte had four performances in Hamburg, the first three of which were Leonore, Elisabeth and Eva. Then she went to London for a Lieder Recital at Queen's Hall. Bruno Walter was not able to accompany her this time, but she accepted Harold Craxton whose reputation was good. Unfortunately they did not hit it off at all, and even *The Times* critic noticed that 'pianist and singer were not together.' Coming fresh to Lotte's methods cannot have been an enviable task for anybody. Three groups of songs by Brahms, Schubert and Strauss respectively were crowned by the 'Frauenliebe und-leben'.

Her swansong performance in Hamburg was as the Marschallin on 23 October. She had not said goodbye to the Alster for ever, only to the stage of the old Stadttheater which still held so many memories for her.

Two days after Christmas, Lotte sang an Ariadne with Piccaver as Bacchus and Adele Kern as Zerbinetta, Strauss conducting. In the opera, Ariadne has the greeting to sing to Bacchus: 'Ich grüsse dich, du Bote aller Boten!' ('I greet you, messenger of all messengers!') but when it came to her cue, she was convinced that the next line, which was in her head, was going to be sung by Piccaver! She wondered what was wrong with him, especially as the prompter was hissing the words angrily. Strauss and Piccaver picked it up and carried on, until the end of the opera when Lotte had forgotten about the extraordinary incident.[43] But Strauss hadn't.

The following day he sent her a note:

Because 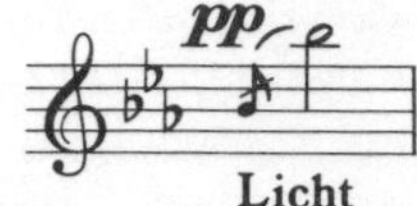

was so beautiful, Lottchen's penalty is diminished so at the next performance of Ariadne the lines 'I greet you, messenger of all messengers' need be sung only twice! But in spite of this it was *very beautiful*! In gratitude, your most faithful admirer,

Richard Strauss

The reference he quoted was to an awkward octave leap in Ariadne's aria near the beginning of the opera (which she did not record).

Rose Pauly had now joined the Opera and was singing Salome, Tosca, Helena, the *Figaro* Countess, Carmen and Elektra. Lotte, meanwhile, continued with her 'quieter' roles of Elsa, Manon, Margarethe and Eva. However, she was a little surprised to find a newcomer, protégée of Clemens Krauss, arriving as a guest soprano from Frankfort to sing Manon *opposite Piccaver* on 22 December. Her name was Viorica Ursuleac and she was Rumanian.

She was born in 1894 to a Greek orthodox priest and his wife but received her strict vocal and musical training at the Vienna Music Academy and from Lilli Lehmann in Berlin. Strict was certainly the word with this Lehmann whose discipline was severe but whose instruction was ideal for Ursuleac. Her début was in Zagreb in 1918, and between 1922–25 she was at the Vienna Volksoper, that excellent training ground for any singer who aspires to greater things. She married and had a daughter. In 1925 she joined the Frankfort-on-Main Opera where Clemens Krauss was Director. He and Ursuleac had already met in Vienna, were now both married, but were strongly attracted to one another. He obtained a divorce from his wife round about 1928 but did not marry Ursuleac for some years.[44]

Ursuleac's advantage over Lotte was a very bright and free top to the voice; but on the other hand she was not an immediately warm and welcoming person (such as she later became) and some singers who worked for years with her have described her as 'not a good colleague'. But here she was, as a guest singer in Vienna, mistress of the Director and almost certainly come to stay.[45]

Chapter Seven

Singing to the World

1930–1932

Viorica Ursuleac's arrival at the Vienna Opera was a blow to Lotte who was thinking that her troubles would soon be over when Jeritza retired in the coming year. (In fact this retiral was postponed.) Lotte and Ursuleac took an instant dislike to one another and for the whole of their time together in Vienna and Salzburg, each accused the other of trying to ruin her career. Lotte never mentions Ursuleac by name in any of her books; Ursuleac is more forthcoming and states that her first role in Vienna was 'substituting for Lehmann in *Manon Lescaut*.' It was in Massenet's *Manon* and the use of the word 'substituting' suggests either that Lotte was indisposed (which she wasn't); or not in Vienna (which she was); or that Ursuleac regarded Lotte as a senior member of the Company. Later, she continues;[1]

> I always loved Lehmann for her intensity and fire on the stage, but alas it was not reciprocal. As I have a philosophical attitude, I never look back, and I forgive her for all the harm she caused me. I believe her hatred for me originated when I exploded on the Viennese horizon with my easy top register just as she was beginning to have a very difficult time with hers. One must remember that at that time, with Jeritza in the United States, she considered herself to be the undisputed queen, and in many ways she was.

While no two singers' roles exactly match, there were far too many of Ursuleac's that coincided with Lotte's own, and to find Ursuleac making her début in the cherished *Manon* with Piccaver was calculated to start relationships on the wrong foot. Ursuleac followed this with Desdemona (Slezak as Otello) and then as Chrysothemis in *Elektra* with Strauss conducting. She had a way with this role that greatly pleased the composer who told her that the manner in which she handled the parlando passages, beyond other singers' powers, was exactly as he had imagined it. (Many years later, Lotte stated that of all the roles she had never sung but most wishes she had, was Chrysothemis.[2] It would have suited her admirably.)

Ursuleac's conquest continued with a strictly non-Lotte role: Leonora in *Forza del Destino*, the Verdi opera which had not been heard in Germany until 1926.

Otto Krause was with Lotte on her first visit to America, arriving in New York during the height of the prohibition of alcohol, that involved stringent customs searches as soon as they had disembarked from the liner. Not only their personal luggage, but also their costumes and properties were gone through, resulting in a tedious delay before they were all allowed to proceed. Frida Leider, Maria Olszewska, Eduard Habich and the conductor, Eugen Pollak, were there.

She was greatly impressed by the luxury train that took them to Chicago, and even more astonished by the opera house there, where they were going to be for a month. Each dressing-room was well appointed and had its own bathroom, but the heating arrangements seemed overdone. This was to counteract the freezing winds that swept round every corner of the city. Even Lotte's fur coat offered little protection from the cold. As she said: 'This land of "unlimited possibilities" seems to deal only in superlatives!'[3]

On 28 October, Lotte gave her début performance in Chicago to a house of 3,500, and as Sieglinde. There was nothing but praise for her performance: 'Her Sieglinde is perfection itself – perfection of voice and action.'[4] Another critic considered that she had 'one of the loveliest voices ever heard on the Civic Opera stage. It is of a freedom and purity seldom discovered in German singers and employed with an eloquence and artistry that moved the audience to a great demonstration.'[5]

Four days later she followed this success with another: in *Tannhäuser* 'her Elisabeth was a spiritual figure. . . . Her singing was of a superb order, tonally beautiful, emotionally warm, yet always informed by authoritative musicianship.'[6]

This was the first occasion, on 1 November, when a young man called Isidore Lichtmann heard Lotte. He lived in Chicago and

> worked at our opera house as an usher. (No pay involved; just the opportunity to see the performance.) I was then a student in Junior College, and being able to attend opera performances gratis during those bleak depression-days was unbelievable good fortune. I remember being bored to near-tears during the endless first act. The Venus (Coe Glade) had the habit of punctuating each high note (most of them sung off pitch) by imitating the Statue of Liberty, with outstretched arm. The ballet belonged in a Marx Brothers

> movie and the tenor must have known better days. But when the second act began, I was struck by lightning. The insipid libretto suddenly didn't matter as that radiant woman took center-stage, and filled that huge auditorium with some of the most rapturous sounds that have ever been heard there.
>
> A week or so later I made my own 'début' in that house – as a super in *Lohengrin*. I had to hold a spear during that interminable first act, and, good trouper that I was, I didn't even try to wipe my face, although I was directly in line of the prodigious spray of Elsa, Elisabeth Rethberg . . .[7]

Lotte had sung an Elsa before that event, and further performances of both *Die Walküre* and *Tannhäuser*, she appeared as Eva in the first Chicago production of *Die Meistersinger*. For eight or nine years, the management had tried unsuccessfully to cast and mount the opera, and now it had at last arrived. The critic of *Musical America* believed that the listeners' thoughts had not been directed to any one performer, but only to 'the colossal genius of Richard Wagner, which had been so lucidly and affectionately revealed' – a compliment to all concerned.

Before the end of the Chicago season, in which Lotte gave eight performances, Otto had to return to Europe, so she spent her free time with an old friend and onetime fan from Vienna, who had now settled down in the USA and married an American. In spite of the cold weather, the receptions and parties and friendship with Samuel Insull[8] and his wife, the excellence of the Drake Hotel overlooking Lake Michigan and the great interest caused by the recent invention of thermostatic controls for heating, all made it a memorable visit. Before Lotte left, she had a contract for 1931 in her pocket.

At the end of November, Lotte travelled to Minneapolis to give a Lieder recital under the auspices of Coppicus. She expected it to be well received and was treating it as a 'warm-up' for the New York concert. But even after her operatic *éclat* in Chicago, her concert failed to awaken the audience to anything like the same approval. Lotte wisely came to terms with the fact that American audiences must be 'different', for she knew that her performance had been the best she could give – as always – and so decided, with her agent's approval, that it was better to wait before going to New York for a lukewarm reception. That would scarcely help her acceptance from the Met, which was still her ambition. 'A good average success' was how she described the Chicago visit.[9]

Whatever doubts she may still have had were soon swept away when she reached Vienna. On 16 December she sat in the artists' box for a performance of *Otello* with Slezak and Ursuleac, and conducted by the exciting (and rather terrifying) Victor De Sabata from La Scala. When Ursuleac took her solo call at the end, the audience rose, turned to the artists' box, and cried 'Hoch Lehmann!' (perhaps best translated as 'Three cheers for Lehmann!' and implying that her version of Desdemona was far preferable to Ursuleac's). It was certainly a hearty welcome back for Lotte.[10]

Her return performance was in *Tannhäuser*, with Schalk conducting, on 21 December; then on Christmas Day there was a *Rosenkavalier* with Lotte and the usual cast and, by now, the usual conductor: Krauss. For two seasons Lotte had not attempted a new role, but now she was revising her Angèle, from Hamburg days, in *Der Opernball* ('the Opera Ball' – an annual New Year's Day event of social significance in Vienna). The opera is as Viennese as they come, and was to be a revival of the work which had met with such success in 1898, during Mahler's era.

But there were those who found that Lotte and Margit Angerer 'were all at sea in operetta',[11] and this may be the reason why Lotte did not approach her successful London Rosalinde on home ground. After giving three performances of Angèle in two weeks, she sang it no more. But Ursuleac did, for her rough-and-tumble experience at the Vienna Volksoper equipped her better.

At the end of February 1931, Krauss put on six performances of the *Frau ohne Schatten*, an opera of which he was especially fond, and in which with Strauss's permission (for Hofmannsthal had died in 1929) Krauss made several alterations in the staging. His motives were thoroughly sensible, artistic, and showed a thorough grasp of the theatre, not always to be found in conductors. Lotte sang the Dyer's Wife on the first night, 25 February, but in none of the succeeding performances. This was the first time that she and Ursuleac appeared together in the same opera, for Dyer's Wife and Empress are in several scenes together and at close quarters. Kalenberg sang the Emperor and Manowarda was Barak – he who had been the first Spirit Messenger. Once Lotte had left the cast, it was without any of the original singers among the leading characters, pointing to the 'them and us' state of affairs.

It has been said that this was Krauss's policy: to attract his 'own singers' round him until they became more faithful to him than to the Opera House. But Vienna expected the man who ran their most important institution to be something of an autocrat.

After an Ariadne, two Leonores, a Butterfly and an Elsa, Lotte went to London where she opened the season with *Rosenkavalier* and on 2 May sang Sieglinde with a sprained ankle – not easy with all that running about in the second act – and then suffered a bad cold so that she was forced to omit the Csardas in the *Fledermaus* first performance, and cancelled her last appearance, so sang only three. Bruno Walter conducted as usual, and Marcel Wittrisch from Berlin made a very acceptable Alfred.

As it transpired, the first *Rosenkavalier*, conducted by Walter, was his last performance of this opera in London.

On Sunday 17 May Lotte was invited to lunch at Chequers by the Prime Minister, Ramsay MacDonald. Bruno Walter, Colonel Blois and Lady Snowden were also there, and Lotte greatly enjoyed seeing round the British Prime Minister's weekend residence in Buckinghamshire.

Lotte could afford only a few days in Berlin for recording before her contractual Elsa in Vienna on 31 May. They included some folk songs, two Brahms songs, two *Mignon* arias, and two numbers from *Fledermaus* (Discog 206–210).

The Vienna Festival Week began on 7 June and Jeritza arrived back from America in time to take part. It opened with Ursuleac as the Countess in *Figaro*. Lotte sang a *Walküre* opposite Gunnar Graarud as Siegmund, now a member of the company, and Mayr was the Wotan. Four days later there was a repetition of *Die Frau ohne Schatten* with the same cast as in February, and with Lotte back as the Dyer's Wife.

On 15 June, Lotte sang an *Ariadne* which was conducted by Schalk. He was ill and had not long to live. This was the last time that Lotte watched the long, slim baton in his delicate hands, saw the light catching those pince-nez, the goatee beard and full moustache. His former strength was much diminished. One cannot help wondering whether he was not a little in love with Lotte as a woman. He was certainly in love with her voice. In spite of her attachment to Strauss, and the animosity which existed between these two men (Strauss refused to write a note of regret over Schalk's resignation) Lotte remained on close terms with them both.

On 21 June, right at the end of the season, Lauritz Melchior made his first appearance in Vienna as a guest from Berlin, in *Tristan und Isolde*, with Henny Trundt. She had also been a pupil of Mathilde Mallinger. Schalk conducted, and seemed to rally for the performance. Lotte, who heard it, for she was still contemplating Isolde, said that Schalk regained all his old fire, and at the end he received enormous applause.

Afterwards, instead of disappearing with the orchestra, he remained at the conductor's desk, looking round the auditorium and taking in all the glories and beauties of that building which had been his very life and purpose since the first year of the century. He remained there until the last member of the audience had gone, and was himself the last person to leave the Opera that night.[12] Soon afterwards he was taken to a sanatorium where Lotte visited him at the end of June, following her last performance of the season in *Rosenkavalier*.

She told Schalk that she had decided to sing Isolde in the next season, and wouldn't he conduct it?

'It's too late . . . too late,' the old man said, stroking Lotte's hand lovingly, though with little strength, for he seemed tired of life.[13]

Salzburg seemed empty without Schalk. As one of the original founders of the Salzburg Festivals in 1917, his absence this year was all the more remarkable, almost tangible, so far as Lotte was concerned. There were others who thought differently and were pressing forward in a revolutionary spirit.

Max Reinhardt produced two plays by Hofmannsthal (the perennial 'Jedermann', and 'Der Schwierige') as well as two others; Krauss conducted four operas; Bruno Walter conducted three; and Robert Heger one. Ernst von Dohnányi gave three concerts; Krauss gave two; Bruno Walter conducted three; Robert Heger and Sir Thomas Beecham each gave one. The musical part of the interesting and well-planned Festival began with operas by an Italian Opera Company, Rossini, Donizetti and Cimarosa. There were many other events, too.

The Vienna Opera's opening performance on 1 August was *Der Rosenkavalier* with Ursuleac as the Marschallin getting the first night notices and yielding the other two performances to Lotte.[14] Otherwise the cast remained constant and included Mayr, Angerer and Kern, as Ochs, Octavian and Sophie respectively. Lotte's other opera – two performances of *Fidelio* – had Franz Völker as Florestan and either Georg Hann or Wilhelm Rode as Pizarro. Krauss conducted. Ursuleac also sang the *Figaro* Countess and Fiordiligi in *Così*, the latter being a role entirely unsuited to her, but one which she continued to sing under Krauss's guidance for many years.

Krauss's colleague and stage producer, Lothar Wallerstein, had been responsible for five of the 'Viennese' operas and objected to a new producer, Karl Heinz Martin, whom Walter had introduced and used for *Zauberflöte* and *Orpheus und Eurydice*. Wallerstein's vendetta against Martin was paralleled by one against Bruno Walter by Krauss, who also disliked the influence and long-standing image of Reinhardt. It may be noted that Reinhardt, Walter and Martin were all Jewish. (So was Wallerstein, but he and Krauss were Austrian!)

Schalk had gone; Krauss knew that he had Richard Strauss's full support; Max Reinhardt lorded it over Salzburg from his Schloss Leopoldskron and would be difficult to move. But Krauss was the

Festival Director and disliked challenges. There was no room for them both among those open squares where Mozart had once walked.

When Lotte returned to Vienna, she opened the season there opposite Franz Völker again, in *Fidelio* on 2 September. He had been attracted from Frankfort to Vienna by Krauss. Völker had, without any formal training, won a singing competition on the radio, and had afterwards essayed Florestan with such success that Krauss's confidence was assured. Völker was a short, dark and slightly sinister looking man who wore rimless spectacles offstage, had been a bank clerk and, most people thought, still behaved like one. Money mattered a terrible lot to him. He carried an extra-large head and – like Slezak who was similarly endowed – was obliged to have a special helmet for each opera that required one. But he had a fabulous tenor voice, strong and sweet, which made him an ideal Walter von Stolzing, Parsifal, Siegmund and Lohengrin; the Emperor in *Frau ohne Schatten*; Florestan; and Hermann in *Queen of Spades*. Only his acting ability failed to reach the heights of his vocal accomplishment.

On the day after this performance, Franz Schalk died, and on 5 September a black flag hung at half-mast over the Opera House. Hundreds of mourners, including Lotte, followed his remains to the village church at Reichenau, in the mountains near Semmering, to the south-west of Vienna, where he wished to be buried.

Lotte was scheduled to sing Eva that evening and was so upset about her old friend that she requested leave of absence from Krauss. He was unsympathetic – but logical.

'Do you imagine that Herr Direktor Schalk would have wished you to place the Opera in a predicament?' he asked her. And there was only one answer: Lotte knew he would not have done. All the same, she got back at Krauss by telling him he had no right to authorise a performance on the day of the burial – the House should have been closed as a token of respect. Krauss merely shrugged his shoulders.[15]

Nevertheless, the *Meistersinger* that evening was a memorial performance for Schalk which Krauss conducted with full pomp. It was prefaced by Siegfried's Funeral March from *Götterdämmerung*. In the course of the *Meistersinger*, Lotte had got herself very wound up with emotion. At one moment she imagined that the Hans Sachs (Wilhelm Rode) was Schalk, who had been a kind of Sachs to her: adviser, supporter, good friend – her operatic father in Vienna. But when they reached the last act and the Chorus greeted Sachs' arrival, Lotte suddenly felt ill, and in a kind of vision she thought it was Schalk who was conducting and drawing the wonderful, well-known sounds from the instruments of the orchestra and the throats of the singers. She was ready to collapse, and in a fit of tears turned away to face upstage where several members of the cast surrounded her and helped her to recover her composure.[16]

Lotte confessed that Krauss had become repugnant to her, especially upon this occasion. She considered him to be 'unworthy, self-seeking, for whom the beloved Vienna Opera was nothing sacred, as it had been to Schalk.'[17]

A fortnight after this bitter and heart-rending event, Lotte pulled off an unexpected double role, a half-début, because she had already studied both but had sung only one: Georgetta and Sister Angelica in Puccini's *Trittico*. It will be recalled that in 1920 Puccini had decided to take away Georgetta from Lotte and give her to Jeritza.

Robert Heger conducted, and in her new opera, *Il Tabarro*, Georgetta's lover was sung by the Hungarian lyric tenor, Koloman von Pataky, and Michele by Hans Duhan. Jeritza was in Vienna at the time, and one wonders whether somehow Lotte had prevailed upon Krauss to let her sing Georgetta in preference to Jeritza. Krauss did not care for that lady who could so easily outsmart Ursuleac. It is a theory. As for Lotte's Angelica, that was as beautiful as ever, perhaps more so, for she could now better express grief.

In November Lotte gave a Lieder recital in Rome and in mid-December she was one of the casualties of an influenza epidemic which raged in Vienna. On 14 December she was 'off' as Leonore when Wildbrunn deputised for her, and although she sang an Elsa on 17th, Lotte was off again as Mimi.

She sailed to America over the turn of the year and at last gave her début recital in Town Hall, New York on 7 January 1932. Her programme was this:

Brahms	Von ewiger Liebe
Schumann	Ich grolle nicht
	Der Nussbaum
	Aufträge
Brahms	Der Schmied
Schubert	Tod und das Mädchen
Strauss	Traum durch die Dämmerung
	Wiegenlied
	Zueignung
	Ständchen

also Hahn, Chausson and Fauré

This was such a success that a return visit was immediately planned after Lotte had concluded her opera season in Chicago.

There she sang three *Lohengrins* and one *Meistersinger*. A tenor called Paolo Marion sang Lohengrin; Maria Olszewska was Ortrud, as usual, and just as powerful; and Hans Hermann Nissen was the Telramund. Otto Erhardt, who had been the producer (called stage director) for the first time in the previous season, had returned with several of the singers from Vienna. In the *Meistersinger*, Nissen was Sachs, Alexander Kipnis the Pogner; and René Maison, the Belgian tenor, sang Walter.

As the financial climate worsened in the USA, singers at both the Met and Chicago Operas agreed to take salary cuts of between 10–20%, and an active fund-raising campaign seemed to be keeping the Opera in Chicago afloat. But the crash came in April with the entire collapse of Insull's huge empire, once estimated at three billion dollars. He fled first to Paris and then to Athens to avoid charges of fraud and embezzlement. But this was in the future.

Lotte gave her second Town Hall recital in New York and then went straight to Berlin where she sang Eva in a splendid première of Furtwängler's new production of *Meistersinger* at the Lindenoper. Alexander Kipnis was dogging Lotte's footsteps as Pogner again; the Sachs was Rudolf Bockelmann and Fritz Wolff the Walter. Lotte believed that the high-point of the production was her scene with Bockelmann in the second act. Alfred Einstein, who was representing the *Berliner Tageblatt*, was very well disposed towards her. He considered 'her Ev'chen so full of character that it would not seem possible to improve on her, with dark hair (officially ordered to be changed by the next performance) decided, stylish, passionate, and with threatening eyebrows. She would undoubtedly rule her Knight as his wife.'

Lotte went over to the other part of Berlin, to which she was more accustomed, and sang a *Rosenkavalier* for Bruno Walter in the Charlottenburg Opera, followed by a *Fidelio*. Lotte also sang in a concert conducted by Furtwängler and gave two Lieder concerts. After only four performances in Vienna, Lotte was back in Berlin to record eleven sides in two days (Discog.212–22) with the 'Orchestra of the Staatsoper' conducted by Manfred Gurlitt: four re-makes of operatic arias and eight songs.

The world depression had its effect on the Vienna Opera, with consequent need for restraint over the singers' salaries. Lotte was among six with a top figure of 1,026 Austrian Schillings a performance. The others were Nemeth, Piccaver, Pauly, Trundt, and Rode. However, some singers' performances had been reduced in number, particularly those in the top bracket of salaries, and among them Nemeth and

Piccaver (the 'old guard') were being deprived of sixty performances. Lotte lost only twelve. By contrast, Ursuleac had managed a financial miracle by having her salary *raised* during this time of economy. Although she was shown as being paid 900 AS a performance, she was 'now owed by acceptance of 12 appearances between 1.9 and 31.12 . . . 13,500 AS' and this meant 1,125 AS each – more than any other singer on the payroll – except one. And that was Jeritza. Her name did not appear on the sheet at all, otherwise it would have turned everything topsy-turvy, for she still demanded 6,000 AS a performance! Jeritza's days in Vienna were numbered, though, with economy as a fine reason for diminishing her number of appearances and substituting Ursuleac. The Krauss clan looked after its own.[18]

In London there had been grave doubts as to whether there was going to be a Summer Season of opera at all. Sir Thomas Beecham, who had recently emerged from a period of bankruptcy, was looking round for the greenest musical pastures, and now agreed to becoming principal conductor of a short season of Wagnerian operas at Covent Garden. They had always pulled in better houses than the Italian and French repertoire.

Rather than do without engagements at all, the singers agreed to take reduced fees – which seemed to be *de rigueur* everywhere – and the season opened with *Die Meistersinger*, after Sir Thomas's rousing and inimitable performance of the National Anthem, for which he was applauded.[19] Lotte sang Eva, Fritz Wolff was Walter and Friedrich Schorr was a marvellous Sachs. In the two cycles of the *Ring* Lotte sang Sieglinde first with Melchior and Schorr, and then with Walter Widdop and Ludwig Hofmann. Frida Leider and Maria Olszewska were the Brünnhilde and Fricka – old friends from both sides of the Atlantic, and good friends as well. Robert Heger conducted the first three operas in the *Ring* cycles, and then Beecham swept in for the *Götterdämmerungs* to make certain that the cycles ended in appropriate fashion. Lotte also sang two *Tannhäusers* with Melchior and Janssen, conducted very comfortably by Beecham who had decided, at short notice, to withdraw from the last *Meistersinger* and give it to one of his assistants, John Barbirolli. This was an old trick of his which went back to the days of the Beecham Opera Company in the First War. Barbirolli was not at all pleased because he had never conducted the opera in German before, and all he had by way of preparation was a piano rehearsal with the soloists on the morning of the performance.

'During this he corrected Lotte Lehmann on a small point. She raised an eyebrow but did what he wanted. Afterwards she said, "It would have been all right tonight, you know." John replied, "Of course, I know that. But if I had not let you know I had noticed your mistake, what would you have thought of me?"' Afterwards Lotte wrote to him, 'Your *Meistersinger* performance was marvellous. I hope to have the chance to sing very often with you.'[20] She never sang with him again.

The 1932 Wagner season at Covent Garden ended triumphantly with a declaration that every seat had been sold. As a result, Beecham and Geoffrey Toye were appointed directors of a new syndicate which planned to give another season in 1933, amid complicated musical politics involving two London orchestras and the BBC.

The Vienna season ended for Lotte with the Dyer's Wife on 10 June (Ursuleac, Kalenberg, Manowarda). Both Ursuleac and Jeritza had been singing a good deal, in preparation for the economies about to be forced on the Opera directorate by the Austrian Government. Lotte had sung only twenty-five times in the past season, quite a scaling-down process, even before it was financially demanded.

While she was on holiday in Sylt, Lotte received a letter from Clemens Krauss asking her what roles, including Isolde, she was hoping to sing in the 1932–33 Vienna season beginning at the end of August. His accusations about her refusing good roles continued, with Marie in *Wozzeck*, Dorota in *Schwanda the Bagpiper*, the Countess in *Figaro*, Lisa in *Queen of Spades* and Agathe in *Freischütz* all being cited.[21] He also mentioned *Bakchantinnen* by Egon Wellesz, the Austrian composer and musicologist, which was far too advanced and 'twentieth Century' for Lotte, in any case.

Lotte had already made known her views on *Wozzeck*. She would not sing in *Schwanda* because Ursuleac had it in her repertory (even if Lotte cared for the work and her role was not Ursuleac's). That left Lisa, the Countess and Agathe, all of which she had sung before. The Countess, especially was one of Ursuleac's favourite roles, and we all know that it had its memories for Lotte.

She replied to Krauss[22] from Westerland, Sylt that she would definitely sing Isolde in Vienna on her return from America at the end of March 1933 for which she wanted intensive rehearsals in the coming September and October. She also wanted very much to sing the Queen in Robert Heger's *Bettler Namenlos* (*The Beggar without a Name*), possibly after Isolde.

'If *Tristan* can come at the beginning of April, I can manage it, but I shall not burn all my bridges in Europe. Berlin was a colossal success for me. I sang there a couple of evenings in spite of the fact that the "highest" fee remains an appalling condition.'

Their correspondence was carried out in an apparently friendly tone with Krauss 'kissing his hand' to her in the normal Viennese manner which might, in fact, mean the very opposite from the heart. Lotte, in exchange, said how much she looked forward to riding with him in the Prater (although she did not use the Marschallin's words for this invitation!). They were both genuinely keen equestrians.

Still intent on her suicidal vocal course with Isolde, Lotte went to Zoppot for the first time since 1914 to sing one performance of *Lohengrin* under Karl Elmendorff,[23] a distinguished Wagnerian conductor whom Siegfried and Winifred Wagner called to Bayreuth between 1927–42.

Eyvind Laholm was Lotte's Lohengrin, but apart from Herbert Janssen the rest of the principals were unfamiliar to her, except for Gertrud Bindernagel, the Ortrud, from Bruno Walter's company in Berlin.

Bindernagel returned to Berlin after the short Zoppot season and was leaving the theatre one night in the following November when she was shot by her jealous banker husband, and died shortly afterwards.[24] Trajan Grosavescu in reverse.

The 1932 Salzburg Festival was all set to be a lavish one. Max Reinhardt's 'Jedermann' production took place as usual but there were no other plays. Karl Heinz Martin repeated his production of *Orpheus*, and as well as conducting three performances of this opera, Bruno Walter undertook *Die Zauberflöte* and Weber's *Oberon*. Fritz Busch and Carl Ebert, the team from Dresden, were responsible for an outstandingly successful *Entführung*. Ebert was a Reinhardt pupil and had recently held the post of general director and producer at the Charlottenburg (Walter's) Opera.

Richard Strauss returned to conduct at Salzburg, to everybody's delight, and chose *Fidelio*. There were two performances at the end of the Festival with Lotte, Völker as Florestan, Rode as Pizzaro and Mayr as Don Fernando. Krauss conducted *Der Rosenkavalier* (first two performances with Ursuleac, third and fourth with Lotte); two performances of *Così* and one of *Figaro*; two performances of *Die Frau ohne Schatten*. Ursuleac was in them all. Lotte sang the Dyer's Wife, Völker was a beautiful Emperor and Helge Roswaenge had the telling, though short role of the Vision of a Young Man who tempts the Dyer's Wife. Owing to technical difficulties in mounting the Vienna production on the smaller and less-well equipped Salzburg stage (no bridges, for example) the première was delayed by a day.

This opera was being given for the first time in Salzburg and was an ambitious undertaking for a mere couple of performances. But the critic of the *Salzburger Volksblatt* singled out Lotte for exceptional praise above the other artists. He considered that 'she achieved an extraordinary comprehension of the role through the beguiling sound of her voice and by means of her singing-art.'

The last opera performance of this Festival was on 31 August. It was the second *Fidelio* and it turned out to have been the last occasion upon which Lotte sang to Richard Strauss's direction, though for that to have been suggested at the time would never have been believed possible.

There were some new voices – and faces – when Lotte returned to Vienna, for Krauss had been having a recruiting drive. Her first appearance was on 3 September as Sieglinde with Völker and Henny Trundt (now a member of the Company) as Brünnhilde. Apart from Völker, who was being worked hard, Lotte sang opposite another tenor, new to the Company, who was said to be the finest lyrico-dramatic in the world at the time. This was Helge Roswange, a Dane of such short stature that he had to wear high 'lifts' in his boots so that he might nearly approach sopranos on an equal level. He had a mournful countenance and prominent eyes, but one entirely forgot the unprepossessing appearance as soon as he began to sing. He was a member of the Vienna Opera until 1958; a member of the Berlin Staatsoper between 1929–45; and sang Parsifal at Bayreuth in 1934 and 1936. He sang Rodolfo and 'Linkerton' with Lotte during the first month.

Jeritza returned on 8 October in the *Tote Stadt* (she also had recorded the celebrated number, though not the duet). It does not 'shine' like Lotte's. On that evening she was created an *Ehrenmitglied* of the Vienna Opera. One might think that, in view of her superior status and her seniority since 1911 – and her magnanimous salary – that she might have deserved it sooner. But she had retired from the Metropolitan Opera because they could no longer afford her and Vienna expected her to sing more than before on home ground – if *they* could afford her also. Lotte's earlier honour with life membership had no such strings attached.

Ursuleac was singing a wide variety of roles: Fiordiligi, Marschallin, Sieglinde, Eva, Elisabetta in *Don Carlos* (one of her really great parts), Senta and in *Bettler Namenlos* which Lotte had specially requested from Krauss for herself. Ursuleac also appeared, strangely enough, as Butterfly which was probably vocally suitable, but not physically. She was a large lady. Lotte was furious about the Heger opera which the wits in Vienna referred to as 'Bettler Samenlos' (referring to Heger himself, and meaning 'The Beggarly Eunuch'). It looked as though Ursuleac had stolen the role from her.

Lotte had still made no definite arrangements with Krauss for her projected Isolde. Henny Trundt was singing it, so the role was covered.

After the last Färberin of her career on 17 October, Lotte wrote to Krauss from Paris,[25] expressing grave doubts as to her ability to undertake Isolde: it would spoil her concert career, she said. Also her interpretation of the true Isolde would have to be sung against 'a whole world of mistrust. Here in Paris everyone I meet utters a cry of warning against Isolde.'

They told her that she would be absolutely marvellous and would undoubtedly have an enormous success *but* time will take its toll and she would no longer be a sought-after lyric soprano. She would no longer be able to sing, even Lieder, for the luscious quality of her voice would have been lost.

'These are not ill-wishers,' she goes on, 'but *friends*, and I don't know what the answer is . . . *Es ist ein Traum*. ['It is a dream' – she is quoting from *Rosenkavalier*] . . . I must not place my concert career in any danger.'

At the end of this letter, Lotte sent greetings to Dr Wallerstein and to one of the officials at the Opera, but none to Frau Ursuleac.

Krauss's reaction to this letter can easily be imagined. Lotte rivalled and, in certain important respects, excelled, the artistic merits of Ursuleac. Lotte had denied her complete allegiance to the Vienna Opera – *ergo* to Krauss himself – by stating unequivocally that her concert career mattered more to her than anything else. Krauss's desire for Lotte to sing Isolde is impossible to define, and had better be left like that. 'Of course he had to support Ursuleac.'

Lotte was eventually persuaded against Isolde for good and all by two Tristans: Leo Slezak and Lauritz Melchior. They had witnessed a number of crumbling Isoldes in the past and knew all the dangers. They could certainly be acknowledged as true friends and, more important, Lotte listened to them both.

All the same, Isolde could not be discarded from Lotte's life as easily as that. They had practically merged into one in Lotte's mind, and Isolde would need exorcising.

Lotte did not wait to hear from Krauss, and went to Berlin where she gave what she called a *Liederabend/Arienabend* – an Evening of Songs and Arias, accompanied by Leo Rosenek.

Then she left for the United States and on 17 November there was an instance of rapid promotion in the Vienna Opera when Clemens Krauss was elevated to the noble ranks of the *Ehrenmitglieder*.

Chapter Eight

The Krauss Régime

1933–1934

On 30 January 1933 Adolf Hitler came to power in Germany as Reichschancellor. Nominal control still existed in the 85-year-old President, Field Marshal Hindenburg, who possessed the constitutional power to veto any decree he considered objectionable. The cabinet consisted mainly of anti-Nazis except for Wilhelm Frick and Hermann Göring. Yet Hitler was able by trickery, bullying and false promises to get everything he wanted.

Lotte did not hear about this until the day after. She was not alarmed because she could not visualise that Germany was going to change very much whoever was in power. She gave a concert in Symphony Hall, Boston on 21 February: a programme of Lieder by Brahms, Schubert, Schumann and Strauss – four to each composer.

Six days later the Reichstag Fire in Berlin inflamed public opinion against the Communists, and on 3 March Göring's infamous speech in Frankfort contained the words: 'My mission is to destroy and exterminate!' On the next day Hitler made his first territorial demands on the Sudetenland.

These fast-flowing political events had an effect upon the whole of Europe but, as we shall see, a more immediate and personal effect on Lotte. Racism was now becoming a significant factor of German life. 'I am an Aryan,' she used to remark with a wry expression, hating the word with its divisive connotation, and implying – as Richard Strauss did far more directly – that it did not matter to her who her audiences happened to be so long as they applauded and enjoyed themselves.

Lotte returned to Vienna in March for a single performance of *Fidelio* on 21st, the opera which extols Freedom above all. On 23 March Hitler's enabling bill was passed by the Reichstag giving him full powers as Chancellor of the Reich. So far as music in Berlin and throughout Germany was concerned, these 'full powers' were invested in Hermann Göring and were weekly becoming more rigorous.

On 28 March Lotte listened to a performance of *Tristan* from the artists' box. It had Henny Trundt and Gunnar Graarud as the lovers, with Richard Mayr as an unforgettable Kurwenal and Emil Schipper as King Mark. The performance was conducted by a guest from Hamburg called Karl Böhm, and was his first appearance there. He was an Austrian from Graz and had been trained at the Vienna Music Academy, now on his way to becoming Music Director of the Dresden Opera.

Lotte had six performances during April including her 'double' of Georgetta-Angelica, and then went to Covent Garden, away from the man she referred to as 'Schalk's successor'.

Colonel Blois, who had done so much to keep the London Summer Seasons of opera alive, had recently died, and Sir Thomas Beecham was now in full command at the Royal Opera House. He conducted the season's opener, *Der Rosenkavalier* with Lotte, Hadrabova, Kern and Mayr. Apart from a single performance of this opera which Beecham had given at Hamburg in November 1930 (without a score)[1] his last *Rosenkavalier* had been at Drury Lane Theatre in 1914 when Lotte sang Sophie. This time she also sang two Sieglindes, under Heger's baton.

After three appearances in Vienna again, she gave a recital of arias at the Augusteo in Rome on 29 May. Alec Robertson heard it and recalls:[2]

> The most memorable experience I had at the Augusteo was hearing Lotte Lehmann sing the *Liebestod*. Her voice had not sufficient weight to undertake the part of Isolde on the stage, being lyrical rather than dramatic in the Wagnerian sense, and I wondered how she would fare at the big climax of the *Liebestod*. Lehmann came on, before the Prelude, gracious and beautiful in a wine-coloured dress, and stood immobile before us while it was played. During those twelve minutes or so, as the music gradually moved to its climax in that tremendous crescendo of passion, we saw Lehmann visibly becoming Isolde, so that when the orchestra made the quiet modulation into the *Liebestod* and she began, as if in a trance, 'Mild und leise wie er lächelt', she *was* Isolde. It was the most astonishing metamorphosis of the kind I had ever witnessed and I realised what immense artistic discipline it must have required. Lehmann held us so spellbound that the lack of volume at the huge climax passed almost unnoticed. Few Isoldes have ended the *Liebestod* with such an exquisite high note – 'höchste Lust' – as she gave us. This was indeed the 'highest bliss'.

Lotte returned to Vienna for only two more performances that season, an Eva and an Elisabeth, but also to receive a snub from the Directorate. She must have known it was coming.

Richard Strauss's next opera, *Arabella*, was scheduled for its world première at Dresden in July and most of the month of June was given over to rehearsals. Lotte would have perfectly well been able to rehearse and Krauss was in Vienna – he had conducted that *Meistersinger* on 4 June. In her first autobiographical book *On Wings of Song* Lotte declares that she was unable to fulfil Strauss's request for her to sing the first *Arabella* in Dresden because of 'over-fatigue after the heavy season'.[3] It had been a particularly light season so far, (only twelve performances, though of course she had been abroad). This excuse was Lotte putting on a brave face by not admitting the real facts. They were these.

Strauss wanted his *Arabella* première to be in Dresden again because this house had proved itself to be the ideal one for launching six of his operas already. But the management had always proved difficult about engaging leading singers from elsewhere – Lotte for Christine in *Intermezzo* was an example. They had also refused to negotiate with Jeritza over the *Helena* première, and the Dresdener, Elisabeth Rethberg had taken it.

Viorica Ursuleac had been singing in Dresden since 1930, was known there and liked, so there was no objection to her singing *Arabella*. Berlin had planned their production at the Staatsoper a few months later, and wanted Krauss to conduct – *ergo*, Ursuleac to sing in it also. Lotte was still convinced that Strauss had promised her *Arabella*, though by now she was well aware of the strength of opposition facing her. Krauss was a thoroughly devious operator when the business in hand concerned his own career, and he was bound, of course, to support Ursuleac.

She was not actually his wife until 1944, though she lived with him in Vienna at Modena Park[4] and was, to all intents and purposes, married to him. Consequently Dresden was 'out' for Lotte.

On 13 June, Lotte was invited to Paris to sing Sieglinde in a performance of *Die Walküre* with Melchior, Leider and Schorr, conducted by Furtwängler. There had been two *Tristans* and two *Walküres*, but Lotte sang only in the last performance, though enjoyed meeting her old friends again, and Furtwängler, who was greatly troubled about the events in Germany. They stayed together at the Villa Majestic and enjoyed a happy time, away from 'the witches' cauldron' of Berlin.[5]

But it was to Berlin where Lotte went afterwards, to make six sides (Discog. 225–230) of which the *Toten Augen* item was a remarkable success. The Antonia aria from *Hoffmann*, which she had not sung on stage since 1925, was a re-make of her first, 1921 essay; while Susanna's 'Deh vieni' was (although a re-make also) a curious choice at this date in her career. The *Werther* aria was first-time.

Sylt was calling and for the first time since 1925, Lotte had a long, long holiday there with only minimal rehearsals scheduled for Salzburg. A contract from Gatti-Casazza of the Met was waiting for Lotte's signature, and on 27 June she wrote her large, free, generous and flowing name for two performances there between 1 January and 31 March 1934 at $600 each. She had to guarantee not to sing in New York City, Brooklyn or Philadelphia during this period. The operas she was offered were all by Wagner.

On 29 June, 'The Night of the Long Knives', Hitler ordered the execution (more like an assassination) of the leaders of his own bodyguard, the *Sturm Abteilung* or SA, because they were getting out of hand, and had to be completely crushed. The significant result of this was that the German army, who feared the power of the SA, now stood solidly behind Hitler and gave him their oath of allegiance. When on 2 August, old Hindenburg died, Hitler was the undisputed master of Germany and 'the Thousand-Year Reich', with the offices of Chancellor and President merged in himself.

When Lotte arrived in Salzburg at the end of August she was surprised by people looking curiously at her and asking tenderly after her health. She was so brown and burnt by daily rides over the sands and under the sun of Sylt that there should have been no doubt about her welfare. Rumours had persisted since the beginning of the summer in Vienna and since the beginning of the Festival in Salzburg (it started on 28 July) that Lotte had contracted some dreadful illness which had kept her away for ten weeks. She records with some amusement the reports that 'she was sinking fast from some hopeless lung-trouble in Davos' or that she and her husband had divorced. There was quite a sensation when Lotte and Otto arrived together in Salzburg, arm in arm.[6]

It was small wonder that there was anxiety over Lotte because she had been given no more than a single operatic appearance in the 1933 Salzburg Festival: one Marschallin. Even the Dyer's Wife had gone to Rose Pauly. In the previous year, Lotte and Bruno Walter had put their heads together and concocted a small scheme which appealed to the Festival Management because it was, in a sense, a semi-private affair and would have no production costs.

'I do dislike this new régime in Salzburg,' said Walter.

'And Vienna,' Lotte added.

The plan was for a Liederabend on 27 August, and 'the two darlings of Salzburg' showed themselves to be perfectionists in the delicate art. The programme consisted of twenty-five Lieder, in groups by Schubert,

Schumann, Brahms and Hugo Wolf, expertly chosen to give variety of range, colour, expression, mood and key. The general opinion among critics, racking their brains for different superlatives, was – in the words of one who simply gave up – 'Es war unsagbar schön!' ('It was unspeakably beautiful!')

About half the items in this programme were later recorded from time to time by Lotte on 78, but others were never committed to disc. Consequently there were members of that audience who could afterwards and always boast: 'Ah, but *I* heard Lotte Lehmann sing Brahms's "Salamander"!'

Her single Marschallin was on 29 August. Despite the fact that Krauss was conducting, Lotte was well able to draw her audience as always, even to outshine her competitor who had preceded her twice in the role that season. Aenne Michalsky, the Leitmetzerin of these performances sums up the difference between Ursuleac and Lotte in a few words: 'As a person and as a singer, Ursuleac wasn't immediately likeable, she was too cold; whereas Lotte, a marvellous colleague, was always warm and sunny – she opened her arms!'[7]

The 1933–34 Vienna Season opened for Lotte with *Fidelio* conducted by Josef Krips who was now on the musical staff in place of Reichenberger, at last pensioned off. Although Ursuleac was singing Helena in Krauss's 'revised version' of Strauss's doubtful success on 20 September, Lotte gave no thought to it, for she was somewhere else, engaged in a four-day task which was going to ensure her immortality.

His Master's Voice had decided to record about half the *Rosenkavalier* score in Vienna and to use the Vienna Philharmonic Orchestra and the most Viennese of the singers familiar with the work. The excerpts chosen lacked the Levée Scene and the Tenor Singer, which came in for some criticism later, but it was for sound financial reasons. Such an enterprise would demand a superb Italian tenor under contract to HMV – even Beniamino Gigli (Melchior's exact twin by birth day) – and for less than a whole 12" side. It would unbalance the budget. HMV approached Strauss to conduct, but his fee was too high. The choice went to Bruno Walter, but he was a Berliner in spite of his facility with this opera, and a Columbia recording artist too – so it came down to Robert Heger, safe and sound and knowing the score intimately. Nobody seemed to realise that Lotte was not strictly Viennese. She had become one – and now she was Austrian by marriage.

The cast does not need listing here (Discog. pp. 282–84), though the Octavian, Olszewska, was somewhat unusual casting. One incident during the recording sessions which has often been misquoted, may be of interest. When the Marschallin crosses the stage with Faninal for her exit line between the two strophes of the Love Duet, she speaks – or almost speaks – the two words 'Ja, Ja!' The old 78 records bear numbers (matrix numbers) in the wax that show the sequence in which all the sides were recorded – seldom the chronological sequence of the score. The last side with 'Ja, ja!' shows from its matrix number that it was recorded on the second day, 21 September. Lotte loved to recount how she left the Mittlerer Sall after having recorded the Trio, forgetting that she had still to sing these two words, and how Elisabeth Schumann sang them for her, mimicking her voice. Time had played tricks with her memory, however, for the recording sheets show that this side was the first recording of the day, not the last, so that Schumann sang the 'Ja, ja!' because Lotte had not yet arrived. Lotte sang her words on a later recording which proved to be defective and could not be used. It became a private joke between Schumann and Lehmann that they had both sung all three soprano roles in *Der Rosenkavalier*. Lotte had, of course, and many times; Elisabeth had sung many, many Sophies, one Octavian (in Hamburg with Klemperer) and two words of the Marschallin for a gramophone record.

After a muted reception to the first *Arabella* in Dresden on 31 July, Krauss and Ursuleac repeated their performances with the Berlin première at the Lindenoper on 12 October.

As early as March 1933, Strauss had confirmed to Krauss that the General Dress Rehearsal would be on 10 October, and the first Berlin *Arabella* on 12th. Then he had (naïvely it seems) asked Krauss: 'Is Frau Lehmann going to sing Arabella?'[8] It was an important State Gala and the Führer was present. For some time he had exercised his magnetism over Ursuleac, who was a party member, but now she had entranced him by her performance, and *Arabella* replaced *Tiefland* as Hitler's favourite opera. He heard Ursuleac sing it ten times.

Lotte recalls that rehearsals for the Viennese première of *Arabella*, in which she and Ursuleac would alternate, were undertaken in such an unpleasant atmosphere that it was 'one of the most ungratifying recollections' of her whole stage career. 'I am sure' she went on 'that he [Krauss] would have preferred it if the singer who took my place at Dresden had done the Vienna première as well . . .'

What made it far worse for Lotte was the health of her mother, who was dying. Otto sat at the bedside while Lotte was rehearsing and Brother Fritz, who had recently become a widower, also attended whenever he was able. Frau Lehmann, now nearly eighty-three, had little to live for and died on the day before the *Arabella* première.

Ursuleac was singing it in Berlin, there was no understudy in Vienna, and Lotte simply had to go on. The house was sold out and many critics from all over Europe had come to hear Strauss's next opera about Vienna *in* Vienna. That was the point of this première.

So Lotte forgot her grief in the transference of her own character and person to that of Arabella Waldner. She became Arabella in 'this miracle of rebirth' as Caruso had shown her and as Alec Robertson has explained after his experience in Rome.

She took few curtain calls at the end of the performance when Richard Strauss came out and told the audience how Lotte had saved the performance for him and for all of them. She had maintained the basic theatrical creed: 'The Show Must Go On.'

Of the eight performances of *Arabella* in Vienna before the end of the year, Ursuleac sang the next four and Lotte the last three. In the early part of 1934 and until the end of that year there were nine more performances. None was scheduled for April, when Lotte came back from America and could have sung, but she gave one more in June – her last. Score: Ursuleac 12, Lotte 5.

There was one entirely unexpected, but subsequently very fruitful result from the *Arabella* première in Vienna. Toscanini was present and fell in love with Lotte. It was the first time he had heard her sing.

Before completing her contract with Odeon and moving over entirely to HMV, Lotte made two 10" records of the aria 'Mein Elemer' and the duet 'Aber der Richtige' from *Arabella*. They match and complement Ursuleac's two 10" discs, also for Odeon, the Act I duet with Bokor and the Act II duet 'Wie Sie sind', as well as the Act III finale, both with Alfred Jerger. From these four records it is easy to determine the different styles of Lotte and Ursuleac and their approaches to the role of Arabella. (Discog.231–34).

On 30 October Lotte had an orchestral concert with Furtwängler and the Berlin Philharmonic Orchestra in the Philharmonie. She sang Katharine's aria from *The Taming of the Shrew* (Discog. 30) and after the interval, three Strauss songs, 'Allerseelen', 'Traum durch die Dämmerung' and 'Zueignung'. She also had a Lieder recital after the recordings when she was accompanied by Franz Rupp. She could not help noticing a change in the audiences there, with a large sprinkling of black-shirted men in evidence. This was on 13 December, and was her last Berlin concert.

After Lotte's last performance at the Opera on Boxing Day – it was a *Rosenkavalier* under Krips – she sailed to the USA with Otto and met her accompanist, Ernö Balogh, a Hungarian. He and Otto had engaged a personal representative via Francis Coppicus, her American manager, knowing that life for Lotte was going to be extremely difficult without someone who was abreast of the inside knowledge and contacts in this land which was still strange to her. Lotte was entirely opposed to any such idea, and was astonished to meet Constance Hope (who was understandably nervous) and to discover that it was all a *fait accompli*. The choice of Miss Hope was ideal. She and Lotte quickly became firm friends and remained so, working together harmoniously and greatly to Lotte's benefit. Miss Hope had just the right touch for her and was always able to persuade her to forget certain European ways of going about things and to take her advice in American habits and customs.

Lotte had never felt that she belonged to the vertical city of New York but now she began to absorb the particular atmosphere of the Metropolitan Opera (the old building, of course) which was only five years older than herself and peopled with the ghosts of singers long departed.

One of them haunted Lotte in a peculiar – and silly – way. She was not accustomed to being confused with other Lehmanns although the name is common in Germany. Now she was mistaken for *Lilli* Lehmann (born in 1848 and died in 1929): 'Remarkably well preserved; I thought she was dead. How old could she be?' This was among the audience at Lotte's début as Sieglinde.[10]

That night for her was like being at Covent Garden or in Chicago so far as the other singers were concerned, which was an enormous comfort. Melchior, Schorr, Gertrud Kappel and Karin Branzell were all in the cast, old Wagnerian friends. Lotte found that she got on well with Artur Bodanzky from Vienna, and chief conductor of German operas at the Met since 1915.

This *Walküre* was a huge success for Lotte. She 'was applauded madly for ten minutes, recalled to the stage many times and actually cheered by hundreds who frantically waved their programmes at her.' Bodanzky conducted with care and 'kindness', for which Lotte thanked him, though it was definitely her evening. People noticed how she sparkled. 'She radiates health,' wrote a columnist, '"Swim for Safety, Sanity and Success" is her slogan.' She gave two recitals in Buffalo, then flew from Miami to Havana 'in a few hours by a giant plane that held thirty-six people;' from the intense heat of Cuba they then encountered the freezing cold of Milwaukee.

On hearing that Lotte was going to be in New York in February, Toscanini asked her to sing for him on his General Motors radio programme (as yet there was no television). Lotte regarded this in two ways. At first she was thrilled at the idea, especially as she knew that he was going to be at the Salzburg Festival in 1934. But then she recalled how she had turned down flat his invitation to sing Eva for him at La Scala in 1926. His reputation for being a martinet had scared her and she was unwilling to risk it – then. But now it was different, and she accepted.

She was to meet him and rehearse on the morning of the concert: 11 February.[11] Lotte knew that she was not in her best voice that day, but she need not have worried about the Maestro. He was courtesy itself and put her entirely at ease. She sang Elisabeth's Act II aria from *Tannhäuser* and Leonore's 'Abscheulicher!'

This concert marked the beginning of a deep and dear friendship. Toscanini insisted that the Salzburg Festival authorities engage Lotte to sing in his Wagner concert there in August, and told her that they would be working together a good deal in the future.

On the day following the Toscanini broadcast concert, Lotte sang for the New York Beethoven Society. As she was going on to the platform with Ernö Balogh, she said: 'Well, here's a fairly straightforward concert to sing and no Toscanini to be breathing down my neck!' And the first person she set eyes on in the audience was – Toscanini!

After that she had an Elisabeth and an Eva at the Met; and with a new contract in her pocket for a concert tour and opera performances in San Francisco, Chicago and the Met again during the 1934–35 season, Lotte sailed home.

Just before she left, she received a cable from Bruno Walter, telling her that she must be note perfect in the role of Tatiana for his new production of *Eugen Onegin* opening on 10 April.[12] Lotte did not know it, but managed to buy a score and settled down on the ship during her return voyage. As the only piano on board was in the dining-room she was forced to learn it to the accompaniment of clashing dishes as the tables were cleared and set.

Jeritza was no longer at the Met, and Lotte felt that much of the troubles she had been suffering lately were not really as bad as all that. With her Lieder recitals in demand throughout Germany, and the beginning of a flourishing career in the USA, she need concentrate less upon the Vienna Opera and all that meant nowadays.

Since the beginning of the Nazi 'take-over' of Germany, Joseph Goebbels, the Minister for Propaganda and a distinctly unsavoury person, had taken over all theatre and music in the Reich. He and Göring were rivals for opera in Berlin. Goebbels controlled the

Charlottenburg Opera but Göring had the Staatsoper unter den Linden, a far more prestigious house. Furtwängler held great musical sway in Berlin as conductor of the Berlin Philharmonic Orchestra, Director of the Staatsoper, and as a Prussian State Councillor.

Furtwängler had championed Paul Hindemith's new opera *Mathis der Maler*, which was about a great painter who sides with a revolutionary faction against the authority of the State. After the first concert performance of a symphonic synthesis of the work in March, he scheduled it for performance at the Staatsoper, but the new authority of the State forbade *Mathis der Maler* to be staged for its message was too close to the Nazi knuckle.

During Lotte's absence abroad, political opponents of the Austrian Chancellor, Dr. Dollfuss, had been crushed by his hard-line government with bloodshed and disturbances. Austria was on Hitler's shopping-list and his supporters there were acting on instructions to help pave the way for the takeover. Austria stood alone in Europe, unable to rely on her old ally Italy, because of Mussolini's admiration for Hitler; uncertain altogether about England and France; and living under the shadow of Hitler's personal hatred and contempt for Dollfuss. Hitler's retreat at Berchtesgaden, the 'Eagle's Nest', was plainly visible from Salzburg and constituted a permanent, ocular threat.

On 2 April, Lotte sang Leonore in Vienna and went into rehearsal for the new production of *Eugen Onegin* which she had absorbed on board. She was at home one morning when the telephone rang.[13] It was Heinz Tietjen, Intendant of all the Berlin Opera Houses, which only he can have managed considering the Goebbels-Göring situation between two houses which Tietjen had to administer. He expressed an invitation to Lotte from the Minister of Education (Hermann Göring) for a few guest performances at his opera house. Lotte refused with some banter, although she was promised anything at all by way of payment. She rejected the possibility of travelling to Berlin immediately because of her forthcoming first night. Tietjen was very persistent but all Lotte said was 'No! And definitely not until after 10 April.'

Tietjen had an awkward time with Göring for failing to produce Lotte in Berlin. Her *Eugen Onegin* was a success, and after another performance and an *Ariadne*, Lotte had a concert engagement to fulfil. This was on 19 April, when a curious thing happened.

She was in the middle of a Lied before a large and most enthusiastic audience when she became 'aware of a curious unrest' among them. A man was attempting, in a thoroughly crude and ill-mannered way, to attract her attention. Such a thing had never happened to her before and she was insulted. After finishing this particular song she crossly asked him what he wanted. He was trembling, seemed to be some sort of local official and said that Reichminister Göring was on the telephone – that she must speak to him immediately.

Lotte laughed, turned away and continued to the end of her group of songs. But there was *no applause*. Word had got round the entire audience and everybody assumed that Lotte was under some political cloud. Nobody wished to associate with her. Lotte did not hurry to reach the telephone but when she eventually answered the long-delayed call, she heard the exasperated voice of Göring's adjutant. He told her curtly that the Reichminister's private aeroplane would be at the local airfield on the following morning at eleven to take her to Berlin.

Lotte was still considering it in a lighthearted manner the next day, for she had not yet absorbed the fear which had permeated most men, women and children in Germany. When she arrived at Tempelhof airfield in Berlin, Tietjen was there to meet her, twitching away and not looking her in the eyes. This time, she saw, he was more unsettled than usual and, in the car on the way to the Ministry, he tried several times to warn Lotte that 'things have changed drastically'. All the time he seemed to be looking out of the corner of one eye at the driver, who was presumably an informer.

Lotte tells this story and what follows with abandon, great humour and not a little artistic licence that epitomizes, all the same, her frivolous attitude towards the Nazis in their early years of power.

Göring kept her waiting for a long time, and she was already famished. At last he appeared, gorgeously arrayed in parade uniform, for it was the Führer's birthday, 20 April, then disappeared for the military event. Later, after a bath, Göring had changed into unconventional shorts, a hunting-knife in his belt and a whip in his hand. At last he gave his full attention to Lotte and they lunched.

They were joined by Göring's future wife, the celebrated German actress, Emmy Sonnemann, but Lotte was surprised to discover that there seemed to be no common ground for conversation between them as she expected. Only later did she discover that Sonnemann was very friendly with Ursuleac.

Göring was expansive, promised Lotte anything she demanded – so she surprised him by asking for a castle on the Rhine. At this, Tietjen looked scared to death, for nobody dared speak to the Reichminister in such a fashion. He did not seem to mind. As an ace Luftwaffe pilot in the First War he had been a good sport and was the nearest approach to one in the whole of the Nazi hierarchy. Lotte would be their first

Nationalsängerin (national singer) a new title for a most favoured artist. Göring guaranteed to stand surety for her high salary, pension, villa and never a bad notice: 'If a critic dares, he will be liquidated!'

Lotte laughed, and Tietjens curled up. She imagined this to be a joke from such a 'perfectly harmless and amiable young man.' (Göring was forty, Lotte was forty-five). Her admitted preference for the Vienna Opera caused Göring to sneer and to mention Chancellor Dollfuss's name with contempt. He went on to talk about the contract which he would have drawn up. Once Lotte had signed it she could expect all his promises to be made good immediately. In exchange for this bounty, he expected her never to sing again outside the Reich: the world would have to come to Germany to hear her.

This was impossible and Lotte rejected the idea instantly. 'Music is an international language,' she told Göring, 'and as one of its messengers I wish to sing everywhere, all over the world.'

Göring didn't like that at all, and Lotte caught sight of Tietjen, visibly trembling and cautioning her to be quiet. After a pause, she agreed to see a contract drawn up according to what had been said. After an amusing incident with the Minister's pet lioness, which Lotte asked to see and with which she made friends at once (unlike Tietjen who was scared of it) she bade Göring farewell and was flown out of Berlin.

The contract, when it arrived, contained no mention of the advantages which Göring had promised her and was not at all a true settlement for such a 'deal'. Lotte wrote, as usual, in a very frank and open manner to Tietjen, complaining at the interpretation in the contract. He passed on her letter to Göring's office as though it was red hot. Then Göring dictated a reply to Lotte which she found to be 'a terrible letter, full of insults and low abuse'. Perhaps he didn't like the question she put to Tietjen: 'What would happen to me if Reichminister Göring were to lose his position?'

The upshot was devastating.

Göring turned it all round so that Lotte was forbidden to sing anywhere *in* the Reich. There could be no more guest performances for her in any German opera houses and no recitals, just as she had built up a reliable circuit and was in great demand.

Although Lotte hints that Göring had taken a fancy to her as a woman, his main idea behind this had undoubtedly been to improve the standard of singing at the Berlin Staatsoper – his house. He was – or had been made – fully aware that Lotte was of the *Weltklasse* and he meant to extract her from Vienna before Austria came under German domination (as it obviously soon would do). Frau Kammersängerin Charlotte

Krause-Lehmann had been thoroughly investigated by the Gestapo, who knew that her husband was Jewish. This might eventually be a way of securing her obedience, as Göring used to say: 'It is for me to decide who is a Jew'.[14] If he found any Jews who might be useful to him, directly or indirectly, he would allow them to remain at his beck and call, suspended between life and death at his pleasure.

Other reasons have been suggested or given[15] why Lotte refused to accept the offer from Göring, and one concerns the repertoire. Lotte is said to have told him that her conditions for coming to Berlin (before she had heard the restrictive clause) depended upon her being first-cast Marschallin, Arabella, Leonore and Sieglinde. This made Göring antagonistic because they were Ursuleac roles (except for Leonore) and she was already a member of his Opera. After her success in *Arabella* and the Führer's pleasure, Ursuleac was expected to be singing in Berlin more often. It has been stated that Lotte tore up Göring's contract in front of him.

A week after this unreal kind of interview, Lotte was in Paris for the last concert of the season at the Théâtre des Champs Elysées. Her performance of Schumann's 'Frauenliebe und -leben' was discussed with animation for a long time afterwards. Then she went to Covent Garden to sing Leonore on the opening night, 30 April, in a new production of *Fidelio* with elegant sets designed by Rex Whistler.

Lotte was not feeling at all well. She was in a 'nervous depression' according to the producer, Otto Erhardt,[16] and no wonder. Sir Thomas Beecham was informed.

Early on the evening of the first night he asked Lotte to meet him in the conductor's room where, to her astonishment, she found the principal woodwind and horn players, and a repetiteur at the piano with the string parts. Beecham was standing as though on the rostrum, facing them, and already in evening dress. He took Lotte carefully through the treacherous 'Abscheulicher!' aria, which he knew was bound to be worrying her, conducting her as he was going to do very shortly before the audience, and marking the parts to suit her voice. This made her feel happy again and thoroughly reassured.

This was the night when some latecomers were kicking up an unnecessary noise while trying to find their seats during the Overture. Beecham turned round to them and shouted 'Shut up, you barbarians!'[17] It was all being broadcast, and in the auditorium as well as over the air in hundreds of genteel homes, the noun sounded like 'buggers'. This received far more lineage in the national press on the following morning than the performance itself, though it was enthusiastically received.

Lotte's Leonore was especially admired, for she gave it with a full heart and complete confidence, thanks to Sir Thomas's understanding.

Lotte's Covent Garden engagement ended on 1 June with a performance of *Die Meistersinger* under Beecham that put her on her mettle. She was the third of three Evas that season, following Käthe Heidersbach and Maria Müller, but the press found her incomparable and the opera-goers thought her preferable in every way to the other two.

Lotte found herself uncomfortably close in London to some of those who favoured the new régime in Germany. Ursuleac was there to sing all four performances of *Arabella*, in the Dresden production which was new to London, and also in *Schwanda*; she gave two performances as Desdemona (opposite Melchior) but was so disliked in the role that Joan Cross was brought over from Sadler's Wells to take over the third,[18] which she sang in English most beautifully.

After her London commitments, Lotte went to Paris for two performances of Eva in a mainly Berlin-cast *Meistersinger* which Furtwängler conducted. The other principals were Max Lorenz, Rudolf Bockelmann, and Alexander Kipnis, Herbert Janssen and Marta Fuchs. It was an engaging compliment for Lotte to be invited. It was reported that 'the gradual awakening of Eva from girlhood was again revealed in miraculous fashion, and the scenes with Sachs were beautifully done, avoiding any suggestion of the minx, but clearly showing her fondness for the old man, with simple naïveté in her appeal to him for help.'

Lotte gave five of her favourite roles in Vienna, in quick succession, to close the season there: Sieglinde, Arabella, the Marschallin, Tatiana and Leonore. Then, after a brief rest, to Salzburg, where she enjoyed the company of a new friend, the American-born and trained soprano Dusolina Giannini.

Bruno Walter was there to conduct three operas, though Lotte did not appear in any of them. Krauss conducted the other six including two *Fidelios* and three *Rosenkavaliers*, all with Lotte. Ursuleac did not sing any Marschallins this year because she was otherwise engaged in *Figaro*, the *Egyptian Helen*, *Cosi* and *Elektra*, and there was an atmosphere of great uncertainty, even fear, at this Salzburg Festival – so unlike anything of the kind there before.

Chancellor Dollfuss had been murdered, there were riots and some shooting within earshot of Salzburg, a bomb was let off in the Hotel Bristol during a performance of *Tristan* on 30 July, and a number of visitors turned in their tickets and left.

Richard Strauss had fallen out with the Nazis and was under a political cloud. He was forbidden to conduct this year in Salzburg and it

Baron and Baroness (above), Erika & Elizabeth (below) zu Putlitz

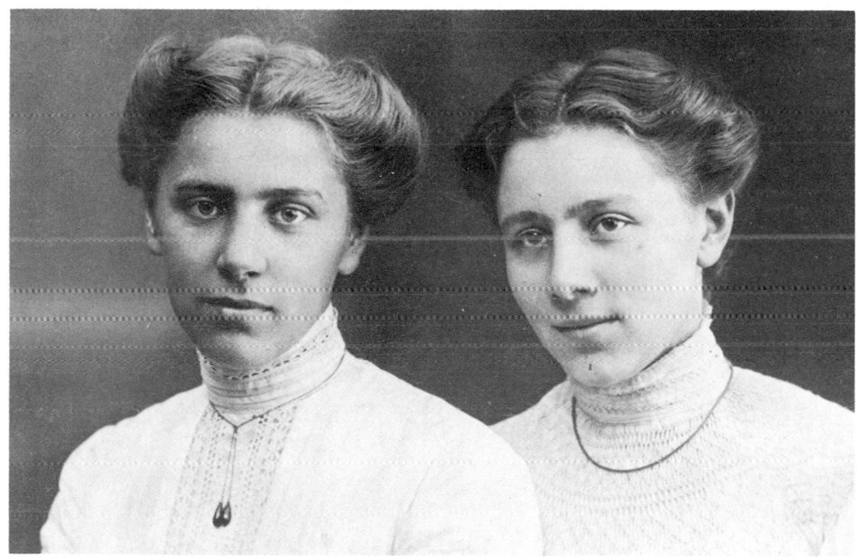

Gross-Pankow

Richard Strauss in 1910

Otto Klemperer in Hamburg, 1910

The Composer, *Ariadne auf Naxos*

Maria Jeritza in *Die Frau ohne Schatten*

Viorica Ursuleac as Arabella

Lehmann in *Manon Lescaut*

Lehmann in *Turandot*

Lehmann as Sieglinde

Lehmann as the Marschallin

Royal Opera Covent Garden

Proprietors: The Grand Opera Syndicate, Ltd.

LONDON OPERA SYNDICATE, Ltd. SEASON

THIS EVENING'S PERFORMANCE

Friday, June 11, 1926, at 7.45

MOZART'S OPERA

DON GIOVANNI

(In Italian)

Donna Anna . . . . . FRIDA LEIDER
Donna Elvira . . . . . LOTTE LEHMANN
Zerlina . . . . . ELISABETH SCHUMANN
Don Giovanni . . . . . MARIANO STABILE
Don Ottavio . . . . . FRITZ KRAUSS
Leporello . . . . . JEAN AQUISTAPACE
Masetto . . . . . POMPILIO MALATESTA
l Commendatore . . . EDOUARD COTREUIL

Conductor . . BRUNO WALTER

SALZBURGER FESTSPIELE 1929

Im Festspielhaus

FIDELIO

Oper in zwei Akten von L. van Beethoven

Dirigent: Franz Schalk
Inszenierung: Lothar Wallerstein
Bühnenbilder: Clemens Holzmeister

Florestan, ein Gefangener . . . . Josef Kalenberg
Leonore, seine Gemahlin (Fidelio) . . Lotte Lehmann
Don Fernando, Minister . . . . Franz Markhoff
Don Pizarro, Kommandant eines Staatsgefängnisses . . . . Ludwig Hofmann
Rocco, Kerkermeister . . . . Josef Manowarda
Marzelline, seine Tochter . . . . Luise Helletsgruber
Jaquino, Pförtner . . . . Hermann Gallos
Erster Gefangener . . . . William Wernigk
Zweiter Gefangener . . . . Viktor Madin
Staatsgefangene, Wachen, Volk

Ort und Zeit: Spanien zur Zeit Karls III. um 1770

Orchester: Wiener Philharmoniker
Chor der Wiener Staatsoper

KONZERTDIREKTION HERMANN WOLFF
(vorm. Konzertdirektion Hermann Wolff u. Jules Sachs), G.m.b.H., Berlin W, Linkstr. 42

Bernburger Str. 22 **PHILHARMONIE** Bernburger Str. 22

Montag, den 30. Oktober 1933, abends 8 Uhr

2. Philharmonisches Konzert

Leitung: **Wilhelm Furtwängler**

Solistin: **Lotte Lehmann**

I.

Symphonie Nr. 39 Es-dur . . . . . . **W. A. Mozart**
Adagio — Allegro
Andante con moto
Menuett
Finale

II.

Arie der Katharina aus „Der Widerspenstigen Zähmung" . . . . . **H. Götz**

— Pause —

III.

3 Gesänge mit Orchester . . . . **R. Strauß**
a) Allerseelen
b) Traum durch die Dämmerung
c) Zueignung

IV.

„Also sprach Zarathustra"
Tondichtung (frei nach Friedrich Nietzsche) . . . . **R. Strauß**

Orgel: Johannes Ernst Köhler

PHILHARMONIE, Montag, den 20. November 1933, abends 8 Uhr

3. Philharmonisches Konzert

Leitung: **Wilhelm Furtwängler**
Solist: **Wilhelm Backhaus**
Bach: Suite D-dur / **Graener:** Sinfonia brevis (zum 1. Mal)
Brahms: Klavier-Konzert B-dur / Akademische Festouvertüre

QUEEN'S HALL

LANGHAM PLACE, W.1

Sole Lessees - Messrs. CHAPPELL & CO. Ltd.

Tuesday Subscription Concerts

APRIL 28th, at 8.15 p.m.

LOTTE LEHMANN

At the Piano - LEO ROSENEK

Lehmann in *Fidelio*, 1934, with Joseph Kalenberg

Fidelio, with Richard Strauss conducting, 1932

Fidelio, rehearsing with Toscanini, 1935

Clemens Krauss

Lehmann with Thomas Mann, Bruno Walter and family

Alfred Jerger, Lotte Lehmann and Lothar Wallerstein with Richard Strauss after the first Vienna performance of *Arabella*, 1933

Otto Klemperer and Lotte Lehmann, Lucerne, 1972

Lotte Lehmann in her limousine

LOTTE

LEHMANN

TWELVE
MASTER
CLASSES

in

Opera and Lieder

presented by

THE NATIONAL
SCHOOL OF
OPERA

at the

WIGMORE
HALL

from

4th May

to

3rd June, 1959

"Interpreter, producer, instructor and inspiration in one"
THE TIMES, 24th September, 1957

Management IBBS and TILLETT LTD., 124 Wigmore Street, London, W.1.

The 1959 Master Classes in London

was announced that he was ill. Krauss took over his proposed direction of *Fidelio*. But when he was seen, as large as life and looking particularly healthy, in the audience for *Elektra*, there was incomprehension as well as applause.

One very potent addition to the Festival was Arturo Toscanini, making his first appearance there. He gave two evening orchestral concerts with the Vienna Philharmonic Orchestra and between them, at eleven in the morning on 26 August, an all-Wagner concert. Toscanini's clear, subtle and perfectly-judged performances astonished all those who had never heard him before. Lotte sang Elisabeth's aria from *Tannhäuser*, then three of the Wesendonek *Gedichte*: 'Im Treibhaus', 'Schmerzen' and 'Träume'.

The Toscanini concerts were regarded as the artistic culmination of the Festival; and from the general public's point of view he and Bruno Walter performed with greater satisfaction than 'the Krauss clique'. Indeed, the *New York Times* correspondent, in a round-up of the Festival,[19] did not disguise the fact that 'Clemens Krauss and his partisans are greatly cut-up over the unbroken succession of Walter and Toscanini triumphs and are excogitating counter-measures for future emergencies. Rightly or wrongly, Krauss is convinced that the victories of his rivals have elbowed him into a shadowy background – an intolerable location for the Pooh-Bah of the Vienna Staatsoper . . . and the withdrawal of *The Woman without a Shadow* – one of his pet hobbies – in favor of still another Walter *Don Giovanni* came near breaking the camel's back.

'The consequences of Krauss's present irritation may be far-reaching and, so far as the artistic distinction of the Salzburg Festival is concerned, dangerous.'

Other critics also noticed the 'Krauss Zorn' (Krauss's wrath) while the unwelcome, political interference caused a temporary curfew for foreign visitors, on holiday in an artistic and historical city, that could do great damage to future years' trade.

Lotte still had a Lieder Recital with Bruno Walter, demanded after their success in the previous year. Their programme was again skilfully put together with the 'Frauenliebe und leben' in the centre; Beethoven, Schubert, Brahms and Hugo Wolf surrounding it. The press was again ecstatic, blessing the conjunction of two such perfect artists, for whose performance every scrap of space was taken in the Mozarteum, and whose every song was delivered with joy and freshness as at a first hearing.

The 1934 Salzburg Festival ended shortly before lunchtime on 2 September with the last notes of Wolf's 'Er ist's'.

The beginning of the 1934–35 Vienna Opera Season was one of displayed rivalry between Lotte and Ursuleac against an evident feeling of great disgruntlement on Krauss's part. So far as the two sopranos were concerned they produced a tension in the House until the middle of October, with each one doing her utmost to outface the other. Of course this is meat and drink to the Viennese who positively revelled in it. Although Ursuleac had the full support of the Musical Director, her bill of fare was no more varied, no more highly coloured than Lotte's:

Ursuleac	*Lehmann*
Elisabeth × 2	Tatiana × 2
Fiordiligi × 2	Elisabeth × 2
Countess	Leonore × 2
Chrysothemis	Elsa
Empress	Manon
Eva × 2	Marschallin
Marschallin	Sieglinde
Sieglinde	Madeleine
Arabella	Mimi

With twelve performances each and in the order shown above, 11 of Lotte's were all crowded into the month of September with the last Elisabeth in October. (Her last *Manon* with Piccaver was on 15 September, so ending the legend (that they *always* sang it together)[20] which still goes on.)

By contrast, Ursuleac's dozen performances were spread over more than twice that time, giving her the advantage of vocal rest. Not that she needed it all that much, for the instrument was solid and she was resourceful. Hildegard Ranczak remarks:[21]

> She had a lovely facile top. I was constantly amazed at the two hours' vocalizing she went through before each performance. Hers was, in my opinion, a marvellously constructed, not really natural voice which she used with uncanny intelligence.

Lotte was still convinced that Ursuleac had 'filched her Arabella performances and was smarting under this injustice; then the one *Frau ohne Schatten* scheduled for the autumn was placed on 9 October, which she swore was done purposely because on 10th she had a concert in

Vienna with Toscanini. So she missed that *Frau*, because the concert could not be given her best voice after singing the Dyer's Wife.

For the first time, Lotte was going to sing Isolde's Liebestod under Toscanini's baton. This followed Wagner's own composite arrangement of Prelude and lead-in to the opera's closing 'aria'. The singer's entrance is a little difficult to pitch but Toscanini said to Lotte, 'Don't worry, when the time comes, I will give you the note.'

But when the time came, at the concert, all Lotte heard from Toscanini was a gruff, buzzing sound that was not a properly pitched note at all. When Lotte told people about this after, and they asked her how she managed, she replied, 'I prayed to God, and He gave me the note!'[22]

This was the concert for which Toscanini had persuaded her to sing the complete Wesendonck Lieder of five songs, with orchestra. Lotte did not normally sing 'Im Treibhaus' (No.3) and disliked No 4, 'Schmerzen', especially after the Maestro had told her that he considered it to be musically weak.[23] 'You *must* sing 'Im Treibhaus', he wrote to her, promising a tempo to suit her voice, telling her it was going to be very beautiful, and persuading her to give him the great pleasure of hearing her sing it – for him. She could not refuse on that occasion, though it is unlikely that she sang it again very often, if at all, in spite of the fact that she recorded 'Im Treibhaus' in 1941. (Discog. 395)

After the very successful Toscanini concert in Vienna, Lotte went to London for a Lieder recital at Queen's Hall – which was packed – accompanied by Leo Rosenek, on 23 October. She then left Europe for San Francisco.

In her absence there was a remarkable upheaval at the Opera in Vienna, resulting from another in Berlin, both of which were to have a decidedly helpful effect – albeit temporarily – on Lotte's peace of mind when she returned.

When Wilhelm Furtwängler had been forbidden to stage the Hindemith opera *Mathis der Maler*, he had fulminated against the decision for months – he was a great procrastinator – until, in November, he wrote a long article about the work and its importance to twentieth century German music. This appeared on the front page of the *Deutsche Allgemeine Zeitung* on 25th, and was repeated in many foreign newspapers on the following day. *Der Fall Hindemith* (the Hindemith Case) became a *cause célèbre*, and Furtwängler's position and offices were all in jeopardy. Hindemith, though he was an Aryan, left Nazi Germany as an example to those whose freedom of thought and of action were in danger, and emigrated to the USA. He thus undermined the position of Furtwängler who had so gallantly – though stupidly – spoken out in his defence.

Goebbels used the event to his own advantage, referring to Hindemith as 'a cultural Bolshevist, spiritually non-Aryan'. Furtwängler's artistic fate hung in the balance and needed only a push to send him down.

Clemens Krauss saw the advantage of proposing himself as the new, loyal Music Director of the Berlin Staatsoper and Erich Kleiber averred that Krauss's bag had been packed for some weeks, that he was only waiting his chance to jump in.

The chance was not long in coming. Ursuleac was on very friendly terms with Emmy Sonnemann and had managed, through her, to arrange a meeting with Hitler at Berchtesgaden.[24] In a pleasant and relaxed atmosphere, Hitler and an aide (but not Tietjen), Göring and Frau Sonnemann, Krauss and Ursuleac made up the group which broke Furtwängler and completely altered the balance of power at the Berlin State Opera.

On 4 December Furtwängler was ordered to resign and Krauss was immediately appointed in his place, with Tietjen remaining as the Intendant – and a not too friendly one at that. But Furtwängler had his supporters, who were furious, and the musical staff at the Opera were seriously alarmed, so were the orchestra, many of them Jewish and previously safe under Furtwängler's protection of them which – with difficulty and a personal roasting – he had obtained from Hitler.

Erich Kleiber also resigned on 4 December.[25] On 30 November he had given a performance of Alban Berg's 'Five Symphonic Pieces from *Lulu*' to a surprisingly passive audience when he had expected a demonstration; but he knew that it was high time he left Berlin. Still an Austrian citizen, under contract there until the beginning of January, he knew 'it was not possible to carry on in a country where music was not, like air and sunlight, free to all'.

On 8 December Kleiber conducted a performance of *Otello* for the Reich's 'National Day of Solidarity'. When Göring walked into his box before the last act he was roundly hissed by the Fourth Gallery while Kleiber was lustily cheered.

Lotte was, in many ways, fortunate to have missed all this upset, though she might have been amused to see Ursuleac scuttling off to Berlin, on Krauss's instructions and in advance of him, after her final Viennese performance as Eva on 13 November.

It was three days after this when Lotte made her début at the San Francisco Opera as Tosca. It cannot be said that this was her best creation although at least one of the critics was kind about it:[26]

> 'an unusually interesting one. . . . She did not wallow as Jeritza had when she sang "Vissi d'Arte". What she did was to give us a Tosca

evolved out of her inner consciousness . . . . She is a personality . . . . She constructs the role as it should be constructed with human conviction.'

All the hallmarks of a Lehmann-conceived role are here, but the Butterfly which followed was not as well received. Her acting, it was said[27]

'verged on the melodramatic in tragic moments but she was amazingly youthful and girlishly animated in the first act. . . .

It may have been assigned to her

'more because of her presence in San Francisco than for her utter aptness for the role.'

There were other critics and certainly members of that audience on 22 November who thought it was a mistake for Lotte, nearly forty-seven years old, to undertake the role. Dino Borgioli supported her beautifully in both instances.

On 8 December, Lotte appeared in *Tannhäuser* in Chicago, but a proposed performance as Elsa did not take place. She then travelled to New York to prepare for her Met roles in January.

Meanwhile, in Vienna, Krauss (now known as the 'Frankfurt-wangler') had encouraged Anny Konetzni – one of the two robust soprano sisters of that name – to take over the Leonores in *Fidelio* while Lotte was absent (she was to sing it only once more in Vienna). Krauss then had a première to overcome before he roughly tied together his loose ends and left the city. He merely left a letter addressed to singers, orchestra and staff saying that he had taken up a new appointment in Berlin and would not be coming back. It was extraordinarily badly received.

Chapter Nine

Chaos

1935–1938

It is ironical to find Ursuleac, in 1935, at the top of the operatic soprano tree in Berlin, in precisely the same position in which Lotte might have found herself, had she agreed to Göring's terms. Ursuleac now had a salary of RM50,000 a year, a firm list of roles that were hers alone (Arabella, the Empress, the Marschallin, Chrysothemis and Helena) and a ten-year contract with the Staatsoper. This was by Hitler's personal order, overriding the maximum contractual fees and term previously imposed by Goebbels.[1] Although Ursuleac was now the most favoured singer in the Third Reich, others had come north from Vienna with her and Krauss: Gertrude Rünger, the best Nurse in the *Frau ohne Schatten*; Franz Völker, that superb tenor; Karl Hammes, a very useful and distinguished baritone; Erich Zimmermann, a buffo tenor of quality; and Josef von Manowarda, an accomplished leading bass, and a professor at the Vienna Music Academy since 1932. He and his wife were ardent Nazis: she always wore a perspex shield over the wrist that Hitler had once kissed.

Krauss had thus not come to Berlin empty-handed, but with a strong nucleus of voices which he immediately cast in leading roles to suit them in his new opera company. Needless to say, none of them was at all popular among the resident members of the Staatsoper, who disliked their intrusion and the favouritism accorded them. It was the same 'them and us' methods of Krauss.

All the same, for Krauss and Ursuleac it was a sensible appointment in spite of their natural, human ambitions and they settled down very happily in the atmosphere of Berlin. Ursuleac, who was by far the more forceful of the pair, had concentrated upon Strauss roles in order that she might capitalise upon this accomplishment, expecting him to compose leading roles in his next operas for her. Krauss, too, considered himself, quite rightly, to have become Strauss's chief disciple and champion, but they had both over-estimated the composer's immunity from artistic persecution.

For Lotte in Vienna, it was as though a warm light had gone on and a great weight had been lifted from her. Berlin did not matter any longer to her and, for all she cared, Ursuleac might sing herself hoarse there. Nor would 'Schalk's successor' be at Salzburg in 1935. It all seemed a blessed relief after the shock of Göring's dictat in the previous autumn.

Lotte now felt secure in planning her annual engagements, with January and February in New York; Spring at Covent Garden and visits to Paris and perhaps Stockholm; July in her beloved Salzburg and, after that, Vienna for the start of the new season. Lieder recitals were also built in to this programme as a matter of course.

But in this form it was only a dream.

Lotte was in good voice and gave some memorable performances at the Met in January 1935. Originally there were to have been four performances, but they were extended to ten, some of which were to be on tour, in Boston.

Lotte had crossed out of her contract the role of Recha in *Die Jüdin*, but had especially requested *Tosca* during these negotiations. She also demanded between three to four days' 'repose' before her first Tosca and before her first appearance in Boston.[2] Her agent at the time was Erich Simon in Paris, which was a little remote. Later on Constance Hope took over all Lotte's business arrangements. For every performance, whether at the Met or on tour, Lotte was to receive $700.

Her present expectation of a happy future without any rivals was dealt a sharp blow a month later. On 2 February, a new Sieglinde made her début at the Met. It was a very different performance from Lotte's, lacking the golden sound, the feminine warmth and sexuality, the stifled longing of an unloved wife. This singer poured out a stream of silver tone in a huge voice, bigger than the Brünnhilde's, but her acting was of the statuesque kind, her dramatic pointing of the music was left partly to the imagination. The Met had not heard such a voice as Kirsten Flagstad's for fifty years.

Flagstad's appearance at the Met followed her first appearance in a major role at Bayreuth in the previous summer. She was thirty-nine, and had been on the point of retiring from a career in the Norwegian Opera, first in Oslo where she sang mainly in operetta, and then in Göteborg. After singing small parts at Bayreuth in 1933 she was 'discovered' and in the next season was snapped up by Gatti-Casazza for the Met, thanks to the recommendation of Kipnis.

On 6 February 1935, Flagstad's association with this company was assured, when she sang a ravishing Isolde – vocally ravishing. It was partly because of Isolde that Flagstad had been engaged for the Met at all, and Lotte had reason privately to curse this Irish princess of legend who had eluded her altogether on stage when she wanted to grasp her; now she was the cause of Lotte's anxiety in the personality of another singer.

Gatti-Casazza had fallen out with Frida Leider, his regular Isolde, and this necessitated calling in another singer able to replace her and, if possible, with panache. But from Lotte's point of view it was a disaster: Frida Leider did not sing Sieglinde – Flagstad did. The great Norwegian soprano had once been to a performance of Lotte's Sieglinde and was disgusted. Lotte, she said, did things on stage which only a married woman should do with her husband in the privacy of their bedroom. This is the only mention which Lotte receives in the two Flagstad biographies.

Lotte, on the other hand, was generous about Flagstad in a tiny piece of a dozen lines, written much later. She declared that Flagstad's voice was unique, she never knew her well as a person, though she seemed 'kind and very uncomplicated'. When in the third act of *Walküre*, singing alternate phrases, 'Sieglinde felt oh so greatly Brünnhilde's inferior'.[3] And that was a very friendly remark.

Lotte stayed in the USA until early April, fulfilling her engagements in Boston, and returned to a Vienna empty of Flagstad, swept clean of Krauss and Ursuleac and, most mercifully, Jeritza was about to retire.

While Clemens Krauss had been 'waiting in the wings' for his big opportunity in Berlin, another conductor was also on the *qui vive* to replace him in Vienna. Many people, including Lotte, hoped that it was going to be Bruno Walter who, as a Jew, had been obliged to quit the Charlottenburg Opera in 1934. But no, it was Felix Weingartner who was well situated to spring from the Volksoper, where he had been since 1919, back to the Opera House on the Ring. Those who had been glad to see him go in the first year of the Strauss-Schalk directorate thought better of him now. Weingartner no longer expressed his animosity towards Richard Strauss, and seemed altogether to be of a more generous and friendly disposition. Perhaps this was as a result of his fifth marriage to one of his conducting students, Carmen Studer. Weingartner was seventy-one, and Carmen was in her early twenties. So after Clemens Krauss's 'insults' and 'treachery', and his never-to-be-forgotten exit from Vienna, the familiar and by now patriarchal figure of Weingartner was not only acceptable, but welcome.

Lotte came back for a *Tosca* and a *Lohengrin* in Vienna, then went to

London for her usual summer season performances with Sir Thomas Beecham. She nearly had to call off her opening *Lohengrin* on 29 April because of a bad cold. Joan Cross, who sang Elsa in English at Sadler's Wells, was summoned to the Hyde Park Hotel (where Lotte always stayed whilst in London). Lotte asked Joan Cross whether she would be prepared to hold herself in readiness, should the performance become too taxing for her health. In the event she managed it, but it was not an enviable experience for Joan Cross, either. She realised that their interpretations were entirely different, and for her to have taken over in the middle of the opera and carried on in her own way would have led to confusion in the minds of the audience, quite apart from the language. Lotte was extremely grateful and wrote Joan Cross a charming letter of appreciation afterwards, one of many, for they remained good friends.[4]

1935 was King George V's Silver Jubilee Year, and the celebrations were at their height during the opera season. The night of Lotte's first *Walküre* coincided with the start of the festivities and everybody was in high spirits. It was good, too, to see old friends there again: Melchior, Janssen, Kipnis and Emanuel List. *Der Rosenkavalier* was absent from the bill for the second year running, much to Lotte's disappointment, but it was with a light heart and an important new recording contract from His Master's Voice in her pocket that she returned to Vienna to give three performances of Desdemona and one of Sieglinde at the beginning of June.

It is sad, in some ways, to reflect on the fact that Desdemona was Lotte's only Verdian role; yet when one looks at his heroines they are all much too big for Lotte's voice as it was when the Verdi revival took place in Germany and Austria. And there was one curious thing about her performance as Desdemona. How often it happened, or whether it was always necessary, cannot be known. In the last act, when Desdemona is left alone to pray, her Ave Maria ends with a top A flat after the majority of the range has been in the comfortable low register of the voice. Before her 'Amen' she rose from her prie-Dieu and walked upstage, back to the audience, then sang 'A-a-a-' on the tonic triad of A flat but with a flick of her wrists, arms uplifted, gave the impression of actually singing the top A flat, which she did not! Then she turned round to face the audience to sing the last 'Amen' on a comfortable Soprano C.[5] She did not record this Ave Maria, only an abbreviated version of the 'Willow Song' without the Emilia that precedes it. (See Discog. 62 & 216.)

Lotte's Desdemonas in Vienna were all with the splendid tenor from the Charlottenburg Opera, Gotthelf Pistor (a native of Cologne) who had sung the Heldentenor roles at Bayreuth between 1927–31. Victor De Sabata conducted. He was being tried out as a possible permanent conductor in Vienna, and this opera was a speciality of his.

It was the Sieglinde that had a special significance. The casting of this performance of *Walküre* was unusual: Richard Schubert as Siegmund; Friedrich Schorr as Wotan, (a guest from the Met); and Anny Konetzni as Brünnhilde. But the significance lay in this being a Sieglinde that has been preserved for ever. Lotte's contract with HMV was for a recording of the whole of Act I of *Walküre* and a part of Act II, preparatory to the whole opera being committed to disc with the best Wagnerian singers then available.

With Melchior as Siegmund, Emanuel List as Hunding and the Vienna Philharmonic Orchestra conducted by Bruno Walter, the recording was rapidly made in the Grosse Musikvereinsaal in Vienna between 20–22 June. All Act I was made in two days; and on 22 June they went on to the Sieglinde passages from Act II, altogether some of the most vivid recordings that Lotte ever achieved. Much has been said about her smouldering interpretation at the beginning of Act I which literally bursts into flames with the love duet as all Sieglinde's pent-up emotions at last find their release in this unexpected love for her long-lost twin brother. Then, in the second act, she expresses such fear for their safety from Hunding and such remorse for the incestuous relationship that Lotte seems to come out of the records in her terror and anguish. (See Discog. 262–282.)

On the second day of this recording, Alfred Roller died, and there were two more significant deaths before the end of the year: Gutheil-Schoder passed away in October and Richard Mayr in December.

Lotte rounded off her season in Vienna with a *Rosenkavalier* that was a kind of preparation for Salzburg, with Jarmila Novotná as Octavian and Fritz Krenn as Ochs. Josef Krips conducted, and was again in charge of the first two performances of that opera which began the Salzburg Festival of 1935. The highlight though, was Toscanini's production of *Fidelio*.

The little Maestro was also going to produce and conduct *Falstaff* with Mariano Stabile and a cast from La Scala, Milan. Toscanini demanded absolute authority in casting and rehearsing in both operas, in return for which he required no fee. His only desire was for perfection in all he did. He planned all the rehearsal schedules himself for singers and sections of the orchestra. The accompanist for the singers at early rehearsals was a very talented Austrian pianist, only twenty-two years of age, named Erich Leinsdorf.

Toscanini was sixty-eight and had not conducted any opera since he stormed out of La Scala in 1929 because he was unable to tolerate their slackness, and was not empowered to change it. His grip on every aspect of the two operas that season in Salzburg was quite extraordinary: he was tireless and he was ruthless. He was staying in Liefering, a village not far away, surrounded by his large family of daughters, sons-in-law, children, his wife, her sister and husband, as well as other, more distant relatives. Sitting next to his chauffeur, Emilio, he motored to the Festspielhaus in his Cadillac, wearing a beret and smiling in a friendly manner at the crowds who lined the streets to welcome him.[6] For Toscanini was, at this time, the most idolised man in this part of Austria, as well as being one of Adolf Hitler's most hated opponents.

When Toscanini had seen the way things were going in Nazi Germany, he refused to conduct again at Bayreuth in 1934. His *Tannhäuser, Tristan* and *Parsifal* in 1931 and 1933 had been revelations to everyone there, not excepting the bassoons for *Parsifal*. Toscanini stopped an orchestral rehearsal and checked them for playing a wrong note, 'B natural' he said, 'B flat' they replied, 'we have been playing this for years and we have the Bayreuth parts.' Toscanini, who always had the score in his head was certain that he was right, and proved himself to be correct and the parts incorrect when he sent for Wagner's own score and examined it in front of the orchestra. Conductors of *Parsifal* since 1882 had failed to notice this one wrong note, but Toscanini heard it instantly.

Naturally everybody wanted Toscanini back at Bayreuth in 1934 but he refused. It is said that Hitler telephoned him personally with the invitation. What Toscanini said has never been divulged, but witnesses reported that Hitler went purple in the face with rage and did not allow Toscanini's name to be mentioned in his presence thereafter. Richard Strauss took over the *Parsifal* that year, for purely musical, not political reasons.

Toscanini's 'spiritual surrender to the music' had been described by Lotte. Having worked with him before only in concert, she was amazed to find that he was a man of the theatre to his fingertips and every rehearsal was as near to the actual performance as possible 'and every performance is a "festival performance".'[7] Whenever he arrived at the Festspielhaus for a rehearsal, photographers and autograph hunters swarmed round him, but he pushed them aside, arriving in the rehearsal room out of sorts. But as soon as Leinsdorf began to play and the singers were launched into their music, Toscanini mellowed, and at once became 'under the spell, . . . his anger transformed to beaming smiles.'

There was no Richard Mayr in *Rosenkavalier* any more, for he was dying in his house in Salzburg, and Lotte spent as much time as she could sitting beside his bed. He was bound to be in the minds of all those who knew him and had seen his extraordinary assumption of Baron Ochs, the greatest one there has ever been. For Strauss had Mayr in mind when he was composing it. When Strauss told him this, Mayr replied that he didn't quite know how to take that kind of remark. He had sung every Ochs at Salzburg since the first *Rosenkavalier* there in 1929, consequently he and Lotte had developed a wonderful partnership, particularly as they often sang together in Vienna. It was not easy for her to adapt to Fritz Krenn's altogether different approach, for although Krenn was Viennese the *Salzburger Volksblatt*'s critic thought he seemed less so than the true Salzburger, Mayr.

There were, of course, a good many arguments for and against the (German) Schalk production of *Fidelio* in previous years, and the (Italian) Toscanini production which astonished all[8] who first heard it on 7 August 1935. But opinions of Lotte's performance remained unanimous.

Her 'fermata on B in Leonore's big aria was like a banner on the mountain-top streaming in the wind' said the critic of the *Salzburger Volksblatt*, 'a strong, glorious wind. Everything is clear, is spacious and bright. Brave new world!' Hers was an 'overpowering accomplishment' in every way, including her spoken words that sounded like music, especially in the climax of the dialogue when the heroine's love for her husband shone through them. When Florestan asks Leonore, knowing her strength but fearing the terrible time she has had before finding him: 'What have you done for me, my Leonore?' she replies simply and directly, but with tremendous understatement: 'Nichts, nichts mein Florestan' ('Nothing, nothing at all, my own Florestan').[9] The way in which Lotte spoke this simple sentence is said to have reduced sensitive members of the audience to tears.

According to the newspaper, it was 'Toscanini's fire which engulfed everything and everybody, including the producer, Dr. Wallerstein', who was acting reluctantly under Toscanini's instructions but had to be there as a member of the festival staff. All four performances were sold out and tickets were being sold for extremely high prices outside the theatre.

Between the second and third *Fidelios*, on 20 August, Lotte and Bruno Walter gave their usual Lieder Recital. It began at 11 am in the Mozarteum with four Mozart songs, four Schumann songs, and then ranged widely from Duparc's 'L'Invitation au Voyage' and 'Extase', to Mussorgsky, Berlioz and finally four Brahms Lieder, of which the last was the joyous 'Meine Liebe ist grün'. It was considered that the 'two darlings of Salzburg' had brought music and words together to make 'a new art-form' before a large, critical but enthusiastic audience.

The critic of the *Salzburger Chronik* noted that in 'Widmung' (the first of the group of Schumann songs) 'mein bess'res Ich' was sung by 'Leonore-Lehmann' in the same glorious manner as her fondest line to Florestan had been in the opera.

It had been the happiest month in Salzburg that Lotte could remember and she returned to Vienna for nine performances in eight different roles – including a Leonore – throughout the month of September. On 1 October, Jeritza made her last (pre-war) appearance at the Vienna Opera as Tosca. She and Lotte then sailed to the United States – but not together.

Lotte had some recordings for Victor in New York on 17 October. Victor was the American affiliate of HMV. The recordings were all Lieder (see Discog. Nos. 283–292) and her accompanist was still Ernö Balogh.

For the first time she took her two Viennese maids, Resi and Marie, with her to New York, together with her small brown Pomeranian called Mohrle that had belonged to her mother. When Lotte reached Chicago for three performances there (a *Lohengrin* and two *Rosenkavaliers*) she was given another Pomeranian which she called Jimmy, because that sounded a suitably American name for an American dog. Resi had stayed in New York and Marie was with Lotte in Chicago.

During the first act of *Rosenkavalier* on 16 November, Marie was standing in the wings with Jimmy in her arms, watching the first act, when the stage manager came towards her. 'Just what I want,' he said, snatching Jimmy from her and giving it to the Animal Vendor in the Levée Scene. Jimmy was absolutely terrified and remained perfectly still during his stage début, but Lotte was horrified, and so was Marie, dancing about and gesticulating in the wings.[10]

In Vienna an unusual event had occurred overnight on 21/22 November. Up to the *Rheingold* of 21st, all surnames on the posters and programmes of the Court – and afterwards the State – Opera had been prefaced by Dr. Herr, Frau or Fräulein (the latter two abbreviated to Fr. and Frl.). But for the *Orpheus* on 22nd, and thereafter, the cosier forename was added between each prefix-title and surname.

Lotte was at the Met for two performances round Christmas: an Elsa beforehand and an Elisabeth on Boxing Day. Then on 31 January came Lotte's Tosca. For a generation and more of audiences innured to the extravagances of Jeritza's Roman diva, Lotte's seemed flat and tame. It was more thoughtful, more emotional in a controlled way, dramatic on a different plane. In both intervals, odious comparisons were made, and most of them to Lotte's disadvantage. Lanfranco Rasponi, who heard her Tosca at San Francisco, expressed surprise that 'she had allowed Edward Johnson to talk her into repeating her error in New York. . . . The temperament and the passion were very much there, but she could not help turning the Roman prima donna into a provincial character.'[11]

Lotte made twenty-seven song recordings for Victor in March (Discog. 293–314) before going down to Boston again. Returning to Vienna in April, she was off for Madeleine in *Andrea Chénier* on 20th, one of the few times she was unable to sing when billed. Zdenka Zika took her place. Lotte's Sieglinde on 16 April had been conducted by Hans Knappertsbusch as a guest, and he also took the *Rosenkavalier* on 22nd with Berthold Sternick as a new Ochs: one who did not return.

On 28 April she was at Queen's Hall in London, with Leo Rosenek, and in a programme that was not only a popular one, but seemed to be advertising her gramophone records:

Schubert	Nähe des Geliebten
	Auflösung
	Im Abendrot*
	Rastlose Liebe
Brahms	Von ewiger Liebe*
	Der Tod, das ist die kühle Nacht
	Das Mädchen spricht
	Meine Liebe ist grün*
Schumann	Widmung*
	Die Kartenlegerin*
	Ich grolle nicht*
	Frühlingsnacht*
Tchaikovsky	Nur wer die Sehnsucht kennt
Rubinstein	Es blinkt der Thau
Worth	Midsummer*
Cimara	Canto di Primavera

The encores were:

Brahms	Botschaft*
	Der Schmied*
Schumann	An den Sonnenschein*
Gretchaninov	My native land*
R. Strauss	Zueignung*
Brahms	Wiegenlied*

The songs marked * were available on records. The Cimara song had been recorded, but was unpublished (Discog. 296).

The number of encores displays the affection which Lotte had gained in London. *The Daily Telegraph* critic said of this recital:[12]

> So exquisite and so poignant can her voice be that at times a single note sufficed to enhance the effect of a whole song. The whole of Brahms's 'Der Tod, das ist die kühle Nacht' was excellent, but the ravishing softness of its last phrase sealed the success of that performance and made one wonder where and by whom it could ever be equalled.

Lotte returned to Vienna, having promised London another recital, and sang two Desdemonas opposite the Swedish tenor, Carl Martin Öhmann and under Victor De Sabata's baton once more. But she was indisposed for *Manon* on 22 May. It is sad to see how the political stresses of the time seem to have caused far more singers than usual to be off, even the resilient Lotte.

The Vienna management were trying out a great number of principal singers, as well as conductors such as De Sabata, and Furtwängler who had come for three *Tannhäusers* while Lotte was abroad. There was a new Minnie in Jeritza's old saddle for *The Girl of the Golden West* in Vera Schwarz; Jussi Björling from Stockholm sang his incomparably sweet Rodolfo and Radames with about as much stage movement and interest as Piccaver possessed; and Bruno Walter conducted *Eugen Onegin* as a guest, at the close of the season in June, with Lotte in her famous role of Tatiana. She was nearly off again – programmes and bills were slipped: 'Fr. Lotte Lehmann fühlt sich indisponiert und bittet um gütige Nachsicht'. But this was a much-beloved and famous interpretation so Lotte overcame all her 'indispositions' and did not let down her audience.

For once, she had not sung at Covent Garden during the Summer Season in London because her Met and Vienna dates had made it impossible. Nevertheless, her two Lieder Recitals did much to keep her well to the front of her fans' minds. After her second recital on 25 May, Lotte went to Paris with the Vienna Opera where she sang a single Leonore on 4 June. This was the first time it had been heard at l'Opéra since this company's visit of 1928. This time Franz Völker (on loan from Berlin) was the Florestan, since this was an important occasion for friendship, and Bruno Walter conducted.

The sensitive and astute French composer, Reynaldo Hahn has left a short account of his impressions from this performance:[13]

> Bruno Walter gave the second *Leonore* Overture and from its playing the conductor seemed more attuned to Beethoven than he was to Mozart. As for Mme Lotte Lehmann, I have already had the opportunity of praising the talent and the fire which she produces in the fine role of Fidelio. But this time, did she let us have them with as much generosity as before, at l'Opéra, or, let me add, as she has done recently in Vienna? I thought I perceived her necessity to err on the side of caution, both in movement and in breathing. Her richly-endowed voice and her profound singing technique combined with her superb lyric ability are enough to allow her to 'give' more without risking the slightest danger.

So this was in the nature of a criticism of her unwillingness to 'let go', something which she was not accustomed to reading.

Since her childhood, Lotte had wondered whether she was going to be a writer, and now she decided to write not one, but two books. The first, which she called 'Anfang und Aufstieg' was to be an autobiography, and because she never kept a diary, all dates and events had to be remembered. But this was not all. Isolde had so got hold of Lotte, and would not leave her, that she had the idea of a novel, undoubtedly based on certain events in her own life and with characters (especially the American ones) who were known to her. It was to be about two sisters, dancers, and of very different temperament; as well as a beautiful, lonely, silent and tragic operatic soprano, famed for her Isolde. This was to be called 'Orplid, mein Land', a quotation from the beginning of Eduard Mörike's poem set by Hugo Wolf about a make-up land in a song by an invented person. Thus 'Gesang Weylas' (Weyla's Song) is without dramatic or operatic provenance, and Orplid occurs in no atlas. This partly fairy-tale element goes no further in Lotte's novel, which is frankly novelettish.

The harsh wheels of the Vienna Opera management, which still sometimes grind their chief conductors into the dust, performed this function on Weingartner by appointing a kind of dual directorship once more, with Bruno Walter and Dr Erwin Kerber. Kerber was a good administrator and had been connected with the Salzburg Festival for some years. He liked Walter, and got on well with him. It would probably have been a golden era of the Vienna Opera, had it lasted, but in any case Kerber was obliged to accept Walter, whose personal patron and protector was no less a person than Kurt von Schuschnigg, the Austrian Chancellor.

For once there was no animosity between the departing Weingartner and the incoming Kerber and Walter, for as well as Toscanini at the 1936

Salzburg Festival, Weingartner was invited to conduct *Figaro* and *Cosi*. Bruno Walter had *Don Giovanni*, Gluck's *Orpheus* and Hugo Wolf's seldom-heard and only completed opera *Der Corregidor*.

The Festival opened with *Fidelio* on 25 July, but somehow Lotte did not rise to the occasion throughout the first act. Critics found it all stiff, some of the characters poorly cast (except for Luise Helletsgruber's Marzelline). The scenery was regarded as indifferent, and several critics noticed that the singers seemed frightened by Toscanini, 'a musician of the first magnitude and color' according to the *New York Times* (also stated elsewhere) who went on to declare that *Fidelio* came to life 'the instant Toscanini lifted his baton for the second act.' Then Lotte 'threw caution to the winds and her voice took on all of its womanly strength and color, and as an actress she became a great tragedienne.'

It was another opera which attracted the main attention this year. After Toscanini had repeated his previous year's *Falstaff* with much the same cast as in 1935, he presented *Die Meistersinger* for the first time in Salzburg. The American author Marcia Davenport, a friend of both Toscanini and of Lotte, has described her impression of the conductor at this time:[14]

> I used to think as I watched him at the most exhaustive and exacting labour I have ever seen how he had said at the age of sixty that he was too old for the Philharmonic; but three months after that retirement he was driving himself and the huge complex of elements in *Die Meistersinger* with the energy of a man of thirty, and a demonic one besides. After the first preparatory work with the singers, and the first orchestral rehearsals, the stage rehearsals began. There was no detail of the production that did not get his minute attention and show the effects of his insistence on perfection. He was all over the place. He stayed in his pit so long as the work went to his satisfaction. If not, if he wanted a change on the stage in action, lighting, setting, business (the riot in the second act!) he was up on the stage. Sometimes we heard his hoarse voice call 'Graf!' from the dark back of the theatre where he had run to see how the scene looked in perspective; and he did see no matter what he insisted about his own poor eyesight or what legend has said of it. Herbert Graf, the stage director, and all the company slaved for him. Lotte was the Eva, a part she had never liked much, but this time she had potent reason to change her mind. The rehearsals culminated in the historic dress rehearsal which has been cited time and again as one of the great moments of operatic history.

For Lotte the dress rehearsal was unforgettable, 'one of life's precious gifts'. She describes the rehearsals for this *Meistersinger* as 'nerve-shattering' because Toscanini was thoroughly dissatisfied with everything they did. Instead of breaking into one of those passionate tempers for which he was infamous, he merely sat in the pit in 'icy silence' looking at them with the kind of scornful expression which a school-teacher might wear before a class of naughty children who were purposely misbehaving so as to annoy him. As a result of Toscanini's impenetrable expression, and the fact that he did not say what was wrong, the singers all became nervous, making the most stupid mistakes and wishing that the Maestro would erupt. But he continued to sit there looking personally affronted.

It says much for Lotte's courage, or perhaps the relationship between Lotte and Toscanini allowed her, and her alone, to make an approach from the stage. She asked him directly, and in front of the cast and orchestra, 'Won't you please tell us *what* you want?' Lotte says that he looked at her with the eyes of 'a dying fawn' and replied: 'There is no fire!'

Then Toscanini smiled, and the fire was thereby kindled.[15]

The Hans Sachs for this production was to have been Friedrich Schorr, but Toscanini refused to accept him. He was reckoned to be the finest Sachs alive, but his voice no longer had the bloom which Toscanini required. Hans-Hermann Nissen was summoned from Munich,[16] a placid man who seemed never to suffer from stage-fright nor nervousness of any kind. For the first time he was caught up in the general excitement of this rehearsal and as he turned round after the 'Wach auf' chorus, he cried: 'My God, how shall I be able to sing any more? That demon has devastated me with his fire!' Marcia Davenport was there:[17]

> . . . the memory of Maestro in his black cassock-like rehearsal coat with the light on his face remains as vivid as on that day . . . But when the curtain fell on the finale, and then went up again as curtains do at rehearsals for technical reasons, there stood the entire company on stage, every one of them in tears. Maestro himself stood motionless in his place with his right hand covering his eyes. I do not know what may have lain in the hearts of those singers and musicians but I have often sensed that for some of them this was their defiant defence of their German heritage in the face of the obscenities across the frontier.

Lotte was absolutely delirious after the rehearsal and rushed heedlessly into Toscanini's dressing-room to find him with practically no clothes on (he always perspired profusely). Neither of them cared, but Emilio was horrified.[18] Lotte tearfully embraced Toscanini and merely stammered 'Thank you, Maestro . . .'

For those who were not present at that rehearsal, the four performances of that season's *Meistersinger* were declared a *miracle*. Lotte had been singing Eva since 1914 and consistently in Vienna (some fifty times to be precise), so it was odd to find Marcia Davenport believing that Lotte did not care for the role.[19] Furthermore the critic of the Basle *National Zeitung* complained that Lotte 'was not born to the part or perhaps she had been born too early', which was nasty. All this may have begun a campaign to put Lotte off singing Eva any more, the first such opposition from outside the opera house that she had encountered.

The première was an extraordinary success, more so than the *Fidelio* in 1935, and possibly on account of the subject. A social note gave a turnout for the *Meistersinger* performance on 8 August as 370 motor-cars, two omnibuses, seven horsedrawn cabs – and Marlene Dietrich.[20]

The *Vienna Reichpost*'s critic, reviewing the recital of 12 August had this to say: [21]

> The annual Liederabend by Lotte Lehmann and Bruno Walter came earlier than usual in the Festival progamme, between the first and second *Meistersinger* performances. There were four groups of songs, by Brahms, Mendelssohn, Cornelius and Franz and Hugo Wolf. Thus it was a recital for connoisseurs insofar as Schubert, Schumann, Mozart and Richard Strauss were not represented. The great opera star descended among the mortals and stood with them, but so much was she still the great artist that they never for a moment doubted the perfection of her singing. Besides, with Bruno Walter as her accompanist, there was complete safety and a unison of minds. The enormous ovation rose above the banks of flowers which formed a barricade between audience and performers. Bruno Walter was decorated with a laurel-wreath and Lotte Lehmann with yet more flowers. Walter was not merely an accompanist, but a partner, drawing from the singer yet more wonder and beauty by means of his own poetic playing.

1936 was the year when Toscanini added his voice and his artistic weight towards plans for a new Festspielhaus in Salzburg, and both he and Lotte were among many who subscribed handsomely to the building fund. As long before that as 1880, Hans Richter had advocated a proper festival theatre in Salzburg but it had never got further than architects' drawings, nor was it to be realised until 1960.[22]

Lotte returned to Vienna feeling happy and elated after the Festival only to find that Flagstad had arrived to sing Brünnhilde as a guest from the Met, with Max Lorenz, Siegmund and another soprano singing Sieglinde. This 1936/37 season in Vienna was the leanest that Lotte had ever been given, with a total of only five performances and all in September, but it was really her own fault. She had told the management of her plans for the coming year which precluded any length of time in Vienna at all. (In fact, after her performance as Tatiana on 27 September 1936, Lotte was not heard again in Vienna until 1 September 1937.)

Toscanini came in September 1936 to conduct two *Fidelios* with mainly the same cast as at Salzburg, and a guest from the Charlottenburg Opera in Berlin (now known as the Deutsche Oper), Anton Baumann, sang Rocco again.

15 September 1936 was Bruno Walter's sixtieth birthday and Lotte attended his party at Semmering's Südbahn Hotel outside Vienna. Alma and Fritz Werfel were there, as well as Walter's family and it was a very happy occasion. Chancellor Schuschnigg sent a congratulatory telegram for he had reason to be particularly grateful to Walter, in a sentimental way. Since the Chancellor's wife died, he had been to every possible performance Walter had given of Gluck's *Orpheus,* seeing the story as a reflection of his own sad bereavement, though not comprehending the music at all.

Schuschnigg was becoming more and more the target for adverse propaganda from Berlin and, perhaps unwisely, he made a number of changes and restrictions which were inclined to undermine his position even further. One of these was a move away from the German Gothic typeface, so favoured by Hitler, and on 1 November, *Parsifal* became the first work at the Vienna Opera to be billed, and to have its programme printed, in Roman characters.

By then, Lotte was in the United States again where she appeared in San Francisco for two performances of *Die Walküre* on 13 and 22 November, and one of *Tosca* on 18th. She seemed determined to overcome disapproval of her *Tosca* by repetition, but again it received only lukewarm notices.

The *Walküre* performances, on the other hand, were acclaimed. Under Fritz Reiner's confident and experienced hand, Flagstad, Lotte, Kathryn Meisle (Fricka), Melchior and Emanuel List gave performances of enormous stature, accompanied by Schorr's sadly worn voice. Most of the second act of the second performance has been preserved.

Lotte then moved eastwards to New York and the Met where she gave a matinée performance of *Walküre* on 16 January. The *New York Times* critic enthused over her Sieglinde:

> Perhaps the most magical of Wagner's women is Sieglinde. She is not the greatest, but she haunts us longest. Like the Iphigenia of Euripides, she is passionate and tender, simple and complex, piteous and wise, strong and weak, heroic and shrinking; and her purity is as elemental as her passion . . . No singing-actress of our time, I think, has achieved a more telling and veracious Sieglinde than Lotte Lehmann . . . It gives us the essence of the character, this remarkable and deeply touching embodiment of Mme Lehmann's . . . In certain moments of exceptional exactness and felicity of suggestion, she colors her voice and shapes her gestures with something of the primitive magic and strangeness and wonder of those who were daughters of earth in old, far-off, forgotten, times . . . It was one of the signals of Mme Lehmann's achievement yesterday that she was most piercing and most memorable when the music was. Wagner . . . speaks of the agonizing utterances of sorrow that this score contains – 'I have had to pay for the expression of these sorrows,' he remarks parenthetically. Mme Lehmann's delivery of Sieglinde's music in her frenzied scene with Siegmund in the Second Act made us realize with peculiar vividness what Wagner must have meant. In such measures as . . . 'Wo bist du, Siegmund?' she charged the music with an almost insupportable intensity of tragic woe.

On 25 January she sang Elisabeth; then her last Eva at the Met was on 12 February, a matinée. In March she had some recordings to make for Victor, an astonishing session of eighteen assorted Lieder (Discog. 301–314) all made on 16 March, but not released in the UK.

Lotte seldom travelled anywhere these days without her last Christmas present from Otto, a typewriter. Admittedly she found it a bit of a struggle to get the right letters to come out on the paper, but she found it useful when writing her books.

It was at Christmas time, too, that the jealousy and the upsets caused by Krauss and Ursuleac in Berlin resulted in their both being hustled out of the Nazi capital. Goebbels and Tietjen were said to have engineered it although the details are still confused.[23] Tietjen and Krauss had had an angry debate in the Intendant's office which, unknown to Krauss, was being recorded. Later, Tietjen played back part of this squabble, and Krauss is said to have gone pale. It was used as an instrument of blackmail.[24] There had nearly been a strike among the 'old guard' at the Berlin Staatsoper over Krauss's favouritism to his followers and especially over salaries, so Hitler had been obliged to sanction the dismissal while making it look like an artistic transfer. Krauss and Ursuleac were 'posted' to Munich in the form of a promotion to start at the beginning of 1937 with an unprecedented salary for Krauss of RM50,000 per annum for ten years (the normal length was three). The papers signed by Hitler still exist.[25]

Munich was close to Garmisch where Strauss lived, and accordingly Krauss conceived the idea of mounting all the composer's stage works, operas and ballets, in ideal performances under ideal conditions, and with the assistance and the approval of Strauss himself, down to the last detail.

Ursuleac came at the right time for the composer. She sang ten principal Strauss roles (including – surprisingly – the Composer in *Ariadne*, though never Christine). The Marschallin tops the Ursuleac list as compiled by Signe von Scanzoni who gives a total of 482 Strauss performances in Ursuleac's career.[26] Outside Strauss, though, her repertoire was small compared to Lotte's and her sphere of operations was much narrower, especially as their voices were entirely different. If anything, Ursuleac's more closely resembled Jeritza's with their 'brilliance and rainbow colour – defying mechanical reproduction' as Ida Cook describes them.[27] That is true. None of Jeritza's nor Ursuleac's gramophone records matches even the less successful of Lotte's, for full-bodied, full-hearted exuberance; though probably both Lotte's adversaries possessed firmer singing techniques and were just as effective on stage in their own ways.

Richard Strauss admired Ursuleac, not only for her vocal ability and intelligence, but for her complete willingness to sing his roles in the critical year when he was *persona non grata* with the Nazis. Strauss's letters to singers and directors of opera houses all emphasise his supreme desire to have his works sung and staged consistently. His praise is fulsome when they are: but snappy when there seems to be a falling off in performances of his works. 'Du bist meine beste/schönste/liebste Arabella' Strauss wrote with one adjective on each of three different dedications,[28] so that they would all go on singing this role in the belief that each was his favourite. Who said that Strauss was no businessman?

Lotte and Otto had a quiet holiday in Santa Barbara before embarking on the SS *Monterey* in San Francisco for Hawaii, Fiji and Auckland for Sidney. This was for a concert tour of Australia which was being sponsored by the Australian Broadcasting Commission.[29] In previous years, other international singers had visited Australia and Lotte was to be the 'star' for 1937. The tour was to last for six weeks and embraced appearances in Sydney, Melbourne and Canberra. Lotte was so full of enthusiasm for it that she resolved to keep a diary of events, the only careful one she ever made.

They arrived in Sydney Harbour on 19 April, and as soon as the liner had berthed, a microphone was run out on deck where Lotte appeared with Otto and Ulanowsky, who was to be her accompanist for the tour. There they were met by the Chairman and Managing Director of ABC. They introduced Lotte, in a live broadcast, to the Australian listeners, then turned to Otto Krause. He made distress signals and when the microphone was brought to him, all he provided was a torrent of German.

'Forgive my poor husband,' laughed Lotte, coming to his rescue, 'he cannot speak English!' Later, though, he was persuaded to allow Ulanowsky to translate for him over the air when he declared that he had never missed a single one of his wife's performances in the opera house or the concert hall during the past sixteen years. Australia, he said, was like a fairy-tale land to most Europeans, and he and his wife had heard something of it from other singers who had been there already, notably Richard Crooks, Elisabeth Rethberg and Ezio Pinza.

When Lotte was then asked to pose for photographs, she regretted that she was unable to smile because she was – they both were – so *hungry*. It was two o'clock and they had not lunched – yet. So with that tactful *valete*, the broadcast came to an end.

That evening there was a reception at which the building of a Sydney Opera House was discussed in the hope that Lotte would support the idea and further the cause, especially as 1938 was to be the 150th anniversary of the founding of the city.

Four events had been arranged for Lotte in Sydney: three Lieder Recitals and one concert with the Sydney Symphony Orchestra. Lotte had wanted all-Lieder Recitals, but the organisers knew that their audiences would want some operatic arias, even though it was only a piano accompanying them. Lotte eventually agreed, though with some reluctance.

The first recital at the Town Hall on 22 April was given to an expectant, capacity audience – one that eventually proved Lotte's wish to perform only Lieder with piano. She held the audience rapt. They liked the simplicity – a 'noble simplicity, there were no artificial effects, no straining after bravura' said the *Sydney Morning Herald*'s critic. The very intimacy of her expression, in songs that may have been entirely unfamiliar, seemed to stem from her own 'rich, sympathetic and serene personality'. The most gripping moment of the evening was her interpretation of Schubert's 'Erlkönig', demonstrating her versatility of style and Ulanowsky's mastery of the piano. The concert should have ended with Wolf's 'In dem Schatten meiner Locken' but there was so much applause that two English songs formed separate encores. The last of these, 'Do not chide me', ended with 'Goodnight' sung three times, which conveniently took Lotte, laughing, off the platform and back to her dressing room.

On the following day, Lotte visited the Randwick Military Hospital and sang to the patients, then gave her second public concert.

The first group of Lieder was all Schubert; the second was Schumann-Brahms, and particularly appealed to the audience. Lotte had to give an encore and chose Wolf's roguish 'Du denkst mit einem Fädchen'. Perhaps it was the next item, though, which many people had come to hear: Lotte's Sieglinde in 'Du bist der Lenz'. Ulanowsky did his best at the piano, and they followed the Wagner with Massenet's 'Il est doux, il est bon' from *Hérodiade*, a curious choice, one might think, for it was a Jeritza role that Lotte never assumed on stage, nor recorded. (In the 'Pasadena Set', Discog. p. 307, it is a student). All the same it was considered to be one of the most 'arresting' performances of the evening.

As a result of the tremendous success of these two concerts, the Commission extended the series by two more Lieder Recitals following the concert on 6 May. Lotte expanded her repertoire at these recitals (29 April and 1 May) but gave repeat or encore performances of the songs that had previously gone down particularly well, such as 'Erlkönig' and 'In dem Schatten'. The 'Frauenliebe und -leben' cycle, always one of Lotte's specialities, was a huge success on 1 May. At all these concerts Ulanowsky contributed a number of piano pieces such as Brahms Intermezzi, Chopin Mazurkas and even a Scriabin Study, but it was thought that he was less successful as a concert pianist than as an accompanist.

It had always been Ulanowsky's intention to become a virtuoso pianist, and for a while he was the staff pianist with the Vienna Philharmonic Orchestra; but one day he visited a clairvoyant who told him that he would travel across the world, accompanying one of the most famous singers of the age. Of course he did not believe it at the time.

The Sydney Symphony Orchestral Concert on 6 May produced scenes 'of extraordinary enthusiasm'. Dr. Edgar Bainton, the conductor, gave a number of orchestral works ranging from Mozart and Beethoven to Wagner, between Lotte's items. As she had to use more voice over the orchestra, Lotte had reduced the number of her songs, which were all by Strauss, with 'Cäcilie' last. No sooner had Lotte finished singing than a young woman in the front of the auditorium handed up a large, brown toy kangaroo holding a pink cactus. There was a roar of laughter and applause, and Lotte was so surprised that it took her a moment to compose herself before launching into her encore, 'Traum durch die Dämmerung'. That was not enough, so she gave them Gretchaninov's 'My Native Land'. Again they demanded more, and Lotte smilingly admitted that since she had not expected so many requests, she would have to repeat 'Cäcilie'.

Her operatic excerpts at this concert were 'Du bist der Lenz', now heard properly with orchestral accompaniment; and Elisabeth's 'Hallenarie', both sure-fire successes before she had even begun them. The audience went wild with delight.

The last concert, on the Saturday, was a matinée at which Lotte announced that she had to leave them for Canberra that afternoon. The tour included Brisbane, Canberra, Melbourne, Adelaide, Hobart and Perth.

During Lotte's absence from Europe, she was invested as an Officer of the Legion of Honour in Paris, by decree, later to be conferred upon her officially. And in Vienna there was an event that turned out to be perfectly ridiculous.

When Lotte left the USA to travel to Australia, she sent her maid Marie back to Europe with the two dogs because quarantine regulations applied in Australia. 'Lotte Lehmann's car' as the imposing vehicle was known to all, arrived at the railway station in Vienna, and a woman carrying much luggage and two dogs was seen entering it and driving to the Ahrenbergring.

Instantly the city was full of rumours: Lotte had cancelled her Australian tour . . . she had travelled alone from New York under an assumed name . . . she had separated from Otto Krause . . . she didn't want anybody to know she was back, and so on. When the scandal-mongers realised they had made a mistake, one of the newspapers carried the (very unreasonable) double-column headlines: 'Lotte Lehmann hoaxes Vienna!'

The Australian adventure had been a great success for Lotte and, as usual, she sought a holiday after it. She and Otto travelled by sea to Suez, which they reached in early July. Instead of staying on board for the journey down the Canal, they disembarked and travelled slowly by land to Cairo. It seems that they encountered the 'Hamsin' or desert storm on their way to Port Said, for Otto contracted an infection from sand in his lungs. It rather spoiled their holiday, and so they returned more quickly than had been planned, from Egypt to Italy, landing at Genoa and travelling by train to Vienna.

Otto was not at all well, and consulted a doctor who diagnosed a damaged lung for which rest was essential.[30] This was not their only misfortune. Lotte received some extremely unpleasant and vicious anonymous letters about her unsuitability to go on singing Eva in *Meistersinger*. In commenting on this briefly in his book, *Cadenza*, Erich Leinsdorf mentions that Maria Reining was the 'Eva in *Meistersinger* – after Lotte Lehmann had resigned from the role due to some nasty mail that considered her too matronly – . . .' It may have been the work of Nazi sympathisers in Saizburg and her connection with the 'Jewish Krause'; it may have been members of an antagonistic fan-club. Whatever the cause, it was too much for Lotte, and in spite of her acclaim in the role of Eva in 1936, she cancelled.

Consequently she had only four performances of opera at the Salzburg Festival: two *Fidelios* under Toscanini with a month between them, and two Marschallins with almost as long a gap. The Strauss was conducted by Knappertsbusch, with Krenn as Ochs and Novotna as Octavian again. Between the two pairs of operas Lotte and Bruno Walter gave two Lieder recitals and the programme for the first one on 1 August was:

Brahms	O wüsst' ich doch den Weg zurück Wir wandelten* Sonntag* O liebliche Wangen*
Schumann	Dichterliebe**
Schubert	Der Lindenbaum Frühlingsglaube Gretchen am Spinnrade*
R. Strauss	Befreit Freundliche Vision
Wolf	Der Gärtner* Storchenbotschaft*

(** recording by both, Discog. 407–414)

Regarding the Lieder Recital, the *Salzburger Volksblatt* had much to say about Lotte's part in the event, while admitting that so much had been said already about her exquisite singing, all over the world, 'She is, by nature, womanly, gentle and heroic, and just like Leonore.' And for Bruno Walter: 'he is no "accompanist" but partner in the duo. Piano and voice are of one mind, exactly as the composer envisaged: neither one inferior to the other, nor superior . . . One might say that Bruno Walter, a poet of the piano, plays another instrument, in Lotte Lehmann's voice; and Lotte Lehmann, on the other hand, sings in Bruno Walter's piano playing. This piano playing has a grand nobility and belongs in the secret realm of dreams, yet quivers with laughter. These two blessed ones gave a supernatural concert beneath a sea of flowers and cataracts of approbation.' Perhaps this was something of a fanciful notice, but it shows how difficult it had become for the press to come up with anything new about 'the two darlings of Salzburg'.

For their second concert on 20 August, they again made the 'Dichterliebe' the core of the programme and repeated three songs:

Schubert	An Sylvia An die Musik* Der Doppelgänger* Im Abendroth*
Schumann	Dichterliebe**
Brahms	Ach, wende diesen Blick Bitteres zu sagen denkst du Mainacht* Therese* O liebliche Wangen*
R. Strauss	Befreit Freundliche Vision Die Georgine Ständchen*

On 27 August, Wilhelm Furtwängler made his first, and somewhat unexpected appearance in Salzburg to conduct one of his specialities: Beethoven's 'Choral' Symphony. As usual, he was full of apologies over the various political disasters that had overtaken him, and attempted to get into conversation with Toscanini about the Italian Maestro's firm *dictat*: 'Salzburg or Bayreuth'. In his opinion, one's loyalties were implicit in one of those places, and it was inconceivable that anybody could conduct at both and retain a clear conscience. Furtwängler had conducted at Bayreuth in 1936 and 1937, but was already contemplating resigning from the 1938 festival there. Toscanini was not taken in and

shunned Furtwängler who, so far as he was concerned, remained a Nazi sympathiser.[31]

What made it worse was the breakdown in a proposed exchange of radio broadcasts between Germany's Bayreuth performances and Austria's Salzburg Festival concerts and operas. When the German Radio refused any event conducted by 'the Jew, Walter', Toscanini cancelled the whole arrangement.

At the end of the Salzburg Festival of 1937, Bruno Walter and Lotte were talking about the next one in 1938. Toscanini, who was with them, shook his head sadly and told them quite plainly that he would not be there, and was making no representation to return in twelve months' time. He seemed to have a prescience about the turn of events in Austria.

Walter did not understand this, and Lotte was unconvinced. Nor did she realise – how could she? – that the last Leonore of her life had been the performance under Toscanini on 26 August just past.

The next finality was Lotte's short season in Vienna. The six performances she gave, all in September, between 1st and 28th, were the Marschallin with Esther Réthy, Margit Bokor and Alfred Jerger, conducted by Knappertsbusch as guest; Elsa with Kirsten Thorborg and August Seider, conducted by Weingartner; Tatiana twice, with Anton Dermota, Alexander Sved and Alexander Kipnis, conducted by Bruno Walter: Sieglinde with a guest Siegmund and Kipnis as Hunding, conducted again by Weingartner; then last of all, and rightly so, the Marschallin with Elisabeth Schumann as Sophie, Margit Bokor as Octavian and Alexander Kipnis as Ochs. Josef Krips conducted.

On 8 October Lotte left Europe on the liner *Europa* for the United States, with two maids and two dogs, but leaving Otto behind in a sanatorium. Because she was anxious to maintain her contacts with Australia, Lotte wrote several rather flirtatious letters to Mr Cleary of the Australian Broadcasting Commission who had been kind to her when she was there before.[32] Perhaps it was a feeling of loneliness, of being abandoned, that caused her to write in a manner so evident later and for the rest of her life: a pestering of people if they did not reply promptly and in full to her last communication.

Lotte's 'Have you forgotten me?' or 'Don't you remember me?' or 'Don't you love me any longer?' and 'Why have you not written to me? / answered my last two letters? / given me your answer to my questions?' – flowed all round the world.

Lotte sang one Marschallin at the Met on 1 December before going to Chicago for another, and then back to the Met for Elisabeth, another

Marschallin at a matinée in Chicago, and two more at the Met. She was living in Upper Fifth Avenue, New York, and fulfilled her engagements there and in Boston up to the end of March.

She was at her hairdresser's in New York on the morning of 11 March 1938 when news of the Nazi Anschluss first reached the American public. The promised plebiscite never took place, the blackshirts steam-rollered their way so as to take over 'democratically'. On that night, Karl Alwin conducted a performance of *Eugen Onegin*, Kurt von Schuschnigg broadcast his resignation and was taken away to prison for the next seven years. The swastika now flew over the Chancellor's office in Vienna, symbolising the centre of this new territorial addition to the Third Reich.

On 12 April, Hitler arrived in Vienna to enjoy the bloodless coup in his native land, and Knappertsbusch conducted a performance of *Tristan* that evening. Kerstin Thorborg was due to sing Brangäne, but although she looked thoroughly Aryan, she left Vienna hastily and managed to reach Sweden unharmed.

On 13 April the main body of German troops entered Vienna and then the Opera was closed for a fortnight. It reopened with the 'freedom opera', *Fidelio* on 27 March, conducted again by Knappertsbusch and in the presence of Hermann Göring. Baldur von Schirach, a great music-lover, had been appointed Gauleiter of Vienna, for Hitler had sensibly decreed that music and opera be left alone, as far as possible, as a means of impressing the Viennese with his wisdom and sympathy with their most important occupation and asset.

From then on, many strange – and artistically fleeting – names appeared on the cast-lists. Some were from Berlin, others (presumably ambitious Nazis) were from smaller houses, determined to capitalise on the political events which had now overtaken Vienna. The general policy, though an unwieldy one, was to co-ordinate all opera-house personnel in the Reich and make them interchangeable – all right on paper, but practically impossible artistically. Those who stayed in Vienna found, at first, that life went on much the same as usual (unless they were Jewish) and there were now boundless opportunities for Viennese jokes about an all-too obvious subject.

This news was sickening to Lotte. She was an Austrian citizen, an adopted Viennese with honours from that city. All her precious possessions were still there: her dogs, her horses,[33] and Otto, languishing in a sanatorium with his lung complaint. Although he had become a Catholic convert (and so had Lotte) he was still tainted in the eyes of the new authorities, and so were his four children. America was still a supposed friendly nation towards Nazi Germany, and American reporters for both press and radio were able, within limits, to report on events in Vienna, so Lotte was kept up to date.

After her Boston Marschallin on 31 March, Lotte had some engagements of her own and general tidying up to do before leaving the USA for Europe and Covent Garden.

There was a gala performance of *Die Meistersinger* at the Vienna Opera on 20 April, Hitler's birthday, which Furtwängler conducted. (One wonders how Toscanini responded to that information). Maria Reining, who had taken over many of Lotte's roles, sang Eva and Ludwig Hofmann was the Sachs.

Lotte arrived in London after a bad Atlantic crossing, feeling unwell. She had a great deal on her mind and was fearful about Otto in Vienna. She had four Marschallins, two Leonores and two Sieglindes to sing for Beecham between 4 May and 1 June.

I well remember listening to the broadcast of that first *Rosenkavalier* from Covent Garden. Only the first act was being relayed live, but the whole of that was not achieved. It was a thoroughly wretched evening for Lotte. Several members of the cast were strongly pro-Nazi and behaved abominably towards her. The Octavian, especially, did her best to upset Lotte further by whispering to her during the performance: 'What is the matter with your voice? Why are you singing so faintly? You don't look very well. Would you like me to take your high notes for you?' and so on, spoken as if meant to be helpful. But Lotte knew that she was not.

Apart from this off-putting and irritating cross-talk, Lotte had also to contend with the sofa on the stage. The Marschallin sits on it for quite a lot of the action but one of its legs came off, and the piece of furniture had to be carefully balanced to prevent it from tipping over and presenting a ludicrous situation.

It all became too much for her. After the Levée, when Ochs had followed the rest of the 'Bagagi' (as the Marschallin's Major-Domo calls the begging visitors) and we were expecting to hear Lotte sing 'Da geht er hin . . .' there was only her muffled voice uttering in agonised tones: 'Kann nichts mehr – Schluss!' ('I can't go on – finish!'). Erich Kleiber was making his conducting début at Covent Garden: another Aryan who had seen enough of Germany, he had now left the Berlin Staatsoper, and was beginning an international career outside it. Kleiber stopped the orchestra and the house curtains came down. After a babble of surprised voices, Walter Legge made an announcement to the audience in the Opera House and over the air. He was Beecham's Artistic Director for the Season. Madame Lehmann had been taken ill, he told us, and there would be a short interval of about twenty minutes while Mme. Hilde Konetzni, who was fortunately present among the audience and had agreed to take over, changed into the Marschallin's costume. The performance would then be resumed, although unfortunately not broadcast.

In those days the nine o'clock news was sacrosanct on the Home Service (there was no Third) and any music or talk which accidentally overran was faded out for Big Ben. There was no hope of finishing the first act before nine-thirty at the earliest.

It is amusing to read the careful account of this event by Hilde Konetzni. She was present, in the management box, with her current *amour*, Walter Legge, and had instantly been persuaded by him to take over the Marschallin as soon as he saw what had happened to Lotte. Konetzni says this:[34]

> Perhaps the most incredible experience I ever had was in London in 1938, when I was engaged to sing at Covent Garden, and it made me internationally famous overnight. I was due to make my début as Chrysothemis and had gone to the theatre by myself very inconspicuously the night before to hear *Der Rosenkavalier* with Lotte Lehmann as the Marschallin. Suddenly she stopped in the middle of the act and walked out. There was pandemonium and the curtain came down. She simply announced she did not feel in good form and could not continue. Someone remembered that I had asked for a ticket so I must be in the house. I had been very successful in this part even in Salzburg.[35] My name was called out, and I left my seat to see what was wanted. Somehow it all happened so fast that I did not even have the time to think that they were going to ask me to replace her. But they did . . . I have always enjoyed challenges and this was the greatest ever. Lehmann's Marschallin was considered, right or wrong, the greatest, and no one in London knew me. I accepted. But there were no costumes. Lehmann had left the theatre in a tearing hurry and, amazingly enough, had carried them off with her. But that was Lotte! She only thought of herself . . .

Dr. Berta Geissmar had been Furtwängler's loyal and trusted private secretary for years, and had almost managed the Berlin Philharmonic Orchestra for him. As a German Jew she had just managed to leave the Reich and was instantly employed by Beecham in London. He was extremely kind to her. She carries on the story:[36]

> I went backstage at once to look after Lotte Lehmann, and then went to Konetzni's room. She was, of course, much plumper than Lehmann and when I entered her room she was just being 'sewn' into her costume; but there was still a large expanse of her back uncovered. I happened to be wearing a long, black velvet cape over my evening dress and Miss Newbery 'the very capable wardrobe supervisor' suggested: 'If you would not mind, Doctor, I think your cape will be just the thing.' We draped it down Hilde's back, and she walked on to the stage, an imposing Marschallin.

Now back to Hilde Konetzni:[37]

> You cannot believe the triumph I had. I thought they would never allow me to go home and have a good sleep, before the *Elektra* the next night. When I awoke late in the morning, I had to move out of my room and take another one, for there were literally dozens and dozens of bouquets and baskets of flowers, including a bunch of roses from Lehmann herself . . .

At this point, the stories of what really happened that night began to differ and to proliferate. *The Times* report on the following morning stated that:

> A specialist who examined Mme Lehmann said that she had a chill and he advised her not to continue. He said she would be quite well again in a few days.

This was Sir Milsom Rees, the Harley Street laryngologist who was retained by the Royal Opera House during the Season to help any singer in difficulty. So it seems unlikely that Lotte had left the Opera House, especially as Richard Tauber had gone round to comfort her.[38]

The several reasons that have been given for Lotte's unique abandonment of a performance in its course, are these:

1. Covent Garden's official statement: 'Mme Lehmann felt ill and saw that it was impossible for her to sing the end of the act to the audience's and her own satisfaction.'
2. Sir Milsom Rees's diagnosis of a chill.
3. Lotte's account of a terrible Atlantic crossing.
4. Lotte's account of having just heard about her husband's imprisonment and the destruction of their possessions in Vienna.
5. Lotte's account of the cruel behaviour of pro-Nazis in the cast.
6. Walter Legge's account:[39]

> Next day Lotte, in good spirits, gave a small lunch party. She said she needed a rest and explained privately (not the usually published, politically coloured version of the incident) that a few minutes before the performance she had been told that relations of hers who were trying to smuggle valuables out of Austria had been held up at the customs, but now she knew they were safely through.

Although Lotte seems to have recovered overnight, she refused to sing the two *Fidelios* and two *Walküres* for which she was contracted. But she went on again for two more Marschallins on 10 and 12 May, the latter being her last appearance at Covent Garden. Pauly sang the two Leonores and Anny Konetzni and Tiana Lemnitz covered the two Sieglindes.

In his biography of Erich Kleiber, John Russell strikes a sober note on the whole affair:[40]

> Madame Lehmann's breakdown seemed to many sensitive observers to symbolise the general collapse and overthrow of European tradition.

Lotte's autobiography, up to the end of the year 1936, and with rosy hopes of a settled future, was published simultaneously in London (as *Wings of Song*) and in New York (as *Midway in my Song*). The original German text had been published in Vienna, Leipzig and Zürich in the previous year and had been reviewed during the 1937 Salzburg Festival.

Concurrently with this, Lotte's novel *Orplid, mein Land* had appeared in Austria and Germany, and an American edition followed, in an English translation that is not always to be trusted and called *Eternal Flight*.

In June 1938, Lotte was staying at the Grand Hotel, Cap Martin, on the Côte d'Azur. Otto had been able to leave Austria with the four children only after they had all been ransomed for a huge sum. His health did not improve during this time of great worry and distress. Lotte mentions in a letter to the Australian Mr. Cleary that he was taken to another sanatorium in France at the end of June, as he was still not yet fit enough to travel any further.[41]

Lotte left for the USA on 4 July on the liner *Scharnhorst* so as to be able to fulfil her engagements at the Met, and took the four children with her. She was able to find jobs for the three boys in the USA, while she looked after Manon, the only girl. At the time she seemed to be revelling in her 'readymade family' but this did not last.

On 6 January 1939, she continued with her recording schedule for Victor in New York, the first of many with Paul Ulanowsky who had now superseded Ernö Balogh. The first session was all Wolf Lieder (Discog. 315–324) the results of which make it seem sad that she was not invited by Walter Legge to participate in the pre-War HMV Wolf Society Recordings.

It is also curious to note that Lotte never appeared at Bayreuth as Flagstad did; was not invited to Glyndebourne; received no dedication of a song from Richard Strauss as Jeritza and Ursuleac did. But compared with what she did do, these omissions can be set aside as relatively unimportant.

Otto arrived in the USA at Christmas time, but his strength did not last. His lung complaint proved fatal and he died at Saranac Lake, in the Adirondack Mountains between Albany and Montreal, on 22 January.

Chapter Ten

Exile

1938–1944

It is not altogether surprising that the duets which Lotte recorded with Melchior eight days after Otto's death cannot be regarded as completely satisfactory. She had once loved her husband passionately, but in the course of time their association had become one of convenience, with Otto in the (often trying) role of husband to the world-famous artist. Lotte had her flings but, once she had met Toscanini, Otto found himself more in the background than before.

Now that he had gone, there was the inevitable remorse and self-pity, but Lotte was determined to keep working and to retain her usual image before the public which, to give her full credit, she managed to do.

There were four more Met performances before she left the USA for her second Australian tour with Ulanowsky. On 20 March 1939 they arrived in Sydney on the SS *Mariposa*.

Mr. Cleary, the Chairman of ABC, who had written in such a friendly manner to Lotte between tours, was not in evidence, but he had arranged for the first concert to be an orchestral one: a far better beginning than a recital, when the proper accompaniment to Elisabeth's and Sieglinde's arias produced the right effect.

Lotte and Ulanowsky gave six Lieder recitals in Sydney[1] and at the penultimate concert she had placed the 'Frauenliebe und -leben cycle in the centre of the programme. She was singing the last song, 'Nun hast du mir den ersten Schmerz getan' which then continues 'du schläfst, du harter, unbarmherz'ger Mann, den Todesschlaf' ('You sleep, you hard and pitiless man, the sleep of death') but it was too much for her and she broke down. 'Tears streamed down her cheeks but she restrained herself and finished the cycle. She afterwards explained that the songs poignantly reminded her of her own life . . . The audience was profoundly moved, and many women wept openly.'[2]

After the last Sydney concert, Lotte travelled overnight to Melbourne by train, arriving there on the morning of 10 April for another seven recitals. They were followed by three more each in Perth and Adelaide before returing to Melbourne, not to sing, but to rest for a day before going back by sleeper to Sydney. One of the three concerts planned for her there had been cancelled, but the tour was not yet over. There were three more concerts in Brisbane and another in Canberra on 31 May, then Lotte left Sydney on the *Wanganella* for New Zealand on 3 June when, after a four-day voyage, she reached Wellington.

An enthusiastic reception was awaiting her (and Ulanowsky). She found hundreds of letters from local admirers as well as many flowers. At the first concert, which was a gala attended by the High Commissioner and his staff with their wives, everybody had taken special care with their dress. 'It was pleasing to note the number of younger music lovers who attended with such evident enjoyment. Groups of schoolgirls were also seen there.'[3] It was a predictable programme:

Brahms	Von ewiger Liebe O lieblicher Wangen
Schubert	Ständchen Der Erlkönig (dramatised)
Schumann	Ich grolle nicht
Martini	Plaisir d'Amour
Trad.	My Lovely Celia
Trad.	The Plague of Love
Purcell	There's not a swain on the plain
Trad.	Drink to me only
Schubert	Ungeduld (as encore)
Thomas	*Mignon* Connais-tu le pays?
Puccini	*Tosca* Vissi d'arte
Trad.	The Last Rose of Summer (as encore)
Hageman	Music I heard with you
James	Covent Garden
Rogers	The Star

Worth	Midsummer
Brahms	Wiegenlied Vergebliches Ständchen (as encores)

After the second concert, which was even more enthusiastically and wildly received because it was less 'dressy', the audience waited for Lotte afterwards.[4]

> They filled the foyer and wide footpath outside the Opera House, and just stood there in a solid mass. At last the diva appeared, looking radiantly happy in her long ermine evening cloak, carrying an armful of flowers. With one accord the crowd applauded and cheered her as she made her way smilingly through the crush to her limousine. Few saw this incident, but it is typical of the occasion: as she passed across the footpath, one young woman stooped and kissed the hem of her coat. Madame Lehmann was unaware of the incident, but realizing the enthusiasm of the crowd, she said, with a smile, after acknowledging the homage paid her, that she hoped the people in other parts of New Zealand were going to be as kind as those of Wellington whose welcome she never could forget.

On account of this tumultuous reception, the New Zealand management arranged for an extra Wellington concert for 18th after Lotte's return from the South Island in the next week. She gave a concert in the packed Dunedin Main Hall on 15 June, and in travelling north again, met and sang to some Maoris who sang to her, too. They greeted her 'Widmung' with enthusiasm – and recognition.

After the extra Wellington concert and two more in Auckland, on 22 and 24 June, Lotte sailed from Wellington for Honolulu on the *Monterey*. The Hawaiian concert was her last before returning home via San Francisco. She had been away from her new home for nearly five months.

In September, Britain and France were at war with Nazi Germany, and although the West Coast of the United States was far away from troubled Europe, and seemingly quite safe, there was the invisible bogey of Japan over the western horizon.

Lotte travelled to the Met in December for three performances of *Rosenkavalier* which Constance Hope had arranged and authorised for her while Lotte was in Australia. The Met were now paying her $750 a performance and Lotte was obliged, even though she was not an American citizen, to join AGMA (the American Guild of Musical Artists).

Helen Traubel recalls:[5] 'Lotte Lehmann, that remarkably sweet singer, comes to me in a remembrance of her silently wringing her hands before her entrance in the opera, the symbol of nervousness that possessed all of us under such circumstances . . . – and her superlative performances the instant she set foot on the stage.'

In the previous April, Constance Hope had specially asked the Met to give Lotte another Sieglinde to sing, and for the first time since 1937 she again appeared in this famous role on 19 January 1940. Otherwise she seemed to have become solely identified with the Marschallin, a state of affairs that did not altogether please her.

The Press Bureau of the Metropolitan Opera New York had – almost certainly still has – a form for artists to complete and return to them as an aid to answering questions to the Press. Lotte refused to take some of these questions seriously, and left several unanswered. These are some of her choicest replies:[6]

Q. Do you recall the dates of any roles that you sang for the first time at the Met. . . . with whom you sang . . . conductor and principals?
A. *No idea*
Q. Do you like to dance? A. *No.*
Q. What is your favorite dish? A. *Filet Mignon.*
Can you cook it? A. *For Heaven's sake!*
Have you the receipe? A. *No.*
Q. What kind of cooking do you like best? A. *American*
Which foods do you dislike? A. *Onions and garlic (Pfui)*
Q. Did you ever win prizes for sports? A. Certainly not
Q. What kind of motion picture do you like?
A. *My taste is versatile*
Q. Who is your favorite star? A. *Mickeymouse. Cleo the goldfish*
Q. Do you want your children to follow in your footsteps?
A. *My dog does not like music*
Q. What are your antipathies? A. *Questionnaires*
Q. What is your height? A. *5*[8]
What is your weight? A. *Are you crazy?*
Q. Name of Manager? A. *Coppicus*
Press Representive
Personal Rep:
Person authorized to speak for you in your absence
A. *Constance*
Remarks: *Now give me my peace.*

Lotte admitted that although she had seemed to receive her expected kind of reception at her Met début, it had not *all* continued according to her expectations. Her attempt to become recognised there as something other than a totally Wagner-Strauss singer had been short-lived with the unhappy *Tosca*, and after that she had been entirely restricted to the German repertoire. The lack of an ensemble, of stylish productions, of a whole-hearted belief in their Opera from the city of New York were results of the financial malaise there, according to which, each season stumbled forward to the next one. It was plain that New York was not Vienna, for there, during the immediate post-war years of the early 20s there was never any doubt in the artists' minds about *next* season: it was bound to happen.

Lotte admitted that she appeared to have no real association with the Metropolitan Opera, and never felt more than a guest. They ignored her until 1934 in spite of the fact that she was loved and famous throughout Europe, but when she was at last – and late – invited there, and her 'burning ambition' was achieved, it was all rather an anti-climax. The many singers she met and worked with there and elsewhere were still unable to make Lotte feel at home on the stage of the 'Diamond Horseshoe' which she had always imagined to be the very Mecca for opera singers. As for her *Tosca*, she admitted:[7]

> I never really made this role my own. Perhaps because its very superficial theatricalism is entirely foreign to my being. It always seemed to me too much. One must have another kind of temperament to do justice to it – a flaring and nervous temperament which is capable of throwing things around, stamping the feet and tearing the hair, perhaps . . . That I don't have at all . . . It must have been this lack of flashing temperament which made me always feel foreign to the role. . . .

However, after singing a few more Marschallins at the Met, Lotte exhibited something like the 'temperament' that she denied herself in print when she heard that Flagstad was going to sing Leonore there. She told Edward Johnson, face to face, that she would never, *never* sing Leonore for him at the Met or on one of the Met's tours.

On 26 February 1940, Lotte recorded eleven of the Schubert 'Winterreise' songs with Paul Ulanowsky for Victor. Even considering that the work was thoroughly familiar to them both as partners, it was a fine achievement for one day. Ultimately Nos. 5, 20, 21, 8 and 17 were not issued in the UK, but very soon appeared on Victor in the USA; they already had catalogue numbers allocated (see Discog. 329–336). That left thirteen songs to record in order to complete the cycle.

At the end of March, Lotte went on a wide Met Opera tour to Baltimore and Boston in the north east; down to Dallas in Texas and to New Orleans in Louisiana; then across to Atlanta in Georgia. She sang, in sequence, two Marschallins, two Sieglindes and two Elisabeths (and for the same fee as she was getting in New York). Travelling expenses were generous.

In the following October, she appeared twice as the Marschallin in San Francisco, where she had not before been heard in this role. She had a strong supporting cast: Risë Stevens as Octavian, Margit Bokor – another refugee from Vienna – as Sophie, and Alexander Kipnis as Baron Ochs. The conductor was Erich Leinsdorf.

Fortunately, Lotte had some substantial recording sessions for Columbia – having switched from Victor – with Paul Ulanowsky accompanying her as usual. After what was probably a kind of 'social' session on 4 March, when she got to know the record producer and engineers, and they her, she made two Schubert Lieder, 'Die junge Nonne' and 'Der Doppelgänger' the latter being one of only three songs she recorded in the studio from Schubert's 'Schwanengesang' (see Discog. 337–38). They then launched into a continuation of the 'Winterreise', an unusual switch to a different recording company, and their main competitor in the USA. They then made mostly Brahms Lieder, with the two concluding songs from the 'Winterreise' on 19 March.

Two more Marschallins at the Met and an Elisabeth in Boston were followed by the exciting news that Lotte's friend in Santa Barbara had bought a property there in which they both would live.

From the end of June until the middle of July, Lotte's recording schedule with Columbia was more concentrated than ever before and she made no less than thirty-three Lieder ranging from Beethoven to Hugo Wolf. This was in the six sessions (Discog. 368–96) and it will be seen that fifteen Lieder were never issued on 78s. Lotte often sang the Wesendonck Lieder at recitals, but never the complete five at any one time. She did not record No. 2 ('Stehe still') at all, and No. 1 ('Der Engel') was not published as a 78 although it was recorded on 9 July. The connection with (Tristan and) Isolde is implicit in these songs.

On 14 July, Lotte's recordings consisted of four songs from Old Vienna and some other numbers such as delighted her audiences in the Antipodes (Discog. 398–406).

In August, Lotte and Bruno Walter made a recording of Schumann's 'Dichterliebe' cycle in a single session (Discog. 407–414); while it is a precious recording to have, the performance which they gave at Salzburg in 1937 was, it is said, to be preferred.

San Francisco gave Lotte only one performance at the start of their 1941–2 season which was the Marschallin again, with the same cast and conductor as in 1940 (when she appeared twice). The Met had offered her 'a minimum of five performances between November 24, 1940, and March 15, 1942 at a fee of $750 each'. And typed on the bottom of the contract was the statement, rather than question, 'Your repertoire is to include "Fidelio".' Lotte had put ? beside that having, as she thought, made it abundantly clear to Johnson that she was not going to do any such thing.

On 6 December, Lotte was scheduled to sing Sieglinde at the Met but, unusually for her, cancelled at short notice. There was no cover. The Swedish soprano, Astrid Varnay, was the closest possibility but had never sung the role on stage. She agreed to 'mark' the part and to save the performance.[8] Thanks to the help she received from the Siegmund (Melchior) and also from Erich Leinsdorf, there were no disasters, but it was a scrappy affair. Varnay went on to become a celebrated Brünnhilde.[9]

On 7 December, Japanese suicide pilots attacked the US naval base at Pearl Harbor in Hawaii and did a great deal of damage. This brought America into the war with Japan immediately, and with Nazi Germany four days later. At once, almost every artist in the USA began giving concerts and recitals to help the war effort: among them was Lotte.

Artur Rubinstein recalls[10] that not long after Pearl Harbor there was a particularly colourful concert in

> the swimming pool of the Beverly Wilshire Hotel. A round building containing a large number of dressing rooms for the swimmers was converted into elegant boxes and the seats were sold at exorbitant prices. A platform was erected at one end of the swimming pool and the program consisted of Beethoven's Kreutzer Sonata played by Jascha Heifetz and me, two cycles of Lieder sung by Lotte Lehmann and accompanied by Bruno Walter and, in between, solo pieces by Heifetz with his own accompanist and by me . . . it indeed yielded a large sum of money . . .

In Vienna, Clemens Krauss came back to the Opera in spite of all that had been said against him, to conduct a fine performance of *Così* (with Ursuleac as Fiordiligi) during a week of Mozart to celebrate the 150th year of the composer's birth. This began to pave the way for his return for, as always, the Viennese soon forget past enemies and in Krauss's case they found him 'not so bad after all'!

That summer he had been in charge of a summer course of music held jointly at Potsdam and Salzburg, especially for foreigners.[11] America was not yet at war with Germany and the event was well advertised in the USA where many people were interested in the idea, either as performers or listeners. Switzerland and Sweden were also canvassed – being neutral countries – for this was partly a propaganda exercise, aimed at impressing the world with the Nazis' humanitarian support of the arts. At Salzburg the professors – under Krauss's directorship – were Rudolf Hartmann and Ludwig Sievert for opera direction and scenery respectively; operatic interpretation by Anna Bahr-Mildenburg; singing by Felicie Hüni-Mihacsek and piano, Elly Ney. It cost 250RM for performers and 125RM for listeners. Accommodation was extra and could be in a variety of hotels, pensions or in families. It seemed an attractive way of extending a holiday immediately after the 1941 Salzburg Festival had ended.

The personnel of the Festival came from Vienna as usual, which is why Krauss was not involved with its planning. But he gave one concert of Strauss's orchestral music with the Vienna Philharmonic Orchestra (but no opera) while he laid plans to take over the whole Festival in 1942.

After Lotte had sung her Marschallins at the Met, she received a letter from Edward Johnson telling her that she was contracted to sing a Sieglinde and a Marschallin in Boston in March, and a Marschallin in Cleveland in early April. Her relationship with Johnson had deteriorated, and she wrote a typical version of a 'Lotte business-letter' to him:[12]

> Since you seem to like very much formalities and have written to me such a formal letter, I will try to become also a formal member of the Metropolitan Opera House . . . under no circumstances I am willing to sing on 9th of April the 'Marschallin' in Cleveland . . . I would be terribly sorry if I should cause you any embarrassment, but I must really ask you to inform the Cleveland Manager that I am not going to sing the 'Marschallin' there . . . So nothing on earth can force me, even not you, yes, even not your smile can seduce me to say 'Yes' to Cleveland . . .
>
> In spite of the fact that we all seem to hate each other, I send you and Mr. Ziegler as usual much love and I am
>
> privately helpless,
> but officially very determined
> Lotte Lehmann

Johnson and Ziegler appealed to Constance Hope to mediate because they really wanted Lotte to sing in Cleveland and why she so objected was not clear. Miss Hope produced a scheme whereby Lotte was practically bribed with a fee of $1,000 (instead of the usual $750) intended to cover the luxury of a 'Battle Creek siesta' afterwards. Ziegler wrote to thank Lotte saying how much they had all appreciated what she had done and agreed to, etc., etc.[13]

In June 1942, Ulanowsky returned to the Columbia studies to accompany Lotte in a recording of Schubert's song-cycle 'Die Schöne Müllerin' which they almost completed in two sessions on 22 and 25 (Discog. 415–428). They left out No. 7, 'Ungeduld', and when this recording came to be transferred to LP, Columbia had to beg Victor for the only version of this celebrated song (made for them in 1935 and always selling well) so that the 'Müllerin' would not be abridged. Lotte knew that if she attempted another 'Ungeduld' now, even in a more comfortable key (as she did with very nearly all the other songs) it could not better her first and only recording of it.

On the afternoon of 6 December 1942, Lotte gave her annual concert at New York's Town Hall. The critic of *The New York Times* wrote:

> That Lotte Lehmann's hold on the public is as strong as ever after a decade of appearances here was evidenced by the size and enthusiasm of her audience at her recital yesterday afternoon in Town Hall. The passing years have not robbed her in the slightest of her warmth of temperament, or diminished the spontaneity of her singing, and today as heretofore, she occupies a niche of her own in the vocal field . . .
>
> The mood and atmosphere of 'An den Mond' could hardly be more completely captured and maintained. It was filled with inner intensity, but though deeply felt, was never subjected to more than just the right amount of emotional stress. Every phrase was subtly molded, the melodic line was finely sustained, and the entire song moved with remarkable rhythmic grace . . .
>
> . . . her excursions into the field of French song was anticipated with interest. 'La Flûte de Pan' of Debussy was the most successful of her ventures in the Gallic group . . .

A week later, also in the afternoon, she was at Jordan Hall, Boston where her programme consisted of:

Schubert	An die Musik
	Lachen und Weinen
Schumann	Alte Laute
	Die Kartenlegerin

Debussy	Colloque sentimental La Flûte de Pan
Duparc	L'Invitation au voyage
Weckerlin	Maman, dites-moi
Ravel	Nicolette
Tchaikovsky	None but the Lonely Heart
Gretchaninoff	Cradle Song
Rubinstein	The Dew is Sparkling
Rachmaninoff	In the Silence of the Night
Brahms	An die Nachtigall Meine Liebe ist grün
Wolf	Verborgenheit Morgenstimmung

There were also many encores, given generously. The critics of the Boston newspapers were ecstatic and from the *Herald* came this:

> Every time Lotte Lehmann comes back to Boston she proves anew – as though she needed to – her position as the greatest Lieder singer of the day . . .
>
> While it may be true her voice is not as it was, the intelligence with which she uses it has somehow added stature to it purely as an instrument. She does not make excessive demands upon it by singing 'big' songs of former years, yet her program yesterday was distinguished and was of sufficient demand upon her voice to demonstrate all but the most trying aspects of vocalise, and she negotiated every song with magnificent technic, erring but once (in the Rubinstein) and then only in pitch.

In January 1943 Lotte sang the Marschallin in three performances in a fortnight at the Met, and younger members of those audiences might be forgiven for thinking that she had no other role there, until February when, after three years she sang Sieglinde and after four, Elisabeth again. This was more like it, a good clutch of performances in three roles and all within a couple of months, which was most convenient for her.

Each summer, Lotte expected to hear from the Met about the forthcoming season. In 1943, July and August went by, then November and still there was no contract. She asked Constance Hope what was happening, but there simply was no request for her in the 1943–4 season. It was not until she had almost given up hearing from them again that she received a letter from Edward Johnson dated 13 November 1944 offering her *one* Marschallin in February, with rehearsal on the day before. In this letter the sentence claiming the right to engage her for performances outside New York, after the Met season, was crossed out.[14]

This performance of *Rosenkavalier* was conducted by George Szell, now also an exile in the USA, who had lost none of his skill – or acerbity. Lotte was fifty-seven and, one might think, on the elderly side for Hofmannsthal's and Strauss's creation of about thirty-five, 'between ages'. Lotte continued to maintain that her Marschallin was always exactly the same age as herself.

On 12 March, at eleven o'clock in the morning, there occurred a disaster in Vienna without comparison. American bombers, flying back from a raid further south, scattered some incendiary bombs while passing over the city, and many of them landed on the Opera. The House had been closed since it had suffered from slight damage in the previous June, though the structure was sound. The closure had been mainly a political one since the unsuccessful bomb-plot on Hitler's life on 22 July. But now, seven years to the day since Hitler had entered Vienna, the beloved building was totally destroyed.

Totally? Well, the entrance foyer and part of the staircase remained, but the rest had gone: all the scenery, properties, armoury and contents of that marvellous wardrobe. It was the greatest calamity that could have befallen the city and every citizen was affected by it. Yet the spirit of the Vienna State Opera remained alive; but for Lotte who had now received the fearful news it was particularly distressing because American airmen had been responsible.

Six days later, Lotte gave an afternoon recital with Paul Ulanowsky at the Emery Auditorium in Cincinnati. Isidore Lichtmann from Chicago who had heard so many of Lotte's performances there (see Chapter VII page 124) was now in the US armed forces,[15]

> stationed at Camp Atterbury, in Indiana, at that time, about 100 miles from Cincinnati and hitch-hiked to attend all three concerts. Tickets were free to Servicemen, and I remember that the rather large hall rarely had more than fifty people in attendance. This was an all-Schumann program, from which the ubiquitous *Frauenliebe* was happily absent; and I soon discovered that the distinguished old man sitting next to me [on 11 March] was Sir Eugene Goossens. He was quite impressed with the fact that I had thumbed a ride to

> be able to attend the concert, and insisted that I accompany him backstage 'to pay homage to Lotte'. She asked what I would like to hear her sing at the last recital, the following week, and I requested 'Die Krähe'. And the following week she announced 'For a very special friend, I shall sing *Die Krähe*'. You can imagine how moved I was.

And it was an all-Schumann programme!

On 1 May the reborn Vienna State Opera opened at the Volksoper with a performance of *Figaro*. That building and all it contained were safe and were in the Russian sector of the city. Alfred Jerger had been nominated as the Intendant and piloted the institution under the most difficult conditions, giving performances with enormous courage.

A week later, the war in Europe – or rather the war against the Nazis – was over, but not before the Russians, in their advance across Brandenburg, had reached Gross Pankow. Old Baron Konrad zu Putlitz had died there in 1924, and the present Baron, his eldest son Waldemar, decided to remain. He 'died, most probably shot by the Russians';[16] but the other members of the family and their children managed to get away to safety at the last moment. Every member of the staff who stayed was strung up from the window frames[17] and then the Schloss was looted and despoiled.

Chapter Eleven

American Citizen

1945–1976

It took not quite seven years for Lotte Lehmann to become accepted as an American citizen. On her way to the Santa Barbara County Courthouse, she told reporters, 'I can hardly wait to become a full-fledged American citizen. As far as Germany and the rest of Europe are concerned, I want to forget everything I know about them. This, I hope, is to be my final "visit" to America because now it is to be my permanent home.'[1]

The simple ceremony was over in a very short time, and then Lotte had reached her third and final nationality. It was 13 June 1945 and, quite by chance, Elisabeth Schumann's fifty-seventh birthday.

Elisabeth was living in New York and teaching. She had been divorced from Karl Alwin in 1936, and he died in this year, 1945. From time to time, Lotte and Elisabeth met and exchanged jokes, reminiscences and presents. But now, with the war in Europe over, they were both thinking about when they might return there with the possibility of rescueing assets from Vienna. This was not likely for the time being, but all the same, Lotte was far from wanting 'to forget everything I know about' Europe.

In the peaceful climate of unrationed California, compared with the horrors that were being uncovered in the former Nazi-occupied countries, Lotte sang two performances of the Marschallin in San Francisco. Act III of the second one was privately recorded (see Discog. p. 303)

And between the dates of these two *Rosenkavaliers*, on 6 October, there was a stirring event in Vienna. *Fidelio* was staged in another manifestation of the Vienna State Opera, in the Theater an der Wien, outside the Russian sector of occupation and with far greater scope and freedom. Anny Konetzni sang Leonore and Josef Krips conducted.

In the following February, Lotte gave a Liederabend for 'The Friends of Music' accompanied by Paul Ulanowsky, in New York (see Discog. pp. 303–4). This, too, was recorded.

Exactly a week later on 17 February, there was a celebration at the Met for Melchior's twentieth anniversary of his first appearance there. Lotte was invited to sing in *Die Walküre* Act I, and was glad to accept, although she fully realised that she was there in the nature of a supporting artist.[2] Melchior was the star, but for her 'Siegmund' she would do anything.

In that June, Leo Slezak passed quietly away, that giant of a man with a giant of a voice, with humour and kindness to match. Lotte loved him dearly. He was one of the last 'originals' and his going upset her deeply especially as, in his last letter to her, he had suggested a visit to Santa Barbara.

On 11 August 1946, Lotte sang at an orchestral concert in Seattle. The conductor was Carl Brickner and the orchestra that which Sir Thomas Beecham had controlled from 1941–43, having encouraged it to play rather well. Lotte's contribution to this event has been preserved (see Discog. p. 304).

In October, Lotte had two more *Rosenkavaliers* in San Francisco, on 8th and 13th matinée. Novotná was the Octavian, Nadine Conner the Sophie and Lorenzo Alvary, Ochs. The conductor was again George Sebastian. He and Alvary were only two of the numerous Hungarian musicians who had enriched American life on account of Nazi persecution. This last *Rosenkavalier* was, to Lotte, the end of a season, not an era.

She had given only one set-piece Farewell Performance in her life: in Hamburg when she left that company to go to Vienna in 1916. It was the only performance in her career that had attracted all the acclaim and emotion of an 'Abschiedsvorstellung' or farewell performance. Her actual last (guest) appearance there had been in 1929 as the Marschallin; her last performance in Vienna in 1937 had been as the Marschallin (though nobody at the time ever imagined that she would not return); she gave her last performance at the Met as the Marschallin in 1945 and now, a year later, it was exactly the same story in San Francisco, although the American public automatically assumed that she would be singing again – at both houses. These two managements did it kindly by merely failing to engage her any more, though Lotte should have taken the hint in 1944.

Meanwhile, and until the operatic situation had fully struck home to her, Lotte devoted more time to the concert platform. Victor had not altogether forgotten her so far as recordings were concerned, though there had been none since 1942 (Columbia) while her last Victor session had been in February 1940. In February 1947, her Liederabend with Ulanowsky has been preserved in part (see Discog. p. 304), and her commercial recordings in June appear like a straightforward continuation of her previous Victor song-making (Discog. 429–38).

Lotte appeared in the MGM film *Big City*, having landed a seven-year contract with that company. 'Made up to look much older than she is, as a dramatic actress in motion pictures, she makes her screen début as a warm-hearted grandmother to small Margaret O'Brien. Naturally she sings in the film – "Kerry Dance", Brahms' "Cradle Song", and "God Bless America". "I have never been one to live in the past", she said recently. "It is today and tomorrow that are important and interesting. Now I am finding this all so new, so . . . so exciting!"'[3]

On 8 January 1948, Richard Tauber passed gently away. He had sung for the last time at Covent Garden on 27 September 1947 during the visit of the Vienna State Opera (and Krauss was one of its conductors) in a performance of *Don Giovanni*. He was dying as he sang that wonderful Don Ottavio, not as a member of the company, but as a resident in London. His old friends urged him to join them for one performance. In early December Tauber had a lung removed, but the most careful treatment could not save him.[4]

Lotte mentions that the house, Hope Ranch Park, that had been bought in Santa Barbara was undergoing alterations, but they were to be finished by the middle of April. Its magnificent view of the Pacific, its gentle climate and general feeling of tranquility all brought about a physical and mental well being. It was the ideal place for Lotte.

Yet she could not rest. That was never in her nature. So she wrote, and she wondered whether, after all, the Met had finished with her. In August 1948 there was a concert in the Hollywood Bowl, Ulanowsky at the piano and Eugene Ormandy conducting the orchestra, but still nothing from the Met.

In May 1949, Lotte expressed her distress, for it hurt her professional pride, that the last *Rosenkavalier*, after her own in 1945, had been with Rose Bampton as the Marschallin. She had helped Rose Bampton with the role, she liked her, but regarded her as very much a junior. Then the opera had been dropped from the repertoire. *Nobody had informed her.* That is what upset her. But was Edward Johnson obliged to do so?

It was common knowledge that he had only one more season to complete at the Met before Rudolf Bing, a naturalised Englishman, formerly a Viennese Jew, was to succeed him. Lotte had first met Bing when he was an artist's agent in Vienna in 1923 or so, and had shown her dislike for him. He had not forgotten. When he founded the new Edinburgh Festival in 1946 (and controlled it thereafter) he had invited Elisabeth Schumann to sing there, but he had not invited Lotte. Even before that, when he was general manager of the Glyndebourne Opera from its inception in 1934 and until 1938 when Lotte was forbidden to sing in the Reich, it would have been nice to have received an invitation to sing there. But she had received none. So she did not expect any favours from Rudolf Bing at the Met, and it rankled that she seemed to have been put on the shelf already.

In March 1950, Lotte gave a concert which was acclaimed as her fiftieth in Manhattan in ten years. It was to honour the memory of Richard Strauss who had died in the previous September. She sang the Marschallin's first act monologues without properties, costume or very much gesture, but with her former brio and finesse.

Meanwhile, Lotte was working on a new novel, *Of Heaven, Hell and Hollywood* which was never published. It was considered by her agent to be out of fashion with the times and the demand, although such extracts as have been printed[5] demonstrate her clear knowledge of singers, and her roguish ability to caricature their foibles. She appreciated that most singers, given ideal circumstances in which to work, would probably devote most of their time and energies to some other occupation altogether, believing it to be far more interesting – if not more important – than their own God-given gift.

The story, or the 'Heaven' part of it, is about a tenor called Reinhold (the name of Lotte's first teacher) who meets Melchior, Schubert, Goethe, Lotte and others in Heaven. He is amazed to find Lotte painting, instead of singing, and with tongue in cheek she allows this Reinhold to admit that Lotte's painting is not as good as her singing. Melchior is hunting game, but thanks to a special arrangement with The Almighty, the great tenor only *thinks* he has shot his prey. Goethe praises Schubert's 'Erlkönig' setting, and tells the shy composer that he is misinformed about the poet's dislike of it, and that he does not want to hear it re-composed. And so on.

Lotte's generous stroke about her painting was unexpected, for this occupation had become almost an obsession to her in real life, and was later extended to ceramics. Even her most fervent friends and well-wishers tended to express the same views of it as Reinhold had done.

Lotte also painted portraits and pictures of opera singers in costume which she gave as presents. On the other hand, her *bought* presents seemed to be subject to financial control.

'Gustl' Breuer, musician and writer as well as exile in America from Austria, says:[6]

> I remember one Christmas at Schumann's in New York, when a gift from Lehmann was unwrapped. It was from a drugstore or Wool-

worths, a metal clasp which fits on to a table from which dangled a hook to take a lady's handbag. 'Ah, that's the new régime at Santa Barbara' Schumann laughed, and that was that.

Lotte was still bubbling over with energy. Each day had to show something achieved, and it was a famous one for her when she was invited to join the staff of the Music Academy of the West in Santa Barbara. At first she had strong reservations.[7]

> Teaching was to me very far from my thoughts. I said 'Oh no! I would never in my life teach. I don't know how to do that: I would never like it.' And they persuaded me to come just once a week and talk to the students or to read them my books or to just be there and tell them about my experiences. And I said 'No. If I do that, then I really would like a Master Class.' And so I started a Master Class without having any idea what to do with them. And it took me a year really to learn to organise and to force them to have a repertory ready because you will not believe it the singers come and have no repertory. They come and generally they know all the old war horses, the same old Lieder. To make them learn something new is something which one has to do each time. And I enjoy it tremendously. It is a great satisfaction and a great frustration, both . . . The talent has to be inborn. One can awaken the talent but one cannot create it: one can only re-create.

On 16 February 1951, Lotte gave a concert, as usual in the Town Hall, New York, accompanied by Paul Ulanowsky. It was not until the interval, when she spoke to the audience, that they realised that there was something very unusual about it.[8]

> This is my farewell recital . . . (Cries of 'No! No!') I had hoped you would protest, but please don't argue with me. After 41 years of anxiety, nerves, strain and hard work, I think I deserve to take it easy. The Marschallin looks into her mirror and says 'It is time!' I look into my mirror and say 'It is time!'

Her last song was Schubert's 'An die Musik', but she was unable to complete the last line, for the emotion in the Hall was palpable, and Lotte burst into tears.

She was practically mobbed afterwards by the hundreds of her fans, supporters and even ordinary members of the public who had attended this concert, and when she had recovered her composure, Lotte remarked, with all her old spirit: 'It is good that I do not wait for the people to say,

"My God, when will that Lotte Lehmann shut up!"[9] For many concert-goers this certainly seemed to mark the end of an era.

It was not that altogether, for Lotte had already agreed to start her classes, only Lieder to begin with, but opera as well, later on.

In July of that year she noticed that her voice was not behaving normally, though there was nothing wrong with her vocal cords. Even so, she had an ice-pack round her neck for several days, as the condition seemed to come and go, irrespective of whether she was using her voice or not. The new medical word 'allergy' was given to explain it away to her.[10]

All the same, she gave another concert in Santa Barbara in August, then listened to the test pressings of her New York Farewell, but could not bear to hear her speech. The very last concert in August had been at the Lobero Theatre with Gwen Koldovsky accompanying her and it was recorded privately (see Discog. p. 305).

In January 1952, Lotte and a friend visited Death Valley in the mountains between Santa Barbara and Las Vegas, the hottest, dryest and lowest area in the USA, so that the only comfortable time to visit it is during the winter. Lotte found it 'overwhelmingly beautiful' and the two of them picked up all kinds of stones, the one choosing very small pieces of mineral, but Lotte dragging huge lumps about because, characteristically she found the large, glistening objects more dramatic.[11]

In February she gave some classes at Pasadena which were very successful. They went on into March, and they were recorded and made available to the public. Their contents are given in the Discography on pages 306–8.

Then on 23 April, Elisabeth Schumann died in New York, after a lingering illness. According to Gustl Breuer who was with her when she passed away, she seemed to have no idea of her condition. Lotte was shocked. She described Elisabeth as 'gaiety impersonated. I have never in my life heard anybody laugh as she could. She was like a happy bird and every one who knew her loved her. It seems quite impossible that she should now be just a heapful of ashes. I cannot get the sense of it.'[12] Elisabeth had one son by her first husband, Puritz (Klemperer's antagonist) and he arranged for a memorial service to his mother in London, where she was also loved and remembered.

Lotte was busy arranging programmes for her students who were due to start their course in June, and was overwhelmed by the larger number of applicants than had been foreseen.

She went to San Francisco to hear a performance of *Rosenkavalier* in English. The translation upset her at first, but after about ten minutes she was able to accept it. Only Ochs's 'Leopold, wir geh'n!' in Act III was unfortunately turned into 'Leopold, let's beat it!' which Lotte found most unpalatable, like the sets, which compared very unfavourably with Roller's.

In the following year, Lotte went on lecture-recital tours, following the première of 'Opera, Song and Life' in Santa Barbara in October.[13] Two young and keen impresarios called Russell Lewis and Howard Young presented this dramatisation of Lotte's life, with herself as narrator and six of her students singing the key songs and arias in her life. There was also one scene devoted to the rehearsal of *La Bohème*.

Lewis and Young were good company and Lotte loved travelling from place to place with them in their 'Show'. They all had a good deal of laughter. She discussed with them, and with others, the possibility of a Lotte Lehmann Opera Company, but as it was felt such an enterprise would only be feasible if it were set up as a nationwide tour, Lotte felt she could not possibly undertake such an exhausting enterprise. Lewis and Young often came to talk about it to her, even though they had lost a lot of money with the 'Show'.

'I never was a real *prima donna*', she wrote to a friend, and went on to say that she thought she had had rather a drab life, and felt like 'a little mousy dressmaker'.[14]

In early 1955 she had to have an operation on one of her feet. Two of her toes were cut open, the bones reset and wires put in to hold them in position. She hated being in hospital, and especially disliked having to ask for a bed-pan, but her nurse astonished her by saying, comfortingly, 'Don't think twice about it. It's just the same for us as it would be for you to go out and sing in front of an audience.'[15]

The Vienna State Opera House was nearing completion, having been rebuilt. In October 1955 the last occupation troops had left there and the reopening was scheduled for 5 November. The building cost 260 million Austrian Schillings (by today's rate of exchange about £10 million) but was not, as rebuilt opera houses are in East Germany, a replica of the old one. The architects wisely decided to incorporate many visual features of the old house, such as the colour scheme in crimson and ivory; but the seating had to be reduced to conform to the new safety regulations, and many of the boxes had been omitted in keeping with the demands of the age. The stage was entirely remodelled and incorporates as many modern devices as possible.

A seat in the house for the opening night cost 5,000 AS and anticipation of the event whipped up the Viennese to a high pitch of excitement.[16] As a life- and honorary-member of the Opera, as well as a recipient of its honours, Lotte was invited as a special guest. She travelled to Europe well in advance of the opening date, her first journey to Austria since before the war.

She started in Italy where she[17]

> acquired on the way a chauffeur with a floridly Italian (or at least histrionic) temperament. On her first night in Austria, at the border town of Villach, she experienced a foretaste of what was coming: the innkeeper brought her flowers, there was a cluster of eager townspeople around the car in the morning to see her off to Vienna. . . .
>
> The Italian chauffeur discovered . . . that Mme Lehmann was a great singer and a national glory – he had previously thought her a painter because she sketched all the way through Italy. Everywhere the car stopped the same kind of thing happened. In a village where the waiter asked her to sign his memory book she asked him, in some surprise, how he could know her after all these years. He said, all offended dignity: 'You think I cannot recognise Lotte Lehmann?'[18]

She arrived in Semmering, about fifty miles (eighty kilometres) from Vienna and waited there for two days, anxious for news from friends that would either speed her on her way to them, or else might make her change her mind and her plans altogether.

Maria Jeritza was still alive and, Lotte knew, had also been invited to the reopening. Lotte also knew that her rival had not yet accepted. The last thing that Lotte was prepared to do was to be seen next to Jeritza in the guests' box, and she had to know what to do.

Then the news came through.[19] Jeritza had been refused a second ticket for her husband, Mr. Seery (a very rich American-European) and in a pet had refused to cross the Atlantic. This was Lotte's cue, and she acted on it immediately,[20]

> . . . with her companion and her flamboyant chauffeur, she arrived at the Ambassador Krantz Hotel in Vienna, in the royal suite.
>
> 'I am sure you know that in Europe and especially in Vienna one has always very many servants. Domestic help is no problem over there. So my maids from former years had made enquiries when I would arrive. And there they were – all of them. They had decorated the door of the apartment with garlands and had put a big sign above it: "Welcome home in Vienna!" . . . My rooms were so filled with flowers that it was difficult to put anything down. Two of my maids who had always been terribly jealous of each

other continued exactly the same thing after these apparently quite unimportant eighteen years. . . . I explained to them how easy it is nowadays to take care of myself. They paled. The looked at each other and then at me with stricken eyes . . .'

Lotte also found many of her old fans, now grown up and with children of their own, but they still came round to see her as in the old days.[21]

'There is a very strong bondage between the audience and the singer
– stronger than in any country, I believe. Music is so very much a part of their lives. All the people feel music in their own blood, necessary for them like the air they breathe. And the artist who brings this music to them becomes much more an idol who, in a certain sense, is their own, a part of their lives . . .'

The official opening of the Opera took place in the morning of November 5th – a ceremony of great solemnity for invited guests, with the President of the Republic and all the officials present. Mme Lehmann seems to have been even more moved at the ceremony in the morning than at the first performance (*Fidelio*) that night.

'It was an unforgettable moment when the iron curtain rose,' she says of the morning. 'Even now in memory it chokes me. This wonderful old house which has served only beauty, which has given joy and uplift to thousands of music loving people, had been mute for so long . . . When Ministerialrat Marboe, the General Manager greeted the guests of honour, I felt proudly the surge of love and loyal admiration which came up to my box in big waves of applause. In the end the wonderful Philharmonic Orchestra played the Prelude to the *Meistersinger*. It almost killed me.'

Lehmann was so stormed by emotions of every kind that she seems to have been unable to give full attention to the performance of *Fidelio*, which, in any case, heard after these momentous eighteen years, must in itself have set her mind and heart wandering . . . As she says, 'Beauty has awakened in ruins,' and 'the heart of Austria was beating again.'

The Italian chauffeur . . . took full advantage of his position. He obtained free seats at theatres, disobeyed traffic rules, discarded his old clothes for new, and did everything he could to take advantage of the fact that he was chauffeur to the great lady. On the night of the Fidelio, when Lehmann's name was mentioned on the loud-speakers and the crowd in the streets outside cheered, he rose and made a speech as being her chauffeur. And on his last night in Vienna he was given a farewell party by all the new acquaintances and friends he had made – forty people were present, he told Lehmann proudly.[22]

It was a blessing that Lotte had never seen the Opera in its state of ruin after the American air raid; she merely came back to a refurbished building which, from the outside, looked very much the same as it had always done. To coincide with the reopening, an Austrian brand of cigarettes produced cards picturing the great singers of the past at the Vienna Opera. No. 1 in the series was Lotte Lehmann.[23]

After this exciting and emotionally disturbing event, Lotte went to Gastein and some of her old haunts before returning to California. One day Anna Russell sat in at one of the master classes and was so impressed by what she saw that she gave a handsome scholarship of $600 a year, to continue as long as she remained an entertainer. And as a display of gratitude from another quarter, the University of California made her a Doctor of Fine Arts in June. In a letter to a friend, Lotte expressed her humorous disappointment that nobody was addressing her as 'Doctor Lehmann'.

In the summer of 1956, she went back to Austria, and now that the ice had been broken by last year's excursion, it was to become an annual event, partly for enjoyment, partly for health reasons. She was suffering from a bad knee and benefited from the treatment she obtained at Bad Gastein. Afterwards she went to Venice, carrying with her a bad cold virus which, she said, 'fell desperately in love with me, and I seemed to be dreadfully attractive to him . . . !' She did not enjoy Venice on account of the 'unsympathetic people' and the consequent lack of the romantic atmosphere which she had expected to find there, as in the past.

Vienna was 'not so crazy' as in 1955, and more like the easy-going city she knew so well. She went to the Opera for a performance of *Meistersinger*, but was not at all pleased.

For the first time since long before the war, Lotte went to Hamburg. She mourned the destruction and disappearance of the old Stadttheater where she had sung the 'trembling pages' in *Lohengrin* and *Tannhäuser*. When she had left the company in 1916, and, of course, had visited there frequently afterwards as a guest, a young and pretty girl called Else had been her dresser and even her confidante at times. Lotte happened to ask whether Else was still alive – still there? They called her, and an old, fat, white-haired woman came shyly down the staircase. It gave cause for Lotte to reflect, like the Marschallin, on age: 'we always see in others how we look ourselves.'[24]

From Hamburg, Lotte flew to London where she had not been for eighteen years, and was delighted to find that there she was 'quite unforgotten'. She was entertained by old friends and also by the Austrian Ambassador at a party in the Embassy where she met the conductor Rafael Kubelik. He promised to send any talented young singers from Covent Garden to her. Kubelik was then the Music Director at the Royal Opera. She was interviewed, made a radio broadcast and was thoroughly happy among many old friends.

In October, Lotte branched out into a new sphere by reciting the words of 'Dichterliebe', 'Winterreise' and some Hugo Wolf songs as well as poems by Mörike and Goethe. She also spoke, very feelingly, the words of the Marschallin's three monologues from *Der Rosenkavalier*. They were all recorded (see Discog. page 308); and it is, perhaps, worth noting that in 1961 the whole *Rosenkavalier* was performed as 'A Comedy in Three Acts' in the Schloss Schönbrunn, Vienna, by a company of distinguished Austrian actors and actresses.[25]

So far as Lotte's recitations were concerned, she believed it to be perfectly legitimate because, for her, the words had always been as important as the music. She credits her dear friend Judith Anderson (the actress) with the idea, for although there was no music to be heard, Lotte declared that 'in my inside I always sang. The music was too strong in me, I could not kill it.'

One of Lotte's pupils was emerging as an exceptional artist, and was given every form of help, encouragement – and love. Her name was Grace Bumbry and Lotte regarded her almost as a daughter. She had been a pupil at Santa Barbara since 1956 and was going to remain there until the end of the summer of 1958. Lotte was absolutely certain that Grace was 'a great and sensational artist ready to conquer the world. . . . She is thrilling beyond words' Her voice was described by Lotte as being of a 'strange, earthy quality, dark vibrant and alive, which generally gives me the shivers as though it had come out of the depths of her being.'[26]

Grace was to have a recital at the Academy in July and a public one in Santa Barbara in November. Lotte was not in the best of health, always getting colds and viruses, but being an old trouper, she carried on through them.

She took Grace with her to London in September 1957 where Joan Cross, of the London Opera School, had arranged some master classes for Lotte at the Wigmore Hall. There were twelve classes between 23 September and 19 October and they were packed. Many people had not seen or heard Lotte since the summer of 1938, many others had never seen her before, and it was a momentous opportunity for 'meeting' the famous interpreter of the Marschallin and Sieglinde on records.

Ivor Newton, who accompanied all the classes, has this to say:[27]

> Time passed, and Lehmann retired; there were many things, like painting, which was a long standing hobby of hers, to which she intended to devote long, leisurely days in California. Her vitality, her histrionic power and her devotion to music, however, had not tired, and the world can count itself fortunate that she was persuaded to hold some master classes to which the public should be admitted. She was a delight to her audience and an inspiration to her pupils; in addition she seemed to enjoy herself. . . . During the lessons she sang often, but usually in a quiet voice an octave, or even two, below the real note, but with the perfection of phrasing and inflection which had made her performances . . . unforgettable. . . . Once, and only once, she seemed to forget herself and sang out as though more than thirty years had not passed since she had first won our devotion on Covent Garden stage; apparently automatically she broke onto a phrase at its proper pitch and in full voice; when she stopped, she was rewarded with a fervour of applause from her students and audience. Much as this seemed to please her, she did not repeat the effect. With facial expression, gestures, enunciation and her low, quiet voice, she could convey the essence of the opera in a way that was deeply moving; the beautiful singing she seemed prepared to leave to the young singers whom she was teaching . . .

On the last afternoon of the 1957 classes in London, Grace Bumbry sang the 'Frauenliebe und- leben, looking young and fresh and extremely handsome in a plain, daffodil-yellow dress, and this Schumann cycle was the culmination of the classes. Some people thought that the final display piece by a pupil of Lotte's from California, not by one of the London Theatre School for which these classes were intended, was a little bit off-side.

Lotte took Grace to Vienna for a week before returning to Santa Barbara at the end of October. Many agents and important opera people in London had expressed an interest in Grace, and Lotte was certain that it was only a matter of time before her protégée was safely placed to begin her career.[28]

On 20 November, Grace gave her recital in Santa Barbara before a completely sold-out house. It was a tremendous success, so much so that the poor girl (she was only twenty) was overwhelmed. Her nerves were affected and Lotte felt – in spite of the huge ovation – that Grace had not been on her top form.

In December, Lotte was left the sizeable legacy of $78,000 by Dr Ernst Schwarz, the president of Agfa in the USA with a note 'in appreciation of our long and wonderful friendship'. Lotte received an outright gift of $12,000 and one sixth of the residuary estate, but nothing else has emerged about their relationship. Schwarz died at the age of seventy-three.[29]

Lotte's seventieth birthday was celebrated quietly in the following February, but a month later she gave one of her several interviews to the loquacious John Gutman of the Met, for inclusion in intervals during opera broadcasts. Then, in the Spring, she was approached by a thirty-five year old Englishman called Archie Drake.[30] He had been a merchant seaman and was something of a Captain Balstrode from Great Yarmouth, and he had a voice. He told Lotte that he had been recommended to apply to her for an audition, and would she give him one?

She heard him in the next few weeks and said shortly, 'We-ll, yes, stay here and work with me.' So that Summer, Archie moved in and met the other members of the Music Academy of the West who were closely connected with Lotte's classes.

The Music Director was Maurice Abravanel. He had been born in 1903 in Thessalonika, and his musical career had embraced the works of Busoni and Weill in Berlin up to 1934, when he was obliged to leave Germany and went to direct the ballet in Paris. Thereafter he directed opera in Australia. He was a conductor at the Met for four operas but became the 'victim of internal politics' and transferred to Broadway where he continued to champion the compositions of Kurt Weill. In 1947 he became the conductor of the Utah Symphony and achieved the 'highest rate of concert attendance in the poorest artistic state of the USA'. And now, with all this experience behind him, Abravanel was in California.

He was a key figure to Archie Drake in more ways than one, because he arranged a scholarship from the Academy for the impecunious Englishman who did not think he stood a chance of attracting one.

The other leading personalities at Santa Barbara Academy were Carl Zitowsky, chorus master and conductor; Jan Popper, of the University of California in Los Angeles's Opera workshop. The Armenian lyric tenor, Armand Tokatyan, took voice. He had been a member of the Met from 1923 to 1946 and had toured for a substantial part of his career. Bill Eddy was the senior vocal coach and worked closely with Lotte.

One of the most lovable people there, after Lotte herself, was

Gwendoline Williams Koldovsky, a Welsh woman who had married the violinist, Adolf Koldovsky. He had died in 1954. According to Archie Drake she was 'sweet, simple, self-effacing and an immaculate accompanist.' She was sensitive and supportive, knowing intuitively how the singer felt and what he needed at any moment.

Each student spent a week preparing to sing a song on the following Saturday afternoon, and an operatic aria or concerted number on the following Sunday afternoon, both before an invited audience. Irving Beckmann was in charge of preparing the operatic items.

The hall, where the 'public examinations' took place, seated some two hundred rather close together, when it was full. There was a good acoustic and the place was comfortable. The students and piano were on a daïs some two feet six inches from the floor (76cm). Lotte sat in a large chair, with a music stand in front of her if the piece was unfamiliar, and she listened carefully. Usually she made very little correction, more often praising the singer and adding a few words such as 'with greater acquaintanceship the interpretation of this song (or aria) will grow.'

If, on the other hand, the piece being sung was one of Lotte's 'own', she might say 'What about this? – let's think of it like this, perhaps'; but very occasionally she would say, 'Let me show you!' Then she sang it, an octave down, but very occasionally she forgot (as in London) and sang out at the proper pitch, to everybody's delight. Because of this, and possibly because of the manner in which she offers instruction in her books, Lotte attracted the reputation, in some quarters, of being dogmatic. But this was not so. It was 'an exploration together', she told them, 'we are looking for ways to help you to find *your* interpretation. But please, whatever you do, *don't* imitate me!'

Some of the pupils, who either were in awe of Lotte, or couldn't develop an interpretation of their own, for one reason or another, received less of her interest. She loved best those who took her advice and built upon it.

Apart from Grace Bumbry, there was a young baritone called Douglas Miller, whom Lotte adored. He was one of the finest interpreters of Lieder that any of the students had heard, and Lotte loved both his methods and his voice. When he sang, all she said was, 'Now here is Douglas Miller to sing. I know he will do it beautifully.' It was a very light, lyric voice, and too light for the opera stage.

Another interesting and important student was Ronald Holgate. He was a very good singing actor with a flexible voice, though unsuitable for opera because of a somewhat harsh quality. He had a great success in musical comedy later, on Broadway, and was seen in London in 'Lend me a Tenor'. He has a great turn of comedy, a good presence, and is an extremely pleasant man. Also he is the only singer mentioned by name in Lotte's book 'Singing with Richard Strauss' after his marvellous student performance as Mandryka in the Academy's production of *Arabella*.

Lotte really enjoyed putting back the clock by getting up on to the platform and demonstrating one of her favourite scenes. One day she showed Mary Beth Piel how she (Lotte) had done the scene with Hans Sachs and the shoe in the second act of *Die Meistersinger* (who said that Lotte disliked the character of Eva?). It was a glorious moment. Lotte was so young and 'coquettish, and she *sang* in a voice that was still silver and wonderful.'

One afternoon the students performed the entire last act of *La Bohème* for Lotte. Mary Beth Piel was the Mimi, Ron Holgate sang Schaunard, and Archie Drake was the Colline. They expected to be interrupted, but as it went on, and on and Lotte allowed them to continue, they became more and more confident. Even when they had reached the Coat Song and Archie thought this to be an ideal place to stop, she still let them continue, right to the very end. 'Mind you,' said Archie, 'it had been well rehearsed, but the last thing we expected was a complete, uninterrupted performance.'

At the end, 'Lotte was sitting in her chair crying. Tears were rolling down her cheeks. After a while she said, "My young friends, you have moved me more than I've been moved in many years. What you did – your youth and freshness and innocence have moved me to tears."'

It was shattering for the students, who were practically in tears too, and it was not the only occasion on which everyone in that room was in tears.

'In this particular year, as a teaching vehicle, she chose the *Toten Augen* of d'Albert on account of the interesting characters in it. Myrtocle, the blind Jewish girl, decides that in order to preserve her marriage to her deformed Roman husband, whom she has seen at last during the temporary time she had her sight, she must go blind again.

'Lotte decided that she would demonstrate that afternoon how this scene should be played. She got up on to the daïs and stood in what we used for the doorway of the house, and just stood there. There is nothing to sing at all, there is d'Albert's music to listen to. But this figure, standing in the doorway and staring into the sun – it was all there. She did not move a muscle – not a muscle. It was all there in the face, in the expression and in the eyes that you could *see* gradually becoming blind! It was uncanny! In the end, the whole assembly was reduced to an emotional shambles. It was an indescribable scene. Bill Eddy was sitting next to me – sobbing. We all were. I will never forget that afternoon. It was one of the most extraordinary things that ever happened to me and it epitomized the *power* of the art of Lotte Lehmann.'

Although Richard Strauss's Salome was not one of Lotte's roles, she sometimes coached student dramatic sopranos in the closing scene with Jokanaan's head. Archie Drake remembers one day in 1959 (with a certain horror) when from her collection of historic mementos, Lotte seized Napoleon's death-mask, put it on a meat-dish and served it up to Dorothy Sanden at Santa Barbara.

Archie Drake's most cherished – yet most painful – memories of his time with Lotte Lehmann in Santa Barbara was in the winter of 1960–61 when he studied Schubert's 'Winterreise' cycle of twenty-four songs with her. 'We worked on three songs a week, with an accompanist, for eight weeks on end. Her insight was remarkable, and I lived through the cycle in those eight weeks. I became so depressed that one afternoon I burst into tears and walked out, but she understood. At the end, the last song, the 'Leiermann' (Hurdy-gurdy) is a retreat into insanity, but then I realised I'd done it – I'd gone through it all with her and a huge load dropped off me.' He remarked on the twenty-four paintings of the 'Winterreise' which Lotte did, each her concept of a song. Her two-dimensional version of Wilhelm Müller's words and Franz Schubert's setting of this tragic and morbid cycle was in 'different tones of blue: not an especially favourite colour of Lotte's but one which, to her, signalled the central core of agonised and desperate resignation in the deep, dark shades.'

When asked about Mozart, Lotte confessed that she did not find enough romantic warmth in his music, but her interpretation of his 'Wiegenlied' (Lullaby) was extremely novel – and romantic. Instead of a straightforward cradle-song, it was the 'for goodness sake go to sleep' of a young mother to her new baby while she got ready to go out for the evening and hoped it would soon drop off before she was ready to leave the house.

Lotte only once sang Mahler – it lay too low for her – but she loved coaching it. Douglas Miller and Grace Bumbry were both superb in the 'Kindertotenlieder'.

Yet among her successes and the undoubted joy it gave Lotte to see her students blossoming under her care, she had her disappointments. A young American Heldentenor called Myron Slater obtained an audition and sang 'In fernem Land' from *Lohengrin*. Lotte was delighted and considered it a major talent. He began to work, then slowly withdrew from his fellow-students, walking alone along the beach which lay a few yards away from the Academy. This was in 1960. Eventually he stopped working altogether and wrote to Lotte, telling her that he had been thinking about it all the Summer, but had received a *Call*. He was immediately released, and was ordained into the Presbyterian Church in course of time. Lotte was deeply disappointed: 'God should have kept out of it', was her comment.

Leila McCormack, a Canadian soprano, arrived in Santa Barbara one day to give an audition to Bill Eddy. She sang the Hall of Song aria from *Tannhäuser*. It was the sound 'of an enormous, Wagnerian soprano, a fantastic voice. Bill couldn't believe it. Pitch and quality were gorgeous, but it was the *size* of the voice. Bill phoned Lotte and said she must come over and listen.

'Lotte gave her a private audition. She sat and listened, then said, "Mein Gott! What have we here?"'

She set to work at once to teach Leila, but those who know Hergé's *Tintin* books will recognise in Mme McCormack the one-aria *prima donna*. Lotte could do nothing with her, for she had not a glimmer of understanding about anything. She could neither learn anything else nor sing anything else, and the voice was all in the throat. After a short time Lotte became so frustrated that she could not bear even to see Leila, especially as she had a true Isolde voice that she could never use properly. It was a terrible, wasteful, agonising disappointment.

'Find your own way. If I can help you, I will,' Lotte used to say, but for Leila McCormack – never!

In 1959, Lotte had been to Bayreuth for the first time, as a guest of the Wagner family, for a performance of *Tristan und Isolde* with Wolfgang Windgassen and Birgit Nilsson. She met Windgassen's father there, now Kammersänger Professor Fritz Windgassen, whom Lotte had known long ago when they were both at the Hamburg Opera. Lotte was entraced by the 'mystical effect of the Prelude to *Tristan* rising from an invisible orchestra'.[31] Certainly the singing was of a high order, and once more, if only temporarily, she was grasped and held by the wonder of Isolde. This was the performance of 27 July.

1962 was a full year: Lotte was determined, it seems, to make full use of her time. In April she went to Zürich and Vienna again, after appearing in New York in a big TV show; and on 23 May was awarded 'a very high medal' – the Ring of Honour of the City of Vienna. She was in Bad Gastein for the whole of June but, much as she loved Austria, Santa Barbara called, and she returned there to prepare for a new venture.

She had been invited to help stage *Der Rosenkavalier* at the Met:[32]

> Grayhaired, portly, nearing 75, she sat just behind the footlights, an elbow planted on a dingy table, one hand gesturing delicately as she offered suggestions to stars too young to have heard her anywhere but on records . . .
>
> 'Sehr gut', Lehmann said crisply and often. But occasionally she shook her head . . . and murmured to herself, 'Sehr schlecht.' . . .
>
> In the breaks between scenes she would beckon the women to her, one at a time, and they would come with a little rush, kneeling beside her to confer in whispers . . .
>
> To the Octavian, Austria's handsome Herta Toepper, who is making her début in the *Rosenkavalier* revival, November 19, Lehmann said softly: 'You cannot do it like zat. You must be brighter . . .'
>
> She rose to demonstrate what she wanted, an old lady in black with a blue chiffon scarf looped around her throat. Then, suddenly, Lehmann vanished: there was Octavian, striding across the stage, lithe and impetuous, in the springtime of life.

And another article added:[32]

> To her right sat the young American conductor Lorin Maazel, who will lead the opera. He munched an apple. Mr Herbert . . . her colleague, concerned himself mainly with blocking out the broad lines for the action. Ralph Herbert is also a singer and has appeared many times as Faninal. Under Miss Lehmann's direction . . . she worked particularly with the intimate aspects of the singers' performance . . .

Among the many flowers which arrived for Lotte at the Met on the first night of this *Rosenkavalier* was a silver rose with the words 'Because we cannot forget'. She did not know who had sent it. Régine Crespin, a very willing pupil, was the Marschallin; Herta Toepper, not so willing; but Anneliese Rothenberger as Sophie – just adorable. 'I came home deeply exhausted,' wrote Lotte, 'and you can be sure that I never do that again.'[34]

On 4 January 1962, Grace Bumbry had been twenty-five. Lotte simply couldn't understand why no opera management had taken her up. Covent Garden seemed likely to do so, after her audition with Lord Harewood, and Lotte's prodding of David Webster. But before they had concluded matters, Grace had made her own arrangements with the Paris Opéra, but without telling Lotte. Grace's international career began as Amneris in *Aida* in Paris, though Lotte felt that Covent Garden would have been a more sensible start.

Archie Drake had not been settled either. Lotte spent a lot of time in trying to persuade people she knew, like the London artist's manager, Emmie Tillett of Ibbs and Tillett, to take an interest in him. Lotte suggested the second London opera house, which was rather affectingly referred to as 'Sadler Wells', but there was nothing there for him either. And Archie Drake has still not sung in opera in the land of his birth.

After her experience at the Met, Lotte was persuaded to do another of John Gutman's radio interviews, but this time with Jeritza there as well. It was a horrible experience. Lotte referred to them as 'two old cats in the form of two half-dead *prima donnas*, giggling the whole time like teenagers.'[35] Jeritza concealed behind large, dark glasses and innumerable jewels, was determined not to let the conversation become serious, in spite of Lotte's wish to do so. After all, it was something of an historic event.

'How is it possible that after four decades she is the same beast she always was?' Lotte complained to John Gutman afterwards. But Lotte managed to get in the date of 1916 which Jeritza, for some reason, did not want mentioned in case somebody was able to calculate her age. How the date of *Ariadne* in Vienna can have done so is incomprehensible. Jeritza had said, 'We always were good friends, Lottchen'. She replied, 'That is news to me.' But that was cut. Lotte was so disgusted afterwards that she broke down in her hotel. Jeritza had upstaged her yet again, but for the last time.

On 27 April 1963, Lotte's brother Fritz died in Santa Barbara. He also had fled from Austria in 1938, with his Austrian wife, and all they owned was confiscated. Fritz had been teaching dramatic interpretation at the High School for Music and Interpretation and had been giving private instruction.

Lotte was receiving new awards almost yearly. In 1960 she had been given the Bon Ami for that year; the Third Ring of Honour for 1963, and on 8 February 1964, the imposing Commanders' Cross of the Order of Merit of the Federal Republic of Germany, known as 'The Great Cross of Germany'. This was bestowed upon her at a ceremony in the German Consulate in Los Angeles.

She went back to Europe in the summer of 1964, first to Vienna and then on to Salzburg for Grace Bumbry's first *Macbeth* on 7 August, where she met an old friend from long ago, Charles Kullman, the lyric tenor of German birth who became an American.

'Grace is now, of course, a great *prima donna* . . . to me she was very sweet and quite humble . . . Do you like Karajan? There's a *Prima Donna* if ever there was one.'[36] He was conducting, and Fischer-Dieskau sang Macbeth. It was a great success for Grace and began her connection with the Salzburg Festival that was to continue until 1967.

In the Autumn, Lotte again went to hear Grace, this time in Chicago as Carmen, and as Eboli in *Don Carlos*. 'All I want in this world is to have Mme Lehmann satisfied with what I do', declared Grace. And Lotte expounded on her 'fantastic success at the Met. O God! How happy I was. I really have never heard such applause. This girl is the one for whom alone it is worthwhile to have taught her and worried about her (and worry yet!)'

On 27 February 1965, 'Lotte Lehmann Day' was proclaimed in Santa Barbara. Then she sprained her ankle rather badly, and was laid up for some time.

The Metropolitan Opera House on Broadway, between the 39th and 40th Streets, which had been the Mecca for American singers since October 1883, was about to close down, the site cleared to be occupied by an office block, and the New Met established in the Lincoln Center. There had been many people who attempted to resist burocracy, but Lotte was not one of them. Alas, she had no fond memories of the old building and did not lend her name to any campaigns to keep the old building. 'One does not sit on tombstones and weep', she said.

On 16 April, Lotte was invited to attend the last performance, at what was now becoming known as 'The Old Met', as a guest of honour, at Rudolf Bing's request. She found herself among Marjorie Lawrence, Lily Pons, Elisabeth Rethberg, Risë Stevens, Giovanni Martinelli, John Brownlee, Richard Crooks and Alexander Kipnis, and many tears were shed that night.

But when she was invited to the reopening of the New Met on 16 September, she declined. As a building and as a place for opera, it meant nothing to her. Nor did Samuel Barber's new work for the occasion, *Antony and Cleopatra*, mean much either.

In November she went to hear Grace in San Francisco, and in the following February she celebrated her seventy-ninth birthday – quietly. Another birthday celebration and a more festive one, followed in June in Hamburg. The buffo-tenor, Paul Schwarz was eighty; he had been a member of the company there from 1912 until the house had been destroyed in 1945, singing David in *Meistersinger*, Monostatos in the *Zauberflöte*, and Mime in *Der Ring*. consequently he and Lotte had been colleagues there for four years, and he was especially delighted that she was able to join him and his wife Adele.

Lotte's own eightieth birthday was celebrated in the following February in great style. Zubin Mehta conducted the Los Angeles Philharmonic Orchestra in a concert 'dedicated to Lotte Lehmann in recognition of her invaluable contribution to the world of music as both performer and teacher.' The programme was a little unexpected: Haydn's Symphony 95 in c minor; *Der Rosenkavalier* Act III – the Trio and Final Duet with three of Lotte's pupils; and Tchaikovsky's Symphony No. 5 in e minor. Afterwards, the principal guests and the committee went to Montecito for a celebration feast. In the following April, there was a performance of *Die Walküre* in San Francisco, dedicated to her.

It was also in San Francisco where Archie Drake got a firm engagement, and Lotte was so delighted that she went there to congratulate him in person.

In February 1969, a fortnight before Lotte's eighty-first birthday, the University Concert Hall in Santa Barbara was dedicated to her. She was her usual humorous self about that: 'Generations from now will be puzzled who Lotte Lehmann was, and I hope somebody may have heard about me and that I was once upon a time a rather good singer.'[37]

She regarded the whole business somewhat wryly with the remark: 'I really don't think one has to be congratulated to be so old. Pfui!! 81!!! Sometimes I feel like 100, sometimes not at all.'

In May she flew to Europe for the centenary celebrations of the Vienna Opera on 25 May. In the morning, Leonard Bernstein conducted a performance of Beethoven's Missa Solemnis, and in the evening, Karl Böhm's *Fidelio* was the highlight of the occasion. At the end of July in Salzburg, a book by Berndt W. Wessling called 'Lotte Lehmann – mehr als eine Sängerin' (. . . more than a singer) was published with a party 'in great style'. They had wanted the party at midnight, but Lotte declined, saying that she never stayed up that late any more, and if she had done so, she 'would only have looked like an old hag – which I am.'[38] After this, Lotte was presented with the Great Silver Medal of Salzburg.

She also published, on her own account, and mainly to give to friends as a very personal kind of present, a book of her own poems. It is called *Ruckblick* (Looking Back) and contains more than fifty utterances, some quite personal, reflecting on places, events, pictures, songs she sang and people in her life. It has a plain, grey paper cover and a rose on the front, drawn by herself.

'Isn't it awful, this blessed Christmas?' she asked in December, a propos having to send and to receive hundreds of cards. And for her it also meant the innumerable letters which she felt she had to write afterwards. In April she had an attack of arthritis and went to Bad Gastein again, hoping for complete relief, but it was only partial.

Lotte was writing yet another book, this time about Lieder cycles for the London publisher, Cassell. The Director who was her editor was David Ascoli, and he found Lotte's continual pressuring of him most uncomfortable. While the book was going through production in English, Lotte was busily translating it into German. Ascoli gave a party for her at the Hyde Park Hotel on 29 July 1971. Among those present were Desmond Shawe-Taylor, Neville Cardus, Janet Baker and Mr and Mrs Robert Speaight. Two chairs were set out in the middle of the room after the toast to Lotte, and one guest at a time occupied the chair next to her for a few minutes' personal talk. As soon as she gave the hint that the 'audition' was at an end, and the incumbent vacated the chair, there was a tactful pause before the next person slid gently in, until everybody there had received their individual attention from Lotte. She looked very alert and alive in mind, through her eyes, which sparkled as of old, but the body was clearly a burden to her.

By Christmas that year, her handwriting on envelopes was very strained; and thanking Archie Drake for his eighty-fourth birthday greeting in February 1972, she remarked, 'Is it true in the Bible that life is only happy when it is a busy one?'

Since 1968 Lotte and Otto Klemperer had been corresponding. It was, at first, on Lotte's part rather tentative, for she still regarded him as the impressive and remote conductor of the Hamburg Opera who had so tirelessly forced her into the role of Elsa. But gradually she found herself able to address him as 'Dear Otto', and to join him in recollections of those 'good old days'. Remembering that then Lotte was in love with him but he did not reciprocate it, one cannot help wondering whether now he had at last come round to feeling fondly for Lotte while she had no such ideas about him any longer. It is a charming, often humorous correspondence,[39] with Klemperer telling her about his production of *Fidelio* at Covent Garden, and Lotte telling him her (blasphemous) ideas about the last act of *Tristan und Isolde*! They met in Zürich in August 1972. Klemperer came to see Lotte and a photograph (q.v.) shows them to be enjoying each other's company enormously.

Lotte managed to visit Europe every summer, sometimes for as long as three months at a time. Both sides of the world attracted her: the old world to which she had formerly belonged, *still* belonged; the new world with its sunshine and *home* in Santa Barbara. When she had been in one of these two places for any length of time, the other called her and begged her to return.

After her eight-seventh birthday in 1975, Lotte wrote to Archie Drake: 'I am now an old woman and never go out any more in the evening and have not been at the Academy for months.' By Christmas, her handwriting was barely recognisable.

Shortly before Easter in 1976, the writing is shaky, small and scraggy, no large, generous, flowing shapes any more. After some discomfort, rather than pain, Lotte passed away at 8.35 in the morning of 26 August 1976, exactly on the other side of the calendar from her birthday. This is considered to be a beneficial sign, but does not very often occur.[40]

A very tiny envelope containing an indifferently typed invitation to the memorial service was sent to each of Lotte's friends: the tribute was at the Musical Academy of the West in Santa Barbara, who had so much to thank her for.

But that was a transitory affair. Santa Barbara does not hold the mortal part of Lotte, which was taken to the Friedhof in Vienna and placed in Austrian soil. Lotte has not gone, though, for her voice remains everywhere when, alive and full of her true spirit it can be heard anywhere and when there is one of her records to play.

The *Rosenkavalier*, in spite of everything it means, is not to me as moving, as inspiring, as her recording of the *Walküre*. And that first act with the essence of Lotte contained in it is only equalled by the scenes from the second act, immensely tragic and affecting.

Sieglinde's last utterance in Act III begins with these words:

> O hehrstes Wunder!
> Herrlichste Maid!
> Dir Treuen dank' ich heiligen Trost!

They represent one of Lotte Lehmann's most astonishing artistic achievements on the opera stage – and my own valediction to her.

Abbreviations

A und A	LL, *Anfang und Aufstieg* (1937)
Heyworth, *OK L&T*	Peter Heyworth, *Otto Klemperer: His Life and Times*, Vol. I (1983)
HUTC	Hamburg University Theatre Collection
MML	LL, *My Many Lives* (1948)
Prawy, *VO*	Marcel Prawy, *The Vienna Opera* (1970)
S w.RS	LL, *Singing with Richard Strauss* (1964)
Strauss-Schalk Corr.	Richard Strauss and Franz Schalk, *Briefwechsel* (1983)
Strauss-Hofmannsthal Corr.	Richard Strauss and H. von Hofmannsthal, *Correspondence* (1961)
W of S	LL, *Wings of Song* (1938)

Notes

Chapter One

1. *Perleberg: Ein Führer durch die Stadt* (1978), pp. 5, 8.
2. ibid., pp. 16–17.
3. Much of Lotte's early life is taken from her autobiography *Anfang und Aufstieg*, translated in the UK as *Wings of Song* and in the USA as *Midway in my Song*. All references are to the original German edition.
4. The Königliche Hochschule für Musik was incorporated into the Akademie der Künste; it was destroyed by bombs on Advent Sunday 1942, and rebuilt in the 1950s.
5. H. Rosenthal & J. Warrack, *Concise Oxford Dictionary of Opera* (1980)
6. *Record Collector*, June 1986.
7. Rosenthal & Warrack, op.cit., p. 301.
8. B.W. Wessling, *Lotte Lehmann . . . mehr als eine Sängerin* (1969), p. 45
9. Professor Dr B. von Barsewisch (a descendant of the zu Putlitz family: letters.
10. A und A, pp. 92–3.

Chapter Two

1. Heyworth, *OK L&T*, p. 49.
2. HUTC Archive.
3. ibid. and local research.
4. Heyworth, *OK L&T*, pp. 49–50.
5. *A und A*, p. 94.
6. All information about operas and casts from HUTC Archive.
7. HUTC Archive.
8. HUTC Archive, *OK L&T*
9. K.J. Kutsch & L. Riemens, *Unvergängliche Stimmen* (1975)
10. ibid.
11. *OK L&T*, pp. 63–4.
12. LL's first important role, of more substance than Freia.
13. LL's forceful personality demonstrated.
14. *A und A*, p. 107. She did not sing it that often in Altona.
15. HUTC Archive.

16. *A und A*, p. 109.
17. HUTC Archive.
18. J. Russell, *Erich Kleiber* (157), p. 163: 'Weingartner's great merits have never quite been those of an opera director.'
19 *A und A*, p. 117; Heyworth, *OK L&T*, p. 75
20. BBC broadcast of 12.6.79: excerpts from three interviews with LL made on 20.10.56, 26.7.59 and 27.9.65.
21. *Hamburger Fremdenblatt*, 30.11.12, quoted by Heyworth, *OK L&T*, p. 75.

Chapter Three

1. Heyworth, *OK L&T*, p. 78,
2. Conversation with K.A. Pollak.
3. *Hamburger Fremdenblatt*, 27.12.12; but the curtain had come down before Klemperer can have emerged from the pit!
4. Gustl Breuer who was at Elisabeth Schumann's death-bed when she told him this: letter.
5. F. von Weingartner, trans. M. Wolff, *Buffets and Rewards* (1937), p. 291.
6. Professor Dr B. von Barsewisch: letter.
7. A. Jefferson, *Der Rosenkavalier* (1985), pp. 134–5.
8. A. Jefferson, *The Operas of Richard Strauss in Great Britain* 1910–1963 (1963).
9. Weingartner, op.cit., p. 165.
10. HUTC Archive.
11. Kutsch & Riemens, op.cit.
12. HUTC Archive.
13. *A und A*, p. 120.
14. ibid., p. 121.
15. H. Riemann, *Musik-Lexikon* Vol 2. p. 452 (1972)
16. *A und A*, pp. 122–3.
17. Jefferson, *Operas of Strauss*, p. 74.
18. *A und A*, pp.124–5.
19. *Opera* Magazine, Festival issue, 1966 p. 7–20.
20. F. Leider, *Playing My Part* (1966), p. 65.
21. *A und A*, pp. 125–7; BBC broadcast of 12.6.79.
22. *A und A*, p. 129.
23. ibid.
24. ibid.
25. V. Sheean, *First and Last Love* (1956), p. 204.
26. *Die Bühne* (1914).
27. HUTC Archive.
28. Hamburg Opera programme, 1968.
29. Letter in possession of Herr Horst Wahl.
30. Weingartner, op.cit., p. 157.
31. *A und A*, pp. 135–6.
32. ibid., pp. 137–8.

Notes

Chapter Four

1. *Die Bühne* (1916).
2. *A und A*, p. 139.
3. *Riemann*, op.cit. p. 452 Vol.II.
4. J. Culshaw, *Ring Resounding* (1967), pp. 66–7.
5. *A und A*, pp. 139–40.
6. Kutsch & Riemens, op.cit.; Prawy, *VO*, p. 96.
7. M. Jeritza, *Sunlight and Song*, pp. 162–74 and p. 202.
8. Discovery of Jeritza's birth certificate after death showed that she was born in 1882, not in 1887 as she had always claimed.
9. IRSG Blätter, no. 7 (1976), p. 5 (Strauss-Karpath correspondence).
10. All information about operas and casts in Vienna are from the Music Collection in the State Library, Vienna.
11. Kutsch & Riemens, op.cit.
12. Prawy, *VO*, p. 108.
13. H. Gregor, *Die Welt der Oper: Die Oper der Welt* (1931), p. 29
14. Conversation with Jim Pearce, London.
15. Prawy, *VO*, p. 96
16. *Strauss-Hofmannsthal Corr.*, pp. 152–3.
17. Gregor, op.cit., p. 177
18. Heyworth, *OK L&T*, p. 118n.
19. Deduction from castlists.
20. *Encyclopedia Britannica*, s.u.*Austria* Vol. 14., p. 515.
21. LL, *MML*, p. 197.
22. Kutsch & Riemens, op.cit.
23. Prawy, *VO*, p. 164.

Chapter Five

1. J. Kapp, *Richard Strauss und der Berliner Oper*, II (1939), pp. 40–6.
2. *Strauss-Hofmannsthal Corr.*, pp. 311–12.
3. ibid., p. 310.
4. *Strauss-Schalk Corr.: letter from RS:* 29.10.18.
5. *Strauss-Hoffmannsthal Corr.*, p. 297.
6. Prawy, *VO*, p. 100, who also notes her 'erotic aura': p. 96.
7. *Strauss-Hofmannsthal Corr.*, p. 312.
8. *Strauss-Schalk Corr.*: letter from RS: 15.12.18.
9. *MML*, p. 33.
10. *Strauss-Hofmannsthal Corr.*, p. 76.
11. LL, *S w.RS*, p. 21.
12. *Salzburger Nachrichten*, 29.8.64; *Strauss-Hofmannsthal Corr.*, p. 326.
13. *S w.RS*, pp. 22–3.
14. ibid., p. 23.
15. *S w.RS*, pp. 24–7 *inter alia*.
16. *MML*, p. 197.

17. ibid.
18. ibid., p. 198.
19. M. Carner, *Puccini: A Critical Biography* (1958), p. 67.
20. *IRSG Blätter*, no. 11(1978), p. 2.
21. Gustl Breuer: letter, 1984.
22. *MML*, p. 169.
23. Jefferson, *Der Rosenkavalier*, p. 128.
24. C. Castle with D.Tauber, *This was Richard Tauber* (1971), p. 37.
25. See LL's interesting description of a similar scene which she saw performed by the distinguished mime, Ruth Draper, in *MML*, pp. 170–1.
26. Jeritza, op.cit., p. 169; S.Jackson, *Monsieur Butterfly* (1974), p. 238.
27. Carner, op.cit., p. 202.
28. ibid.
29. *Tiefland* was Hitler's favourite opera until 1933.
30. This whole episode was related to the author by the late Frau Dr Schneider, Vienna, 1986.
31. Weingartner, op.cit., p. 329 *et seqq*.
32. ibid., p. 331.
33. *A und A*, p. 151.
34. Metropolitan Opera Archive, New York.
35. Prawy, *VO*, p. 133.
36. *Strauss-Hofmannsthal Corr.*, p. 331.
37. *MML*, p. 165.
38. Their records were issued in Britain under the Parlophone label.
39. It had, of course, been as Sophie at Drury Lane Theatre, London in May 1914.
40. *A und A*, p. 154.
41. *S w. RS*, p. 69.
42. Dresden State Opera Archive (Elisabeth, Desdemona, Eva and Mimi).
43. *S w.RS*, p. 68; BBC broadcast, 12.6.79.
44. *IRSG Blätter*, no. 10 (1977), pp. 13–14.

Chapter Six

1. L. Rasponi, *The Last Prima Donnas* (1984), p. 122.
2. Jackson, op.cit., pp. 237–8.
3. R. Christiansen, *Prima Donna* (1984), p. 246.
4. Rasponi, op.cit., p. 96.
5. Lubin, when asked about LL's Marschallin, *à propos* her own, paused and then replied: 'Moi, j'étais belle; Lotte Lehmann n'était pas belle.'
6. H.D. Rosenthal, *Two Centuries of Opera at Covent Garden* (1958), p. 436.
7. *MML*, pp. 201–62.
8. *S w.RS*, pp. 109–80.
9. Schwarzkopf, *On and Off the Record: A Memoir of Walter Legge* (1982), p. 20.
10. EMI confirmed this in December 1986.
11. Ida Cook in conversation, 1984.

12. Rasponi, op.cit., p. 326.
13. *MML*, p. 89.
14. *Die Bühne* (1926)
15. Later Lady Diana Cooper and mother of Viscount (John Julius) Norwich.
16. *Strauss-Hofmannsthal Corr.*, p. 419.
17. ibid., p. 418.
18. Lotte is not in it.
19. Schwarzkopf, op.cit., p. 124 (quoted by Walter Legge).
20. Rasponi, op.cit., p. 482.
21. ibid., p. 22.
22. Prawy, *VO*, p. 118.
23. ibid., p. 120.
24. Between 1919 and 1929 this was so.
25. Gustl Breuer: letter, 1984.
26. *IRSG Blätter*, no. 6 (1975), p. 22 (letter no. 92).
27. Heyworth, OK L&T, p. 249 *et seqq*.
28. B. Walter, *Briefe 1894–1962*(1969), p. 298.
29. British Institute of Recorded Sound *Bulletin* (Spring 1958), p. 2.
30. *Strauss-Hofmannsthal Corr.*, pp. 365–6; Strauss later wrote 'Jeritza . . . the only one'. ibid., p. 443.
31. ibid., p. 448.
32. ibid., p. 447.
33. ibid., p. 469.
34. ibid., p. 467.
35. ibid., p. 468.
36. ibid., p. 520.
37. ibid., p. XX
38. Prawy, *VO*, p. 129.
39. *IRSG Blätter*, no. 7 (1967), p. 6 (letter no. 145): Strauss to Karpath on 19.10.28: '. . . Dass die arme Lehmann so verblendet ist, ist eine Jammer! Schade um dieses schöne Talent u. diese selten kostbare Stimme! Aber da Kann man eben nichts machen! . . .'
40. ibid. (letter no. 144): Karpath to Strauss on 17.10.28: ' . . . Streng vertraulich muss ich Ihnen sagen, dass Lotte die Helena nicht lernen will. Sie hat sich die Isolde in den Kopf gesetzt und will an dieser Partie arbeiten. Ich sagte ihr ganz offen, dass sie ihrem Ruin entgegengeht, aber sie ist einmal von der Isolde nicht abzubringen . . .'
41. E. Sackville-West & D.Shawe-Taylor, *The Record Guide* (1950), p. 566.
42. *Suddeutsche Zeitung*, 4.9.29, translated from *Sunday Times*, 18.8.29.
43. *S w.RS*, p. 15.
44. Provided by the late Viorica Ursuleac.
45. How Krauss bested Furtwängler for control of the Vienna Opera is told in some detail by B. Geissmar, *The Baton and the Jackboot* (1944), and by Prawy, *VO*.

Chapter Seven

1. Rasponi, op.cit., p. 130.
2. Avant Scène Opéra: *Les Introuvables du Chant Wagnérien*, no. 67 September 1984, p. 11.
3. *A und A*, p. 182.
4. R.L. Davis, *Opera in Chicago* (1966), p. 188 (from *Musical Courier*).
5. ibid. (from *Musical America*).
6. ibid.
7. Lichtman: letter, 1986.
8. Millionaire-philanthropist who, at one time, controlled all the electricity – among other commodities – in Chicago.
9. *A und A*, pp. 185.
10. Gustl Breuer: letter, 1984.
11. Prawy, *VO*, p. 142.
12. *A und A*, pp. 186–7.
13. ibid., p. 187.
14. In her interview with Rasponi (op.cit., p. 136) Ursuleac complained bitterly about how badly LL had behaved towards her, especially at Salzburg, but her quoted example is not borne out by the Festival archive.
15. *A und A*, p. 188; *MML*, p. 85.
16. ibid., pp. 85–6.
17. LL moderated and regretted her previous attitude towards Krauss, many years later: *S w.RS*, pp. 44–5.
18. Prawy, *VO*, p. 134.
19. *The Times*, 10.5.32.
20. M. Kennedy, *Barbirolli* (1971), p. 74.
21. G.K. Kende, *Clemens Krauss – Briefe* (1971). CK: letter of 27.6.32.
22. ibid.; LL: letter of 1.7.32.
23. *Opera* Magazine, cit. pp. 11–21.
24. Kutsch & Riemens, op.cit.,
25. Kende, op.cit.; LL: letter of 30.12.32. The singing teacher who had been encouraging Lotte in Isolde was Felicia Kaszowska.

Chapter Eight

1. A. Jefferson, *Sir Thomas Beecham: A Centenary Tribute* (1979), p. 210.
2. A. Robertson, *More than Music* (1961) p. 142; Tortelier also noticed her dramatic powers on the platform.
3. *A und A*, pp. 206–7.
4. *Die Bühne* (1933).
5. Geissmar, op.cit., p. 87.
6. *W of S*, p. 194.
7. Conversation with Michalsky, Vienna 1985.
8. G.K. Kende & W. Schuh, *Richard Strauss – Clemens Krauss Briefwechsel* (1963): RS to CK: 10.9.33.

9. *A und A*, p. 207.
10. *New York Evening Post*, 15.1.34 (front page).
11. G. Marek, *Toscanini* (1976), p. 158.
12. *MML*, p. 175.
13. C. Osborne (ed.) *Opera 66* (1966), pp. 187–99; Rasponi, op.cit., p. 136, *inter alia*.
14. Geissmar, op.cit., p. 138.
15. Conversations with Walter Legge and K.A. Pollak, 1978.
16. *Tagesspiegel*, 28.8.76.
17. Jefferson, *Beecham*, p. 173.
18. Conversation with Joan Cross, 1986.
19. *New York Times*, 2.9.34.
20. Of her 60 *Manons* in Vienna, LL sang 46 with Piccaver; 8 with Környey (between 1916–18 only); and 6 with five other tenors (Rogatchewsky, Riavez, Tokatayan, Pataky, and twice with Ardelli, the last in place of Piccaver who was billed to sing).
21. Rasponi, op.cit., p. 232.
22. Conversation with Archie Drake, 1986.
23. *Eighteen Song Cycles* (1971), p. 131.
24. Wiener Library, London.
25. Geissmar, op.cit., p. 143.
26. A. Bloomfield, *50 Years of the San Francisco Opera*, p. 60 (Redfern Mason, critic).
27. ibid. (Marjorie Fisher, critic).

Chapter Nine

1. Wiener Library, London.
2. Contract is in the Metropolitan Opera Archive, New York.
3. Osborne, op.cit., pp. 75–6.
4. Conversation with Joan Cross, 1986.
5. ibid.
6. M. Davenport, *Too Strong for Fantasy* (1958), p. 180.
7. *A und A*, p. 224.
8. Except for Oskar Kokoschka, according to Erich Leindsdorf, *Cadenza* (1976), p. 43.
9. Marek, *Toscanini*, pp. 202–3; Robertson, op.cit., p. 43.
10. *A und A*, p. 227.
11. Rasponi, op.cit., p. 479.
12. *Daily Telegraph*, 29.4.36.
13. R. Hahn, *L'Oreille au Guet* (1937), p. 38.
14. Davenport, op.cit., p. 195.
15. *MML*, p. 92.
16. Leinsdorf, op.cit., p. 44.
17. Davenport, op.cit., pp. 195–6.
18. *MML*, p. 93.

19. *MML*, p. 69, LL states: 'Eva was for years one of my favourite roles.'
20. *Salzburger Volksblatt*, 30.9.36.
21. Vienna *Reichspost*, 14.8.36.
22. The new Festspielhaus was opened on Tuesday 26 July 1960. After an opening ceremony in the morning there was a performance of *Der Rosenkavalier* that evening, conducted by Herbert von Karajan, with Della Casa, Jurináč, Gueden and Edelmann.
23. Krauss's favouritism and greed also contributed.
24. Conversation with Walter Legge, 1978.
25. Wiener Library, London.
26. S. von Scanzoni, *Richard Strauss und seine Sängerin* (1969) p. 282.
27. *Opera* Magazine, December 1985, p. 24.
28. Ursuleac, Lemnitz, Reining.
29. Australian Broadcasting Corporation Archive, Sidney.
30. Private Collection.
31. H.Sachs, *Toscanini* (1978), p. 261.
32. Australian Broadcasting Corporation Archive, Sydney.
33. All were subsequently destroyed by the Gestapo, including the animals.
34. Rasponi, op.cit., pp. 103–4.
35. Where she had sung it only once in August 1937 between two other performances by Lotte. (It was, however, to lead to Konetzni singing all four Marschallins there in 1938, and four out of five in 1939).
36. Geissmar, op.cit., p. 274.
37. Rasponi, op.cit., p. 104.
38. Schwarzkopf, op.cit., p. 127.
39. ibid.
40. Russell, op.cit., p. 166.
41. ABC Archive, Sydney.

Chapter Ten

1. Australian Broadcasting Corporation Archive, Sydney.
2. *Sydney Telegraph*, 6.4.39; LL, *MML*, p. 64.
3. *Dominion*, 12.3.39.
4. ibid.
5. H. Traubel & R.G. Hubler, *St. Louis Woman* (1977), p. 271.
6. Extract from publicity questionnaire in Metropolitan Opera Archive, New York.
7. *MML*, pp. 164–5.
8. Rasponi, op.cit., p. 12.
9. Varnay was the first post-Second World War Brünnhilde at Bayreuth on 1.8.51.
10. A.Rubinstein, *My Many Years* (1980), p. 487.
11. Illustrated promotional booklet in author's collection.
12. Metropolitan Opera Archive, New York.

13. ibid.
14. ibid.
15. Lichtman: letter, 1986.
16. Professor Dr B.Barsewisch: letter, 1987.
17. Wessling, op.cit., p. 49.

Chapter Eleven

1. Metropolitan Opera, 'Press Book for Lotte Lehmann, Prima Donna Metropolitan Opera', issued by the Met's Press Department, p. 14.
2. W.H. Seltsam, *Metropolitan Opera Annals 1883–1947*(1947) p. 718.
3. *Woman* (NY), 21.6.48.
4. Richard Tauber Foundation of London.
5. *Opera* Magazine, February 1968, pp. 97–104.
6. Gustl Breuer: letter, 1984.
7. BBC broadcast, 12.6.79.
8. R. Gelatt, *Music Masters* (1950), p. 121.
9. Unidentified American magazine, March 1951.
10. Private collection.
11. ibid.
12. ibid.
13. Cutting of 'Opera, Song & Life' from unidentified Santa Barbara newspaper, September 1953.
14. Private collection.
15. ibid.
16. Prawy, *VO*, p. 179.
17. Sheean, op.cit., pp. 206, 202.
18. ibid.
19. Recounted by Christopher Raeburn, 1987.
20. Sheean, op.cit., pp. 202–3.
21. ibid., pp. 203–5.
22. ibid. p. 206.
23. ibid., p. 207.
24. Private collection.
25. Issued on two Preiser records in Austria.
26. Private collection.
27. I. Newton, *At the Piano – Ivor Newton* (1966), pp. 178–9.
28. They included Lord Harewood and David Webster.
29. AGFA-Gevaert, Leverkusen.
30. Conversations with Archie Drake, summers of 1985 and 1986.
31. *Bayreuther Blätter* (1959)
32. *New York Post*, 13.11.62.
33. *New York Times*, 10.11.62.
34. Private collection.
35. ibid.

36. ibid.
37. ibid.
38. ibid.
39. Lotte Klemperer (OK's daughter).
40. It also applied to Erich Korngold (information from F.N.M. Juynboll).

Appendix A

Hamburg Performances

I. Lotte Lehmann's Operas in Hamburg 1910–1916

d'Albert, Eugen	*Tiefland* Pepa / Marta
	Toten Augen Myrtocle
Bizet, Georges	*Carmen* Micaëla
Blech, Leo	*Versiegelt* Else
Cornelius, Peter	*Barber of Bagdad* Margiana
Gluck, Christoph	*Orpheus und Euridike* Eurydice
Goldmark, Karl	*Cricket on the Hearth* May
Halévy, Fromental	*Jüdin* Recha
Heuberger, Richard	*Opernball* Angèle
Humperdinck, Engelbert	*Hänsel und Gretel* Sandman / Dew Fairy
Kaiser, Alfred	*Theodor Körner* Christine
Kienzl, Wilhelm	*Evangelimann* Martha
Mascagni, Pietro	*Cavalleria Rusticana* Lola
Meyerbeer, Giacomo	*Prophet* 2 Choirboy
Mozart, Wolfgang Amadeus	*Così fan Tutte* Dorabella
	Figaro Countess
	Zauberflöte 2 Boy / 1 Boy / Pamina
Nicolai, Otto	*Merry Wives of Windsor* Anna / Fr. Fluth
Offenbach, Jacques	*Hoffmanns Erzählungen* Antonia
	Fortunios Lied Max
	Orpheus in the Underworld Eurydice
Strauss, Johann	*Gipsy Baron* Irma
	Fledermaus Orlovsky
Strauss, Richard	*Ariadne auf Naxos I* Echo
	Rosenkavalier Sophie / Octavian
Wagner, Richard	*Lohengrin* 1 Esquire / Elsa
	Götterdämmerung Gutrune / 3 Norn
	Meistersinger Apprentice / Eva
	Parsifal 4 Flower Maiden / 5 Flower Maiden

Wagner (contd.)	*Rienzi* 2 Messenger / Irene
	Rheingold Freia / Wellgunde
	Tannhäuser 2 Page / 1 Page / Elisabeth
	Walküre Ortlinde / Gerhilde / Sieglinde
Weber, Carl Maria von	*Freischütz* 1 Bridesmaid / Agathe
Weingartner, Felix	*Kain und Abel* Ada
Wolf-Ferrari, Ermanno	*Jewels of the Madonna* 2 Girl / Stella

II. Lotte Lehmann's Guest Performances in Hamburg 1917–1929

Season	
1916–17	Elsa
1917–18	Mignon
	Myrtocle
	Margarethe
	Else
	Eva
	Sieglinde
	Myrtocle
	Elsa
1918–19	Myrtocle
	Octavian
	Elisabeth
	Myrtocle
	Myrtocle
	Eva
	Myrtocle
	Elsa
1919–20	Elsa
	Mimi
	Elisabeth
	Octavian
	Eva
	Myrtocle
	Sieglinde
1920–21	Rachel
	Marta
	Octavian
	Myrtocle
	Elsa
	Elisabeth
	Eva
1921–22	Elsa
	Eva
	Octavian
	Butterfly
1925–26	Eva
	Tosca
1926–27	Elisabeth
	Elsa
	Leonore
	Turandot
1927–28	Leonore
	Elsa
	Turandot
	Heliane
	Elisabeth
	Myrtocle
	Heliane
1928–29	Marschallin
	Sieglinde
	Elsa
1929–(30)	Leonore
	Elisabeth
	Eva
	Marschallin

A total of 55 guest performances between 16 May 1917 and 29 October 1929.

III. *Lotte Lehmann: Opera in Hamburg* 1910–1916

		1910 –11	1911 –12	1912 –13	1913 –14	1914 –15	1915 –16	*Totals*
1	2 Boy, *Zauberflöte*	7						*7*
2	2 Page, *Tannhäuser*	1						*1*
3	Freia, *Rheingold*	2	3	1	9	3	3	*21*
4	1 Bridesmaid, *Freischütz*	6						*6*
5	Apprentice, *Meistersinger*	8	8					*16*
6	2 Choirboy, *Prophet*	4	2					*6*
7	Anna, *Merry Wives*	2	3	7				*12*
8	Max, *Fortunios Lied*	4						*4*
9	1 Esquire, *Lohengrin*	6	11	5				*22*
10	Sandman, *Hansel and Gretel*	5	2					*7*
11	Lola, *Cavalleria Rusticana*	2						*2*
12	1 Page, *Tannhäuser*	4	14	8				*26*
13	Sophie, *Rosenkavalier*	5	8	4	1			*18*
14	Irma, *Gypsy Baron*	4	1					*5*
15	1 Boy, *Zauberflöte*		4					*4*
16	Agathe, *Freischütz*		6	8	4	7	4	*29*
17	May, *Cricket on the Hearth*		5					*5*
18	Eurydice, *Orpheus und Eurydike*		1				2	*3*
19	Dew Fairy, *Hänsel und Gretel*		1					*1*
20	Micaëla, *Carmen*		2	5	11	5	6	*29*
21	2 Girl, *Jewels of the Madonna*		14					*14*
22	2 Messenger, *Rienzi*		2					*2*
23	Shepherd, *Tannhäuser*			7				*7*
24	Wellgunde, *Rheingold*			3				*3*
25	Ortlinde, *Walküre*			4	4			*8*
26	Pepa, *Tiefland*			2				*2*
27	Martha, *Evangelimann*			10	6	1		*17*
28	Elsa, *Lohengrin*			8	8	3	7	*26*
29	Mermaid, *Oberon*			11				*11*
30	Echo, *Ariadne I*			11				*11*
31	Irene, *Rienzi*			2	3	2	3	*10*
32	Antonia, *Tales of Hoffmann*			3	4	6	7	*20*
33	Gerhilde, *Walküre*			5				*5*
34	Dorabella, *Così fan Tutte*			7		2		*9*
35	Elsa, *Versiegelt*			3				*3*
36	Stella, *Jewels of the Madonna*			1				*1*
37	Gutrune, *Götterdämmerung*			1	1	3	1	*6*
38	Iphigenie, *Iphigenie in Aulis*				3			*3*
39	3 Norn, *Götterdämmerung*				3			*3*
40	Countess, *Figaro*				2	6	8	*16*
41	Sieglinde, *Walküre*				4	3	1	*8*

Continued

		1910 –11	1911 –12	1912 –13	1913 –14	1914 –15	1915 –16	*Totals*
42	4 Flower Maiden, *Parsifal*				12	1		*13*
43	Pamina, *Zauberflöte*				2	2	5	*9*
44	Eurydice, *Opheus in the Underworld*				13	3		*16*
45	Eva, *Meistersinger*				1	9	2	*12*
46	Christine, *Theodor Körner*					5		*5*
47	Octavian, *Rosenkavalier*					8	6	*14*
48	Margiana, *Barber von Bagdad*					6		*6*
49	5 Flower Maiden, *Parsifal*					14	7	*21*
50	Angèle, *Opera Ball*					11	3	*14*
51	Elisabeth, *Tannhäuser*					2	3	*5*
52	Orlovsky, *Fledermaus*					4	4	*8*
53	Ada, *Kain und Abel*						3	*3*
54	Recha, *Jüdin*						4	*4*
55	Myrtocle, *Toten Augen*						11	*11*
	TOTALS	*60*	*87*	*116*	*91*	*106*	*90*	*550*

Appendix B

Vienna Performances

I. Lotte Lehmann's Operas in Vienna 1916(1914)–1937

Composer	Opera / Role	Season
d'Albert, Eugen	*Tiefland* Marta	20/21
Beethoven, Ludwig van	*Fidelio* Leonore	26/27
Bittner, Julius	*Kohlhammerin* Witwe Helene	20/21
	Musikant Friederike	18/19
Bizet, Georges	*Carmen* Micaëla	16/17
Brandts-Buys, Jan	*Schneider von Schönau* Veronika	16/17
Branfels, Walter	*Don Gil* Donna Juana	24/25
Cornelius, Peter	*Barbier von Bagdad* Margiana	19/20
Giordano, Umberto	*André Chénier* Madeleine	25/26
Goetz, Hermann	*Widerspenstigen Zähmung* Katharine	27/28
Gounod, Charles	*Faust* Margarethe	16/17
Halévy, Fromental	*Jüdin* Rachel	16/17
Heuberger, Richard	*Opernball* Angèle	30/31
Kienzl, Wilhelm	*Evangelimann* Martha	16/17
	Kuhreigen Blanchefleur	21/22
Korngold, Julius	*Ring des Polykrates* Laura	18/19
	Tote Stadt Mariette/Marie	24/25
	Wunder der Heliane Heliane	27/28
Massenet, Jules	*Manon* Manon	16/17
	Werther Lotte	17/18
Mozart, Wolfgang Amadeus	*Figaro* Countess	17/18
	Zauberflöte Pamina	16/17
Nicolai, Otto	*Merry Wives of Windsor* Fr. Fluth	16/17
Offenbach, Jacques	*Hoffmanns Erzählungen* Antonia/ Giulietta	16/17
Pfitzner, Hans	*Palestrina* Silla	18/19
Puccini, Giacomo	*La Bohème* Mimi	19/20
	Madam Butterfly Butterfly	20/21

Puccini, Giacomo	*Manon Lescaut*	Manon	23/24
	Sister Angelica	Angelica	20/21
	Tosca	Tosca	22/23
	Il Tabarro	Georgette	31/32
	Turandot	Turandot	26/27
Strauss, Richard	*Arabella*	Arabella	33/34
	Ariadne auf Naxos	Composer/	16/17
		Ariadne	22/23
	Frau ohne Schatten	Dyer's Wife	19/20
	Intermezzo	Christine	26/27
	Rosenkavalier	Octavian/	16/17
		Marschallin	24/25
Tchaikovsky, Peter	*Eugen Onegin*	Tatiana	33/34
	Queen of Spades	Lisa	18/19
Thomas, Ambroise	*Mignon*	Mignon	16/17
Verdi, Giuseppe	*Otello*	Desdemona	22/23
Wagner, Richard	*Lohengrin*	Elsa	16/17
	Meistersinger	Eva	1914
	Parsifal	5 Flower Maiden	16/17
	The Ring: Rheingold	Freia	17/18
	Walküre	Sieglinde	17/18
	Götterdämmerung	Gutrune/	16/17
		2 Rhine Maiden	16/17
	Tannhäuser	Elisabeth	16/17
Weber, Carl Maria von	*Freischütz*	Agathe	16/17
Zaiczek-Blankenau, Julius	*Ferdinand und Luise*	Luise	17/18

Analysis

54 roles of which only 17 carried forward from Hamburg, including 5 performances in which she sang 2 roles (1 *Hoffmann*; 4 *Tritticos*).

Most sung roles:		
Manon	60	(47 with Piccaver)
Eva	53	
Mimi	38	
Elsa	37	
Composer	36	
Elisabeth	36	
Leonore	35	
Sieglinde	32	
Ariadne	28	
Butterfly	25	

Total roles in her career: 92, including Donna Elvira and Rosalinde (both unique to London)

II. *Lotte Lehmann: Opera in Vienna 1914–1937*

Seasons:		1914	16-17	17-18	18-19	19-20	20-21	21-22	22-23	23-24	24-25	25-26	26-27	27-28	28-29	29-30	30-31	31-32	32-33	33-34	34-35	35-36	36-37	37-(38)	*Totals*
1 *Eva**	(a.G.)	1	4	1	-	-	4	2	4	3	6	5	5	4	3	4	2	2	2	-	-	1			*53*
2 *Agathe*			4	1	1	2	5	1	-	1															*15*
3 *Martha*			2	-	1	-	-	-	1	-	-	-	1												*5*
4 *Elisabeth*			2	-	-	1	1	2	6	3	1	1	2	-	3	3	3	1	2	2	2	1	1		*37*
5 Guilietta			1																						*1*
6 *Antonia*			4	3	1	3	1	-	1	-	-	1													*14*
7 *Micaela*			4	1	-	4	2	1	1	1	1	1													*16*
8 *Recha*			3	1	2	-	-	-	2	2	3	2	1	-	1	1									*18*
9 Composer			20	6	3	3	5																		*37*
10 2 Rhine Maiden			1																						*1*
11 *Pamina*			2	1	1	3	1	1	1	-	1	1	2	4	2										*20*
12 *Elsa*			1	1	1	3	3	1	3	2	1	2	1	3	1	1	4	2	1	1	3	1	-	1	*37*
13 5 *Flower Maiden*			3	-	4																				*7*
14 Mignon			2	4	2	2	1	1	1	1															*14*
15 *Octavian*			3	-	-	2	1	3	2																*11*
16 *Gutrune*			2	1	2	2																			*7*
17 Veronika			4																						*4*
18 Manon			8	4	2	1	4	4	-	3	5	4	2	1	4	6	3	3	2	1	1	2			*60*
19 Margarethe			1	-	-	3	-	-	3	3	1	1	1	1	-	3	-	-	-	1					*18*
20 Fr. Fluth			2	3	1																				*6*
21 Luise				3																					*3*
22 *Freia*				1	2																				*3*
23 *Sieglinde*				2	2	1	3	-	2	1	1	3	1	1	2	1	2	1	1	2	2	3	-	1	*32*
24 Lotte				2	3	3	1	-	2	-	1	2	-	-	1	1	-	2							*18*
25 *Countess*				2	-	-	-	-	-	-	-	1	1	-	1										*5*
26 Lisa					4																				*4*
27 Friederike					6																				*6*

		1914	16-17	17-18	18-19	19-20	20-21	21-22	22-23	23-24	24-25	25-26	26-27	27-28	28-29	29-30	30-31	31-32	32-33	33-34	34-35	35-36	36-37	37-(38)	*Totals*
28	Silla				5																				*5*
29	Laura				1	1																			*2*
30	Dyer's Wife					8	1	-	-	-	-	-	-	-	-	-	2	1	1						*13*
31	Mimi					5	3	1	3	4	3	3	4	3	3	-	1	-	2	1	1	1			*38*
32	*Margiana*					1	-	1	1	1	3	-	-	1	1										*9*
33	Butterfly						6	1	5	2	2	1	1	2	-	-	2	1	1	1					*25*
34	Angelica						6	-	-	-	1	-	-	-	-	-	-	3	1						*11*
35	Marta						2																		*2*
36	Widow Helen						2																		*2*
37	Blanchefleur							3																	*3*
38	Tosca								5	3	2	2	-	-	-	-	-	-	-	-	1	1	1		*15*
39	Ariadne								3	2	-	3	1	2	2	3	5	2	3	2					*28*
40	Desdemona								1	1	-	-	-	2	3	-	-	1	-	-	3	2			*13*
41	Manon Lescaut									7															*7*
42	Marschallin										1	7	4	5	4	5	5	2	1	5	2	2	-	2	*45*
43	Mariette/Marie										2														*2*
44	Donna Juana										2	1													*3*
45	Madeleine											6	1	-	-	3	1	1	1	-	1	1			*15*
46	Turandot												9	3											*12*
47	Christine												8	3	-	2	1								*14*
48	Leonore												5	4	4	1	6	3	3	4	2	1	2		*35*
49	Heliane													6											*6*
50	Katharine													3											*3*
51	*Angèle*																3								*3*
52	Georgette																	3	1						*4*
53	Arabella																			5					*5*
54	Tatiana																			4	2	2	1	2	*11*
	TOTALS:	*1*	*73*	*37*	*44*	*48*	*52*	*22*	*47*	*40*	*37*	*47*	*50*	*48*	*35*	*34*	*40*	*28*	*22*	*29*	*20*	*18*	*5*	*6*	*782*

**Roles carried forward from Hamburg in italic*

Appendix C

Opera Performances at Other Centres

I. London

Seasons:	1914	1924	1925	1926	1927	1928	1929	1930	1931	1932	1933	1934	1935	1938	*Totals*
Sophie	2														2
Sieglinde		2	-	1	1	1	1	1	1	2	2	2	2		*16*
Marschallin		5	4	-	5	-	3	-	1	-	3	-	-	2+	23+
Ariadne		2													2
Elsa			2	-	-	-	2	-	2	-	-	-	2		*8*
Eva			2	1	-	1	1	2	-	4	-	1			12
Countess				3											3
Desdemona				4											4
Donna Elvira				3											3
Gutrune						1									1
Elisabeth						1	-	-	-	2					3
Rosalinde								4	4						8
TOTALS	2	9	8	12	6	4	7	7	8	8	5	3	4	2+	85+

+ = *unfinished performance of* 4.5.38

II. South America

1922	Buenos Aires	Montevideo	*Totals*
Freia	1		*1*
Sieglinde	1	1	*2*
Gutrune	1		*1*
TOTALS	*3*	*1*	*4*

III. Salzburg

	1926	27	28	29	1930	31	32	33	34	35	36	37	*Totals*
Ariadne	1												*1*
Leonore		4	3	3	2	2	2	1	2	4	3	2	*28*
Marschallin				5	1	2	2	1	3	2	-	2	*18*
Dyer's Wife							2						*2*
Eva											4		*4*
TOTALS	1	4	3	8	3	4	6	2	5	6	7	4	*53*

IV. Chicago

	1930/31	1931/32	1934/35	1935/36	1937/38	*Totals*
Sieglinde	2					*2*
Elisabeth	2	-	1			*3*
Elsa	2	3	-	1		*6*
Eva	2	1				*3*
Marschallin				2	2	*4*
TOTALS	8	4	1	3	2	*18*

V. The Met, New York

	1933 -34	*34 -35*	*35 -36*	*36 -37*	*37 -38*	*38 -39*	*39 -40*	*40 -41*	*41 -42*	*42 -43*	*44 -45*	*Totals*
Sieglinde	1	-	-	2	-	-	2	-	1	1		*7*
Elisabeth	1	1	2	2	2	1	1	1	-	1		*12*
Eva	1	1	-	2								*4*
Marschallin		3	-	-	5	2	4	4	4	3	1	*26*
Elsa		1	1	-	-	1						*3*
Tosca		1	1									*2*
TOTALS	*3*	*7*	*4*	*6*	*7*	*4*	*7*	*5*	*5*	*5*	*1*	*54*

Her last appearance on stage at the Met was in 1946, as a guest, in Lauritz Melchior's anniversary performance of '20 years at the Met' when they sang part of the third scene from *Die Walküre* Act I

VI. *San Francisco*

	1934/35	1936/37	1940/41	1941/42	1945/46	1946/47	*Total*
Tosca	1	1					2
Butterfly	1						1
Sieglinde		2					2
Marschallin			2	1	2	2	7
TOTALS	2	3	2	1	2	2	12

A Discography of
Lotte Lehmann's Sound Recordings

Compiled and introduced by
Floris Juynboll

Introduction

Lotte Lehmann had the kind of soprano voice that made her predestined for the performance of Lieder. Although her earlier recordings show that she could command a D flat above top C (for example, the acoustic Odeon version of 'Butterfly's Entrance', No. 73), her voice had the mellow quality of a mezzo-soprano, the type of voice for which Schubert, Schumann, Brahms and Wolf had composed most of the standard Lieder repertoire. The advantage of this particular voice over the true, high soprano, is that the singer can often more easily colour the tone in order to express the subtle nuances of a song text.

She made her first recordings for Pathé in 1914 just after she had been engaged by the Vienna Court Opera; from 1916 to 1921 she recorded for Polydor, then from 1924 onwards for Odeon in Berlin. The opera sets, *Der Rosenkavalier* and *Die Walküre,* both recorded in Vienna, followed in 1933 and 1935 for Electrola (German HMV), though Act 1 of *Die Walküre* actually first appeared in Germany on the German Columbia label. From 1935 onwards she recorded only in the USA. Recordings are comparatively few after 1944 considering how well known she was, but this lack is made up for to some extent by a number of live concert recitals preserved on record, including an important Wolf recital, which she gave in New York in 1938.

Her earliest records, made before 1927 by the acoustic horn method, contain many gems which she did not later re-record. If we listen carefully to the excellent transfers issued by Preiser in their *Lebendige Vergangenheit* series ('Lotte Lehmann', Vols. II, III, IV and V) we hear a young, warm, beautifully produced voice. However dated they may sound, these discs are technically good for the period and the late acoustics from Odeon come across very well. The accompanying orchestra can be heard in correct perspective and details such as the bells in the 'Entrance of Butterfly' scene (No. 73) and in 'Der Erste, der Lieb' mich gelehrt' from Korngold's opera, *Die Tote Stadt* (No. 65) are clearly audible. At the end of this last aria she sharpens a top C, a lapse in intonation seldom heard in her recordings.

The introduction of electric recordings during 1925 and 1926 brought with it a vast improvement in sound quality and tonal definition. Columbia began to use the new process by the end of 1925 and Odeon followed, rather hesitantly at first, a year later. A week after Lotte's last acoustic session, a recording of the *Rosenlieder* (Nos. 85–87) in August 1926, Odeon produced transfers from a series of recordings of the Concertgebouw Orchestra conducted by Willem Mengelberg made by Columbia, with whom they were affiliated.

The improvement in tonal clarity is at once evident from the first electric recordings made by Lotte Lehmann in February 1927. Unfortunately, the Odeon company did not immediately use the new medium to the best advantage, nor did they seem to realise that electric recording would show up, all too audibly, any defects in the quality of orchestral accompaniments and inadequacies on the part of instrumentalists and conductors.

Odeon began electric recording by following the former acoustic practice of having singers and instrumentalists grouped closely around the microphone, and making the recordings in acoustically 'dead' studios. Horst Wahl, who was employed by Odeon during this period, relates how he used to visit the *Musikerbörse* in Berlin, a kind of exchange where musicians without engagements that day could be hired. If too many players had been hired, thus overcrowding the microphone, some were sent away and the reduced volume of sound available was amplified in order to suggest an 'orchestra' when only a small instrumental ensemble – sometimes only a trio – was actually playing.

The resultant sound-quality was far from as good as it should have been, and matters were not improved by Odeon's current policy of having almost all singers accompanied by instrumentalists even when singing German Lieder. The practice of singing Lieder to orchestral accompaniment seems to have originated from the nineteenth century custom of having songs by Schubert and Schumann orchestrated by well-known composers for performance at symphony concerts. Schubert himself never made orchestrations of his songs as his entire output was intended for performance by a small circle of music-loving friends. Since there was a lack of published song accompaniments arranged for small instrumental groups, the Odeon company had to have them specially prepared, and the words *Eigene Bearbeitung*, which occur frequently in the recording books, meant that the orchestrations were the work of house conductors like Weissmann, Gurlitt, Römer and others, who were paid direct by Odeon for their services. Some Lieder recordings were accompanied by the piano, but the instruments in the Odeon studios seemed to have been in poor shape and, more often than not, sound badly out of tune. This is noticeable even with keyboard recordings by pianists such as Siegfried Grundeis and Cor de Groot.

Few arrangers seemed able to transcribe piano accompaniments without making some 'improvements', most of them in very questionable taste. Frieder Weissmann, for example, when orchestrating the songs of Schumann, not only rearranged the accompaniment and altered the composer's harmonies now and then, but frequently added inner contrapuntal parts. Nor is the conducting beyond criticism. Lack of rehearsal may have been a contributory cause but bad intonation, faulty balance and poor ensemble, which occur too often on the recordings, and which the close microphone positioning exposes, display a quality of musicianship so poor as to be almost inexplicable, especially when it is remembered that these *ad hoc* instrumental ensembles often included members of the Berlin Philharmonic Orchestra.

Not until 1930 did matters improve, at the same time as the recordings themselves improved. But even in June 1930 Schumann's 'Ich grolle nicht' (No. 199) suffers from orchestral maltreatment as well as excessive rubato. Not that the use of piano accompaniment guaranteed satisfactory results, as, for example, in the recording of Schubert's 'Erlkönig' (No. 200). Lotte sings well in what must be the fastest version of this song on record. The famous octave triplets are absent most of the time, and the whole performance is one mad rush by pianist and singer to cram the song on to a ten-inch side.

Odeon's predilection for ten-inch recordings gave rise to endless artistic problems, especially in the performance of Lieder. The playing time is simply too short in, for example, some of the songs in Schumann's song cycle, *Frauenliebe und -leben*, especially at the rather dragging tempo adopted on the 1928 recording (Nos. 137–144), where the preludes and postludes are either cut short or omitted altogether when the song is too long for the side. The recordings of Wagner's *Wesendonck-Lieder* (Nos. 169, 170), otherwise beautifully sung, suffer in exactly the same way. When a song was too short other measures were taken in order to fill the side. In Schumann's 'An meinem Herzen' (No. 143) the accompaniment to the first verse is played as an instrumental prelude, contrary to the composer's intentions, the tempo is slow and the closing *ritardando* is dragged out at length. Even so there is half a minute of empty grooves after the music stops.

In Schubert's 'Der Tod und das Mädchen' (No. 108) the use of a string quartet instead of the piano, which could remind listeners of the well-known set of variations of the second movement of the composer's own string quartet, might have been acceptable, but the intonation of the strings leaves much to be desired.

Richard Strauss's 'Cäcilie' (No. 46), with its rapturous outbursts of melody, which she recorded in 1921, suits her well. 'Morgen', (No. 47) is a song of which she gave more intense performances in later years, though in none of these versions does she display the sense of wonder we hear with Elisabeth Schumann, or the delightful word painting of Dietrich Fischer-Dieskau or Elisabeth Schwarzkopf. This song figured prominently on the farewell programmes of the latter singer, as it did with Lotte, and she made it her last encore at her very last public concert in California in 1951.

Most of the acoustic Lieder recordings Lotte made for Odeon were by Richard Strauss. Although passed for issue none was published owing to technical defects in the masters which prevented satisfactory processing according to the recording books. The loss of Strauss's 'Wiegenlied' and Leo Blech's delightful 'Heimkehr vom Feste' are particularly to be regretted, though the latter was sung as an encore in the Wolf recital she gave in the New York Town Hall in 1938.

The Schumann cycle, *Frauenliebe und -leben*, mentioned above, which she recorded in 1928 (Nos. 137–144) is unsatisfactory. She was not inspired by the trivialised 'tea-shop' orchestral accompaniment – *Salon-Schande*, as it amused her to call it at the time though she was less amused about it later in her book, *Eighteen Song Cycles* (p.10). The beginning of 'Süsser Freund' is promising but she fails to sustain the emotional tone to the end of the song. The last song, 'Nun hast du mir den ersten Schmerz getan', has good moments but the last line is ruined by an 'accident' in the violins after the word *fällt*.

The session of June 1929 went rather better despite the still questionable orchestral arrangements, especially of the Schumann Lieder – there is still the odd tasteless counterpoint played by the horn. But Lotte's performance of Schumann's 'Die Lotosblume' (No. 217) made in April 1932, is beautifully phrased and a gem among her recordings.

These recordings show that she was not inexperienced in Lieder singing during her earlier years, but assurance in that field came only in the early thirties when she worked with Bruno Walter. It was thanks to his presence that they began to give Lieder recitals at the Salzburg Festivals, which resumed the custom of having Lieder recitals as a regular part of the festival programme, and to her making so many Lieder recordings during her career in America.

As regards her work in the opera house, extending the list in Wessling's book to include *Hänsel und Gretel* (Humperdinck), *Heimchen am Herd* (Goldmark), *I Gioielli della Madonna* (Wolf-Ferrari), and *Oberon* (Weber), and not counting boys, pages, messengers and the like which she played during her earliest years in Hamburg, gives her a repertoire of some sixty major roles by 1934 – an impressive total even by today's standards. Though many of her important operatic parts are unrecorded, thirty-four roles have been preserved, most of them it is true in tantalisingly short snatches. But two or three of her major roles, chiefly those which she sang until late in her career, were recorded at length and it is from these that we get the best idea of her capabilities as an operatic singer.

It is fitting that her first recordings for Pathé should have been, 'Einsam in trüben Tagen' and 'Euch Lüften, die mein Klagen', the two big arias from *Lohengrin*, her first success in Hamburg, both of which she re-recorded electrically sixteen years later (Nos. 189, 190). From Act 2 there is an additional excerpt, 'Du Ärmste kannst wohl nie ermessen' (No. 5). These extracts are too short to give more than a superficial idea of her conception of Elsa, but sufficient for us to discern that it differs markedly from that of Eva von der Osten who, in her 1910 recordings, emphasises the more fragile side of the character.

The great role of her early years, however, was undoubtedly the Composer in the *Vorspiel* to Richard Strauss's *Ariadne auf Naxos*. This was her stepping stone to world fame, and while she probably looked less like a boy than, say, Irmgard Seefried or Sena Jurinac, both famous modern interpreters of the role, there was no doubt as to the quality of her acting and singing, a glimpse of which can be obtained from her recording of Ariadne's great scena which she made in 1928 (Nos. 130–132).

Another remarkable creation, one that touched the composer Puccini deeply, was her Angelica in *Suor Angelica*. The two excerpts extant on Polydor (Nos. 36, 37), (available dubbed on to microgroove on the Rococo and Preiser labels) though short, are a worthy memorial in sound of the description given by the composer. The role also demonstrates the extent of Lotte's range, for it takes the singer from A below the stave to top C, a compass of over two octaves.

Along with the usual excerpts from *Tannhäuser, Margarethe (Faust), Mignon, Madama Butterfly, La Bohème* and even *Eugen Onegin* – too short an excerpt from a long scene which usually plays for some fifteen minutes – there is her Micaëla from *Carmen* (No. 21), her performance of which made Gregor engage her for Vienna. It is a pity that she and Richard Tauber did not record the first act duet together.

The single excerpt from Act 2 of *Manon Lescaut* (No. 54) is a reminder of how the opera was heard by the Viennese public. The first performance was given in Vienna in 1908, but it never caught on, in spite of Lotte Lehmann and Alfred Piccaver, in 1923. Puccini, who was present, reported that he found Lotte deficient in coquetry in Act 2 but magnificent in Act 4. His criticism does not apply to the beautiful and famous aria, 'In quelle trine morbide' (No. 54), one of the more tranquil moments in the opera.

Of greater importance is the long excerpt of the scene from Act 2 of *Die Meistersinger* with Michael Bohnen (Nos. 9, 10). Unfortunately, Lotte is further away from the recording horn than her Sachs, but even so this, together with the fragment recorded in October 1925 (No. 68), gives us some idea of her Eva. In *My Many Lives* she expatiates on the role of Eva, and the recordings confirm her conception of the character as more forceful and confident than is usual – when played, for example, by famous post-war singers such as Hilde Gueden and Elisabeth Grümmer. In 'Sachs, mein Freund' from Act 3, which calls for exultant singing, she really comes into her own.

Lotte's Leonora from *Fidelio* (together with the Marschallin and Sieglinde her most famous roles) fares badly on record. The only commercial recording she made, shortly after the Beethoven centenary celebrations, of 'Komm' Hoffnung' from Act 1 (No. 112) seems to have caught her on an off day (some record labels, incidentally, state erroneously that she begins with the recitative, 'Abscheulicher, wo eilst du hin?'). The livelier part towards the end of the aria finds her in technical difficulties, emphasised by extra and frequent audible breathing. Some time later, after she had sung the role under Toscanini at Salzburg in 1935, a complete commercial recording of *Fidelio* with the Vienna State Opera was announced (there is a reference in *The Gramophone Shop Encyclopedia of Recorded Music*, 1936, at the bottom of page 39, first column), to be made by HMV/Victor but nothing has come to light about the project. It is known that a set of test pressings of a complete *Fidelio* went with the singer to Santa Barbara in 1939 but these may have been recorded from a broadcast. The private recording of Act 1 on UORC 218 was made via short-wave radio transmission and the sound quality is heart-breakingly poor.

In Lotte's recordings from Mozart's *Le Nozze di Figaro* her Countess always sounds more convincing than her Susanna, due perhaps to that lack of coquetry which Puccini observed in her Manon in Act 2 of his *Manon Lescaut*.

Korngold's *Das Wunder der Heliane* was never successful and in spite of all Lotte's efforts did not find its way into the repertory in Vienna. The part of Heliane appealed strongly to her and a performance she gave in Hamburg in 1928 was so magnificent that one critic went so far as to declare that performances such as this were among the finest then to be seen on the German stage, and its like had not been experienced since the days of Edyth Walker. Certainly her performance of Heliane's aria from Act 2, 'Ich ging zu ihm' (Nos. 116, 117) makes one of her most exciting records.

Desdemona from Verdi's *Otello* is another of her roles which is insufficiently documented on commercial recordings. Her 'Willow Song' in the acoustic version (No. 62) is far preferable to the electric recording of eight years later (No. 193). In the latter she is far too impassioned for so gentle an aria. Such an interpretation may be appropriate in the long scenes in Act 3, but Act 4 requires the approach she brought to Angelica. Moreover, in 1920 she could still command a *morendo* on high A – or at least take the note *piano*, so far as one can judge from the primitive recording. On a record one cannot turn round and visually suggest a soft top note. It is precisely this feature, somewhat untypical of our diva, that makes her Angelica fragment so precious. She did not easily command the lighter voice of, say, a Hina Spani, who also sang Elsa in *Lohengrin*.

The prayer from Puccini's *Tosca* (No. 52) is notable for the almost uncontrollable sobbing at the end. But as the singer herself remarked of Tosca the role was far too theatrical for her and she never really enjoyed performing it. Her later recordings from the opera are decidedly less distinguished than the earlier, though the Odeon company took considerable trouble over the remakes of 'Vissi d'arte' in 1929 – four recordings in all. The same amount of care was taken over her recordings of Mimi's aria from *La Bohème* (No. 168), and with the two acoustic versions that preceded it.

The Wagner session of February 1930 (Nos. 187–190) yielded some satisfying remakes of the best-known excerpts from *Lohengrin* and *Tannhäuser*, corner-stones of her Wagner repertoire, which she had first recorded as long ago as 1914 and 1916. The closing scene from *Tristan und Isolde*, the *Liebestod* (Nos. 194–195) is, however, only a glimpse of something extraordinary that might have been – if perhaps only once. She had studied the part of Isolde under Bruno Walter. The later live recording under Pierre Monteux (on BWS–729) shows that she had not worked on the score recently, and this suggests that she did not often sing this Wagnerian fragment.

Massenet's operas, *Manon* and *Werther*, were extremely popular in Vienna and the extracts (Nos. 225, 226, 228) and the earlier acoustic versions (Nos. 25, 51,58), though sung in German, are uniformly excellent. It might be objected that the weeping in *Manon* (in No. 58, for example) is overdone, especially as French singers rarely produce such an intense expression of grief, but it must not be forgotten that Massenet himself wrote 'Très troublé' into the score.

The last sessions for Odeon are very fine. These include excerpts, far too short, from Strauss's then new opera, *Arabella*. Comparison with Viorica Ursuleac, who sang the role at the world première (the first world première of an opera to be broadcast live) is perhaps unavoidable, but the difference is all too clear. It is said that Ursuleac 'did not record well', as if the recording machine could not cope with the vibrations in her voice. It is more likely, however, that she was one of those singers who cut a believable figure on the operatic stage but whose voice does not really stand up to the merciless scrutiny of the microphone. There have been, and still are, many such singers.

Details about the HMV recording of scenes from *Der Rosenkavalier* have been given in the text of this book. Outstanding as the performance is, the recording is far from perfect technically, and though Heger conducts competently it can only be regretted that neither Strauss himself nor Bruno Walter was in charge of the orchestra. The fragment from Act 1 (No. 114) is more clearly recorded by Odeon and the singing is not affected by the bad patch that Lotte was experiencing in December 1927. What is more, the side contains music not recorded in the HMV set.

The other operatic venture undertaken by HMV in the mid-1930s, the complete recordings of Acts 1 and 2 of Wagner's *Die Walküre*, is so good that it can justifiably be called one of the glories of the gramophone. Act 1 still deserves to benefit from a remastering and fresh dubbing on to microgroove to do it full justice, the treatment accorded to the *Der Rosenkavalier* excerpts for reissue on the World Record Club label in 1972. The latest refurbishing of Act 2 is satisfactory. It is extraordinary how little one actually notices the transition from the Vienna Philharmonic Orchestra under Bruno Walter to the Berlin Philharmonic Orchestra under Bruno Seidler-Winkler, recorded three years later in Berlin. Musically, the listener could have noticed how much more fire Bruno Walter brought to the introduction to Act 2. In Nazi Germany this act was sold incomplete, with all the parts sung by Lotte Lehmann and conducted by Bruno Walter removed.

These two Wagner acts are a true memorial to the greatness of Lotte Lehmann, who described Sieglinde as the role she most treasured, the one, so she thought, that best matched her own temperament and disposition: *Eine Frau die die Fesseln von sich wirft, die das Haus in dem sie sich gefangen fühlt verlässt und ins Ungewisse davonstürzt mit dem Mann, den sie liebt* (A woman who throws off her fetters, who flees the house in which she feels herself imprisoned, and rushes away into the unknown with the man she loves).

In the autumn of 1935 Lotte Lehmann entered on the last part of her recording career. All the records were made in America, and all were recordings of songs. They were issued for the most part, in albums, in sets of three or more 78 rpm pressings, and in the Discography the album numbers are clearly stated in the heading to each recording session when they apply.

The first two albums from 1935 and 1937 find the singer still in good voice. They contain her finest recordings in the field of German Lieder and include some rare titles by composers such as Pfitzner, Marx and Franz. Except for 'Die Krähe' (No. 333), her abridged recording of Schubert's song cycle, *Winterreise* (Nos. 329–336), made in 1940, is less satisfactory. Age is beginning to take its toll on the voice and a certain uniformity of approach in her interpretations is becoming apparent. When she completed the recording of this cycle for American Columbia a year later, her mannerisms had become even more noticeable, and there is often a want of softer colouring, of mezza voce, the lack of which the close recording does not help to disguise.

One song in particular by Schubert, 'Der Doppelgänger' (No. 338), which she made at this time, should never have been issued. The sound she produces is not pleasant and the song really needs a much larger voice. For once she had overstepped her limitations. Hans Hotter, and after him Dietrich Fischer-Dieskau, have both recorded striking performances. Lotte's rival in singing Lieder written for the male voice, Elena Gerhardt, probably never attempted the song.

Her recordings of Lieder by Brahms are so much better that it can only be concluded that she had a better rapport with this composer than with Schubert. One of her finest interpretations, and the best in Album set M–453 (Nos. 349–356) is 'Auf dem Kirchhofe'. The scene is painted in so remarkable a way as to leave her greatest rivals, Elena Gerhardt and Dietrich Fischer-Dieskau, far behind. One is *in* the graveyard with the chilly gusts of wind and rain, which are underlined by the accompaniment though in the score all one sees is a string of rising arpeggios. In *More than Singing*, she wrote: 'The prelude gives the impression of a storm with its torrents of rain. Take up the storming with your whole being'. This is what she does on the record. Another set of songs to which she was well suited is Brahms' *Zigeunerlieder* (Nos. 431–434, and VOCE 69).

The custom of female singers performing songs, and in particular song cycles (such as Schubert's *Winterreise* and *Die schöne Müllerin*, and Schumann's *Dichterliebe*), the poems for which are intended to be sung by a man, has come in for some criticism, even though Elena Gerhardt sang the *Winterreise* cycle and songs like 'Der Atlas' and 'Der Zwerg'. In the introduction to her last book, *Eighteen Song Cycles*, Lotte Lehmann repudiates such criticism: 'Why should a singer be denied a vast number of wonderful songs, if she has the power to create an illusion, which she makes her audience believe in?' And this she most certainly did – perhaps most successfully in *Dichterliebe*, aided not least by the inspired playing of Bruno Walter. When this set was made only one serious rival had a complete recording in the catalogue: Gerhard Hüsch.

Lotte always begged her friend, Elisabeth Schumann, an unrivalled exponent of Mozart, not to come to her recitals before the interval, that is, after she had sung her Mozart group. And on record, at least, she does not display a true feeling for the classical pulse of the songs. In 'Abendempfindung' (VOCE 99) her rhythmic treatment is so free that the flowing accompaniment loses its impetus as the pianist strives to maintain the ensemble. Mozart singing requires greater rhythmic energy and a more instrumental approach than she gives it.

Towards the end of her career Lotte began to include some French *mélodies* in her repertoire, songs by Duparc and especially by Reynaldo Hahn. It cannot be said that she sounds convincing in this music as her pronunciation of the French language leaves much to be desired. In fact, it is practically unintelligible, something most unusual for her. A great exponent of the French repertoire, Suzanne Danco, once wrote: 'It is extremely difficult – not to say next to impossible – for people who do not speak French to tackle this repertoire. I am terribly critical when French vocal pieces are sung with a faulty accent. French is first and foremost a spoken language, hence the importance of a good diction to express it properly'.

In Section IX of the Discography a number of recordings of live performances have been listed, and it is interesting to compare certain songs with performances of the same music recorded in the studio, for example, Mendelssohn's 'Venetianisches Gondellied' and Schubert's

'Die Männer sind méchant'. In the live performance she tends to use more emphasis to intensify the meaning of the text, and this also makes her sound warmer. The way her audiences react is also revealing. The 1938 Wolf recital, though the sound is no more than adequate, clearly shows how Lotte played on, and with, her audience. She inserts encores after a group of songs, and even repeats two songs during the course of the recital. Finally, for her penultimate encore, she announces Leo Blech's 'Heimkehr vom Feste' in which she is infectiously merry as the character in the song who is returning home from a party, having had too much to drink. Her announcement of the song is impossible to make out, and the title is not printed on the record label.

Outstanding among her public performances is the live recording of Schumann's song cycle, *Frauenliebe und -leben* (on VOCE 99) with Paul Ulanowsky, which is vastly superior to the studio version she made with Bruno Walter. The original masters from which the microgroove record was made were partly damaged, but the listener should not let that deter him from the extraordinary experience of hearing a performance of this well-known work such as one enjoys perhaps only once in a lifetime.

A frequent mannerism in these late recitals, and not noticeable on her acoustic recordings, is a quite audible intake of breath. It was becoming conspicuous in the recording sessions of December 1927 and, by about 1940, had turned into shortness of breath. A Viennese throat specialist is said to have diagnosed nodules on Lotte's vocal cords but she did not have an operation as she thought they enhanced the particular quality of her voice. She mentions this in 1945 in her book, *More than Singing* (p. 17): 'With justice I am reproached for breathing too often and so breaking the phrases. This is one of my unconquerable nervous inadequacies'. In fact, it is often difficult to tell if her frequent breathing is being used as a means of enhancing expression, or a matter of sheer necessity.

A special feature displayed by Lotte Lehmann on most of her records, certainly up to the end of the 1930s, is that of *morbidezza*, an Italian word used to describe, in singing, a particular vibrant quality of tone, which serves to transmit emotion and attract immediate attention. Horst Wahl, who often heard the artist in the Odeon recording studios, refers to this in a letter to the writer in 1985: 'The impression she made on us all with her heavenly voice is indescribable. Even now, after so many years, I can still feel, almost with pain, the wonderful beauty and warmth of her voice. To be standing near her when she was producing that steady stream of golden tone was an experience barely to be endured, and her great personal warmth always ensured that her singing went straight to the heart'.

Acknowledgements

A discography as detailed as this could not have been completed without extensive assistance from record collectors, audio archive libraries and experts in the field of recorded music. For help with recordings made in Germany I am indebted to Horst Wahl, Freiburg-im-Breisgau, Jürgen Schmidt of Preiser Records, Vienna, and Johann Landgraf of EMI, Cologne. Most of the numbers for the American recordings were supplied by William R. Moran and the late Ted Fagan of California, USA, the authors of *The Encyclopedic Discography of Victor Recordings*. To James Seddon, London, I am indebted for research carried out at the National Sound Archive, London, which resulted in numerous corrections to much of the material already assembled.

Others who gave willing assistance are A.G.F. Boersma, Amsterdam, Harold M, Barnes, Paris, Dr Ulrich Dahmen, Rosengarten, Germany, Dr. G. Fraser, Scotland, Dr. G.R.N. Jones, London, Jürgen Grundheber, Munich, Roland Henkels, Solingen, Germany, Alan Jefferson, Alan Kelly, Sheffield, Ewoud Krüsemann, Amsterdam, Barbara Migurska, Secretary of Yale Historical Sound Recordings, USA, Dr. Günther Meyer, Kalletal, Germany, Christopher Norton-Welsh, Vienna, Jim Pearse, London, Brian Rust, Swanage, the late Roland Teuchtler, Vienna, J, Vlaanderen, Amsterdam, Jens-Uwe Völmecke, Remscheid, Germany, Günter Walter, Münster, Germany, and Richard Warren, Curator of Yale Historical Sound Recordings, USA.

All the above-mentioned are heartily thanked for invaluable help and co-operation. Encouragement to prepare the discography was given by the late James F.E. Dennis, and his friend, Horst Wahl, former recording engineer with the Odeon Company, and a lifelong friend of the artist.

Index to main sections:

Section	Label or Company		No. in discog.	No. of sides publ.	unpubl.
I	*Pathé Frères, Berlin*	*1914*	1–2	2	4?
II	*Grammophon-Polydor*	*1916–1921*	3–50	44	4
III	*Odeon (acoustic)*	*1924–1926*	51–89	27	12
IV	*Odeon (electric)*	*1926–1933*	90–235	130	16
V	*His Masters Voice*	*1933–1935*	236–282*	32	—
VI	*Victor U.S.A.*	*1935–1940*	283–336	50	4
VII	*Columbia U.S.A.*	*1941–1943*	337–428	89	3
VIII	*Victor U.S.A.*	*1947–1949*	429–455	24	3
IX	*Non-commercial recordings on microgroove*	*1935–1951*			
X	*Master classes, Pasadena*	*1952*			
XI	*Caedmon U.S.A., speech recordings*	*1956–1958*			

* Lotte Lehmann does not sing at all on 15 sides of the sets of Der Rosenkavalier and Die Walküre, Act I.

SECTION I: *Pathé Frères, Berlin 1914*

Etched label, centre start, 29 cm Ø, probably 87 rpm. Label title: Lotte Lehmann, Stadttheater Hamburg.

1 55978 Einsam in trüben Tagen – Lohengrin, Act 1 (Wagner)
42048, (14): RA–1110, coupling number: 5844

2 55979 Euch Lüften, die mein Klagen – Lohengrin, Act 2 (Wagner)
42048, (14): RA–1008, coupling number: 5844

Reissued on Preiser LV 1336, entitled 'Lotte Lehmann V'.

Note: Pathé usually made recordings in batches of six, which could all be fitted on to a master cylinder. That would imply four unpublished titles. These have not been traced and may have been damaged in the process of transferring them from master cylinder to disc.

SECTION II: *Grammophon/Polydor, Berlin, 1916–1921*

The discography number is followed by the matrix number. Three catalogue numbers are given for each side. Twelve-inch (30 cm) single-sided records are numbered in the 76000 series, double-sided in the 72000 series. Ten-inch (25 cm) single-sided records are numbered in the 74000 series, double-sided in the 70000 or 80000 series. The 040000 series and numbers prefixed 'B' are international catalogue numbers. Speeds vary from 78 to 80 rpm. Most recordings probably play at 80 rpm, but this could not be verified for lack of original pressings. All titles are accompanied by orchestra.

Some titles were recorded twice or three times during the same recording session. Each recording of the same title bearing the same matrix number is technically known as a 'take'. Take 1 is the initial recording, the repeat would be take 2, a second repeat take 3, and so on. A later take could be made at a subsequent session. The take number is hyphenated to the matrix number (e.g. 1221–2 m, xxB 7611–2), and the numbers are usually impressed into the blank surround between the end of the grooves and the label. This applies to all the 78 rpm recordings listed in this discography.

(December) 1916. L and m in the matrix numbers denote that the recording engineer was Franz Hampe.

3	1101 m	Dich teure Halle, Act 2, Tannhäuser (Wagner) 76353/72902, 043294, Amer. Vocalion 35045
4	1102 m	Allmächt'ge Jungfrau, Act 3, Tannhäuser (Wagner) 76354/72902, 043295
5	1103 m	Du Ärmste kannst wohl nie ermessen, Act 2, Lohengrin (Wagner) 76355/72903, 043296
6	1104 m	See Notes
7	1105 m	See Notes
8	1106 m	Alles pflegt schon längst der Ruh', Act 2, Der Freischütz (Weber) 76356/72904, 043297
9	1107 m	Gut'n Abend Meister, Act 2, Die Meistersinger von Nürnberg (Wagner) with Michael Bohnen. 76357/85305, 044299
10	1108 m	Doch starb Eure Frau, Act 2, Die Meistersinger (cont.) w. Bohnen 76364/85305, 044306
11	1109 m	Es war ein König in Thule (Il était un roi de Thulé), Act 3 Margarethe (Faust), (Gounod) 76368/72905, 043309
12	19037 L	Er liebt mich (Il m'aime), Act 3, Margarethe (Faust), (Gounod) 74607/70694, 2–43540
13	19038 L	Auf eilet (Alerte, alerte), Act 5, Margarethe (Faust), (Gounod) Closing trio with M. Bohnen and R. Hutt 74596/80079*, 3–44159 (*on the reverse: Selma Kurz)

Probably 1917

14	1220 m	Man nennt mich jetzt Mimi (Mi chiamano Mimi), Act 1, La Bohème (Puccini) 76402/72907, 043338
15	1221–2 m	Ich schreib' an Sie (I write to you) 'Letter Scene', Act 1 Eugen Onegin, (Tchaikovsky) 76369/72906, 043310
16	1222 m	See Notes
17	1223 m	Kennst du das Land? (Connais-tu le pays où fleurit l'oranger?) Act 1, Mignon (Thomas) one strophe only. In D flat 76403/72907, 043339
18	1224 m	Weh' mir, du weinst! Ach dir fehlet der Glaube . . . Eines Tages sehen wir (Piangi? per che? . . . Un bel di vedremo) Act 2, Madama Butterfly (Puccini) 76411/72909, 043355
19	1225 m	Heil'ge Quelle (Porgi amor) Act 2, Die Hochzeit des Figaro (Le Nozze di Figaro), (Mozart) 76414/72910 043363
20	1226 m	O säume länger nicht (Deh vieni, non tardar), Act 4, Die Hochzeit des Figaro (Le nozze di Figaro), (Mozart) 76477/72910, B 24072
21	1227 m	Ich sprach, dass ich furchtlos mich fühle (Je dis que rien ne m'épouvante), Act 3, Carmen (Bizet) 76478/72914, B 24073
22	1228 m	Dort bei ihm ist sie jetzt (Elle est là près de lui), Act 2, Mignon (Thomas) 76413/72909, 043362
23	1229 m	Wie nahte mir der Schlummer, bevor ich ihn gesehn? Act 2, Der Freischütz (Weber) 76482/72904, B 24088
24	19184 L	Über das Meer und alle Lande (Spira sul mare e sulla terra), Entrance of Butterfly, Act 1, Madama Butterfly (Puccini) 74604/70693, 2–43529
25	19185–2 L	Folget dem Ruf, so lieblich zu hören . . . Nützet die schönen, jungen Tage (Obéissons quand leur voix appelle . . . Profitons bien de la jeunesse) Act 3, Gavotte, Manon (Massenet) 74598/70693, 2–43525
26	19186 L	Du bist der Lenz, Act 1, Die Walküre (Wagner) 74597/70692, 2–43524

1919

27	1377 m	Ozean du Ungeheuer, Rezia's Aria, Act 2, Oberon (Weber) part 1 76455/72913, B 24036
28	1378 m	Rezia's Aria, part 2. 76456/72913, B 24037

29 1379 m See Notes
30 1380 m Es schweige die Klage, Act 4, Der widerspenstigen Zämung (Götz)
76483/72914, B 24089
31 1381 m Nun eilt herbei, Part 1 Act 1, Die lustigen Weiber von Windsor (Nicolai)
76421/72911, B 24011
32 1382 m Ha, ha, ha, er wird mir glauben . . . part 2 Die lustigen Weiber,
76422/72911, B 24012
33 1383 m So wisse dass in allen Elementen es Wesen gibt, part 1 Act 2, Undine (Lortzing)
76484/72915, B 24090
34 1384 m Doch kann auf Erden . . . (part 2) Undine
76485/72915, B 24091
35 19259 L Psyche wandelt durch Säulenhallen, Die toten Augen (d'Albert)
74608/72692, B 4000

1920

36 150 ap Ohne Mutter (Senza mamma, o bimbo) Schwester Angelica (Suor Angelica), (Puccini)
76405/72908, 043346
37 151 ap O Blumen, die ihr Gift (Amici fiori che nel picco seno) Schwester Angelica (Suor Angelica), (Puccini)
76406/72908, 043347
38 152 ap So lang' hab' ich geschmachtet (Crudel, perchè finora farmi languir così), Act 3, Die Hochzeit des Figaro (Le nozze di Figaro), (Mozart) with Heinrich Schlusnus
76412/72933, 044328
39 153 ap Bei Männern welche Liebe fühlen, Act 1, Die Zauberflöte (Mozart) with Heinrich Schlusnus
76415/72932, 044330
40 154 ap Ihr Schwalben in den Lüften (Légères hirondelles, oiseaux bénis de Dieu), Act 1, Mignon (Thomas) with H. Schlusnus
76409/72932, 044326
41 155 ap Reich' mir die Hand mein Leben (Là ci darem la mano), Act 1, Don Juan (Don Giovanni), (Mozart) with H. Schlusnus
76410/72933, 044327

1921

42 416 as O Sachs, mein Freund, Act 3, Die Meistersinger von Nürnberg (Wagner)
76486/72903, B 24092
43 417–2 as Der Männer Sippe, Act 1, Die Walküre (Wagner)
72906, B 24093 (Double-sided only)
44 418 as Und ob die Wolke, Act 3, Der Freischütz (Weber)
76488/72916, B 24094

45 419 as O grausames Geschick . . . Sie entfloh, die Taube so minnig (Image trop cruelle . . . Elle a fui, la tourterelle), Act 3, Hoffmanns Erzählungen (Les Contes d'Hoffmann), (Offenbach)
76489/72916, B 24095

46 420 as Cäcilie (R. Strauss) sung in E flat
76454/72912, B 24029, Amer. Vocalion 35034

47 421 as Morgen, Op. 27 No. 4 (R. Strauss) sung in G
76490/72917, B 24096 (on the reverse: M. Olszewska B 24119)

48 530 as Der Spielmann (Hildach) sung in F (orig: E)
76453/72912, B 24028

49 531 as Er kommt zurück (Il va venir), Act 2, Die Jüdin (La juive), (Halévy)
76464/72905, B 24045

50 1121 ar Ihr die Ihr Triebe (Voi che sapete), Act 2, Die Hochzeit des Figaro (Le Nozze di Figaro), (Mozart)
74615/70694, B 4010

NOTES TO THE GRAMMOPHON/POLYDOR RECORDINGS

As the recording books for the years 1916–21 are lost the accuracy of the recording dates given could not be verified. Those given for Nos. 27–50 are believed to be correct. It should be noted that the dates on test pressings invariably indicate when the pressing itself was made, not when the title was recorded. While it can be assumed that the recording was made shortly before the test pressing was issued, this does not always apply to recordings made during World War I. The dates on many test pressings which reached England during this period are sometimes as much as two years later than the dates of the recording sessions. All titles are sung in German.

6 Believed to be an earlier version of No. 21, which was either rejected or damaged during processing.

7 Probably an earlier version of No. 23.

8 This is the second part of 'Wie nahte mir der Schlummer', See No. 23.

11–12 Matrix No. 1110m is a recording by Michael Bohnen.

16 Believed to be an earlier version of No. 45.

23 The first part of the aria. For the second part see No. 8.

27–35 This session may possibly have taken place during August–September.

29 Probably an earlier version of an aria subsequently re-recorded. The title is unknown.

46 The original key of the version with piano accompaniment is E. The key was changed to E flat when the song was orchestrated.

REISSUES ON LONG PLAYING RECORDS SECTION II: GRAMMOPHON/POLYDOR

The numbers in brackets belong to another section.

Rococo 5217 'A Richard Strauss Memorial' contains No. 46

Rococo 5257 'Lotte Lehmann'
side 1: No. 19, 38, 20, 41, 21, 45, 40
side 2: No. 44, 4, 5, 9–10, 42, 35

Rococo 5356 'Lotte Lehmann, vol II'
side 1: No. 23–8, 33–34, 36, 37, (65)
side 2: No. (62), 26, 14, 30, 27–28, (120)

Preiser, Court Opera Classics, CO 387, 'Michael Bohnen', contains 9–10
Preiser, Court Opera Classics, CO 410, 'Michael Bohner II' contains 13
Preiser, LV 180 'Lotte Lehmann III'
  side 1: No. 19, 20, 44, 27–28, 33–34
  side 2: No. 49, 21, 45, 30, 15, 36, 37
Preiser, LV 294 'Lotte Lehmann IV'
  side 1: No. 50, 38, 41, 39, 31–32, 48, 46* (*not on sleeve only on record label)
  side 2: No. 17, 40, 22, 25, 14, 24, 18
Preiser, LV 1336 'Lotte Lehmann V'
  side 1: No. 23/8, 3, 4, (1), (2), 5, 11
  side 2: No. 12, 9–10, 42, 43, 26, 35, 47
Rubini RDA 003 (2 discs) 'Lotte Lehmann'
  side 1: No. 19, 50, 38, 20, 41, 44
  side 2: No. 27–28, 9–10, 42, 13
  side 3: No. 3, 4, 5, 43, 15, 12
  side 4: No. 49, 45, 25, 24, 18, 30
EMI 137–30704/05 (2 discs) 'Lotte Lehmann 2. Die Lyrikerin der Gesangskunst'. Identical with Seraphim IB 6105. It contains the following acoustic Polydors: No. 5, 9–10. All the remainder belongs to sections 3 and 4.
Top Classics 9052: No. 17
Opera Discs 3086: No. 23 & 8
DG 2721 176 (2 discs) '300 Jahre Staatsoper Hamburg', contains No. 43
Top Artist Platters:
  T–318 'Twenty Great German Singers of the Twentieth Century' No. 17

SECTION III: *Odeon acoustic recordings, Berlin, 1924–1926*

The first catalogue number (prefixed LXX or RXX) is that assigned to single-sided records, the second number (prefixed O–) to double-sided records. The O–9500 series did not come into use until the end of 1926. All records are twelve-inch (30 cm) and all titles are sung in German.

It will be observed that most matrix numbers in this section, and in Section IV (Odeon electric recordings), are shown without a take number. This signifies that take 1 was issued, in keeping with the company's practice of omitting the –1 from the matrix number impressed in the shellac of published copies. It does not mean, however, as it could with other record companies, that only one recording of the title had been made. In fact, Odeon required their artists to make at least two recordings (i.e. takes 1 and 2) of every title, and this is the reason why some copies of an issued title show that it was pressed from take 1, while other copies show take 2, and why this occurred so frequently. All known instances of issued recordings which show both takes are indicated in the notes at the end of the sections. Take 2 is always made on the same day as take 1 unless otherwise stated.

13 February 1924. Members of the Berlin State Opera Orchestra cond. by Carl Besl.

51	xxB 6945	Folget dem Ruf, so lieblich zu hören . . . Nützet die schönen, jungen Tage (Obéissons quand leur voix appelle . . . Profitons bien de la jeunesse) Act 3, Gavotte, Manon (Massenet) Lxx 80934, O–9510
52	xxB 6946	Nur der Schönheit weiht' ich mein Leben (Vissi d'arte, vissi d'amore), Act 2, Tosca (Puccini) Lxx 80935, O–9511
53	xxB 6947	Man nennt mich jetzt Mimi (Mi chiamano Mimi), Act 1, La Bohème (Puccini) Lxx 80933, O–9502
54	xxB 6948	Du bist verlassen . . . Ach, in den kalten Räumen hier (L'ho abbandonato. . . . In quelle trine morbide), Act 2, Manon Lescaut (Puccini) Lxx 80936, O–9503
55	xxB 6949	Eines Tages seh'n wir (Un bel di vedremo), Act 2, Madama Butterfly (Puccini) Lxx 80937, O–9503

18 February 1924. Carl Besl, piano.

56	xxB 6950	Wiegenlied (R. Strauss) Unpublished, see repeat on 7 December 1925
57	xxB 6951	Freundliche Vision (R. Strauss) Unpublished, see repeat on 7 December 1925 with Berlin State Opera Orchestra conducted by Carl Besl
58	xxB 6952	's ist für ihn . . . Leb' wohl, mein liebes kleines Tischchen (Allons! Il le faut! pour lui même . . . Adieu, notre petite table), Act 2, Manon (Massenet) Lxx 80938, O–9510
59	xxB 6953	Dich teure Halle, Act 2, Tannhäuser (Wagner) Lxx 80939, O–9504
60	xxB 6954	Du bist der Lenz Act 1, Die Walküre, (Wagner) Lxx 80940, O–9504

24 March 1924. Members of the Berlin State Opera Orchestra conducted by Georg Széll

61	xxB 6972	Allmächt'ge Jungfrau, Act 3 Tannhäuser (Wagner) Lxx 80947, O–9509
62	xxB 6973	Sie sass mit Leide auf öder Heide (Piangea cantando nell'erma landa), Willow Song, Act 4, Otello (Verdi) Lxx 80955, O–9511
63	xxB 6974	Euch Lüften, die mein Klagen, Act 2, Lohengrin (Wagner) Lxx 80979, O–9509

17 April 1924. Berlin State Opera Orchestra conducted by Georg Széll

64 xxB 6993–2 Glück, das mir verblieb – Die tote Stadt (Korngold). Duet with Richard Tauber, tenor, from Act 1
Lxx 80944, O–9507 (both takes used)

65 xxB 6994–2 Der Erste, der Lieb' mich gelehrt – Die tote Stadt (Korngold). Marietta's aria from Act 3
Lxx 80945, O–9502 (both takes used)

17 October 1925. Members of Berlin State Opera Orchestra conducted by Hermann Weigert

66 xxB 7239 Wie nahte mir der Schlummer, Act 2, Der Freischütz (Weber)
Lxx 81100, O–9516

67 xxB 7240–2 Alles pflegt schon längst der Ruh' . . . leise, leise, fromme Weise, Act 2 Der Freischütz (Weber)
Lxx 81101, O–9516 (both takes used)

68 xxB 7241 O Sachs, mein Freund, Act 3 Die Meistersinger (Wagner)
O–9518

69 xxB 7242 Ach, ich fühl's, es ist entschwunden, Act 2 Die Zauberflöte (Mozart)
Unpublished

70 xxB 7243 Einsam in trüben Tagen, Act 1 Lohengrin, (Wagner)
O–9518

71 xxB 7244 Kann mich auch an ein Mädel erinnern, Act 1 Der Rosenkavalier, (R. Strauss)
Lxx 81103, O–9517

22 October 1925. Members of Berlin State Opera Orchestra conducted by Hermann Weigert.

72 xxB 7250 Kennst du das Land wo die Zitronen blühn? (Connais-tu le pays où fleurit l'oranger?), Act 1, Mignon (Thomas). E flat
Lxx 80997, O–9515

73 xxB 7251–2 Bald sind wir auf der Höhe (Ancora un passo or via) Entrance of Butterfly, Act 1, Madama Butterfly (Puccini) With female chorus.
Lxx 81102, O–9517 (Both takes used)

74 xxB 7252 Ich gäb' was drum . . . Es war ein König in Thule (Je voudrais bien savoir . . . Il était un roi de Thulé), Margarethe (Faust), Act 3, (Gounod)
Lxx 80998, O–9515

75 xxB 7253 Stille Nacht (Gruber)
Rxx 80600 (brown label) later O–8540

76 xxB 7254–2 O du fröhliche (traditional)
Rxx 80601 (brown label) later O–8540 (both takes used)

77 xxB 7255 a) Da unten im Tale (Brahms)
b) Wiegenlied (Brahms)
With Hermann Weigert, piano accompaniment.
Unpublished.

7 December 1925. Hermann Weigert piano accompaniment

78 xxB 6950–2 Wiegenlied (R. Strauss)
Repeat of 18 February 1924. Unpublished
79 xxB 6951–2 Freundliche Vision (R. Strauss)
Repeat of 18 February 1924. Unpublished.

2 March 1926. Hermann Weigert piano and Dajos Bela violin

80 xxB 7432–2 Morgen (R. Strauss)
Unpublished
81 xxB 7433 Mit deinen blauen Augen (R. Strauss)
Unpublished
82 xxB 7434 Allerseelen (R. Strauss)
O–8608 assigned, never catalogued.
83 xxB 7435 a) Zueignung (R. Strauss)
b) Cäcilie (R. Strauss)
O–8608 assigned, never catalogued.
84 xxB 7436 a) Aufträge (Schumann)
b) Heimkehr vom Feste (Leo Blech)
Unpublished

5 August 1926. Piano accompaniment by Mischa Spoliansky

85 xxB 7477 a) Monatsrose (Philipp zu Eulenburg)
(–2) b) Wilde Rose (Philipp zu Eulenburg)
With Dajos Bela violin
O–8703, Am.D. 25800
86 xxB 7478 Weisse und rote Rose (Philipp zu Eulenburg)
O–8703, Am.D. 25800
87 xxB 7479 a) Rankende Rose (Philipp zu Eulenburg)
b) Seerose (Philipp zu Eulenburg)
O–8704, Am. D. 25801
88 xxB 7480 Der Nussbaum (Schumann)
Unpublished
89 xxB 7481 Heidenröslein (Werner) with Dajos Bela violin
O–8704, Am. D. 25801

NOTES TO ACOUSTIC ODEON RECORDINGS

51 Passed by the artist on 24.3.1924, released Oct. 1925
52 Passed by the artist on 24.3.1924, released Nov. 1925
53 Passed by the artist on 5.3.1924, released Apr. 1924
54 Passed by the artist on 24.3.1924, released Jan. 1925
55 Passed by the artist on 24.3.1924, released Jan. 1925
56 Passed by the artist on 17.4.1926, destruction requested 11.5.1926.
58 Passed by the artist on 24.3.1924, released Oct. 1925
59–60 Passed by the artist on 24.3.1924, released May. 1924
61 Passed by the artist on 28.4.1924, released Apr. 1925
62 Passed by the artist on 5.5.1924, released Nov. 1925
63 Passed by the artist on 28.5.1924, released Apr. 1925

64 Take 1, initially in reserve, was also used later. The earlier pressings, with a rim before the music begins, are take 2. Released in June/July 1924. For the three electric transfers of this title (takes II, III and IV) see Nos. 211 and 224 and Notes.

65 Take 1, initially in reserve, was also used later.

66–67 Passed by the artist on 2.11.1925, and released in May/June 1926.

68 Passed by the artist on 17.4.1926. As the record was issued in February 1927 no LXX single-sided number was assigned. The singer is reported to have made electric repeats but there are no entries in the recording books, nor have any electric versions been discovered.

69 Passed by the artist on 17.4.1926. Not issued. The master may have been damaged during processing.

70 Passed by the artist on 17.4.1926. Not issued until February 1927, hence no LXX single-side number was assigned. As with No. 68 an electric repeat has been reported but there is no entry in the recording books, and no copies have shown up.

71 Passed by the artist on 17.4.1926, and by Hermann Weigert on 14.11.1925. Issued in September 1926.

72 Released in April 1926.

73 Released in September 1926.

74 Released in April 1926.

75–76 Released in December 1925.

77 Scheduled to be coupled with xxB 7436 (No. 84).

78–79 Note that a different pianist was used for the repeats.

80 A transfer was made (take 3) but spoiled during processing ('Could only be used for a sample' – 12.8.1926). Destruction was requested on 27.4.1927. Dajos Bela probably played only for this title.

81 Passed by the artist on 17.4.1926, and by Herman Weigert on 11.5.1926.

82–83 A brown label issue. Passed by the artist on 17.4.1926 and by Hermann Weigert on 11.5.1926. Probably never published.

84 Scheduled to be coupled with xxB 7255 (No. 77).

85 Take 2 was spoiled during processing and could be used only as a sample copy. Passed by the artist along with Nos. 86, 87, and 89 on 14.12.1926, and issued in March 1927. Electrical repeats have been reported but copies have not been seen and no entry has been traced in the recording books.

89 Both catalogues and labels give Schubert as the composer. In the recording book his name is crossed out and 'Werner' substituted.

REISSUES ON LONG PLAYING RECORDS
SECTION III: ODEON – ACOUSTIC RECORDINGS

EMI 0–83396. Serie: 'Die goldene Stimme' Lotte Lehmann
side 1: No. 59, 70
The other contents of this disc relate to sections IV and V

Rococo 5356 'Lotte Lehmann, Vol II'
side 1: No. 65
side 2: No. 62
The other titles are taken from Grammophon/Polydor records

EMI 147–29 116/17M Lotte Lehmann I, Die Lyrikerin der Gesangskunst
side 3: No. 59*, 70

* Not No. 187 as the label and sleeve state
The duet from Die tote Stadt is the later version with orchestra conducted by Frieder Weissmann, see No. 224

EMI 137–30704/05 (2 discs), Seraphim IB 6105: Lotte Lehmann II. Die Lyrikerin der Gesangskunst.
side 1: No. 66–67, 68
side 2: No. 65
side 3: No. 58, 54, 71
Further dubbings from electrics appear in the following section.
Preiser LV 94. 'Lotte Lehmann II'
side 1: No. 61, 70, 63, 74, 72, 58, 51, 68
side 2: No. 62, 54, 53, 52, 73, 55, 71, 65
EMI RLS 743 'The Record of Singing, vol II', side 22, band 2: No. 52
Scala 837, Eterna 494 and EMI RLS 7700 'The Art of Richard Tauber' contain No. 64
Top Classics TC 9052: 59, 60, 61 and 66/67
Preiser LV 500 'Vom Hofoper zur Staatsoper' contains No. 54 (record 3)
Top Artists Platters:
T–306 'Twenty great Sopranos' contains No. 51

SECTION IV: *Odeon electric recordings, Berlin, 1927–1933*

Catalogue numbers: the O–8700 series (with matrix numbers prefixed xxB) are 12-inch recordings, the O–48 series (with matrix numbers prefixed Be) are ten-inch. English issues on Parlophone: the R 20000 series are 12-inch recordings, the RO 20000 are ten-inch. Parlophone historic reissues are prefixed PXO and PO for twelve-inch and ten-inch recordings respectively. Affiliated labels: American Columbia, American Decca, French Odeon, American Odeon, Italian, Spanish and Argentine Odeon, Australian Parlophone (AR prefix) etc. All titles are sung in German except the duets with Kiepura, Nos. 110/111

16 February 1927. Members of the orchestra of the Berlin City Opera, conducted by Fritz Zweig. Speed 80 rpm

90	xxB 7609	In diesem Schlosse, vor vielen tausend Jahren (In questa Reggia, or son mill'anni e mille), Act 2, Turandot (Puccini) O–9602 later O–8720, Parl. R 20014, France 123.601
91	xxB 7610	Die ersten Tränen (Del primo pianto), Act 3, Turandot (Puccini) O–9602 later O–8720, Parl. R 20014, France 123.601
92	xxB 7611–2	Ozean du Ungeheuer, Rezia's aria, part 1, Act 2, Oberon (C.M.v. Weber) O–8742, Parl. R 20024, Am. Col. 9055 M, Am.D. 29014
93	xxB 7612–2	Ozean du Ungeheuer, aria part 2. O–8742, Parl. R 20024, Am. Col. 9055M, Am.D. 29014
94	xxB 7613	Von Blut gerötet war meine Schwelle (La mamma morta m'hanno a la porta), Act 3, Andrea Chenier (Giordano) Unpublished in Germany. Parl. R. 20025

18 February 1927. Members of the Berlin State Opera Orchestra conducted by Fritz Zweig. Speed 80 rpm

95	xxB 7618–2	Ach war es nicht ein Traum . . . Am stillen Zufluchtsort – Berceuse, Act 2, Jocelyn (Godard). Sung in g/E flat (a/F) O–8709, Parl. R 20019, Fr. 123.621
96	xxB 7619	O lass dich halten goldene Stunde (Jensen) sung in G flat O–8709, Parl. R 20019, France 123.621
97	xxB 7620–2	Murmelndes Lüftchen (Jensen) F (G flat) Unpublished in Germany, Parl. R 20025
98	xxB 7621	Auf Flügeln des Gesanges (Mendelssohn) G (A flat) O–8713, Parl. R 20013, Am. Col. 9059M, Am.D. 25806, France 123.622, Argentina 177.056
99	xxB 7622	Von ewiger Liebe (Brahms) sung in b O–8713, Parl. R 20013, Am. Col. 9059M, Am. D. 25806, France 123.622, Argentina 177.056 Later also issued on Odeon O–8763 coupled with No. 100

6 December 1927. Chamber orchestra cond. by Manfred Gurlitt. Speed 78 rpm

100	xxB 7873	An die Musik – D.547 (Schubert) sung in D O–8724, Parl. R 20051, Am. Col. 9073M, Am. D. 25798, Col. 50170–D, AR 1019. Odeon O–8763 coupled with No. 99
101	xxB 7874	Ave Maria – D.839 (Schubert) two verses, sung in B flat O–8719, Parl. R 20050, Am. D. 25797, Argentina 177.042 Dutch Od. AA 178.024b (coupled with Helene Cals) Brazil D 7107, Spain 121.025, AR 1009
102	xxB 7875	Du bist die Ruh' – D.776 (Schubert) sung in E flat O–8724, Parl. R 20051, Am.D. 25798, Argentina 177.069
103	xxB 7876	Sei mir gegrüsst – D.741 (Schubert) B flat O–8725, Parl. R 20052, Am. Col. 9073M, Am. D. 25799 Argentina 177.069, AR 1019
104	xxB 7877	Auf dem Wasser zu singen – D.774 (Schubert) a flat O–8725, Parl. R 20052, Am. D. 25799
105	xxB 7878 (–1)	Der Lenz Op. 19 No. 5 (Hildach) Unpublished, see repeat on 13 March 1928
106	xxB 7879	Der Spielmann (Hildach) sung in G (E) O–8727, Am. Col. 9054M, Am.D. 25802
107	xxB 7880	Ständchen, D. 957 No. 4 (Schubert), Sung in d O–8719, Parl. R 20050, Am.D. 25797, AR 1009 Argentina 177.042, Brazil D 7107, Spain 121.025
108	Be 6397	Der Tod und das Mädchen – D.531 (Schubert) d O–4800, Parl. RO 20061, Am.D. 20281, Argentina 196.030

9 December 1927. Chamber Ensemble cond. Manfred Gurlitt

109	Be 6400	Geheimes – D.719 (Schubert) A flat O–4800, Parl. RO 20061, Am.D. 20281, Argentina 196.030

10 December 1927. Members of the Berlin State Opera Orchestra conducted by Manfred Gurlitt

110 xxB 7881–2 Qual' occhio al mondo – Act 1, Love duet, Tosca (Puccini) with Jan Kiepura tenor (in Italian)
O–9603 later O–8743, Parl. R 20048, Am.D. 29016, France 123.602 Argentina 177.068, AR 1054

111 xxB 7882–2 Amaro sol perte m'era il morire – Act 3, Love duet, Tosca (Puccini) with Jan Kiepura tenor (in Italian)
O–9603 later O–8743, Parl. R 20048, Am.D. 29016, France 123.602, Argentina 177.068, AR 1054

13 December 1927. Members of the Berlin State Opera Orchestra conducted by Manfred Gurlitt

112 xxB 7885 Komm' Hoffnung Part 1 – Fidelio (Beethoven)
O–8721, Parl. R 20053 later PXO 1013, Am.D. 25803, France 123.603, Austrian Parl. BX 601, AR 1026

113 xxB 7886 Ich folg' dem inneren Triebe – aria Part 2 (Beethoven)
O–8721, Parl. R 20053 later PXO 1013, Am.D. 25803, France 123.603, Austrian Parl. BX 601, AR 1026

114 xxB 7887–2 O, sei er gut, Quinquin . . . Die Zeit, die ist ein sonderbar Ding Act 1, Der Rosenkavalier (R. Strauss)
O–8726, Parl. R 20054, PXO 1014, Am.D. 25817, AR 1022

115 xxB 7888 (–1) Heil'ge Quelle (Porgi amor), Act 2, Die Hochzeit des Figaro (Le nozze di Figaro), (Mozart)
O–8726, Parl. R 20054, PXO 1014, Am. D. 25817, AR 1022

13 March 1928. Members of the Berlin State Opera Orchestra conducted by Manfred Gurlitt

116 xxB 7997–2 Ich ging zu ihm, Part 1, Act 2, Das Wunder der Heliane (Korngold)
O–8722, Am.D 25805

117 xxB 7998–2 Nicht hab' ich ihn geliebt, Part 2, Das Wunder der Heliane (Korngold)
O–8722, Am.D. 25805

118 xxB 7878–2 Der Lenz, Op. 19 No. 5 (Hildach). Repeat of No. 105. Sung in D
O–8727, Am.D. 25802, Am. Col. 9054–M

119 xxB 7888–2 Heil'ge Quelle (Porgi amor), Act 2, Die Hochzeit des Figaro (Le Nozze di Figaro)
O–8726, Parl. R 20054, PXO 1014, Am.D. 25817, AR 1022

3 September 1928. Members of the Berlin State Opera Orchestra and Chamber Orchestra Hans von Benda cond. by Hermann Weigert

120 xxB 8150 So war meine Mutter . . . (spoken recitative)
Wär es auch nichts als ein Augenblick – Eva (Lehár)
O–8730, Parl. R 20275, AR 1085

121 xxB 8151 Wenn dein ich denk' – Das Zauberlied (Meyer-Helmund) F (D flat?)
O–8730, Parl. R 20275, Am. Col. 9082M, AR 1085
122 Be 7174 (–1) Ave Maria (J.S. Bach, arr. Gounod)
Not accepted. See repeat on 10 November 1928, No. 145
123 Be 7175 (–1) Largo, Serse, (Händel) in German
Not accepted. See repeat on 10 November 1928, No. 146
124 Be 7176 Eine kleine Liebelei (Rotter-Stransky, Ralton)
O–4801
125 Be 7177 Frühling ist es wieder (Beda-W. Engel, Berger)
O–4801
126 Be 7178 Der Nussbaum (Schumann) with piano. In G
O–4821, Parl. RO 20071, Am. Col. 4065M, Am.D. 20375
127 Be 7183 Mit deinen blauen Augen (R. Strauss) with piano & violin acc. in F
O–4846, Parl. RO 20081, Am.D. 20339, AR 128
128 Be 7184–2 Aufträge (Schumann) with piano accompaniment in A
O–4821, Parl. RO 20071, Am. Col. 4065M, Am.D. 20375
129 Be 7189 Morgen (R. Strauss) with piano and violin. In G
O–4846, Parl. RO 20081, Am.D. 20339, AR, 128

4 September 1928. Members of the Berlin State Opera Orchestra conducted by Hermann Weigert

130 xxB 8168 In den schönen Feierkleidern – Ariadne's aria 2nd part, Ariadne auf Naxos (R. Strauss) see below for part one
O–8731, Parl. R 20147, Am.D. 25816, AR 1069
131 xxB 8169 (–1) Sie lebt hier ganz allein . . . Es gibt ein Reich, Part 1, Ariadne auf Naxos (R. Strauss)
O–8731
132 xxB 8169–2 Sie atmet leicht . . . Es gibt ein Reich Part 2, – Ariadne auf Naxos (R. Strauss)
O–8731, Parl. R 20147, Am.D. 25816, AR 1069
133 Be 7185 Zur Drossel sprach der Fink Op. 9 No. 4 (d'Albert) B flat
O–4823
134 Be 7186–2 Ach wer das doch könnte (Wilhelm Berger) F
O–4823, Parl. RO 20263, AR 259
135 Be 7187 O du fröhliche (traditional)
O–4810, Parl. RO 20098, Am.D. 23052, Brazil A 3122
136 Be 7188 Stille Nacht, heilige Nacht (Gruber)
O–4810, Parl. RO 20098, Am.D. 23052, Brazil A 3122

10 November 1928. Instrumental trio cond. Frieder Weissmann. Speed 76 rpm

137 Be 7601 Frauenliebe und -leben (Schumann) Complete.
Seit ich ihn gesehen, B flat

O–4806, Parl. RO 20090, Am.Col. 4070M,Am.D. 20411,
France 188.785, Italy 15013, Argentina 196.274

138 Be 7602 Er, der herrlichste von Allen, E flat
O–4806, Parl. RO 20090, Am. Col. 4070M, Am.D. 20411,
France 188.785, Italy 15013, Argentina 196.274

139 Be 7603 Ich kann's nicht fassen nicht glauben, c
O–4807, Parl. RO 20091, Am. Col. 4071M, Am.D. 20412,
France 188.786, Italy 15014, Argentina 196.275

140 Be 7604 Du Ring an meinem Finger, E flat
O–4807, Parl. RO 20091, Am.Col. 4071M, Am.D. 20412,
France 188.786, Italy 15014, Argentina 196.275

141 Be 7605 Helft mir, ihr Schwestern, B
O–4808, Parl. RO 20092, Am. Col. 4072M, Am.D. 20413,
France 188.787, Italy 15015, Argentina 196.276

142 Be 7606 Süsser Freund, G
O–4808, Parl. RO 20092, Am. Col. 4072M, Am.D. 20413,
France 188.787, Italy 15015, Argentina 196.276

143 Be 7607 An meinem Herzen an meiner Brust, D
O–4809, Parl. RO 20093, Am.Col. 4073M, Am.D. 20414,
France 188.788, Italy 15016, Argentina 196.277

144 Be 7608 Nun hast du mir den ersten Schmerz getan, c
O–4809, Parl. RO 20093, Am. Col. 4073M, Am.D. 20414,
France 188.788, Italy 15016, Argentina 196.277

145 Be 7174–2 Ave Maria (J.S. Bach, arr. Gounod)
O–4802, Parl. RO 20076, Am.D. 20277, France 188.651,
Italy 15005, Chile & Argentina 196.036, Brazil A. 3076,
AR 120

146 Be 7175–2 Largo, Serse, (Händel) in German
O–4802, Parl. RO 20076, Am.D. 20277, France 188.651,
Chile & Argentina 196.036, Brazil A. 3076, AR 120

12 November 1928. Accompanied by the Odeon Church Organ. Speed 75 rpm

147 xxB 8220–2 Halleluia (Hummel) sung in C
O–8733, Parl. R 20265, AR 1082

148 xxB 8221–2 Wo du hingehst – Trauungsgesang (Louis Roessel) in E
O–8733, Parl. R 20265, AR 1082

17 December 1928. Members of the Berlin State Opera Orchestra and Chorus conducted by Frieder Weissmann.

149 xxB 8266 Herr Chevalier, ich grüsse Sie-Finale Act 2, part 1,
–2 Die Fledermaus (J. Strauss) with Richard Tauber tenor,
–3 K. Branzell contralto, M. Nikisch & W. Staegemann
O–8734, Parl. R 20085 later PXO 1032, Am.Od. 3268,
Am.D. 29015, Am.Col. 9078M, Australia AR 1029, France
123.018, Argentina 177.217, Austria, BX 602

150 xxB 8267–2 Genug damit, genug – Finale Act 2, conclusion, Die Fledermaus (Joh. Strauss). Same cast as 149
O–8734, Am.Od. 3268, Am.Col. 9078M, Am.D. 29015, Parl. R 20085 later PXO 1032, France 123.018, Australia AR 1029, Argentina 177.217, Austria, BX 602.

151 xxB 8268–2 Ein Fürstenkind – Finale Act 2, Der Zigeunerbaron (J. Strauss). Same cast as 149 plus Hans Lange.
O–8735, Parl. R 20104 later PXO 1034, Am.Col. 9079M, France 123.019, Am.D. 29013, Australia AR 1035, Od. 5172

152 xxB 8269–2 Er ist Baron – Finale Act 1, Der Zigeunerbaron (J. Strauss) with same cast as 149 & Hans Lange.
O–8735, Parl. R 20104 later PXO 1034, Am.Col. 9079M, France 123.019, Am.D. 29013, Australia AR 1035, Od. 5172

26 February 1929. Members of the Berlin State Opera Orchestra conducted by Manfred Gurlitt. Speed 76 rpm

153 xxB 8305 Wie nahte mir der Schlummer Part 1, Act 2, Der Freischütz (Weber)
O–8741, Parl. R 20087 later PXO 1016, Am.Col. 9060M, Am.D. 29007 Am. Od. 3286, AR 1031. See also No. 235

154 xxB 8306 Alles pflegt schon längst der Ruh', Part 2, Aria, Der Freischütz
O–8741, Parl. R 20087 later PXO 1016, Am.Col. 9060M, Am.D. 29007, Am.Od. 3286, AR 1031

155 Be 8036 Nur der Schönheit (Vissi D'arte), Act 2, Tosca (Puccini)
Unpublished

156 Be 8037 Man nennt mich Mimi (Mi chiamano Mimi), Act 1, La Bohème (Puccini)
Unpublished

157 Be 8038 O Haupt voll Blut und Wunden – religious hymn with organ.
O–4811, Parl. RO 20215, Am.D. 20336, Australia AR 220

158 Be 8039 Christi Mutter stand in Schmerzen – religious hymn w. organ
O–4811, Parl. RO 20215, Am.D. 20336, Australian AR 220

159 Be 8040 Geleite durch die Welle – Marienlied, religious hymn w. organ
O–4803, Parl. RO 20205, Am.D. 20337, AR 203

160 Be 8041 Es blüht der Blumen eine – Marienlied, religious hymn w. organ
O–4803, Parl. RO 20205, Am.D. 20337, AR 203

16 April 1929. Members of the Berlin State Opera Orchestra conducted by Frieder Weissmann.

161 xxB 8321 (–1) Nur der Schönheit (Vissi d'arte), Act 2 Tosca, (Puccini)
See repeat No. 167

162 xxB 8322 (–1) Man nennt mich Mimi (Mi chiamano Mimi), Act 1, La Bohème (Puccini)
See repeat No. 168

163 Be 8143 Es gibt eine Frau, die dich niemals vergisst (Schwabach – Jim Cowler)
O–4805

164 Be 8144 Der Duft der eine schöne Frau begleitet (H. May)
O–4804, France 188.728

165 Be 8145 Wenn du einmal dein Herz verschenkst (W. Rosen)
O–4804, France 188.728

166 Be 8146 Ich hol' dir vom Himmel das Blau – Die lustige Witwe (Lehár)
O–4805

13 June 1929. Members of the Berlin State Opera Orchestra conducted by Frieder Weissmann. Speed 76 rpm

167 xxB 8321–2 Nur der Schönheit (Vissi d'arte), Act 2, Tosca (Puccini)
–3 O–8736, Parl. R 20095, Am. d. 25804, Tonalit NM 7065

168 xxB 8322–2 Man nennt mich Mimi (Mi chiamano Mimi), Act 1, La Bohème
–3 (Puccini)
O–8736, Parl. R 20095, Am.D 25804, Tonalit NM 7065

169 Be 8299–2 Schmerzen (R. Wagner) in C
O–4812, Parl. RO 20100, Am.D. 20284, Am.Col. 4059M

170 Be 8300–2 Träume (R. Wagner) in A flat
O–4812, Parl. RO 20100, Am.D. 20284

171 Be 8301–2 Widmung (R. Schumann) in A flat
O–4824, Parl. RO 20102, Am. Col. 4059M, Am.D. 20376, Australia AR 132

172 Be 8302 Du bist wie eine Blume (R. Schumann) in A flat
O–4824, Parl. RO 20102, Am.D. 20376, Australia AR 132

173 Be 8303 Traum durch die Dämmerung (R. Strauss) in F sharp
O–4820, Parl. RO 20096, Am.D. 20340, AR 129

174 Be 8304 Ständchen (R. Strauss) in F (F sharp)
O–4820, Parl. RO 20096, Am.D. 20340, AR 129

3 October 1929. Acc. by Paul Mania on the Odeon church organ.

175 Be 8590 O heiliger Geist, kehr' bei uns ein (hymn)
O–4814, Parl. RO 20320, Am.Col. 4062M, Am.D. 20334

176 Be 8591 Aus tiefer Not (hymn)
O–4815, Parl. RO 20309, Am.Col. 4057M, Am.D. 20333

177 Be 8592 Ach bleib' mit deiner Gnade (hymn)
O–4815, Parl. RO 20309, Am.D. 20333

178 Be 8593 Jesus, meine Zuversicht (hymn)
O–4816, Am. Col 4057M, Am.D. 20335

179 Be 8594 Wir glauben all' an einen Gott (hymn)
O–4816, Parl. RO 20320, Am.D. 20335

180 Be 8595–2 Bist du bei mir (attr. Stölzel)
O–4814, Parl. RO 20292, Am.Col. 4062M, Am.D. 20334, Australia AR 281.

20 February 1930. Members of the Berlin State Opera Orchestra Chorus, & organ conducted by Dr Römer.

181	Be 8876	Andachtsstunde (The sacred hour) Reverie (Ketèlby)
	(–1)	Unpublished, see No. 197
182	Be 8877	Heiligtum des Herzens (Sanctuary of my heart) (Ketèlby)
	(–1)	Unpublished, see No. 198
183	Be 8878	Es ritten drei Reiter zum Tore hinaus – Scheiden und Meiden (Folksong with chorus, arr. Römer) O–4817, Parl. RO 20166, Am.D. 20278, Argentina 196.134
184	Be 8879	Der rote Sarafan – Näh' nicht, liebes Mütterlein (Russian folksong, arr. Römer) O–4822, Argentina 196.134
185	Be 8880	Es stiess ein Jäger wohl in sein Horn (folksong arr. Römer) O–4817, Am.D. 20278
186	Be 8881	Es waren zwei Königskinder – Zwei Königskinder – Lied (folksong arr. Römer) O–4822

21 February 1930. Members of the Berlin State Opera Orchestra, conducted by Frieder Weissmann. Speed 80 rpm

187	Be 8882	Dich teure Halle – Act 2, Tannhäuser (Wagner) O–4813, Parl. RO 20139 later PO 156, Am.Col. 4063M, Am.D. 20283, Austria B 502, France 188.059, Argentina 196.152
188	Be 8883	Allmächt'ge Jungfrau, Act 3, Tannhäuser (Wagner) O–4813, Parl. RO 20139 later PO 156, France 188.059, Am.Col. 4063M, Am.D. 20283, Austria B 502, Argentina 196.152, Spain 184.180
189	Be 8884	Euch Luften, die mein Klagen – Act 2, Lohengrin (Wagner) O–4819, Parl. RO 20113 later PO 152, France 188.060, Am.Col. 4066M, Am.D. 20282, Austria B 503. Brazil A 3128, AR 139
190	Be 8885	Einsam in trüben Tagen – Act 1, Lohengrin (Wagner) O–4819, Parl. RO 20113 later PO 152, France 188.060, Am.Col. 4066M, Am.D. 20282, Austria B 503, Spain 184.180, AR 139

18 June 1930. Members of the Berlin State Opera Orchestra, conducted by Frieder Weissmann.

191	xxB 8494	Ich gäb' was drum, wenn ich nur wüsst' . . . Es war ein König in Thule (Je voudrais bien savoir quel était ce jeune homme . . . Il était un Roi de Thulé), Act 3, Margarethe (Faust), (Gounod) O–8747, Parl. R 20137, Am.Col. 9082M, Hungary: Tonalit NM 7060–b
192	xxB 8495	Kennst du das Land? (Connais-tu le pays?), Act 1, Mignon (Thomas) D flat O– 8747, Parl. R 20137, Hungary: Tonalit NM 7060–a
193	xxB 8496	Sie sass mit Leide auf öder Heide (Piangea cantando nell'erma landa), Willow song, Act 4, Otello (Verdi) Unpublished

194 xxB 8497 a) Du bist der Lenz, Act 1, Die Walküre (Wagner)
leading without scroll to first part of:
b) Isoldes Liebestod, Act 3, Tristan und Isolde (Wagner)
O–8745, Parl. R 20122, Am.Col. 9049M, Am.D. 25807, Australia AR 1046, Chile & Argentina 177.216

195 xxB 8498 Seht ihr's nicht, Isoldes Liebestod, conclusion.
O–8745, Parl. R 20122, Am. Col. 9049M, Am.D. 25807, Australia AR 1046, Chile & Argentina 177.216

196 xxB 8499 Eines Tages seh'n wir (Un bel di vedremo), Act 2, Madama Butterfly (Puccini)
Not published. Later copied on to 25 cm: Be 9935–O
(See No. 223)

19 June 1930. Members of the State Opera Orchestra, Berlin conducted by Frieder Weissmann, speed 80 rpm.

197 Be 8876–2 Andachtsstunde (The sacred hour) Rêverie (Ketèlby)
O–4818, Am.D. 23058

198 Be 8877–2 Heiligtum des Herzens (Sanctuary of my heart) (Ketèlby)
O–4818, Parl. RO 20166, Am.D. 23058

199 Be 9044 Ich grolle nicht – Dichterliebe No. 7 (Schumann) in C
O–4825, Parl. RO 20185, Am.Col. 4092M, Am.D. 20378

200 Be 9045 Der Erlkönig – D.328 (Fr. Schubert), in G with Frieder Weismann, piano.
O–4825, Parl. RO 20292, Am.Col. 4092M, Italy 15005 AR 281

23 May 1931. Orchestra or trio of members of the Berlin State Opera Orchestra conducted by Frieder Weissmann.

201 Be 9488 Ein feste Burg ist unser Gott (hymn) with chorus & organ
O–4828, Parl. RO 20368, Am.D. 20338, Argentina 196.199, AR 335

202 Be 9489–2 Ich bete an die Macht der Liebe, with chorus & organ
O–4828, Parl. RO 20368, Am.D 20338, Argentina 196.199, AR 335

203 Be 9490 Die Mainacht Op. 43 No. 2 (Brahms) with instrumental trio acc.
O–4829, later also O–4847 coupled with No. 221, Parl. RO 20159, Am. Col. 4094M, Am.D. 20285 F sharp

204 Be 9491–2 Schlaf' Herzenssöhnchen Op. 13 No. 2 – Wiegenlied (Weber)
O–4838, Parl. RO 20185, Am.D. 20378 in D

205 Be 9492 s'Zuschaun – Bavarian folksong Op. 326 No. 27 (Bohm)
O–4838

26 May 1931. Members of the Berlin State Opera Orchestra conducted by Frieder Weissmann.

206 Be 9493 Dort bei ihm ist sie jetzt (Elle est là près de lui), Act 2, Mignon (Thomas)
O–4826, Parl. RO 20174, AR 172

207 Be 9494 Kam ein armes Kind von fern (Je connais un pauvre enfant), Styrienne, Act 2, Mignon (Thomas)
O–4826, Parl. RO 20174, AR 172

208 Be 9495–2 Klänge der Heimat – Czardas Act 2, Die Fledermaus (J. Strauss)
O–4831, Parl. RO 20171 later PO 163, Am.D. 20280, Am.Col. 4101M, Austria B 504, Argentina 196.161, Finland PLE 134
209 Be 9496 Mein Herr, was dächten Sie von mir? Act 1, Die Fledermaus (J. Strauss)
O–4831, Parl. RO 20171 later PO 163, Am.D. 20280, Am.Col. 4101M, Austria B 504, Argentina 196.161, Finland PLE 134
210 Be 9497 Vergebliches Ständchen Op. 84 No. 4 (Brahms) w. instr. trio
O–4829, Parl. RO 20159, Am.D. 20285, Am.Col. 4090. In A

28 January 1932. Recopying: electrical transfers of No. 64, xxB 6993.
211 xxB 6993–II Die tote Stadt (Korngold)
–III OL
–IV OL

23 April 1932. Members of the Berlin State Opera Orchestra conducted by Manfred Gurlitt.

212 Be 9905 Ach, ich fuhl's, es ist verschwunden – Act 2, die Zauberflöte (Mozart)
O–4832, O–4851 coupled to No. 230, Parl. RO 20194 later PO 157, Am.D. 20279, Australia AR 194
213 Be 9906 Nun eilt herbei, Witz heit're Laune – Act 1, Die lustigen Weiber von Windsor (Nicolai) part 1
O–4833, Parl. RO 20303, Am.D. 23025, AR 295
214 Be 9907 Er wird mir glauben – Die lustigen Weiber von Windsor, (Nicolai), Part 2.
O–4833, Parl. RO 20303, Am.D. 23025, AR 295
215 Be 9908–2 Bald sind wir auf der Höh' . . . über das Meer und alle Lande (Ancora un passo or via), Entrance of Butterfly, Act 1, Madama Butterfly (Puccini) with female chorus.
O–4832, later O–4849 coupled to No. 223, Parl. RO 20194 later PO 157, AR 194
216 Be 9909 Sie sass mit Leide auf öder Heide (Piangea cantando nell'erma landa), Willow Song, Act 4, Otello (Verdi)
O–4834, Parl, RO 20248

25 April 1932. Odeon Chamber Orchestra conducted by Manfred Gurlitt. Speed 79 rpm

217 Be 9910 Die Lotosblume Op. 25 No. 7 (Schumann) F (orig key)
O–4839, Parl. RO 20207, Am.D. 20377, Am.Col. 4049M, Australia AR 199
218 Be 9911 a) An den Sonnenschein Op. 36 No. 4 (Schumann) B flat
b) Marienwürmchen Op. 79, No. 13 (Schumann) F
O–4839, Parl. RO 20207, Am.D. 20377, Am.Col. 4049M, Australia AR 199
219 Be 9912 Die Trommel gerührt! Op. 82 No. 2 – Klärchens Lied – Egmont (Beethoven) f

O–4835, Parl. RO 20196, Am.D. 20276, Australia AR 217
220 Be 9913 Freudvoll und leidvoll Op. 84 No. 1, Egmont (Beethoven) A
O–4835, Parl. RO 20196, Am.D. 20276, Australia AR 217
221 Be 9914 Sandmännchen (Brahms) sung in A flat (G)
O–4836, Parl. RO 20403, Am.Col. 4087M, Am.D. 20286 later also O–4847 coupled to No. 203
222 Be 9915 a) Gruss (Leise zieht durch mein Gemüt) (Mendelssohn) in C
b) Der Schmied (Brahms) C (B)
O–4836, Parl. RO 20403, Am.Col. 4087M, Am.D. 20286

25 May 1932. Recopying: transfer of 12 inch xxB 8499, No. 196, onto a 10-inch side

223 Be 9935–O Eines Tages seh'n wir (Un bel dì vedremo), Act 2, Madama Butterfly (Puccini)
O–4834, later O–4849 coupled with No. 215

13 May 1933. Recopying of xxB 6993, No. 64, with added orchestral accompaniment by Frieder Weissmann

224 xxB 8558
–OL Glück das mir verblieb, Die tote Stadt (Erich Korngold)
–II–OL Duet with Richard Tauber, tenor.
O–8613, Parl. R 20258, Am. D. 29012, AR 1081

20 June 1933 Members of the Berlin State Opera Orchestra conducted Frieder Weissmann.

225 Be 10384–2 Werther, Werther . . . Nicht kann ich mir's verhehlen (Werther . . . Qui m'aurait dit la place), Letter Scene Act 3, Werther (Massenet)
O–4845, Parl. RO 20240, Australia AR 237
226 Be 10385 Zum Fenster dringt empor (Des cris joyeux d'enfants), Letter Scene, conclusion, Werther (Massenet)
O–4845, Parl. RO 20240, Australia AR 237
227 Be 10386 Sie entfloh' die Taube so minnig (Elle a fui, la tourterelle) Act 3, Hoffmanns Erzählungen (Les contes d'Hoffmann), (Offenbach)
O–4844, Parl. RO 20263, AR 259
228 Be 10387 Folget dem Ruf . . . Nützet die schönen, jungen Tage (Obéissons quand leur voix appelle . . . Profitons bien de la jeunesse), Act 3, Gavotte, Manon (Massenet)
O–4844 later O–4850 coupled to No. 230, Parl. RO 20248
229 Be 10388 Psyche wandelt durch Säulenhallen, Die toten Augen (d'Albert)
O–4841, Parl. RO 20229 later PO 158, AR 226
230 Be 10389 O säume länger nicht geliebte Seele, (Rosenarie) (Deh vieni non tardar), Act 4, (Le nozze di Figaro), (Mozart)

O–4841 later O–4850 coupled with No. 228, Parl. RO 20229 later PO 158, Am. D. 20279, AR 226. In October 1941: O–4851 coupled with No. 212

11 November 1933. Berlin State Opera Orchestra conducted by Richard Jäger.

231 Be 10468 Mein Elemer! – Arabella, Act 1 (R. Strauss)
O–4842, Parl. RO 20237 later PO 171, Australia AR 234, Am.D. 23043, Argentina 196.230

232 Be 10469 Wie sagt die Zdenka – finale Act 1 concl. Arabella (R. Strauss)
O–4842, Parl. RO 20237 later PO 171, Am.D. 23043, Australia AR 234, Argentina 196.230

233 Be 10470 Er ist der Richtige – duet Act 1, Arabella (R. Strauss)
O–4843, Parl. RO 20236, Am.D. 23048, Australia AR 233, Argentina 196.231

234 Be 10471 Aber der Richtige – duet concl. with K. Heidersbach
O–4843, Parl. RO 20236, Am.D. 23048, Australia AR 233, Argentina 196.231

7 November 1934. Production and copying of:

235 xxB 8564–OP –II –III Sterne der Gesangskunst, ein Hauskonzert mit Künstler von Weltruf. Text spoken by Frank Günther. With Herbert Ernst Groh, Lotte Lehmann and Herbert E. Groh with Gerhard Hüsch. Lotte Lehmann's contribution is from No. 153: Leise, leise, fromme Weise, Der Freischütz (Weber)
O–6950 a

235a xxRek 22–0 Lindström Werbeplatte (trailer), February 1933 with No. 203 (extract).

235b – Odeon Parade (Lindström Werbeplatte, 25cm January 1933). Includes Gitta Alpar, Richard Tauber, Elisabeth Rethberg, Gregor Piatigorsky, Karol Szreter, Lotte Lehmann, Berlin Philharmonic Orchestra cond. F. Weissmann. Spoken commentary by Paul Nikolaus.
O–11756.

NOTES TO THE ELECTRIC ODEON RECORDINGS

When the artist is accompanied by orchestra, the 'orchestra' in question is usually an *ad hoc* assembly of members of various Berlin orchestras working on a free-lance basis. As some players often belonged to the Berlin State Opera Orchestra it looked better on the label to suggest that all were members of this famous ensemble, even if this statement were not strictly true to fact.

When the key is given in which the song is sung on the recording, the original key is sometimes shown in parenthesis. Capital letters indicate major keys and small letters minor keys. A recommended playing speed is suggested for records made at certain sessions. If none is given the speed may be assumed to be 78 rpm.

90–91 O–9602 belongs to an older series of catalogue numbers used only for these two sides and for Nos. 110–111.

92 Take 1 was perhaps also used. Most copies show take 2.
93 Take 2 was perhaps also used. Most copies show take 1.
94 No catalogue number is shown in the recording books.
95 Take 1 was probably held in reserve.
100 The 'D' number after each Schubert title refers to O.E. Deutsch's standard thematic catalogue of Schubert's works.
100–109 The dating of these sessions is believed to be correct though neither the recording books held by Electrola, Cologne, nor the recording sheets supplied by the Lindström Company to HMV, Hayes, are perfectly clear.
102 The now less common Mandyczewski version of the score was used, without the minor third higher note on the repeat of 'deinem Glanz' on the last page of the score.
106 On the 1921 Polydor recording the song is sung in F.
110–111 Both takes were used.
111 On 10 December 1927 Jan Kiepura also recorded the two tenor arias from *Turandot* on xxB 7883 and xxB 7884.
112 Only the aria is recorded. The recitative beginning with 'Abscheulicher! Wo eilst du hin?' is omitted.
114 Both takes were used.
115 Take 1 was used for most issues. Take 2 (No. 119) appears on some others.
116–117 Probably only take 2 was used, with take 1 in reserve.
118 Only take 2 was used.
119 Take 2 was also used, probably for later issues.
120 Probably the earliest recording of Lotte Lehmann's speaking voice.
121 The tenor, Jacques Urlus, sings this in the same key on his Edison recording.
126–129 Where 'piano accompaniment' is indicated it can be assumed that the pianist was the conductor, Hermann Weigert. The violin obbligato is used only for 'Morgen' (No. 129). Nos. 126–8 are with piano only.
130 This is the second part of Ariadne's aria.
131–132 For take 2 the music begins eight bars later than for take 1. Both takes were used but take 2 is more frequent. For difficulties with this particular aria see the broadcast interview of 28 March 1970 (with Maria Jeritza).
134 Take 1 was possibly retained in reserve.
137–144 Some bars in certain songs have been repeated, others omitted completely. Also issued in Australia on AR 143/6, and in Chile on 292545/8, auto coupling, AC 100012/15.
145–146 Repeats of Nos. 122–123, passed for issue.
147–148 Take 1 was probably retained in reserve.
149 Both takes were used.
150 Only take 2 was used.
151 Only take 2 was used.
152 Only take 1 was used.
153 Part of this side was copied on to *Sterne der Gesangskunst*, No. 235.
155–156 The discarded first attempts of Nos. 167–168.
157 The title on the English pressing reads 'O sacred head'.
161–162 Take 1 was not passed. See also Nos. 155–156.
167 Take 3 was accepted.
168 Take 2 was accepted.
169–171 Both takes used. Take 1 probably in reserve.
181–186 Probably also recorded at 80 rpm, as with 187–190.
193 Damaged during processing. See No. 216.
196 Not published in twelve-inch form. See No. 223.

208 Take 1 was probably only in reserve.
211 The three electrical transfers of xxB 6993 (No. 64). xxB 6993–4–O, reported for American Decca 29012.
215 Take 2 probably kept in reserve.
223 The transfer was made by the recording engineers. The artist was not present.
224 An electrically recorded orchestral accompaniment was superimposed on the original acoustic recording (No. 64). Matrix xxB 6993–4–O, which appears on the American Decca release (29012) was probably used for the transfer. DecB
225 Take 2 is used on some copies of AR 237.
231–234 The artist's last session for Odeon took place after she had taken part in the HMV recording of scenes from *Der Rosenkavalier* on 20–24 September 1933.
231–234 Nos. 231–232 play accurately at 78 rpm, but No. 233 starts at 76 rpm and increases speed to 77 rpm by the end of the side; No. 234 begins at 77 rpm and also increases speed, to 78 rpm by the end of the side. These fluctuations in speed have been copied on to the dubbing on microgroove, HQM 1121.

REISSUES ON LONG PLAYING RECORDS
SECTION IV. ODEON – ELECTRIC RECORDINGS

Parlophone-Odeon (EMI) PMA 1057, Angel, COLO 112, Toshiba EMI (Japan) GR 2046 'Great Recordings of the Century'
side 1: No. 153–154, 112–113, 213–214, 225–226
side 2: No. 132–130, 230, 209, 116–117, 194b–195

Odeon (EMI) O–83 396 'Die goldene Stimme' Lotte Lehmann talks about her career (in German). It includes:
side 1: No. (59), (70), 112–113, 213–214, 208
side 2: No. 200, 279 (part)–280, 245–247 and 258 partly

EMI HQM 1121 'Golden Voice Series 10 – Lotte Lehmann', Seraphim 60060 and Toshiba EMI (Japan) GR 2198
side 1: No. 216, 215, 167, 94, 228, 207, 227, 95
side 2: No. 169, 170, 187, 189, 223–234, 231–232

Preiser, LV 10. Unvergängliche Stimmen der Wiener Oper. No. 187.

Preiser, LV 22 Lotte Lehmann (Vol I)
side 1: No. 119, 212, 92–93, 169, 196 (= 223), 91
side 2: No. 107, 108, 217, 218, 126, 222b, 221, 210, 133

Preiser, LV 500 'Von der Hofoper zur Staatsoper', contains No. 206 on record 3 (1969)

Rococo 5356, Lotte Lehmann Vol II contains no. 120 (all other titles are acoustically recorded)

EMI HLM 7026 'The Grand Tradition' contains No. 128

EMI 147–29 116/17M 'Lotte Lehmann I, Die Lyrikerin der Gesangskunst' with Melchior, Kiepura, Tauber, Heidersbach and Olszewska.
side 1: No. 119, 212, 153–154, 92–93, 112–113
side 2: No. 213–214, 228, 207, 169*, 170*, 279 part–280, 194b–195
side 3: No. (59)**, (70), 216, 110, 167, 223, 90, 224***
side 4: No. 132 part & 130, 233–234, 245 & 247, 229, 116–117

* titles transferred on sleeve: Schmerzen, Träume
** not the version from 1930, but the acoustic Odeon from 1925
*** the later version with orchestra conducted by Dr Frieder Weissmann from 1933

EMI 137–30 704/05M, Seraphim IB 6105 'Lotte Lehmann II, Die Lyrikerin der Gesangskunst' with Bohnen and Kiepura.
side 1: No. 230, (66–67), 188, (5), (9–10), (68),
side 2: No. 194a, 192, 206, 191, 227, 94, 95, (65), 209
side 3: No. (58), 225–226, (54), 168, 111, 215, 91, (71)
side 4: No. 114, 231–232, 129, 203, 126, 217, 108, 100

EMI RLS 766 'Schubert Lieder on Record' (1982) 6993–4–O, which appears on the side 4: No. 103, 104 and 109

EMI RLS 7700 'The Art of Richard Tauber' contains No. 149–150 and No. 64.

EMI RLS 7711 'Wagner on record' No. 189, 281–282

EMI RLS 154 7003 'Schumann & Brahms on Record' (1983)
side 4: No. 218, side 11: No. 99

EMI 181–30 669/78M 'Sänger auf dem grünen Hügel. Dokumentation anlässl. d. 100j. Jubiläums d. Bayreuther Festspiele 1867–1967'

EMI 049–30 679M '100 Jahre Bayreuther Festspiele. Historische Dokumente berühmter Wagner-Sänger'

EMI 147–01 259/60M 'Lauritz Melchior; Der Wagner-Tenor des Jahrhunderts'

EMI 147–30 636/37M 'Die Stimme seines Herrn, 75 Jahre EMI'.
All contain No. 194a (Die Walküre: Du bist der Lenz)

EMI 147–30 226/7 'Johannn Strauss: ewig junger Walzerkönig' Nos. 149–50

Odeon OBL 1073/20479 (7", 45 rpm) contains No. 224 (electric version of No. 64)

American Decca DL 9523 (out of order): No. 229, 112–113, 230, 187, 188, 190, 189 and 215

American Decca DL 9524: No. 149–150, 208, 209, 119,
side 2: No. 153–154, 231–232, 114

Belcanto discs U.K. BC 234 No. 116–117

Odeon: Belcanto discs (France):

ORX 123 'L'école allemand du chant' No. 149–150 & 194b 195

ORX 133 'Hommage à la Malibran' No. 112–113

ORX 503–505 'L'age d'or de l'Opéra Comique de Paris' No. 110

Seraphim 6041: No. 132–130, 231–232, 233–234

Top Artists Platters:

T–306 'Twenty great sopranos' No. 228 (possibly No. 51)

Top Classics:

H 679/80 (Historia) Richard Tauber – Band 9 contains No. 149–150

TC–9052: No. 194b–195, 213–214, 230, (59), (60), (66–67)

Pathé Marconi 290 2123 – PM 663 'Les Introuvables du Chant Wagnérien' contains No. 189 and the complete Act 2 of Walküre, including Nos. 278–282

Ritornello Records:

R–1001/2 'A Tribute to Dr Frieder Weissman' contains Nos. 164, 151, 152.

SECTION V: *His Master's Voice recordings, 1933–1935*

Der Rosenkavalier – excerpts (R. Strauss)
Recorded in Vienna, Mittlerer Saal, *20–24 September 1933* on twenty-six sides.
The cast is as follows:

Die Feldmarschallin	(a)	Lotte Lehmann
Der Baron Ochs auf Lerchenau	(b)	Richard Mayr
Octavian	(c)	Marie Olszewska
Herr von Faninal	(d)	Victor Madin
Sophie	(e)	Elisabeth Schumann
Marianne, Leitmetzerin	(f)	Aenne Michalsky
Valzacchi	(g)	Hermann Gallos
Annina	(h)	Bella Paalen
Police Commissary	(i)	Karl Ettl
Innkeeper	(j)	William Wergnick

With members of the chorus (k) of the Vienna State Opera and the Vienna Philharmonic Orchestra conducted by Robert Heger.

Catalogue numbers: DB 2060–72 (auto coupling DB 7547–59).
Issued in America by Victor, set M–196 (7917–29), auto coupling AM–196 (7930–42), auto drop sequence coupling DM–196 (17119–31). Assigned Victor matrix numbers CVS–81418–43. The 'V' was added by Victor to identify European originals. The published take is underlined. Two cutting machines were used during the recording sessions, working in parallel. Recordings made on the second machine are shown by an 'A' following the take number.

20 September 1933

236	2WX 581–1,–1A,–<u>2</u>	Orchestral introduction			DB 2060
	(22 Sept) –3,–4A	Side 1	32–4100		
237	2WX 582–1,–1A,–2,–<u>2A</u>	Mir ist die Ehre		c,e	DB 2065
		Side 12	32–4111		
		(Presentation of the Silver Rose)			
238	2WX 583–1,–1A,–2A	Wo war ich schon einmal		c,e	DB 2066
	(24 Sept) –3,–3A,–4,–<u>4A</u>	Side 13	32–4112		

21 September 1933

239	2WX 584–1,–1A,–2,–<u>2A</u>	Sind halt aso! Ist ein Traum		c, d, e	DB 2072
	–3, –3A			a,c,d,e	
	(24 Sept) –4,–5A	Ist ein Traum	32–4123	c,e	
		Side 26			
240	2WX 585–1,–1A,–2A,	Heut' oder Morgen		a,c,e	DB 2071
	–3, –<u>3A</u>	Side 23	32–4120		
241	2WX 586–1,–1A,–2,–<u>2A</u>	Marie Theres'! (Trio)		a,c,e	DB 2071
		Side 24	32–4121		

No.	Matrix	Title		Performers	Issue
242	2WX 587–1,–1A	Wie du warst!		a,c	DB 2060
		Side 2	32–4101		
243	2WX 588–1,–1A,–2,–2A	Lachst du mich aus?		a,c	DB 2061
		Side 3	32–4102		
244	2WX 589–1,–1A,–2,–2A	Der Feldmarschall sitz		a,c	DB 2061
		Side 4	32–4103		
245	2WX 590–1A,–2,–2A	Ah! du bist wieder da!		a,c	DB 2063
		Side 8	32–4107		
246	2WX 591–1,–1A,–2,–2A	Da geht er hin		a	DB 2063
		Side 7	32–4106		
247	2WX 592–1,–2	Wo sie mich da hat		a,c	DB 2064
	(24 Sept) –3,–3A	Side 9	32–4108		
248	2WX 593–1,–1A	Weiss bereits nicht		a,b,e	DB 2070
		Side 21	32–4118		
249	2WX 594–1	Hat sie schon einmal		a,b,c	DB 2062
	(24 Sept) –2,–2A,–3,–3A	Side 6	32–4105		

22 September 1933

No.	Matrix	Title		Performers	Issue
250	2WX 595–1,–2,–2A	Hab'n euer Gnaden		b,j,k	DB 2068
		Side 18	32–4125		
251	2WX 596–1,–1A*	Wart', dich hau' i' z'samm		b,h,k	DB 2067
		Side 15	32–4114		
252	2WX 597–1,–2,–2A	In dieser feierlichen Stunde		e,f,k	DB 2065
		Side 11	32–4110		
253	2WX 598–1,–1A*	Ich hab' halt schon einmal		b,h	DB 2067
		Side 16	32–4115		
254	2WX 599–1,–1A	Introduction Act 3			DB 2068
		Side 17	32–4124		
	2WX 581–3,–4A	(See 20 September)			

23 September 1933

No.	Matrix	Title		Performers	Issue
255	2WX 600–1,–2,–3,–3A	Ich hab' halt schon einmal		a,b,c,e,	DB 2070
		Side 22	32–4119	g,h,j,k	
256	2WX 601–1,–2,–2A	Die Stimm!		a,b,c,k	DB 2062
		Side 5	32–4104		
257	2WX 602–1,–1A,–2	Zu ihm hätt' ich		c,e	DB 2066
		Side 14	32–4113		
258	2WX 603–1,–1A	Ich werd' jetzt in die			
		Kirchen geh'n		a,c	DB 2064
	(24 Sept) –2,–2A,–3,–3A	Side 10	32–4109		
259	2WX 604–1,–2A	Muss jetzt partout zu ihr		a,b,c,e,i,j	DB 2069
		Side 20	32–4117		

24 September 1933

2WX 583–3,–3A,–4,–4A — See above for earlier takes
2WX 584–4,–5A

260	2WX 605–1,–1A	Nein, nein		b,c	DB 2069
		Side 19	32–4116		
261	2WX 606–1,–1A	Ist ein Traum, Sind halt aso!		a,c,d,e	
	–2	Ist ein Traum	32–4122	c,e	DB 2072
		Side 25			

2WX 594–2,–2A,–3,–3A
2WX 592–3,–3A
2WX 603–2,–2A,–3,–3A
see above for earlier takes
* unusable: defective on arrival at Hayes.

Die Walküre (Wagner), Act 1 (complete), Act 2 (scenes)
Recorded in Vienna, Grosse Musikvereinsaal, *20–22 June 1935*
The cast is as follows:

Siegmund	(a)	Lauritz Melchior
Sieglinde	(b)	Lotte Lehmann
Hunding	(c)	Emmanuel List
Brünnhilde	(d)	Ella Flesch
Wotan	(h)	Alfred Jerger

Vienna Philharmonic Orchestra conducted by Bruno Walter

Catalogue numbers: Act 1 (complete) on DB 2636–43 (auto coupling DB 8039–46). German Columbia, LWX 105–112. Italian Columbia GQX 10889–96. American Victor, Set M–298 (8932–9), auto coupling, AM–298 (8940–47), auto drop sequence coupling, DM–298 (16933–40). Victor assigned matrix numbers: Act 1, CVS 95833–95848, Act 2, CVS 037525/6/7 and CVS 037532/3.

20 June 1935

262	2VH 94–1,–1A,–2	Prelude/Wess' Herd dies auch sei	a	DB 2636
263	2VH 95–1,–1A,–2	Ein fremder Mann?	a,b	DB 2636
264	2VH 96–1,–1A,–2,–2A	Kühlende Labung gab mir	a,b	DB 2637
265	2VH 97–1,–1A	Einen Unseligen	a,b	DB 2637
	(21 June) –2			
266	2VH 98–1,–1A,–2	Müd' am Herd	a,b,c	DB 2638
	(21 June) –3A			
267	2VH 99–1,–2	Trägst du Sorge	a,b,c	DB 2638
268	2VH 100–1,–1A,–2	Wunder und wilde Märe	a,b,c	DB 2639

21 June 1935

269	2VH 101–1,–2,–2A	Die so leidig Loos	a,b,c	DB 2639
270	2VH 102–1,–1A,–2,–2A	Ich weiss ein wildes Geschlecht	c	DB 2640
271	2VH 103–1,–1A,–2	Mit Waffen wehrt sich	a,c	DB 2640
272	2VH 104–1,–2,–2A	Was gleisst dort hell	a,b	DB 2641
273	2VH 105–1,–1A,–2	Der Männer Sippe	b	DB 2641
274	2VH 106–1,–1A,–2	Dich selige Frau	a,b	DB 2642

275	2VH 107–1,–1A,–2	Du bist der Lenz	a,b	DB 2642
276	2VH 108–1,–1A	Wie dir die Stirn	a,b	DB 2643
277	2VH 109–1,–1A	Siegmund heiss' ich	a,b	DB 2643

22 *June 1935*: Scenes from Act 2

278	2VH 110–1A,–2,–2A	Raste nun hier (Scene 3)	a,b	DB 3724
279	2VH 111–1,–1A,–2	Hinweg! Hinweg!	a,b	DB 3725
280	2VH 112–1,–1A	Horch, o Horch	a,b	DB 3725
281	2VH 113–1,–2,–2A	Zauberfest bezähmt (Scene 5)	a,b	DB 3728
282	2VH 114–1,–1A,–2,–2A	Wehwalt! Wehwalt!	a,b,c, d,h	DB 3728

In Act 2 Sieglinde sings only in Scenes 3 and 5. Scenes 1, 2 and 4, which complete the act, were recorded during September 1938 in the Beethovensaal in Berlin with a different cast (except for Melchior who recorded Scene 4, the *Todesverkündigung*, on 19 September) under Bruno Seidler-Winkler and the Berlin State Opera Orchestra.

No. 273 appeared also on Victor 14205 in Album M–329, No. 274 on Victor 14204 in M–329, and No. 275 coupled with 277 on Victor 15817 in M–633

REISSUES ON MICROGROOVE

Der Rosenkavalier: Victor LCT–6005 (1953)
Victor 45 rpm, 7″: WCT–6005 – 18 sides
Victor LCT–1 (10″) contains No. 246, 258
Victor 45 rpm, 7″: WCT–5
His Masters Voice COLH 110–111
'Great Recordings of the Century' (1959)
Pathé Marconi: FALP 50.014/5
Angel GRB 4001 (1960)
Electrola E 80 630–1, WCLP 697–8 (1961)
Seraphim IC 6041 (coupled with excerpts from *Arabella* and *Ariadne auf Naxos*, see previous section)
World Record Club SH 181–2 (1973) (remastered)
EMI SLS 7704 (1983)
Pathé Marconi Référence 143 2943 (1984)
Excerpt 'Selbstverständlich empfängt mich Ihre Gnaden' part of No. 256 & 249 on EMI 187–29 225M. Salzburger Festspiele 1920–1970'
EMI 147–29 116/7M: 'Lotte Lehmann: die Lyrikerin der Gesangskunst', Nos. 245, 247

Die Walküre: Victor LVT–1003, also LCT–1033 Act I
Victor 45 rpm, 7″: WCT–58
Excerpt No. 275 on LCT–1 (10″) and on Victor 45 rpm, 7″: WCT–2

Excerpt No. 277 on LCT–1001
Seraphim 60190, Act I
His Masters Voice COLH 133, 'Great Recordings of the Century'
Act I (1962)
Pathé-Marconi FALP 50013, Act I
Electrola E 80 686–8, WCLP 734–6, Acts I & II
Excerpts No. 268–269 & 266 on Top Classics TC 9048
Excerpts No. 274–277 on EMI 147–01 259
Excerpts No. 281–282 ON RLS 7711 'Wagner on Record'
Pathé-Marconi 2 C 051–03023M Act I
Excerpt No. 278 on EMI EX 29 0 131 3
Excerpts No. 279 (in part) & 280 on Odeon (EMI) 0–83 396
Pathé-Marconi EMI 290 2123 PM 663 (1984)
'Les introuvables du Chant Wagnérien'. Act II complete
EMI 149–29 116/7M: 'Lotte Lehmann I: die Lyrikerin der Gesangskunst'.
279–280

SECTION VI: *Victor electric recordings, New York, 1935–1940*

All are recordings of German Lieder and songs, and all are ten-inch recordings except for Nos. 331, 332, 334, and 336, which are twelve-inch. The Victor catalogue number is listed first, the HMV number second (prefixed DA for ten-inch records and DB for twelve-inch), except for the recording of *Winterreise* (Nos. 329–336) when the second number is Australian HMV (prefixed EC and ED). Note that UK pressings published in Europe carry matrix prefixes OA for ten-inch records and 2A for twelve-inch, instead of the Victor prefixes BS and CS. The adopted take is underlined. For Nos. 283–314 the piano accompanist is Ernö Balogh, for No. 315 onwards Paul Ulanowsky, who became the artist's regular accompanist from 1938. All titles are sung in German apart from Nos. 299–300, which are sung in French, Nos. 293, 294, 313–314, sung in English, and Nos. 295–6 in Italian.

17 October 1935. Album VM 292.

283	BS 95611–1,–2	An Chloe K.524 (Mozart) 1730, DA 1466	E flat
284	BS 95612–1,–2	Die Verschweigung K.518 (Mozart) 1730, DA 1466	F
285	BS 95613–1,–2	Ungeduld – Die schöne Müllerin D.795 No. 7 (Schubert) 1731, DA 1467	A flat (A)
286	BS 95614–1,–2	Im Abendrot D.799 (Schubert) 1731, DA 1467	G flat (A flat)
287	BS 95615–1,–2	Die Kartenlegerin Op. 31 No. 2	E flat

		(Schumann) 1732, DA 1468	
288	BS 95616–1,–2	Waldesgespräch – Liederkreis Op. 39 No. 3 (Schumann) 1732, DA 1468	E
289	BS 95617–1,–2	Der Tod das ist die kühle Nacht Op 96 No. 1 (Brahms) 1733, DA 1469	B (C)
290	BS 95618–1,–2	a) Therese Op. 86 No. 1 (Brahms) b) Meine Liebe ist grün Op. 63 No. 5 (Brahms) 1733, DA 1469	F (D) F (F sharp)
291	BS 95619–1,–2	Anakreons Grab (Goethe-Wolf) 1734, DA 1470	D
292	BS 95620–1,–2	In dem Schatten meiner Locken (Sp. Lb.-Wolf) 1734, DA 1470	B flat

13 March 1936

293	BS 99451–1,–1A,–2	Do not Chide (Balogh) Unpublished	
294	BS 99452–1,–1A	a) My native Land (Gretchnanínoff) b) Midsummer (Amy Worth) 1893, DA 1617	
295	BS 99453–1,–1A,–2	Fa la Nanna, Bambin (Sodero) in Italian Unpublished	
296	BS 99454–1,–1A	Canto di primavera (Cimara) in Italian Unpublished	
297	BS 99455–1,–1A,–2	Ich liebe dich (Beethoven) 1995, DA 1733	G flat (G)
298	BS 99456–1,–1A	Schlafe, mein süsses Kind (traditional, arr. Alwin) 1995, DA 1733	
299	BS 99457–1,–1A	D'une Prison (Hahn) 1972	
300	BS 99458–1,–2,–2A	Vierges d'Athènes (Gounod) Unpublished	

16 March 1937 No. 301 – 312. Album M 419.

301	BS 0957,–2, –2A	Botschaft Op. 47 No. 1 (Brahms) 1857, DA 1604 (take –1 on 16 October 1936 not used)	C (D flat)
302	BS 06656–1,–1A	Gretel (Pfitzner) 1858, DA 1572	E (F)

303	BS 06657–1,–1A, 2,–2A	Selige Nacht (Marx) 1858, DA 1572	G flat
304	BS 06658–1,–1A	Storchenbotschaft (Mörike-Wolf) 1860, DA 1602	A (B flat)
305	BS 06659–1,–1A, 2,–2A	a) Der Gärtner (Mörike-Wolf) b) Du denkst mit einem Fädchen mich zu fangen (It.Lb.-Wolf) 1860, DA 1602	D flat (D) B flat
306	BS 06660–1,–1A	a) Für Musik Op. 10 No. 1 (Franz) b) Gute Nacht Op. 5 No. 7 (Franz) 1861, DA 1573	G flat d
307	BS 06661–1,–1A, –2	Lehn' deine Wang' an meine Wang' (Jensen) 1861, DA 1573	E flat
308	BS 06662–1,–1A	Alte Laute Op. 35 No. 12 (Schumann) 1859, DA 1571	A flat
309	BS 06663–1,–1A, –2, –2A	a) Du bist wie eine Blume Op. 25 No. 24 (Schumann) b) Frühlingsnacht – Liederkreis Op. 39 No. 12 (Schumann) 1859, DA 1571	A flat F sharp
310	BS 06664–1,–1A	Gretchen am Spinnrade D.118 (Schubert) 1856, DA 1603	c sharp (d)
311	BS 06665–1,–1A	Wiegenlied: Schlafe, schlafe . . . D.498 (Schubert) 1856, DA 1603	G (A flat)
312	BS 06666–1,–1A, –2,–2A	a) Das Mädchen spricht Op. 107 No. 3 (Brahms) b) Meine Mädel hat einen Rosemund, Volkslieder (Brahms) 1857, DA 1604	G (A) B flat
313	BS 06667–1,–1A	Tonerna (Visions), Sjøberg-Balogh 1972, DA 1612	D flat
314	BS 06668–1,–1A	Drink to me only (Calcott, arr.:Cohn) 1893, DA 1612 and DA 1617	G flat

6 January 1939. Album M–613 (Nos. 317, 318, 319, 320, 322, 324 only)

315	BS 031403–1,–1A –2,–2A	Gebet (Mörike-Wolf) Not on shellac, see LP Section	E
316	BS 031404–1,–1A	Nun lass uns Frieden schliessen (It.Lb.Wolf) Not on shellac, see LP section	E flat
317	BS 031405–1,–2 –1A, –2A	Frühling übers Jahr (Goethe-Wolf) 2029 (also 1969 but not issued), assigned DA 1734 but not issued	G (A)

318	BS 031406–1, –1A	Auf ein altes Bild (Mörike-Wolf) 2030, DA 1723	A
319	BS 031407–1,–2, –1A,–2A	In der Frühe (Mörike-Wolf) 2029 (also 1969 but not issued), assigned DA 1734 but not issued	d
320	BS 031408–1,–2 –1A,–2A	Auch kleine Dinge (It.Lb.-Wolf) 2031, DA 1724	
321	BS 031409–1, –1A	Und willst du deinen Liebsten sterben sehen (It.Lb.-Wolf) Not on shellac, see LP section	A flat
322	BS 031410–1,–2 –1A,–2A	Peregrina I (Mörike-Wolf) 2031, DA 1724	E flat
323	BS 031411–1, –1A	Der Knabe und das Immlein (Mörike-Wolf) Not on shellac, see LP section	A flat(B flat)
324	BS 031412–1,–2 –1A,–2A	Heimweh (Mörike-Wolf) 2030, DA 1723	F

30 January 1939. Duets (Schumann) with Lauritz Melchior. Victor Orchestra conducted by Bruno Reibold. Album M–560

325	BS 031860–1,–2 –1A	Er und Sie Op 78 No. 2 1906, DA 1716, EC72	E flat
326	BS 031861–1, –1A	a) So wahr die Sonne scheinet Op. 37 No. 12 b) Unterm Fenster Op. 34 No. 3 1907, DA 1717	E flat A
327	BS 031862–1,–2 –1A,–2A	Familien-Gemälde Op. 34 No. 4 1907, DA 1717	F
328	BS 031863–1 –1A	Ich denke dein Op. 78 No. 3 1906, DA 1716, EC72	G

26 February 1940. Eleven songs from Winterreise, D.911 (Schubert) Piano accompaniment by Paul Ulanowsky. Album M–692. American Columbia Albums M–466 and M–587 complete the cycle. Nippon album, LW 45. See section VII

329	BS 047267–1, –1A	Die Nebensonnen, No. 23 2108, EC 124	G (A)
330	BS 047268–1,–1A, –2,–2A	a) Die Post No. 13 b) Der stürmische Morgen, No. 18 2108, EC 124	E flat d
331	CS 047269–1	Der Lindenbaum, No. 5 1190, (DB 5767 assigned but not issued), ED 265	E
332	CS 047270–1	Der Wegweiser, No. 20 17191, (DB 5768 assigned but not issued), ED 266	G
333	BS 047271–1,–2, –2A	Die Krähe, No. 15 2109, EC 125	c

334	CS 047272–1,–2, –1A,–2A	Das Wirtshaus, No. 21 17191, (DB 5768 assigned but not issued), ED 266	F
335	BS 047273–1, –1A	a) Täuschung, No. 19 b) Mut! No. 22 2109, EC 125	A G
336	CS 047274–1, –1A	a) Im Dorfe, No. 17 b) Rückblick, No. 8 17190, (DB 5767 assigned but not issued), ED 265	D g flat (g)

NOTES TO THE VICTOR RECORDINGS

285–286 Issued in Japan on Victor NF 4196.
299 Reported as issued in Japan on JE 215 (possibly coupled with No. 313).
301 Take 1 of matrix BS 0957 is reported as having been made on 16 October 1936, but copies of the Victor recording sheets received at Hayes show only three recording sessions on that day, none with Lotte Lehmann, and a search through the sheets for 1936 and early 1937 showed no trace of the recording. The HMV pressing issued on DA 1604 gives the matrix number with the usual HMV OA prefix.

SECTION VII: *American Columbia recordings, New York, 1941–1943*

The matrix prefix CO denotes a ten-inch side, XCO a twelve-inch side. Where two catalogue numbers are shown in the 71000 series (twelve-inch records) and 17000 series (ten-inch records) the second number is assigned to records issued in automatic couplings. The piano accompanist is Paul Ulanowsky, except for the two Schumann cycles (Nos. 360–367 and 407–414) which are accompanied by Bruno Walter.

4 March 1941.

337	XCO 30013	Die junge Nonne D.828 (Schubert) 71509–D, LOX 654 Australia	e (g)
338	XCO 30016	Der Doppelgänger, Schwanengesang D. 957 No. 13 (Schubert) 71509–D, LOX 654 Australia	b

14 March 1941. Winterreise D.911 (Schubert) in two sets: M–587 (10″) and M–466 (12″) of 3 discs each (these complete the abridged cycle issued by Victor in album M–692. See previous section). Also issued in Canada on 15485/7. (12″ only).

339	CO 29948	Gefror'ne Tränen No. 3 17367–D /17464–D	f
340	XCO 29949	Wasserflut No. 6 71174–D / 72071–D	e
341	CO 29950	Der greise Kopf No. 14 17369–D / 17466–D	c
342	XCO 29951	a) Die Wetterfahne No. 2 b) Letzte Hoffnung No. 16 71175–D / 72072–D	g (a) E flat

343	XCO 29952	Auf dem Flusse No. 7 71175–D / 72072–D	d (e)
344	XCO 29953	Rast No. 10 71176–D / 72073–D	c
345	CO 29954	Einsamkeit No. 12 17368–D / 17465–D	b
346	CO 29955	Irrlicht No. 9 17368–D / 17465–D	b
347	XCO 29956	Frühlingstraum No. 11 71176–D / 72073–D	F (A)
348	XCO 30018	Gute Nacht No. 1 71174–D / 72071–D	c (d)

19 March 1941. Ten Lieder by Brahms. Album M–453 (Two 10-inch and two 12-inch records).

349	XCO 30005	Die Mainacht Op. 43 No. 2 71060–D / 71980–D	F (E flat)
350	XCO 30006	Feinsliebchen, du sollst mir nicht barfuss geh'n – Volkslieder 71059–D / 71979–D	b flat (b)
351	CO 30007	An die Nachtigall Op. 46 No. 4 17274–D / 17439–D	E flat (E)
352	CO 30008	Auf dem Kirchhofe Op. 105 No. 4 17274–D / 17439–D	d (c)
353	CO 30009	Wie bist du meine Königin Op. 32 No. 9 17273–D / 17438–D	E flat
354	CO 30010	Wir wandelten Op. 96 No. 2 17273–D / 17438–D	C (D flat)
355	XCO 30011	a) Erlaube mir, fein's Mädchen – Volksl. b) Da unten im Tale – Volkslieder 71059–D / 71979–D	F (G) F (E)
356	XCO 30012	a) Sonntag Op. 47 No. 3 b) O liebliche Wangen Op. 47 No. 4 71060–D / 71980–D	G flat (F) D flat (D)
357	CO 30014	Der Leiermann – Winterreise (Schubert) 17369–D / 17466–D (set M–587)	g (a)
358	CO 30015	Erstarrung – Winterreise (Schubert) 17367–D / 17464–D (set M–587)	b (c)
359	CO 30017–1	Liebesbotschaft – Schwanengesang D. 957 No. 1 (Schubert) Not in shellac, see LP section	F (G)

24 June 1941. Frauenliebe und –leben Op. 42 – complete (Schumann). Bruno Walter, piano. Album M–539.

360	CO 31508	Seit ich ihn geseh'n 17362– D	B flat
361	CO 31509	Er der Herrlichste von Allen 17362–D	E flat

362	CO 31510	Ich kann's nicht fassen nicht glauben 17363–D	c
363	CO 31511	Du Ring an meinem Finger 17363–D	E flat
364	CO 31512	Helft mir, ihr Schwestern 17364–D	B
365	CO 31513	Süsser Freund, du blickest mich verwundert an 17364–D	G
366	CO 31514	An meinem Herzen, an meiner Brust 17365–D	D
367	CO 31515	Nun hast du mir den ersten Schmerz getan 17365–D	c

26 June 1941.

368	CO 31485–1	a) In der Fremde I: Aus der Heimat . . . Op. 39 No. 1 (Schumann)	f sharp
		b) Wenn ich früh in den Garten gehe – Volksliedchen Op. 51 No. 2 (Schumann) Not in shellac, see LP section	G flat (G)
369	CO 31486–1	Aufträge Op. 77 No. 5 (Schumann) Only test pressings made	
370	CO 31487	Die Lotosblume Op. 25 No. 7 (Schumann) Only test pressings made	

30 June 1941.

371	CO 31699	Morgengruss Op. 47 No. 2 (Mendelssohn) 17344–D	
372	CO 31700–1	Venetianisches Gondellied: Wenn durch die Piazzetta . . . Op. 57 No. 5 (Mendelssohn) Not in shellac, see LP section	b flat (b)
373	CO 31701–1	Neue Liebe: In dem Mondenschein im Walde . . . Op. 19a No. 4 (Mendelssohn) Not in shellac, see LP section	e
374	CO 31702–1	Der Nussbaum Op. 25 No. 3 (Schumann) Not in shellac, see LP section	G flat (G)
375	CO 31703–1	Wonne der Wehmut Op. 83 No. 1 (Beethoven) Not in shellac, see LP section	E
376	CO 31704–1	Andenken: Ich denke dein . . . WoO 136 (Beethoven) Not in shellac, see LP section	D flat
377	CO 31705–1	a) Der Kuss Op. 128 (L.v.Beethoven)	A flat (A)
		b) Die Trommel gerühret, Egmont (Beethoven) Not in shellac, see LP section	G
378	CO 31706–1	In questa tomba oscura WoO 133 (Beethoven) Not in shellac, see LP section	A flat

379	CO 31707–1	Verborgenheit (Mörike-Wolf) Not in shellac	
380	CO 31708–1	Zur Ruh', zur Ruh' (Kerner-Wolf) Not in shellac, see LP section	A flat (G)
381	CO 31709–1	Gesang Weylas (Mörike-Wolf) Not in shellac, see LP section	D flat (E fl)
382	CO 31710–1	a) Wiegenlied Op. 49 No. 4 (Brahms) b) Ständchen Op. 106 No. 1 (Brahms) Only test pressings made	
383	CO 32035	Wiegenlied Op. 49 No. 4 (Brahms) 17300–D	D (E flat)
384	CO 32036	Ständchen Op. 106 No. 1 (Brahms) 17300–D	F (G)

2 July 1941.

385	CO 31693	Auf Flügeln des Gesanges Op. 34 No. 2 (Mendelssohn) 17344–D	G (A flat)
386	CO 31694	Allerseelen Op. 10 No. 8 (R. Strauss) 17385–D, album X–270	
387	CO 31695	Morgen Op 27 No. 4 (R. Strauss) 17384–D, album X–270	G
388	CO 31696	Zueignung Op. 10 No. 1 (R. Struass) 17385–D, album X–270	C
389	CO 31697	Ständchen Op. 17 No. 2 (R. Strauss) 17384–D, album X–270	F (F sharp)
390	CO 31698–1	Schmerzen-Wesendonclieder No. 4 (Wagner) Not in shellac, see LP section	c

9 July 1941.

391	CO 31488	Der Engel-Wesendonclieder No. 1 (Wagner) Not in shellac, see LP section	G flat (G)
392	CO 31489–1	a) Sehnsucht nach dem Frühling K. 596 (Mozart)	E
		b) Warnung K. 453 (Mozart) Not in shellac, see LP section	F
393	CO 31490–1	Das Veilchen K. 476 (Mozart) Not in shellac, see LP section	F
394	XCO 31491	Träume-Wesendonclieder No. 5 (Wagner) 71469–D	A flat
395	XCO 31492	Im Treibhaus-Wesendonclieder No. 3 (Wagner) 71469–D	c
396	CO 31493–1	Wer tat deinem Füsslein weh? (Sp.Lb.–Wolf) Only test pressings made	
397	CO 31494	Wien, du Stadt meiner Träume (Sieczynski) 17304–D, album M–494	F sharp

14 July 1941. Album M–494 Nos. 398, 399, 400, 403, 404

398	CO 31521	Da draussen in der Wachau (Arnold Weill) 17302–D	G flat
399	CO 31522	Im Prater blüh'n wieder die Bäume (Stolz) 17302–D	E
400	CO 31523	Wien, sterbende Märchenstadt (Herm. Leopoldi) 17303–D	A flat
401	CO 31524–1	My lovely Celia (George Monro) Not in shellac, see LP section	F sharp
402	CO 31525–1	She never told her love (Haydn) Not in shellac, see LP section	A flat
403	CO 31526	Ich muss wieder einmal in Grinzing sein (Benatzky) 17304–D	D flat
404	CO 31527	Heut' macht die Welt Sonntag für mich (Nico Dostal after J. Strauss) 17303–D	E
405	XCO 31528–1	a) C'est mon ami (Folksong, arr. Weckerlin) b) Maman dites-moi (Folksong arr. Weckerlin) Not in shellac, see LP section	F d
406	XCO 31529–1	a) La vierge à la crèche (French folksong) b) La mère Michel (Folksong) Not in shellac, see LP section	D A flat

13 August 1941. Dichterliebe – complete (Schumann). Bruno Walter, piano. Album M–486.

407	CO 31377	a) Wenn ich in deine Augen seh' No. 4 b) Ich will meine Seele tauchen No. 5 17295–D / 17440–D	G b
408	CO 31378	a) Ich hab' im Traum geweinet No. 13 b) Allnächtlich im Traume No. 14 17296–D / 17441–D	e flat B
409	XCO 31379	Aus alten Märchen winkt es No. 15 71309–D / 72078–D	E
410	CO 31380	a) Im wunderschönen Monat Mai No. 1 b) Aus meinen Tränen spriessen No. 2 c) Die Rose, die Lilie, die Taube, die Sonne No. 3 17295–D / 17440–D	A A D
411	XCO 31381	a) Und wüssten's die Blumen No. 8 b) Das ist ein Flöten und Geigen No. 9 c) Hör ich das Liedchen No. 10 71308–D / 72077–D	a d g

412	XCO 31382	Die alten bösen Lieder No. 16	c sharp
		71309–D / 72078–D	
413	XCO 31383	a) Im Rhein, im heiligen Strome No. 6	e
		b) Ich grolle nicht No. 7	C
		71308–D / 72077–D	
414	CO 31384	a) Ein Jüngling liebt ein Mädchen No. 11	E flat
		b) Am leuchtenden Sommermorgen No. 12	B flat
		17296–D / 17441–D	

22 June 1942. Die schöne Müllerin D. 795 (Schubert), Paul Ulanowsky piano. Album M–615

415	XCO 32966	a) Das Wandern No. 1	A (B flat)
		b) Wohin? No. 2	G flat (G)
		71771–D / 71778–D	
416	XCO 32967	a) Halt! No. 3	B flat (C)
		b) Danksagung an dem Bach No. 4	F (G)
		71771–D / 71779–D	
417	XCO 32970	a) Morgengruss No. 8	A (C)
		b) Des Müllers Blumen No. 9	G (A)
		71773–D / 71782–D	
418	XCO 32971	Tränenregen No. 10	G (A)
		71773–D / 71783–D	
419	XCO 32972	Pause No. 12	A fl (B fl)
		71774–D / 71784–D	
420	XCO 32973	a) Mein! No. 11	D
		b) Mit dem grünen Lautenbande No. 13	A fl (B fl)
		71774–D / 71784–D	
421	XCO 32975	Die liebe Farbe No. 16	a (b)
		71775–D / 71782–D	
422	XCO 32976	Die böse Farbe No. 17	A (B)
		71776–D / 71781–D	

25 June 1942. Die schöne Müllerin, (Schubert) continued.

423	XCO 32968	Am Feierabend No. 5	G (A)
		71772–D / 71780–D	
424	XCO 32969	Der Neugierige No. 6	A flat (B)
		71772–D / 71781–D	
425	XCO 32974	a) Der Jäger No. 14	c
		b) Eifersucht und Stolz No. 15	A fl (B fl)
		71775–D / 71783–D	
426	XCO 32977	Trock'ne Blumen No. 18	c (e)
		71776–D / 71780–D	
427	XCO 32978	Der Müller und der Bach No. 19	e (g)
		71777–D / 71779–D	
428	XCO 32979	Des Baches Wiegenlied No. 20	c (E)
		71777–D / 71778–D	

SECTION VIII: *Victor recordings, New York, 1947–1949*

All are ten-inch recordings. The titles assigned a number in the 49–000 series are reissues on seven-inch 45 rpm microgroove records.

26 June 1947. Paul Ulanowsky piano.

429	D7–RB–0560–1,–1A	Ständchen: Leise flehen meine Lieder D.957 No. 4 (Schubert) 10–1498 later 19–1498 and 49–0699	
430	D7–RB–0561–1,–1A 11 July –2,–2A	Der Erlkönig D.328 (Schubert) 10–1448 later 19–1448 and 49–1033 (DA 1919 assigned but not issued)	F (G)
431	D7–RB–0562–1,–1A	a) He Zigeuner (Zigeunerlieder Op. 103 No. 1) (Brahms) b) Hochgetürmte Rimaflut No. 2 10–1391, album M–1188 10–1393, album DM–1188 later 49–0846	g (a) c (d)
432	D7–RB–0563–1,–1A	a) Wisst ihr, wann mein Kindchen No. 3 b) Lieber Gott, du weisst No. 4 10–1391, album M–1188 10–1394, album DM–1188 later 49–0847	B (D) D (F)
433	D7–RB–0564–1,–1A	a) Brauner Bursche No. 5 b) Röslein dreie in der Reihe No. 6 10–1392, album M–1188 10–1394, album DM–1188 later 49–0847	C (D) F (G)
434	D7–RB–0565–1,–1A	a) Kommt dir manchmal in den Sinn No. 7 b) Rote Abendwolken No. 11 (one verse) 10–1392, album M–1118 10–1393, Album DM–1188 later 49–0846	D (E flat) B fl (D fl)
435	D7–RB–0566–1,–1A	An den Mond (Hölty) D. 193 (Schubert) 10–1498 later 19–1498 and 49–0699	
436	D7–RB–0567–1,–1A	An die Musik D.547 (Schubert) 10–1448 later 19–1448 and 49–1033 (DA 1919 assigned but not issued)	D flat (D)
437	D7–RB–0568–1,–1A	Feldeinsamkeit Op. 86 No. 2 (Brahms) 10–1405	
438	D7–RB–0569–1,–1A	a) Der Kranz Op. 84 No. 2 (Brahms) b) Der Schmied Op. 19 No. 4 (Brahms) 10–1405	

30 June 1947. The RCA Victor Chamber Orchestra conducted by Richard Lert.

439	D7–RB–0578–1,–1A	Ave Maria (Bach, arr. Grounod) sung in Latin. Unpublished	

440 D7–RB–0579–1,–1A Adeste fideles (O come all ye faithful).
–2,–2A In English, with chorus and orchestra
10–1367, album MO–1226 later 49–0793

441 D7–RB–0580–1,–1A Stille Nacht, heilige Nacht (Gruber).
In German, with chorus and orchestra
10–1367, album MO–1226 later 49–0793

442 D7–RB–0581–1,–1A Es ist ein Ros' entsprungen (arr. Praetorius) in German and in English: 'Lo! How a rose e'er blooming'.
Unpublished

11 July 1947. Paul Ulanowsky piano.

443 D7–RB–1300–1,–1A a) Der Jüngling an der Quelle D.300 (Schubert) G flat (A)
–2,–2A b) An die Nachtigall D.497 (Schubert) E (G)
10–1551 later 49–1277

444 D7–RB–1301–1,–1A Die Männer sind méchant D.866 No. 3 g (a)
10–1551 later 49–1277 (Schubert)

445 D7–RB–1302–1,–1A Nacht and Träume D.827 (Schubert)
–2,–2A Unpublished
1 October –2B,–2C, –2D 'Electrical transfers from D7–RB–1302–2 to furnish new masters'.
D7–RB–0561–2,–2A For details see 26 June above.

22 December 1947. Orchestra conducted by Robert Armbruster.

446 D7–RB–2733–1,–1A God bless America (Irving Berlin) with
–2,–2A the St. Luke Choristers
10–1433, album MO–1226

447 D7–RB–2734–1,–1A The Kerry Dance (Molloy) with the St. Luke Choristers.
10–1433, album MO–1226

448 D7–RB–2735–1,–1A Träumerei (Schumann) no words used,
–2,–2A vocalised, from the MGM film 'Big City'
–3,–3A 10–1432, album MO–1226, HMV DA 1909 key: C

449 D7–RB–2736–1,–1A Wiegenlied Op. 49 No. 4 (Brahms) sung
–2,–2A in English from the MGM film 'Big City'
10–1432, album MO–1226, HMV DA 1909 key: D

9 March 1949. Paul Ulanowsky piano.
Takes 1 OR 1A used for 10–0000 series, takes 1B or 1C used for both 10–0000 and 49–0000 series

450 D9–RB–0263–1,–1A L'enamourée (Hahn)
10–1509, album DM–1342
11 April –1B,–1C used for 49–0769

No.	Matrix	Title / issues	Key
451	D9–RB–0264–1,–1A	Infidélité (Hahn)	
		10–1510, album DM–1342	
	21 May –1B,–1C	used for 10–1510 and 49–0770	
452	D9–RB–0265–1,–1A	La vie antérieure (Duparc)	
		10–1510, album DM–1342	
	21 May –1B,–1C	used for 10–1510 and 49–0770	
453	D9–RB–0266–1,–1A	Psyché (Paladilhe)	
		10–1508, album DM-1342	
	21 May –1B,–1C	used for 49–0768	
454	D9–RB–0267–1,–1A	a) Die Zeitlose, Op. 10 No. 7 (R. Strauss)	f
		b) Wozu noch Mädchen, Op. 19 No. 1 (Strauss)	G fl
		10–1509, album DM–1342, HMV DA 1943	
	23 May –1B,–1C	used for 49–0769	
455	D9–RB–0268–1,–1A	Du meines Herzens Krönelein, Op. 21 No. 2 (R. Strauss)	F
		10–1508, album DM–1342, HMV DA 1943	
	21 May –1B,–1C	used for 49–0768	

Note: On the later dates in April and May transfers (all from the first takes) were made for use on 7″ vinylite.

No. 450–455: the '0' in the matrix numbers is not shown on the recording sheets sent to Hayes, e.g. D9–RB–*263*–1.

REISSUES ON LONG PLAYING RECORDS: SECTIONS VI, VII & VIII

RCA Victor and American Columbia 1935–1949

RCA Camden 378, UK: CDN 1015, Japan: RS 7
- side one: 312, 301, 292, 291, 318, 320, 322
- side two: 302, 297, 303, 307, 444, 430, 436

RCA LCT–1108, France: 430.529S 'Voix immortelles' (1962)
- side one: 284, 283, 285, 286, 332, 333, 335
- side two: 331, 287, 308, 288, 309b, 290, 289, 306

RCA France 430.661
- side one: 325, 328, 327, 326, 312, 301, 444
- side two: 430, 436, 302, 297, 292, 291, 320

RCA LM– 2763, German RCA HR–219, UK: RB 6604 'Flagstad & Melchior, Lehmann & Melchior, Wagner and Schumann duets' (1964)
- contains: Nos. 325, 328, 327, 326

Victrola VICS–1320–E (1968)
- side one: 431–434 (Zigeunerlieder), 437, 438, 289, 290, 301, 312
- side two: 291, 317, 304, 305a, 315*, 319, 318, 322, 323*, 324, 305b, 316*, 321*, 320
- * previously unpublished

Artisco-Artphone (Japan) YD 3016
 360–367 (Frauenliebe und -leben)
 407–414 (Dichterliebe)
Artisco-Artphone (Japan) YD 3017/18 Schubert (1978)
 on three sides the complete Winterreise:
 side one: 348, 342a, 339, 358, 331, 340, 343, 336b
 side two: 346, 344, 347, 345, 330a, 341, 333, 342b
 side three: 336a, 330b, 335a, 332, 334, 335b, 329, 357
 side four, with miscellaneous Schubert: 443, 337, 338, 359*, 310, 286, 311
 *) previously unpublished
Artphone (Japan) C 22 G 0008, Lieder by Brahms
 side one: 431–434 (Zigeunerlieder), 355, 350, 438, 290, 384
 side two: 383, 356, 353, 354, 351, 349, 437, 352, 289
Columbia, America – CBS: A tribute to Lotte Lehmann in honour of her 75th birthday. ML 5778 or UK: BRG 72073 CBS (1963)
 side one: 337, 338, 369*, 374*, 372*, 378*, 377a*
 side two: 384, 383, 380*, 390*, 394, 389, 387, 388
 *) previously unpublished
Odyssey (CBS-Columbia) 32 16 0179 (ca. 1968?)
 side one: 404, 400, 403, 398, 399, 397
 side two: 402*, 401*, 405*, 406*, 385
 *) previously unpublished
American Columbia ML 2182 (10″)
 No. 360–367 (Frauenliebe und -leben – Schumann)
 ML 2183 (10″), UK: 33C 1020, France: FC 1034
 No. 407–414 (Dichterliebe – Schumann)
American Columbia ML 4788, Philips (Holland) A 01265L, Odyssey 32 16 0315 (1957)
 side one: 360–367 (Frauenliebe und -leben)
 side two: 404–417 (Dichterliebe)
American Columbia ML 5996, UK: BRG 72209 CBS (1964)
 415–428 & 285 (RCA) complete cycle 'Die schöne Müllerin'
 285 (Ungeduld) was included by special courtesy of RCA Victor
Bruno Walter Society 'In memoriam Lotte Lehmann' (1976) BWS–729
 side one: 393, 392, 375, 376, 377b, 368, 391, 373, 381 all previously unpublished
 side two: see non-commercial recordings.

Note: On the label of BWS–729 for *Neue Liebe* (see No. 373) the composer is indicated as Wolf. It should read: Mendelssohn.

SECTION IX: *Non-commercial recordings on microgroove, 1935–1951*

All the recordings listed in this section have been issued on long-playing discs or are stored in private archives. The technical quality of the recordings varies enormously and the sound is sometimes downright bad. The recording speeds are even more erratic than those of the commercial recording companies and should not be taken on trust. On some recordings the pitch varies even while a song or an operatic excerpt is being sung, though this is not always noticeable. For example, Wolf's 'Kennst du das Land', which opens the New York Town Hall recital broadcast of 1938, rises by almost half a tone during the course of the performance.

Recordings published by Edward J. Smith in his *Golden Age of Opera* series are designated by the letters EJS, and in his *Unique Opera Record Corporation* series by UORC. Some of these recordings were later taken over by Recital Records (RR), I Grandi Interpreti (IGI) and the Bruno Walter Society (BWS) which subsequently amalgamated as Discocorp, Inc. Berkeley, California, USA.

1 November 1930	Dich teure Halle, Act 2, Tannhäuser (Wagner) Chicago Opera Orchestra. Conductor: G. Polacco.	EJS 444
11 February 1934	New York. Broadcast 'General Motors Symphony Orchestra' conducted by Arturo Toscanini. Komm' Hoffnung, aria from Act 1, Fidelio (Beethoven)	in Toscanini archive
24 October 1935	Lohengrin (Wagner) no details	private archive
1 June 1935	Otello (Verdi) w. Pistor, Conductor: de Sabata	private archive
31 August 1935	Salzburg. Title role in Act 1, Fidelio (Beethoven), Toscanini conducting From the Salzburg Festival	UORC–218
20 September 1935	Die Meistersinger von Nürnberg (Wagner) 2 excerpts, 'Jerum! Jerum!' 1'46" from Act 2 and the Quintet from Act 3 Eva — Lotte Lehmann Magdalena — Kerstin Thorborg Walther — Eyvind Laholm David — William Wernigk Hans Sachs — Ludwig Hofmann Beckmesser — Hermann Wiedemann Orchestra of the Vienna State Opera, conducted by Felix v. Weingartner	Teletheater 6.43 333 AG (Teldec)
8 August 1936	Salzburg Festival. Eva in Act 1, Die Meistersinger (Wagner) with H.-Herm. Nissen, K. Thorborg, H. Alsen, C. Kullmann, A. Dermota. Conductor: Toscanini	UORC–257

Date	Recording	Issue / Key
13 November 1936	San Francisco Opera. Act 2, Die Walküre (Wagner)	EJS 234 RR 426 EL 0042
	Wotan Friedrich Schorr Fricka K. Meisle Brünnhilde Kirsten Flagstad Sieglinde Lotte Lehmann Siegmund Lauritz Melchior Hunding Emmanuel List Orchestra conducted by Fritz Reiner	
	Excerpts from above recording relevant to Lotte Lehmann in 'Lauritz Melchior'.	Pearl GEMM 228–9
5 February 1938	Der Rosenkavalier (R. Strauss) complete	EJS 496 (3)
	Marschallin Lotte Lehmann Baron Ochs Emmanuel List Octavian Kerstin Thorborg Faninal Friedrich Schorr Sophie Susanne Fisher Annina Dorothea Manski Valzacchi Angelo Bada Conductor: Bodanzki	
18 January 1938	New York Town Hall. Wolf recital with P. Ulanowsky, piano	UORC–235
	Kennst du das Land? (Goethe)	G flat
	Frühling übers Jahr (Goethe)	A flat (A)
	Und willst du deinen Liebsten sterben sehen (Ital. Lb.)	A flat
	Wenn du mein Liebster steigst zum Himmel auf (Ital. Lb.)	G flat
	In der Frühe (Mörike)	d/D
	Auch kleine Dinge (Ital.Lb.) postlude cut	A
	Der Knabe und das Immlein (Mörike)	F (G)
	The same song repeated	
	Peregrina I (Mörike) postlude cut	E flat
	Er ist's (Schumann! encore)	A flat (A)
	Storchenbotschaft (Mörike-Wolf)	G flat (B fl)
	An eine Äolsharfe (Mörike)	E
	In dem Schatten miener Locken (Span.Lb.)	B flat
	Gebet (Mörike)	E
	Nun lass uns Frieden schliessen (Ital.Lb.)	E flat
	Der Gärtner (Mörike)	D flat (D)
	Ständchen (R. Strauss)	F (F sharp)
	Therese (Brahms)	F
	Auf ein altes Bild (Mörike)	f sharp
	Du denkst mit einem Fädchen mich zu fangen	B flat

	The same song repeated (Ital.Lb.)	
	Heimweh (Mörike)	F
	Schweig einmal still (Ital.Lb.)	a
	Ich hab' in Penna (Ital.Lb.)	F
	Zueignung (Richard Strauss – encore)	C
	Heimkehr vom Feste (Leo Blech) encore	E flat
	Vergebliches Ständchen (Brahms – encore)	A
3 March 1938	*'In memoriam. Lotte Lehmann 1888–1976'*	BWS–729
	Orchestral concert conducted by Frank Black	
	Vissi d'arte, Act 2, Tosca (Puccini)	
	Zueignung (R. Strauss)	C
(*date unknown*)	Traum durch die Dämmerung (R. Strauss)	F sharp
(*date unknown*)	Ständchen (R. Strauss)	F (F sharp)
1938	Potpourri No. 21 Lotte Lehmann sings:	EJS–425
	Vissi d'arte, Tosca (Puccini)	
	Zueignung (R. Strauss)	
	Das Mädchen spricht (Brahms)	
	Wiegenlied (Schubert)	
7 January 1939	Der Rosenkavalier (R. Strauss), complete	
	With Stevens, Farell, List, Schorr,	
	Metropolitan Opera New York.	
	Conductor: Bodanzky.	MET 5
30 March 1940	Die Walküre (Wagner) complete.	
	Metropolitan Opera at Boston	EJS–178
	Siegmund — Lauritz Melchior	
	Sieglinde — Lotte Lehmann	
	Hunding — Emanuel List	
	Wotan — Friedrich Schorr	
	Brünnhilde — Marjorie Lawrence	
	Fricka — Kerstin Thorborg	
	Walküren — Manski, Votipka, Jessner, Browning, Heidt, Stellman, Olheim and Doe.	
	Metropolitan Opera Orchestra conducted by Erich Leinsdorf.	
1943	Isoldes Liebestod from Tristan und Isolde (Wagner) with San Francisco Symphony Orchestra cond. Monteux. Monteux	BWS–729
	'Lotte Lehmann II' previously unissued selections from New Friends of Music concerts	VOCE–99
20 January 1946	Frauenliebe und – leben (Schumann)	orig. keys
27 February 1949	Als Luise die Briefe K. 520 (Mozart)	c

	Abendempfindung K. 523 (Mozart)	E
	Dans un bois solitaire K.308 (Mozart)	G
	Die Verschweigung K.518 (Mozart)	F
	Dein blaues Auge (Brahms)	E flat
	Komm' bald (Brahms)	G (A)
	Bitteres zu sagen denkst du (Brahms)	E flat (F)
	Schön war, dass ich dir weihte (Brahms)	e (f)
	Am Sonntagmorgen (Brahms)	d (e)
	Es glänzt der Mond nieder (Brahms)	f (e)
	Der Tod das ist die kühle Nacht (Brahms)	B flat (C)
	Liebestreu (Brahms)	c sharp (e flat)
	Frühlingstrost (Brahms)	F sharp (A)
	Der Kuss	G (B flat)
	O wüsst' ich doch den Weg zurück (Brahms)	D (E)
	Wie froh und frisch (Magelone XIV) (Brahms)	F (G)
1944	Recital of songs, all sung in English	EJS–536
	She never told her love (Haydn)	
	Dedication (Widmung), (Schumann)	
	Londonderry Air	
	Drink to me only	
	Serenade (Ständchen, Leise flehen meine Lieder) (Schubert)	
	On wings of song (Auf Flügeln des Gesanges) (Mendelssohn)	
23 February 1945	Der Rosenkavalier (R. Strauss). The artist's last performance at the Metropolitan Opera Act 1: 'Ich sag': Pardon, mein hübsches Kind'	Private archive
18 October 1945	Der Rosenkavalier (R. Strauss). Act 3 complete	EJS–462
	Marschallin Lotte Lehmann	
	Baron Ochs Lorenzo Alvary	
	Octavian Risë Stevens	
	Sophie Nadine Conner	
	Faninal Walter Olitzki	
	Annina Herta Glaz	
	Valzacchi Alessio de Paolis	
	Orchestra of the San Francisco Opera Company conducted by George Sebastian	
10 February 1946	Song recital for the New Friends of Music, New York with Paul Ulanowsky piano.	VOCE–69
	An eine Quelle, D.530 (Schubert)	G (A)
	Der Tod und das Mädchen D.531 (Schubert)	d orig
	Der Jungling und der Tod D.545 (Schubert) b (second version)	(c sh)

	Auflösung D.807 (Schubert)	F (G)
	Die Forelle D.550 (Schubert)	B (D flat)
	Dass sie hier gewesen D.775 (Schubert)	B fl (C)
	Schwanengesang D.744 (Schubert) G flat	(A flat)
	Die Männer sind méchant D.866 No. 3 (Schubert)	g (a)
	Zigeunerlieder op. 103 (Brahms)	
	He, Zigeuner	g (a)
	Hochgetürmte Rimaflut	c (d)
	Wisst ihr, wann mein Kindchen	B (D)
	Lieber Gott, du weisst	D (F)
	Brauner Bursche führt zum Tanze	D orig.
	Röslein dreie in der Reihe	F (G)
	Kommt dir manchmal in den Sinn	D (E flat)
	Rote Abendwolken ziehn am Firmament	B fl (D fl)
	Wie bist du meine Königin (Brahms)	E fl orig.
	Die Kränze (Brahms)	B (D flat)
	Es träumte mir (Brahms)	A fl (B)
	Frühlingslied op. 85 No. 8 (Brahms)	F (G)
	Willst du, dass ich geh' (Brahms)	c sharp (d)
11 August 1946	Orchestral concert with Seattle Symphony Orchestra conducted by Carl Bricker.	EJS–536
	Die junge Nonne D.828 (Schubert)	
	Der Jüngling an der Quelle D.300 (Schubert)	
	Der Erlkönig D.328 (Schubert)	
	Träume (Wagner)	
9 February 1947	From New York song recital for the New Friendsof Music. P. Ulanowsky, piano	VOCE–69
	Wenn durch die Piazzetta, Venetianisches Gondellied (Mendelssohn)	a (b)
	Die Liebende schreibt (Mendelssohn)	E flat orig.
	An die ferne Geliebte, song cycle (Beethoven)	D (E flat)
5 August 1948	From a concert in the Hollywood Bowl, conducted by Eugene Ormandy.	private archive
	Morgen (R. Strauss) violin solo: Sacha Jacobson	
	Allerseelen (R. Strauss)	
	Traum durch die Dämmerung (R.Strauss)	
	Zueignung (R. Strauss)	
	Encores with piano: (Paul Ulanowsky)	
	Ständchen (Schubert)	
	Wiegenlied (Brahms)	
1949	Song recital with Paul Ulanowsky. Paladilhe, Hahn, Duparc, Strauss, Schubert.	private archive

1950	From a Town Hall recital in New York acc. by Bruno Walter.	BWS–729
	Ständchen, leise flehen meine Lieder D.957 No. 4 (Schubert)	d fl (d)
	Auf Flügeln des Gesanges (Mendelssohn)	G (A fl)
	Wiegenlied (Brahms)	D (F)
	Aufträge (Schumann)	G (A)
16 February 1951	Farewell recital at the New York Town Hall with Paul Ulanowsky, piano.	Pembroke (incomplete) Pelican 2009 EMI 1C–027 60386
	Widmung (Schumann)	G (A flat)
	O, Ihr Herren (Schumann)	G (A flat)
	Ständchen (Schumann)	G flat (G)
	Wer machte dich so krank (Schumann)	G (A flat)
	Der Mond (Mendelssohn)	D flat (E)
	Wenn durch die Piazzetta, Venetianisches Gondellied (Mendelssohn)	a (b)
	Ein Ton (Cornelius)	e flat (e)
	Wiegenlied (Cornelius)	E flat
	Träume (Wagner)	A flat or.
	Für Musik (Rob. Franz)	E
	Ständchen (Rob. Franz)	B flat
	Gute Nacht (Rob. Franz)	D flat
	Weisst du noch (Rob. Franz)	D
	Dies und das (Rob. Franz)	F
	Wohin? D.795 No. 2 (Schubert)	G flat (G)
	Danksagung an den Bach D.795 No. 4	F (G)
	Der Neugierige D.795 No. 6 (Schubert)	A flat (B)
	Tränenregen D.795 No. 10 (Schubert)	G (A)
	Die liebe Farbe D.795 No. 16 (Schubert)	a (b)
	Des Baches Wiegenlied D.795 No. 20 (Schubert)	C (E)
	Encore: An die Musik D.547 (Schubert)	C(D)
7 August 1951	Farewell concert at the Lobero Theatre, Santa Barbara with Gwendolyn Koldofsky, piano.	UORC–306
	An mein Klavier D.342 (Schubert)	G flat (A)
	Der Neugierige D.795 No. 6 (Schubert)	A flat (B)
	Fischerweise D.881 (Schubert)	D orig.
	Im Abendrot D.799 (Schubert)	G fl (A fl)
	Seligkeit D.433 (Schubert)	D (E)
	Der Mond (Mendelssohn)	D (E)
	Wenn durch die Piazzetta, Venetianisches Gondellied (Mendelssohn)	a (b)
	Ein Ton (Cornelius)	e flat (e)
	Wiegenlied (Cornelius)	D

	Träume (Wagner)	A flat orig.
	A nos morts ignores (Hahn)	D flat
	Pholoe (Hahn)	a
	Phyllis (Hahn)	F (E flat)
	Offrande (Hahn)	D (C)
	Le Rossignol des Lilas (Hahn)	G (A flat)
encore:	Si mes vers avaient des ailes (Hahn)	D (E)
	Die Mainacht (Brahms)	E (E flat)
	Lerchengesang (Brahms)	A flat (B)
	Es träumte mir (Brahms)	A flat (B)
	Botschaft (Brahms)	B flat (D fl)
encore:	Morgen (R. Strauss)	G flat (G)

Note: The complete recording of Wagner's *Die Walküre* taken from the Metropolitan Opera performance of 30 March, 1940, and issued in The Golden Age of Opera series, usually appears with the catalogue number EJS 178 on the record labels. Complete listings issued by Ed. Smith, however, sometimes show that number allocated to extracts from Ambroise Thomas' *Mignon*, with the Wagner recording listed under EJS 179.

SECTION X: *Master Classes*

Lotte Lehmann's *Art of Song Interpretation* Campbell 1/24

This collection embraces six two-hour classes given by Lotte Lehmann at Pasadena, California in *March and April 1952*.

Sixteen students took part in the two-hour sessions eight at a time, alternately, on these twenty-four LP records. The songs, arias and duets chosen were as follows:

Record	1	*Happy Birthday*	
		Heimkehr	R.Strauss
		Cäcilie	R.Strauss
	2	Marschallin's monologue, Rosenkavalier Act 1,	R. Strauss
		Ich grolle nicht, Dichterliebe Op. 48 No. 7	Schumann
	3	Tu lo sai	Torelli
		La flûte de Pan, Chansons de Bilitis No. 1	Debussy
		Gesang Weylas	Wolf
	4	Im Abendroth D.799	Schubert
		Der Kuss Op. 128	Beethoven
		Männer suchen stets zu naschen K.433	Mozart
	5	Les cloches	Debussy
		Das Veilchen K.476	Mozart
	6	Hat dich die Liebe berührt	Marx
		Anakreons Grab	Wolf

Record	Title	Composer
Record 7	Waldesgespräch Op. 39 No. 3	Schumann
	Heimliche Aufforderung Op. 27 No. 3	R.Strauss
8	Recuerdo	Castelnuovo-Tedesco
	Chanson d'amour	Chausson
	Die Verschweigung K.518	Mozart
9	Mi chiamano Mimi, La Bohème	Puccini
	Zur Ruh! Zur Ruh!	Wolf
	Hist! Hist!	Dr Arnold
10	Zueignung Op. 10 No. 1	R.Strauss
	Maman, dites-moi	Trad. French
11	Ein junger Dichter denkt an der Geliebte	Marx
	Feast of Lanterns	Bantock
	In dem Schatten meiner Locken	Wolf
12	Über Nacht	Wolf
	Der Nussbaum Op. 25 No. 3	Schumann
13	Il est doux, il est bon, Hérodiade	Massenet
	In fernem Land, Act 3, Lohengrin	Wagner
14	Nicht mehr zu dir zu gehen, Op. 32 No. 3	Brahms
	Stresa	Wintter Watts
15	Im wunderschönen Monat Mai, Dichterliebe Op. 48 No. 1	
	Aus meinem Tränen spriessen, Dichterliebe No. 2	
	Die Rose, die Lilie, die Taube, die Sonne, Dichterliebe No. 3	Schumann
	What is Sentimentality?	*Lotte Lehmann*
	Die Nachtigall, Volks-Kinderlieder No. 2	Brahms
16	Die heisse schwüle Sommernacht	Wolf
	Aufenthalt D. 957 No. 5	Schubert
17	Le Tombeau des Naiades, Chanson de Bilitis No. 3	Debussy
	Mandoline	Debussy
	Psyché	Paladilhe
18	Carnaval	Félix Fourdrain
	Duet Act 2, Rosenkavalier	R. Strauss
19	Fischerweise, D. 881	Schubert
	Das Mädchen spricht, Op. 107 No. 3	Brahms
	Träume	Wagner
20	Wiegenlied, Op. 41 No. 1	R.Strauss
	Ruhe, meine Seele, Op. 27 No. 1	R.Strauss

Record	21	Credo in un Dio, Otello Act 2	Verdi
		Auf einer Wanderung	Wolf
		D'une prison	Hahn
	22	Du denkst mit einem Fädchen mich zu fangen	Wolf
		Du bist der Lenz, Act 1, Walküre	Wagner
		Immer leiser wird mein Schlummer Op. 105 No. 2	Brahms
		Die Nacht, Op. 10 No. 3	R.Strauss
	23	Che gelida manina, La Bohème	Puccini
		A nun takes a veil, Op. 13 No. 1	Barber
		Die Krähe, D. 911 No. 15	Schubert
	24	Der Jüngling an der Quelle, D.300	Schubert
		Unbewegte laue Luft, Op. 57 No. 8	Brahms
		Concluding remarks by Lotte Lehmann	

Master classes in London *1957*
Ivor Newton at the piano.
On LP from J.H. Crawley — Spring 1969
(no details available)

SECTION XI: *Speech recordings by Lotte Lehmann on Long Playing Records*

Caedmon October 1956, publ. 1957
Lotte Lehmann reading German lyric poetry. Poems by Goethe, Mörike, Heine, Rilke, von Hofmannsthal and Wilhelm Müller. Caedmon TC 1072

Caedmon FEBRUARY-MARCH 1958
Lotte Lehmann reads Rainer Maria Rilke: Die Weise von liebe und Tod. Das Marienleben (excerpts) Caedmon TC 1128

On Odeon O–83396 Lotte Lehmann talks (in German) about her career as an introduction to some reissues, see above. 4′32″ plus 6′3″

APPENDIX: *Radio interviews*

Interview with Elisabeth Schumann, *5 February 1950* — private archive

Lotte Lehmann tells her feelings about the role of the Marschallin in *Der Rosenkavalier* in an interview with John Gutman on the Metropolitan Opera intermission, *22 March 1958*

Lotte Lehmann is interviewed by John Gutman about *Arabella* during the Metropolitan Opera intermission, *21 January 1961*

Lotte Lehmann discusses her early beginnings in opera and her present activities with Jan Popper in 'Spotlight on Opera', ULCA Lecture series, broadcast on television, *3 September 1961*

Lotte Lehmann discusses *Ariadne auf Naxos* with Maria Jeritza and John Gutman, on the Metropolitan Opera intermission, *3 February 1963*

'Besuch bei Lotte Lehmann, Gedanken und Erinnerungen aus einem grossen Leben' TV interview in German, *1963*, on the occasion of her 75th birthday. Made in Santa Barbara.

Another German TV interview in *1966*, made in Santa Barbara (out of doors)

Lotte Lehmann pays tribute to Toscanini. Recorded in Santa Barbara, played on the Metropolitan Opera intermission on *25 March 1967* (centenary of Toscanini's birth).

Lotte Lehmann in conversation with Walter Slezak on his father Leo's wit and the opera *Die Jüdin* etc. Private archive

Sources of reference used for the discography

Voices of the Past, Vol. 4,
The International Red Label Catalogue,
The Gramophone Co. Ltd., Book I, 'DB'
J. R. Bennett & E. Hughes, Oakwood Press.

Voices of the Past, Vol. 6,
The International Red Label Catalogue,
The Gramophone Co. Ltd. Book II, 'DA'
J. R. Bennett & E. Hughes, Oakwood Press.

Voices of the Past Vol. 7,
The 1898–1925 German Catalogues,
The Gramophone Co. Ltd. & Deutsche Grammophon A.-G.
J. R. Bennett & Wilh. Wimmer, Oakwood Press.

Catálogo Numérico dos Discos Vocais Victor Sêlo Vermêlho
(Numerical Catalogue of Red-seal Victor Vocal Records)
Part 1 (1964) & Part 2 (1968) by Jacques Alain Léon

World Encyclopaedia of Recorded Music by F.F. Clough & G.J. Cuming
Sidgwick and Jackson Ltd., 1952

The Gramophone Shop Encyclopedia of Recorded Music, compiled by
R.D. Darrell, The Gramophone Shop, New York 1936

The same, 3rd edition, Crown, New York 1948

Vertical-cut Cylinders and Discs by V. Girard & H.M. Barnes, British Institute of Recorded Sound, London 1971

Catalogue général Disques microsillon Classiques 1966, Diapason

Berndt W. Wessling: *Lotte Lehmann, mehr als eine Sängerin,* Residenz Verlag 1969, Salzburg.

Schwann Long Playing Record Catalogue, June 1964 and January 1968 Collections, vocal section.

Index to titles

LP's from section IX, for which discography numbers have not been assigned are identified by catalogue numbers. Opera titles are set in italic.

Wiegenlied Op. 49 No. 4	77b, 382a, 383, 449, BWS–729 and tape, Hollywood Bowl archive
Willst du dass ich geh'	VOCE–69
Wir wandelten	354
Zigeunerlieder Op. 103 (8)	429–436, VOCE 69
CALCOTT	
Drink to me only	314, EJS–536
CASTELNUOVO-TEDESCO	
Recuerdo	Campbell 8
CHAUSSON	
Chanson d'amour	Campbell 8
CIMARA	
Canto di primavera	296
CORNELIUS	
Ein Ton	PEL–2009, UORC–306
Wiegenlied	PEL–2009, UORC–306
COWLER	
Es gibt eine Frau, die dich niemals vergisst	163
D'ALBERT	
Die toten Augen: Psyche wandelt	35, 229
Zum Drossel sprach der Fink	133
DEBUSSY	
Les cloches	Campbell 5
La flûte de Pan	Campbell 3
Mandoline	Campbell 17
Le tombeau des Najades	Campbell 17
DUPARC	
La vie antérieure	452
EULENBURG	
Monatsrose	85a
Rankende Rose	87a
Seerose	87b
Weisse und rote Rose	86
Wilde Rose	85b
FOLK SONGS	
France: C'est mon ami	405a
Germany: Es ritten drei Ritter	183
Es stiess ein Jäger	185
Es waren zwei Königskinder	186
Ireland: Londonderry Air	EJS–536
France: Maman, dites-moi	405b, Campbell 10
La mère Michel	406b
Russia: Der rote Sarafan	184
France: La vierge à la crèche	406a
Germany: Schlafe mein süsses Kind	298

HILDACH

Der Lenz, Op. 19 No. 5	105, 118
Der Spielmann	48, 106

HUMMEL

Halleluia	147

HYMNS

Ach bleib mit deiner Gnade	177
Aus tiefer Not	176
Christi Mutter stand in Schmerzen	158
Ein feste Burg ist unser Gott	201
Es blüht der Blumen eine	160
Geleite durch die Welle	159
Ich bete an die Macht der Liebe	202
Jesus, meine Zuversicht	178
O Haupt voll Blut und Wunden	157
O heilger Geist	175
Wir glauben all an einen Gott	179

JENSEN

Lehn' deine Wang an meine Wang	307
Murmelndes Lüftchen	97
O lass dich halten, goldene Stunde	96

KETÉLBY

Andachtsstunde – Reverie	181, 197
Heiligtum des Herzens	182, 198

KORNGOLD

Die tote Stadt: Der Erste, der Lieb' mich gelehrt	65
Glück das mir verblieb	64, 211, 224
Das Wunder der Heliane: Ich ging zu ihm	116
Nicht hab' ich ihn geliebt	117

LÉHAR

Eva: So war meine Mutter... Wär es nichts als ein Augenblick	120
Die lustige Witwe: Ich hol' dir vom Himmel das Blau	166

LEHMANN, Lotte

What is sentimentality? (with reference to 'Dichterliebe') and concluding remarks in master classes, Pasadena 1952	Campbell 15

LEOPOLDI

Wien, du sterbende Märchenstadt	400

LORTZING

Undine: So wisse dass in allen Elementen	33
Doch kann auf Erden	34

MARX

Ein junger Dichter denkt an der Geliebte	Campbell 11
Hat dich die Liebe berührt	Campbell 6
Selige Nacht	303

Sehnsucht nach dem Frühling, K. 596	392a
Das Veilchen K. 476	393, Campbell 5
Die Verschweigung K. 518	284, VOCE 99 Campbell 8
Warnung: Männer suchen stets zu naschen K.433	392b, Campbell 4
Die Zauberflöte: Ach ich fühl's	69, 212
Bei Männern welche Liebe fühlen	39
MONRO	
My lovely Celia	401
NICOLAI	
Die lustigen Weiber von Windsor:	
Nun eilt herbei . . .	31, 213
Ha, ha, ha, er wird mir glauben	32, 214
OFFENBACH	
Hoffmanns Erzählungen:	
Sie entfloh'die Taube	16, 45, 227
PALADILHE	
Psyché	453, Campbell 17
PFITZNER	
Gretel	302
PRAETORIUS	
Es ist ein Ros' entsprungen	442
PUCCINI	
La Bohème: Che gelide manina	Campbell 23
Man nennt mich jetzt Mimi	14, 53, 156, 162, 168
Mi chiamano Mimi	14, 53, 156, 162, 168, Campbell 9
Madama Butterfly:	
Ancora un passo or via	73
Bald sind wir auf der Höh'	73
Eines Tages sehen wir	18, 55, 196, 223
Entrance of Butterfly	24, 73
Über das Meer und alle Lande	24, 73
Un bel di vedremo	18, 55, 196, 223
Weh mir du weinst	18
Manon Lescaut:	
Ach, in den kalten Räumen	54
Du bist verlassen . . .	54
In quelle trine morbide	54
L'ho abbandonato	54
Schwester Angelica (Suor Angelica)	
Amici fiori nel picco seno	37
O Blumen, die ihr Gift	37
Ohne Mutter	36
Senza Mamma	36
Tosca: Amaro sol perte (love duet Act 3)	111

Die Männer sind méchant D. 866 No. 3	444, VOCE 69
Nacht und Träume D. 827	445
Der Neugierige D. 795 No. 6	424, PEL–2009, UORC–306
Die schöne Müllerin D. 795	285, 415–428
Schwanengesang D. 744	VOCE 69
Sei mir gegrüsst D. 741	103
Seligkeit D. 433	UORC–306
Serenade D. 957 No. 4 (in Engl)	EJS–536,
Ständchen: Leise flehen ... D. 957 No. 4	107, 429, BWS–729, EJS–536 tape Hollywood Bowl archive
Der Tod und das Mädchen D. 531	108, VOCE 69
Tränenregen D. 795 No. 10	418, PEL–2009
Ungeduld D. 795 No. 7	285
Wiegenlied D. 498	311, EJS–425
Winterreise D. 911	329–336, 339–348, 357–358
Wohin? D. 795 No. 2	415b, PEL–2009
SCHUMANN	
Alte laute	308, PEL–2009
An den Sonnenschein	218a
Aufträge	84a, 128, 369, BWS–729
Dichterliebe (complete) Op.48	407–414
First three songs of Dichterliebe	Campbell 15
Du bist wie eine Blume	172, 309a
Er ist's	UORC 235
Er und Sie, Op. 78 No. 2	325
Familien-Gemälde, Op. 34 No. 4	327
Frauenliebe und -leben (complete)	137–144, 360–367, VOCE 99
Frühlingsnacht Op. 39 No. 12	309b
Ich denke dein, Op. 78 No. 3	328
Ich grolle nicht Op. 48 No. 7	199, 405b, Campbell 2
In der Fremde I, Op. 39 No. 1	368a
Die Kartenlegerin	287
Die Lotosblume	217, 370
Marienwürmchen	218b
Der Nussbaum	88, 126, 374, Campbell 12
O ihr Herren	PEL–2009
So wahr die Sonne scheinet Op. 37 No. 12	326a
Ständchen: Komm' in die stille Nacht	PEL–2009
Träumerei – vocalised	448
Unterm Fenster Op. 34 No. 3	326b
Volksliedchen Op. 51 No. 2	368b

Ich sag' Pardon, Act 1	256, archive
Monologue (also in sets)	71, 246, Campbell 2
O sei er gut	114, 245
Act 3	EJS–462
Ruhe meine Seele	Campbell 20
Ständchen	174, 389, UORC–235, BWS–729
Traum Durch die Dämmerung	173, with Orch.: BWS–729 and Hollywood Bowl, archive
Wiegenlied	56, 78, Campbell 20
Wozu noch Mädchen	454b
Die Zeitlose	454a
Zueignung	83a, 388, UORC–235, EJS–425 BWS–729 and Hollywood Bowl, archive, Campbell 10
TCHAIKOVSKY	
Eugen Onegin: Letter scene (excerpt)	15
THOMAS, Ambroise	
Mignon: Connais–tu le pays?	17, 72, 192
Dort bei ihm ist sie jetzt	22, 206
Elle est là	22, 206
Je connais un pauvre enfant	207
Kam ein armes Kind, Styrienne	207
Kennst du das Land	17, 72, 192
Légères hirondelles	40
Schwalbenduet	40
TORELLI	
Tu lo sai	Campbell 3
TRADITIONAL	
Adeste fideles	440
Christi Mutter	158
Es blüht der Blumen, Marienlied	160
Geleitet durch die Welle	159
Londonderry air	EJS–536
O du fröhliche	76, 135
O Haupt voll Blut und Wunden	157
Schlafe mein süsses Kind	298
VERDI	
Otello: complete version	private archive
Piangea cantando (Willow song)	62, 193, 216
Bei meiner Mutter	62, 193, 216
Credo in un Dio crudel	Campbell 21

WOLF

Anakreons Grab	291, Campbell 6
An eine Aeolsharfe	UORC–235
Auch kleine Dinge	320, UORC–235
Auf ein altes Bild	318, UORC–235
Auf einer Wanderung	Campbell 21
Der Gärtner	305a, UORC–235
Der Knabe und das Immlein	323, UORC–235 (2x)
Du denkst mit einem Fädchen	305b, UORC–235 (2x) Campbell, 22
Frühling übers Jahr	317, UORC–235
Gebet	315, UORC–235
Gesang Weylas	381, Campbell 3
Heimweh (Mörike)	324, UORC–235
Die heisse schwüle Sommernacht	Campbell 16
Ich hab' in Penna	UORC–235
In dem Schatten meiner Locken	292, UORC–235, Campbell 11
In der Frühe	319, UORC–235
Kennst du das Land?	UORC–235
Nun lass uns Frieden schliessen	316, UORC–235
Peregrina I	322, UORC–235
Schweig' einmal still	UORC–235
Storchenbotschaft	304, UORC–235
Über Nacht	Campbell 12
Und willst du deinen Liebsten	321, UORC–235
Verborgenheit	379, UORC–235
Wenn du mein Liebster steigt zum Himmel auf	UORC–235
Wer tat deinem Füsslein weh'	396
Zur Ruh', zur Ruh'	380, Campbell 9

WORTH

Midsummer	294b

Bibliography

Biancolli, L.: *The Flagstad Manuscript*. Heinemann, London 1953

Bloomfield, Arthur: *50 Years of the San Francisco Opera* San Francisco Book Company, San Francisco 1972

Carner, Mosco: *Puccini: A Critical Biography* Duckworth, London 1958

Castle, Charles with Tauber, Diana Napier: *This was Richard Tauber* W.H. Allen, London 1971

Christiansen, Rupert: *Prima Donna* Bodley Head1984

Culshaw, John: *Ring Resounding* Secker & Warburg, London 1967

Davenport, Marcia: *Too Strong for Fantasy* Collins, London 1958

Davis, Ronald L.: *Opera in Chicago* Appleton-Century, New York 1966

Downes, Olin: *Olin Downes on Music 1906–55* (ed. Downes, Irene) Simon & Schuster, New York 1957

Geissmar, Dr Berta: *The Baton and the Jackboot* Hamish Hamilton, London 1944

Gelatt, Roland: *Music Makers* Knopf, New York 1950

Gregor, Hans: *Die Welt der Oper: Die Oper der Welt* Bote & Bock, Berlin 1931

Hahn, Reynaldo: *L'Oreille au Guet* Gallimard, Paris 1937

Harewood, Lord: *The Tongs and the Bones* Weidenfeld & Nicholson, London 1981

Heyworth, Peter: *Conversations with Klemperer* Gollancz, London 1973

— *Otto Klemperer: His Life & Times* Vol. I, Cambridge 1983

Horne, Marilyn: *My Story* Doubleday, New York 1984

Jackson, Stanley: *Monsieur Butterfly* W.H. Allen, London 1974

Jefferson, Alan: *The Operas of Richard Strauss in Great Britain 1910–1963* Putnam, London 1963

— *Sir Thomas Beecham: A Centenary Tribute* Macdonald & Janes, London 1979

— *Der Rosenkavalier* Cambridge 1985

Jeritza, Maria: *Sunlight and Song* (trans. Martens, F.H.) Appleton, New York 1929

Kende, Götz Klaus (ed.): *Clemens Krauss – Briefe* – Residenz Verlag, Salzburg 1971
Kende, Götz Klaus & Schuh, Willi (eds.): *Richard Strauss – Clemens Krauss Briefwechsel* C.H. Beck Verlag, Munich 1963
Kennedy, Michael: *Barbirolli* Rupert Hart-Davis, London 1971
Lehmann, Lotte: *Anfang und Aufstieg* Herbert Reichner Verlag, Vienna, Leipzig–Zürich 1937
— *Orplid, mein Land* Herbert Reichner Verlag, Vienna. Leipzig–Zürich 1937
— *Eternal Flight* (trans. Krauch, E.) New York 1937
— *On Wings of Song* (trans. Ludwig, M.) Kegan Paul, London 1938
— *More than Singing: The Interpretation of Songs* (trans. Holden, F.) Boosey & Hawkes, New York 1945
— *My Many Lives* (trans. Holden, F.) Boosey and Hawkes, New York 1948
— *Singing with Richard Strauss* (trans. Pawel, E.) Hamish Hamilton, London 1964
— *Gedichte* Rudolf Reischl, Salzburg 1969
— *Eighteen Song Cycles* Cassell, London 1971
Leider, Frida: *Playing My Part* Calder & Boyars, London 1966
Leinsdorf, Erich: *Cadenza* Houghton Mifflin, Boston, Mass. 1976
Lochner, Louis P.: *Fritz Kreisler* Rockliff, London 1951
Marek, George: *Richard Strauss: The Life of a Non-Hero* Gollancz, London 1967
— *Toscanini* Vision Press, London 1976
Mayer, M.: *The Met: 100 Years of Grand Opera* Thames & Hudson, London 1983
MacArthur, Edwin: *Flagstad, A Personal Memoir* Knopf, New York 1965
Newton, Ivor: *At the Piano – Ivor Newton* Hamish Hamilton, London 1966
Pleasants, Henry: *The Great Singers* Macmillan, London 1983
Prawy, Marcel: *The Vienna Opera* Weidenfeld & Nicholson, London 1970
Rasponi, Lanfranco: *The Last Prima Donnas* Gollancz, London 1984
Robertson, Alec: *More than Music* Collins, London 1961
Rubinstein, Artur: *My Many Years* Cape, London 1980
Russell, John: *Erich Kleiber* André Deutsch, London 1957
Sachs, Harvey: *Toscanini* W.H. Allen, London 1978
Scanzoni, Signe von: *Richard Strauss und seine Sängerin* Residenz Verlag, Salzburg 1969
Schwarzkopf, Elisabeth: *On and Off the Record: A Memoir of Walter Legge* Faber & Faber, London 1982
Sheean, Vincent: *First and Last Love* Gollancz, 1957

Skelton, Geoffrey: *Paul Hindemith: The Man Behind the Music* Gollancz, London 1975
Smythe, Colin: *Schnabel* Gerrards Cross 1970
Steane, J.B.: *The Grand Tradition* Duckworth, London 1978
Strauss, Richard and Hofmannsthal, H. von: *Correspondence* (trans. Hammelmann, H. & Osers, E.) Collins, London 1961
Strauss, Richard and Schalk, Franz: *Ein Briefwechsel* (ed. Brosche, G.) Hans Schneider, Tutzing 1983
Tortelier, Paul and Blum, David: *Paul Tortelier* Heinemann, London 1984
Traubel, Helen and Hubler, R.G.: *St. Louis Woman* Arno Press, New York 1977
Walter, Bruno: *Theme and Variations* (trans. Galston, J.A.) Hamish Hamilton, London 1947
Walter, Bruno: *Briefe 1894–1962* S. Fischer Verlag, Vienna 1969
Weingartner, Felix von: *Buffets and Rewards* (trans. Wolff, M.) Hutchinson, London 1937
Wessling, Berndt W.: *Lotte Lehmann . . . mehr als eine Sängerin* Residenz Verlag, Salzburg 1969

Reference Works

Clough, F.F. & Cuming, G.J. *The World's Enclyclopedia of Recorded Music* Sidgwick & Jackson, London 1952–3
Die Bühne (German theatre directory) 1910–14, 1917–39
Bulletin of the British Institute of Recorded Sound no. 8, Spring 1958.
Harewood, Lord (ed.): *Kobbés Complete Opera Book* Putnam, London 1976, Bodley Head, 1987
Kapp, Julius (ed.): *Richard Strauss und der Berliner Oper II*, Max Hesse, Berlin 1939
Kaut, Josef, *Festspiele in Salzburg* Deutsche Taschenbuch Verlag, Salzburg 1970
Kutsch, K.J. & Riemens, L. *Unvergängliche Stimmen* Franke Verlag, Bern-Munich 1975
Der Merkur (German musical journal) 1916
Opera Magazine (ed. Rosenthal, H.D.) London
Perleberg: Ein Führer durch die Stadt 1978
Richard Strauss Blätter (ed. Brosche, G.) old style 6–8, G. Grasl, Baden 1975–6; new style Heft 15, Hans Schneider, Tutzing 1986 (publication of the International Richard Strauss Society – IRSG – of Vienna)
Riemann, Hugo *Musik-Lexikon* B. Schotts Söhne, Mainz 1972

Rosenthal, Harold *Two Centuries of Opera at Covent Garden* Putnam, London 1958
(with Warrack, J.) *The Concise Oxford Dictionary of Opera* Oxford University Press, London 2nd edn. 1979
Sackville-West, Edward & Shawe-Taylor, Desmond *The Record Guide* Collins, London 1951
Sadie, Stanley (ed.) *The New Grove* Macmillan, London 1980
Scholes, Percy A. & Ward, J.O. (eds.) *The Oxford Companion to Music* Oxford University Press, London 10th edn. 1970
Seltsam, William H. *Metropolitan Opera Annals 1883–1947:A Chronicle of Artists and Performances* H.W. Wilson Co., New York, in association with the Metropolitan Opera Guild Inc., New York 1947
Wolff, Stephanie *L' Opéra au Palais Garnier (1875–1962)* Slatkine, Paris 1963

Index